STANLEY COMPLETE WIRING

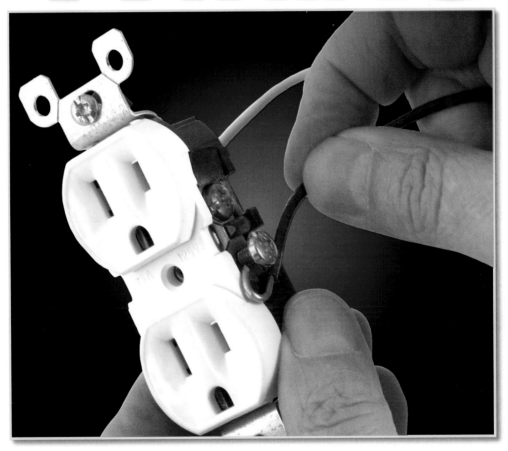

WILEY

John Wiley & Sons, Inc.

CONTENTS

CONTENTS

ISBN 978-0-696-23710-2

Printed in the United States of America

10 9 8 7

Photography Courtesy of:
(Photographers credited may retain copyright © to the listed photographs:

L = Left, R = Right, C = Center, B = Bottom, T = Top

Generace Power Systems, Inc.
www.generac.com
Page 257 - TL, TR, B

National Renewal Energy Laboratory
Department of Energy
www.nrel.gov
Page 152 - T, Astro Power
Page 152 - B, United Solar Systems Corporation
Page 153 - TL, John Haigwood
Page 153 - TR, Warren Gretz

Siemens Energy & Automation, Inc.
www.sea.siemens.com/reselec
Page 256 - BR

Note to the Readers: Due to differing conditions, tools, and individual skills, John Wiley & Sons, Inc., assumes no responsibility for any damages, injuries suffered, or losses incurred as a result of following the information published in this book. Before beginning any project, review the instructions carefully, and if any doubts or questions remain, consult local experts or authorities. Because codes and regulations vary greatly, you always should check with authorities to ensure that your project complies with all applicable local codes and regulations. Always read and observe all of the safety precautions provided by manufacturers of any tools, equipment, or supplies, and follow all accepted safety procedures.

WORKING SAFELY

Approach household electricity with caution and respect. Professional electricians routinely take steps to protect themselves against shocks. You need to be just as cautious while doing electrical work.

Be insulated

The effect of a shock varies according to how much power is present, your physical condition, and how well insulated you are. Of these three variables you have immediate control over insulation. When working with electricity wear rubber-sole shoes, remove jewelry, and keep dry. If the floor of your work area is damp or wet, put down dry boards or a rubber mat to stand on. Use tools with insulated handles.

If you are wearing dry clothes and rubber-sole shoes, receiving a 120-volt shock will grab your attention but probably not harm you. However if you have a heart condition or are particularly sensitive to shock, the effects could be more serious.

If you haven't taken precautions, chances of injury from shock are greater. If you are working on a 240-volt circuit, the danger is much greater.

Maintain respect for electrical power. Even if you have survived one shock, the next one could be a different story.

Shut off the power

Before starting any electrical project, always shut off power to the circuit. Then test to make sure there is no power present in the electrical box or wires (pages 48–49).

You may be tempted to skip this step and save a trip to the service panel. Or you may think you can change a receptacle or light fixture without touching any wires. Don't take that risk. It takes only a few moments to protect yourself against shock.

How circuits work:
For more information see pages 26–27. To learn how to check overloaded circuits, see pages 36–37.

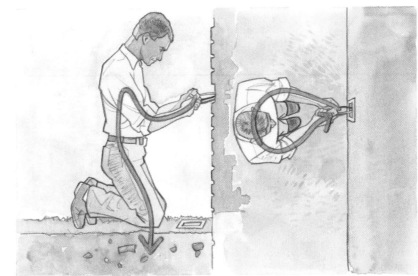

Your body is conductive and can become a path for electricity. Here's how shocks occur:
You become the pathway to ground. If you touch only a hot wire (usually black or colored), current passes through you and toward the ground. To greatly reduce or eliminate a shock, wear rubber-sole shoes and/or stand on a thick, nonconducting surface such as a dry wood floor.

You become part of the circuit. If you touch both a hot (black or colored) wire and a neutral (white) or ground (green or bare copper) wire at the same time, your body completes the circuit and current passes through it, even if you are standing on a nonconductive surface. Avoid touching any bare wire; use rubber-grip tools and hold them only by the handle.

SAFETY FIRST
Safety glasses and insulated tool grips

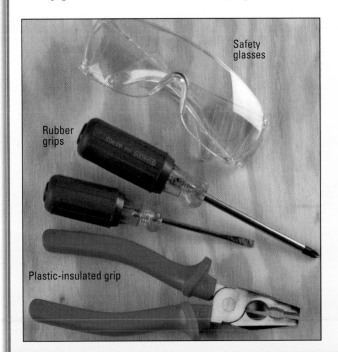

Safety glasses

Rubber grips

Plastic-insulated grip

Electrician's tools have heavy-duty insulated grips to protect hands from wayward power. Use these special tools (pages 12–13) rather than regular carpentry tools. Always hold tools by the rubber grips—never touch the metal parts of the tools.

Wear safety glasses when you're doing any construction work. They protect your eyes from irritants such as drywall or plaster dust that fly up whenever holes are being cut into walls or ceilings. Safety glasses also prevent dangerous bits of metal from flying into your eyes when you saw metal or snip wires. Porcelain and glass fixtures also can chip and pose hazards.

TURNING OFF POWER

Start every electrical project with the most important safety measure— de-energizing the wires and devices you work on. Follow the steps on these pages to make sure the power to your home circuits has been turned off.

The information here also helps you know what to do when receptacles or lights suddenly go dead, which may indicate that a circuit has overloaded. The place to begin is the electrical service panel.

Accessing the service panel
A residential main service panel contains either circuit breakers or fuses and is usually located in a utility area. It should be easily accessible but away from the main traffic flow in the house.

The panel may be in the garage or basement. In warm climates it may be on the outside of the house. In an apartment or condo, it may be recessed into the wall in a closet or laundry area. The service panel probably is a gray metal box or door, unless it has been painted.

You may find more than one service panel, especially in an older home. Subpanels are sometimes added to older systems to expand the number of circuits. De-energize these just as you would a fuse or breaker in a main service panel.

You may need to get at the panel in the dark or in a hurry during an emergency. Make sure all adults in your home know where to find it. Keep the path to the panel clear and don't lean things against it.

Open the door to get to the fuses or breakers inside. **If the panel appears damaged or if loose wires are visible, call a professional electrician** to check it.

Need more help?
If you have trouble locating the service panel, check page 31. If you still can't locate it or if you are confused about how to shut it off, call an electrician.

Breaker box

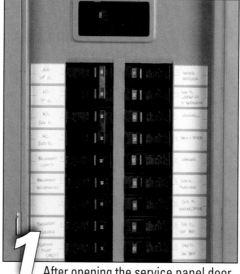

1 After opening the service panel door, you find rows of individual circuit breakers, which look like toggle switches, and a main breaker on top. A list indicates which parts of the house each breaker controls. (If your panel does not have a list, see pages 54–55.)

2 The list should identify which breaker controls the receptacle or fixture you want to de-energize. To shut off an individual breaker, flip the lever to the "off" position. **Test the device to make sure power is off** before working on it. See page 48 to learn how to test for power.

CIRCUIT BREAKERS
Two other types of breakers

Toggle switch

Push-in switch

Breakers vary in the way they shut off when they sense an overload. One toggle type (above left) has a red button that pops up when the breaker has tripped. Reactivate it by turning the switch back on. Some toggles turn partway off

when they blow. To restore power flip the switch all the way off, then on. The button on a pushbutton breaker pops out when the breaker shuts off (above right); push the button in to restore power.

Fuse box

Main fuse block

3 To turn off power to the entire house, flip off the main breaker, usually a double-width switch located at the top of the service panel. You may need to have a flashlight handy when you turn off power.

1 If you have a fuse box, shut off power by unscrewing and removing a fuse. If there is no list telling which fuse you need to remove, see pages 54–55. **Test the device to make sure the power is off** (page 48) before doing any work. If a fuse has blown, replace it with a new one.

2 To turn off power to the entire house, pull out the main fuse block, which looks like a rectangular block with a handle. It is usually located at the top of the panel. Tug hard and straight out on the handle. **Use caution.** If you have just removed the block, its **metal parts may be hot.**

Safety First
Hands off live wires!

When turning off or restoring power in a service panel, take care not to touch any wires. Open only the door: Do not remove the inner cover over the wires. (See page 36 if you need to open the cover.) Touch only the breaker. For added safety wear rubber-sole shoes. If the floor near the box is wet, lay down a dry board or rubber mat and stand on it.

Never touch the thick wires that enter the service panel from outside the home. They are always energized, even if the main breaker is turned off.

What If...
A fuse blows often?

When a fuse blows frequently, it's tempting to replace it with one of a greater amperage. This is dangerous—house wires could burn up before the fuse blows. Instead remove some of the load from the circuit.

The wire gauge in the circuit determines how large a fuse or circuit breaker it can have (page 37). A 15-amp circuit should have 14-gauge or larger wire; a 20-amp circuit, 12-gauge or larger; and a 30-amp circuit, 10-gauge or larger.

Checking the wire gauge is easy if you have nonmetallic cable running into the box. Examine the sheathing for a stamped or printed identification, which includes the gauge. With armored sheathing or conduit, open a receptacle on the circuit (pages 38–39). Check the insulation on the wires for a gauge marking or compare it with a wire of known gauge.

Main Fuse Block
Check the fuses inside

A main block or 240-volt circuit may have a fuse block that has cartridge fuses inside. Remove an individual cartridge fuse by pulling it out from the holders. Test the fuse (page 49) and, if necessary, replace it.

DEVELOPING SAFE HABITS

Most electrical work is not difficult. And if you shut off the power and test to be sure it is off, you are safe from shock. It doesn't take a lot of time or effort to avoid a shock—just a little care and a few simple steps. Learn these steps, then make them habits.

Pretend it's live

Professional electricians have this simple rule: **Even after shutting off power, always act as if the wires are live.** That way if someone accidentally turns on the power or a tester gives the wrong reading, you're still protected.

Pretending each wire is live means you should never touch two wires at once. Nor should you touch a wire and a ground at the same time. In fact it is good practice to only touch the bare end of a wire with an insulated tool, not your fingers. As an added precaution, lightly twist a wire nut onto the bare end of any wire that you are not working on—good assurance that it will cause no harm.

Redundant protection

Get into the habit of taking the time and trouble to provide yourself with double— even triple—protection. In addition to shutting off power and testing to make sure power is off, wear rubber-sole shoes and use tools with rubber grips specifically designed for electrical work. Use safety glasses when dust or debris is a hazard. And wear ear protection when working with power tools.

Maintain concentration

A single lapse of concentration can create a dangerous situation. Eliminate all possible distractions. Keep nonworkers (especially children) away from the worksite. Don't listen to the radio or a music player while you work. Check and recheck your connections before restoring power.

Give yourself plenty of time to finish a job. If you need to leave a job and pick it up again the next day, start at the first step: **Make sure the circuit is shut off and test for power** before proceeding.

Take the extra step to be safe

1 Make sure no one turns on the power while you are working. Tape a note to the service panel door. You may even want to lock the panel.

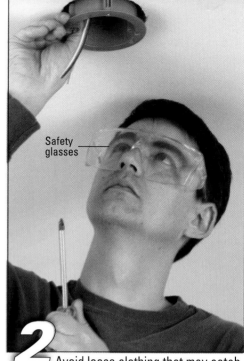

Safety glasses

2 Avoid loose clothing that may catch on wires. Wear safety glasses anytime you might get dust, metal pieces, or other material into your eyes. Wear protective clothing and rubber-sole shoes. Remove all jewelry, including a wristwatch.

STANLEY PRO TIP

Cut with care

Use caution anytime you cut into a wall or ceiling; an electrical cable may lie behind the surface. Use a voltage detector to **check if live wires are present** (opposite page). Another way to check is to drill a hole into the wall or ceiling and insert a bent wire to feel for a cable. Still you may miss a cable. To be safe cut with a handsaw, not a power tool. Stop if you feel any resistance; it might be a cable.

Test all the wires

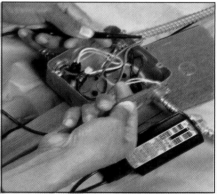

You may find several pairs of wires in an electrical box. This indicates that more than one electrical circuit may be present. So even after you shut off one circuit, some of the wires in the box may still be hot. Take extra care. Shut off the circuit you plan to work on at the service panel. Then open the box, carefully remove wire nuts, and **test all the wires in the box for power.**

Checking that power is off

Circuit index shows which outlets each breaker or fuse controls

MAIN

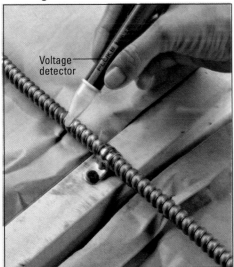

1 At the service panel flip off the breaker or unscrew the fuse controlling the electrical box or device you will work on.

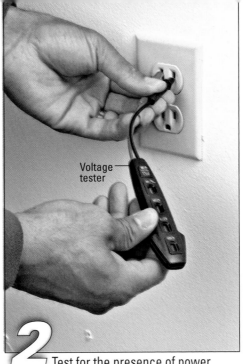

Voltage tester

2 Test for the presence of power using a voltage tester (pages 48–49). If you are working on a receptacle, test both plugs. **Test the tester** too. Touch the probes to a live circuit to make sure the indicator bulb lights.

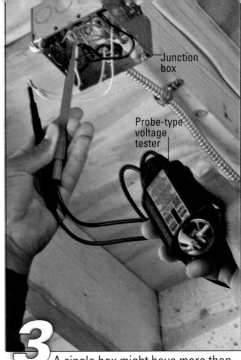

Junction box

Probe-type voltage tester

3 A single box might have more than one circuit running through it. Carefully remove the device or fixture, unscrew the wire nuts, and test all the wires for power.

Testing tools

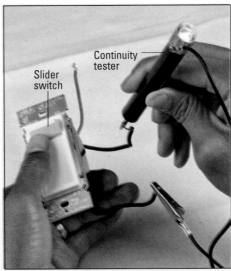

Voltage detector

A voltage detector senses the presence of power inside cables and in some cases even inside walls. Before using it test this battery-powered tool on a line you know to be live. If the end glows the tester is functioning.

Continuity tester

Slider switch

A continuity tester shows when there is a path for current flow. Use it to test a fuse, a switch, or the wiring in a lamp or light fixture. Use it only when the power is off. If the tester lights there is a path for current flow.

Multitester

A multitester does the work of both a voltage tester and a continuity tester. Use it also to test low-voltage wiring such as a door chime. A tester with digital readout (shown) is easier to use than one with a meter.

GETTING READY

Wiring and electrical work are amateur friendly. A handy person who understands some basic information and carefully follows instructions can make safe and reliable electrical installations. Attention to detail is the key.

Wiring help for the whole house
Before you begin a project in this book, read the safety information on page 5 and understand how to shut off power and know how to test that power is off (pages 6–9). This chapter describes the tools and supplies needed for electrical projects. The next chapter, "Checking Your Electrical System," helps you understand your electrical system—and spot problems that may need

attention. "Basic Techniques" shows how to strip wires, splice wires together, and join wires to terminals—essential skills for safe, secure, and reliable electrical connections. Chapters on "Repairs," "Switches & Receptacles," and "Lights & Fans" guide you through basic repairs and upgrades. "Planning New Electrical Service" introduces you to the important preliminary steps for more complex and demanding wiring projects. It also explains how to work with a local building department to ensure that your project meets electrical safety code.

Help extending or adding circuits begins with "Installing Cable & Boxes." The next two chapters show specific projects:

"Installing New Fixtures" and "Installing Fans & Heaters." The final chapters deal with household communication and security, outdoor wiring, and how to connect appliances and new circuits.

How to use this book
Each project includes a Prestart Checklist, which outlines the time, skills, tools, preparations, and materials needed. In addition to the project steps, you'll find Stanley Pro Tips and other extra information. Because no two houses are exactly alike, "What If ..." boxes provide help for different situations you might encounter.

Proper tools and quality materials save time and help ensure a safe and reliable installation.

CHAPTER PREVIEW

Assembling a tool kit
page 12

Special-duty tools
page 14

Cable and wire
page 15

Cable and conduit
page 16

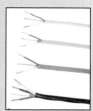
Decoding NM (nonmetallic) cable
page 17

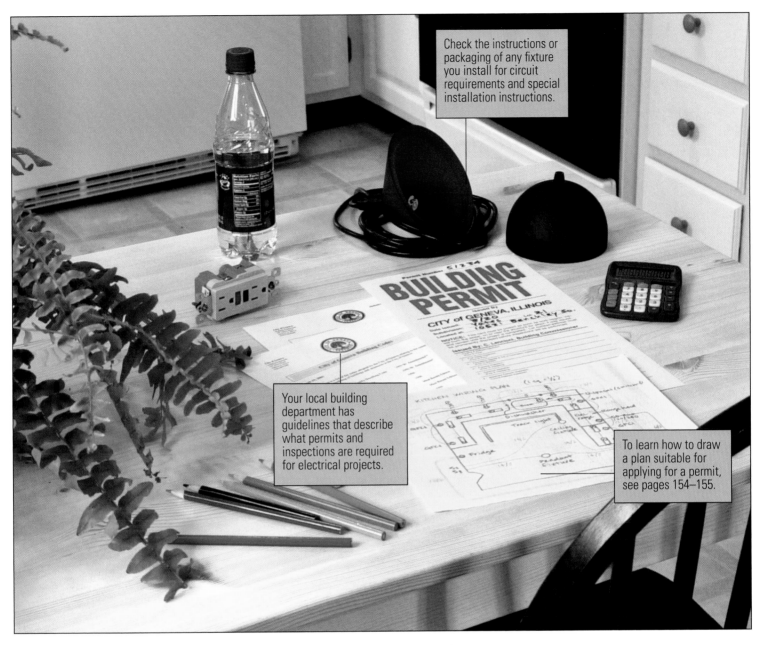

Check the instructions or packaging of any fixture you install for circuit requirements and special installation instructions.

Your local building department has guidelines that describe what permits and inspections are required for electrical projects.

To learn how to draw a plan suitable for applying for a permit, see pages 154–155.

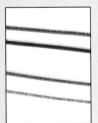

Conduit wire
page 17

Conduit fill
page 18

Electrical boxes
page 19

How many wires?
page 21

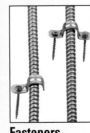

Fasteners and clamps
page 22

Wire nuts
page 23

You can draw plans for an electrical project with the simplest of tools. A pad of graph paper, a ruler, and some colored pencils do the job. You need to find out about building code requirements at the local building department.

ASSEMBLING A TOOL KIT

Buy quality tools for electrical work; your safety and the quality of the installation are at stake. Assembling a complete kit of professional-quality electrician's tools costs far less than hiring a professional to do even a simple installation.

Wiring tools

These tools enable you to cut, strip, and join wires tightly. A pair of **side cutters** (also called diagonal cutters) makes working inside a crowded electrical box or snipping off sheathing from nonmetallic cable easier.

Cutting pliers help with general chores such as snipping armored cable. Use **long-nose pliers** to bend wires into loops before attaching them to terminals. **Combination strippers,** with holes for the wires near the tip, are easier to use than strippers with holes near the handle. For twisting wires together after stripping them, no other tool works as well as **lineman's pliers.** You can also use the pliers to cut wire.

Screwdrivers designed especially for electrical use have thick rubber grips, which shield a hand from shock. You'll most often use screwdrivers with 6- to 7-inch shanks; buy two sizes of **slot screwdrivers** for slotted screws and two sizes of **phillips screwdrivers.** Occasionally you may need a short, stubby one. A **wire-bending screwdriver** quickly forms a perfect loop in a stripped wire end. A **rotary screwdriver** drives screws quickly; use it when you have cover plates to install.

Testers

For most work you need a **voltage tester** to check for the presence of power and a continuity tester (page 9) to see whether a device or fixture is damaged. A multitester

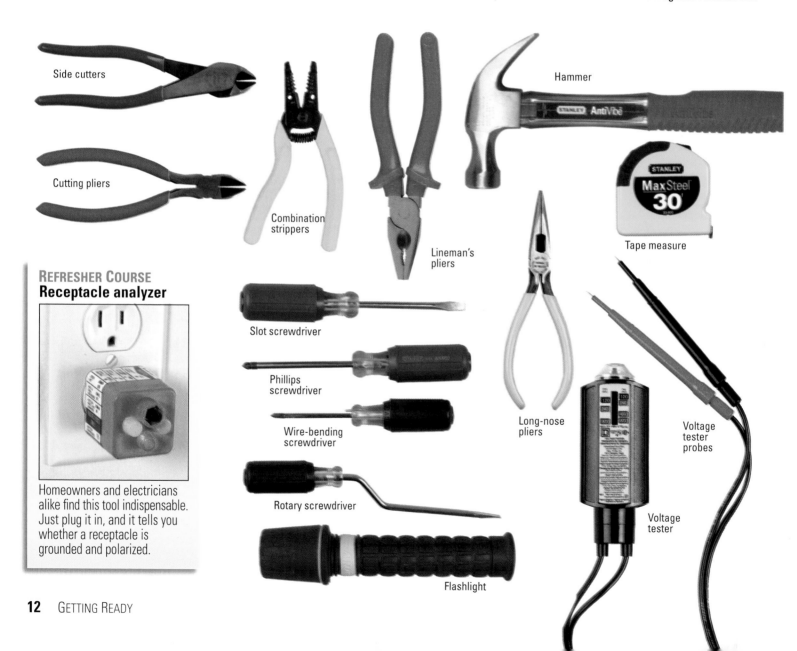

Side cutters

Cutting pliers

Combination strippers

Lineman's pliers

Hammer

Tape measure

Slot screwdriver

Phillips screwdriver

Wire-bending screwdriver

Rotary screwdriver

Long-nose pliers

Voltage tester probes

Voltage tester

Flashlight

(page 9) does the job of both but is a bit more complicated to use. Professional-quality testers have probes and clips with thick rubber grips, and clearly visible lights or readouts.

In addition buy a voltage detector (page 9), which senses power through cable sheathing, a box cover, or even a wall or ceiling. (Testers are shown in use on pages 48–49.) Also buy a **receptacle analyzer** (page 32).

General tools
Keep a reliable **flashlight** within easy reach, in case you have to work with the lights off.

For jobs that involve running cable, you need common carpentry tools. A **hammer** and a pair of **groove-joint pliers** come in handy for just about any wiring job.

To remove moldings with minimal damage, use a **pry bar.** Make initial cuts into walls and ceilings with a **utility knife.** Complete the cuts in plaster walls with a **jigsaw;** use a **drywall saw** to cut through drywall. Use a **hacksaw** to cut rigid conduit and to cut through screws holding boxes.

Fishing tools
These tools help minimize damage to walls and ceilings when running cable. A **⅜-inch drill** is powerful enough for most household projects; rent or buy a ½-inch model for extensive work. In addition to a standard **¾-inch spade bit,** buy a **fishing bit,** which can reach across two studs or joists and pull cable back through the holes it has made (page 177).

You can use a straightened coat hanger wire to fish cable through short runs, but a **fish tape** is easier to use (pages 176–177). Occasionally you may need to run one tape from each direction, so buy two. Also use a fish tape when pulling wires through

Groove-joint pliers

Fishing bit

Drywall saw

Hacksaw

Fish tape

Utility knife

Spade bit

Jigsaw

⅜" drill

Pry bar

STANLEY PRO TIP

Electrician's tool belt

An electrician's tool belt holds all the tools you need and it helps you keep them separate from general tools.

SPECIAL-DUTY TOOLS

The tools shown on pages 12–13 are needed for almost any wiring project. They're essential for any project that involves running new lines. Buy or rent the specialized tools on this page as the need arises.

Cutting tools
If you have old plaster walls, cutting into them to run cable is difficult and messy. There's no simple solution, but many people find a **rotary-cutting tool** handy. It slices through both the lath and plaster without vibrating. It does, however, kick up a good deal of dust.

A **reciprocating saw** cuts notches into walls quickly and is ideal for reaching into tight spots. Use this tool carefully if you suspect electrical cable may lie behind the wall or ceiling surface; if in doubt use a handsaw.

When running outdoor electrical lines, a garden **spade** is usually all you need. Rent a trencher for projects requiring a lot of digging. Use a **clamshell digger** to dig postholes for lamps.

Tools for drilling holes
A ⅜-inch drill is powerful enough to drill six or seven holes in an hour but overheats and even breaks when used continuously. If you have a lot of drilling to do, rent or buy a heavy-duty ½-inch drill. A **right-angle drill** makes it possible to drill holes straight through studs and joists or in other restricted areas. For leveling and plumbing boxes, use a **torpedo level**. To make sure your holes are level with each other, use a 4-foot or longer **carpenter's level**.

Other useful tools
Most electrical components fasten with screws, but some use nuts. For these use a **nut driver** or a socket and ratchet. A **conduit reamer** slips onto a square-shanked screwdriver to clean out pieces of metal conduit cut by a hacksaw. A **cordless screwdriver** saves time if you are installing many devices. Often framing needs notching and trimming—have a ¾-inch **wood chisel** on hand.

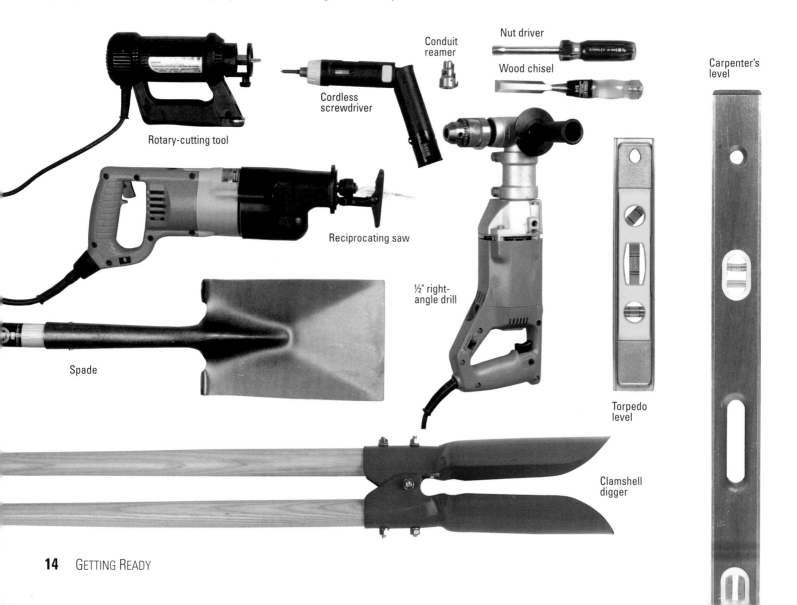

Rotary-cutting tool

Cordless screwdriver

Conduit reamer

Nut driver

Wood chisel

Carpenter's level

Reciprocating saw

½" right-angle drill

Spade

Torpedo level

Clamshell digger

CABLE AND WIRE

Most house wires—the wires that run from the service panel through walls and to electrical boxes—are solid-core, meaning they are made of a single, solid strand. Light fixtures and some switches have leads—wires made of many strands of thin wire, which are more flexible. The thicker a wire, the lower its number; for instance 12-gauge wire is thicker than 14-gauge.

"Cable" refers to two or more wires encased in a protective sheathing. Cable packaging indicates the gauge and number of wires. For example "12/2 WG" means two (black and white) 12-gauge wires plus a ground wire.

Nonmetallic (NM) cable, sometimes called Romex, has two or three insulated wires plus a bare ground wire wrapped in plastic sheathing. Many local codes permit NM cable inside walls or ceilings, and some codes allow it to be exposed in basements and garages. Underground feed (UF) cable has wires wrapped in solid plastic for watertight protection. Use it for outdoor projects.

Armored cable encases insulated wires in metal sheathing for added protection. Metal-clad (MC) and BX (also called AC) have no ground wire, only a thin aluminum bonding wire unsuitable as a ground; the metal sheathing provides the path for grounding. MC may have may have a green-insulated ground wire. Some local codes require armored cable or conduit wherever wiring is exposed.

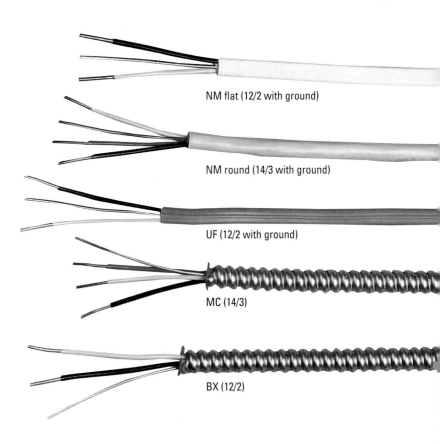

NM flat (12/2 with ground)

NM round (14/3 with ground)

UF (12/2 with ground)

MC (14/3)

BX (12/2)

Conduit types

EMT rigid metal conduit

PVC ½" conduit

Greenfield

EMT ½"

Conduit—pipe that wires run through—offers the best protection against damage to wires. It also makes it easy to change or install new wires: Pull the wires through the conduit rather than cut into walls to run new cable.

Metal conduit (pages 162–163) once was used as a path for grounding; recent codes require a green-insulated ground wire. PVC (plastic) conduit is cheaper but not quite as strong (page 164). Metal Greenfield and plastic EMT tubing are flexible types of conduit. They are useful when working in tight spots.

Wire colors and sizes

The thicker a conductor, the more amperage (amps) it can carry without overheating. A 14-gauge wire can carry up to 15 amps; a 12-gauge wire, up to 20 amps; and a 10-gauge wire, up to 30 amps. Never overload a wire—for instance never wire a 20-amp circuit with 14-gauge wire.

Wires coated with insulation that is black, red, or another color are hot wires, carrying power from the service panel to the electrical device. White wires are neutral, meaning they carry power back to the service panel. Green or bare wires are ground wires. **Beware: If wiring has been done incorrectly, the color of the wires in your house might not indicate which are hot.**

HOT WIRES

14-gauge red

12-gauge blue

10-gauge brown

12-gauge black

GROUND WIRES

12-gauge green insulated

12-gauge copper bare

CABLE AND CONDUIT

Make sure any new cable being installed can handle the electrical load safely and satisfy local building code requirements (pages 146–147).

Nonmetallic (NM) cable has a plastic sheathing and is available in a flat profile or a round profile. Printing on the sheathing of NM cable indicates the gauge and number of wires (page 15). For instance "14/2 WG" means the cable contains two 14-gauge wires plus a bare ground wire; "14/3 WG" indicates three 14-gauge wires plus a ground. The forerunner to NM was fabric-sheathed cable, no longer sold but found in older homes.

Armored cable has a flexible metal sheathing. There are two types: MC, which carries two or three wires plus a ground wire, and older BX, which has no ground wire but has a thin, brittle aluminum wire running through it.

Metal conduit is pipe through which wires run. (Because they are made of metal, BX and metal conduit can be used for grounding, taking the place of a ground wire.)

Underground feed (UF) cable has sheathing that is molded to the wires to protect against moisture in outdoor installations. Telephone cable with four thin wires is increasingly being replaced by Category 5 cable, which can carry lines for telephone, modem, and computer networking. Coaxial cable, used for cable and satellite TV and radio antennas, contains a single solid wire encased in sheathing that includes metal mesh.

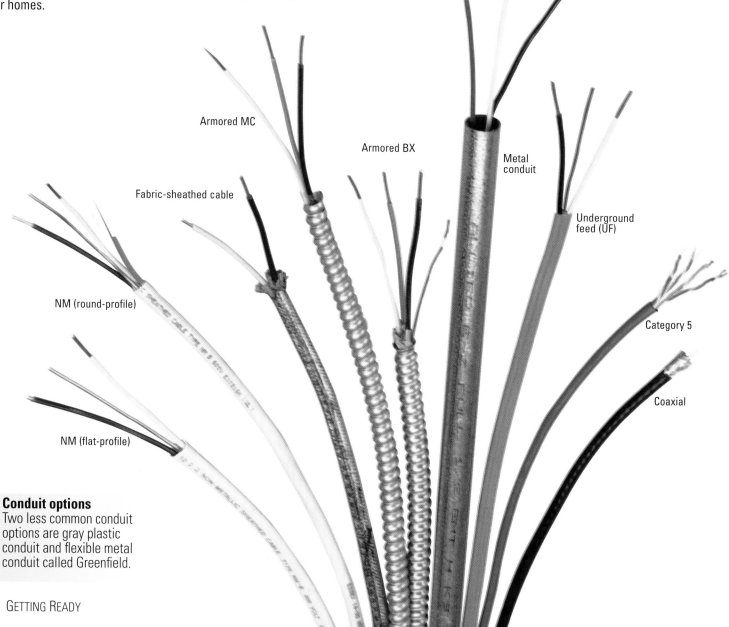

Armored MC

Fabric-sheathed cable

Armored BX

Metal conduit

Underground feed (UF)

NM (round-profile)

Category 5

NM (flat-profile)

Coaxial

Conduit options
Two less common conduit options are gray plastic conduit and flexible metal conduit called Greenfield.

Decoding NM (Nonmetallic) Cable

The color of the sheathing indicates the wire gauge on most NM-B cable made after 2001, though color-coding is voluntary. Color-coded 14-gauge wire has a white jacket; 12-gauge wire is yellow, 10-gauge is orange, and 6- and 8-gauge wires are black. Underground feed (UF) cable is always gray. Double-check by reading the required printing on the sheath: On the white cable (top) 14-2 tells you the conductors are 14-gauge and that there are two of them. (12-gauge three-conductor would be 12-3.) The uninsulated ground wire is never listed. NM means the cable sheathing is nonmetallic; B means the sheath is solid. 600 V is the maximum voltage the wire can carry.

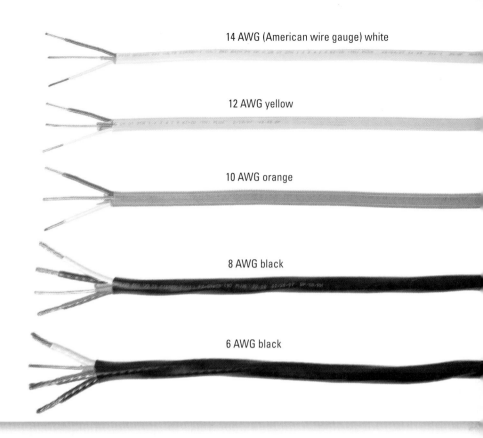

14 AWG (American wire gauge) white

12 AWG yellow

10 AWG orange

8 AWG black

6 AWG black

Conduit Wire

Individual wires are meant to be housed in conduit, and a single piece of conduit can carry wires for several circuits. The color of the insulation indicates the wire's intended use and helps you color-code different circuits. Black, red, blue, and yellow are always hot wires; white and gray are neutral; and bare, green, or green with a yellow stripe are ground.

Labeling on the jacket tells the wire gauge size (12 shown); its conductor material (co, for copper), its maximum voltage capacity (600), and the type of insulation (T, for thermoplastic.) An H indicates it is heat resistant to 167°F; a double H indicates heat resistance to 194°F. N indicates that it has an additional nylon coat to make it oil- and gasoline-resistant, and W indicates a water-resistant cable.

Insulation (this wire meets standards for two classes of wire)

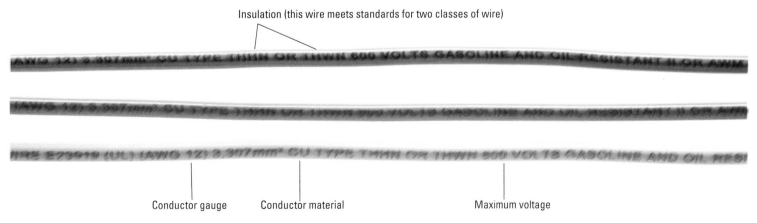

Conductor gauge   Conductor material   Maximum voltage

CONDUIT FILL

The number of wires you can safely put into conduit without overheating is called the conduit fill. Conduit fill depends on the wire size and type and the conduit size and type. While there are hundreds of possible combinations, there are only a few you're likely to use—14-, 12-, or 10-gauge wire, in one of four or five types of conduit. These conduit fill charts describe the allowable fill for common types of conduit.

Conduits and their capacity

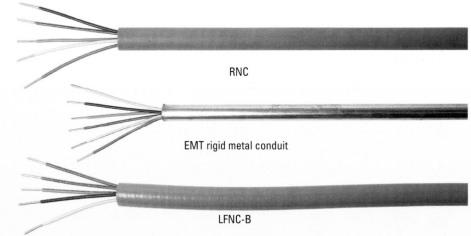

RNC

EMT rigid metal conduit

LFNC-B

All of the conduit shown here is ¾ inch in diameter, but not all can carry the same number of wires without overheating. Electrical metallic tubing, or EMT, dissipates heat well and can carry as many as eleven 12-gauge AWG (American Wire Gauge) conductors. Rigid nonmetallic conduit (RNC), made of PVC, can handle as many as nine 12-gauge wires and meet code. Electrical nonmetallic tubing (ENT) can handle up to 10. Type-A liquidtight flexible nonmetallic conduit (LFNC-A) has a smooth inner core, a layer of reinforcement, and a cover. Code allows you to put up to twelve 12-gauge wires into it. LFNC-B, which has different reinforcement, also can carry up to one dozen 12-gauge wires.

Liquidtight Flexible Metal Conduit

	½" DIA. CONDUIT	¾" DIA. CONDUIT
14 awg	9	15
12 awg	7	12
10 awg	5	9

Liquidtight flexible metal conduit (LFMC) has a liquidtight, nonmetallic, sunlight-resistant jacket over an inner flexible metal core.

Type-A Liquidtight Flexible Nonmetallic Conduit

	⅜" DIA. CONDUIT	½" DIA. CONDUIT	¾" DIA. CONDUIT
14 AWG	5	9	15
12 AWG	4	7	12
10 AWG	3	5	9

Type-A liquidtight flexible nonmetallic conduit (LFNC-A) has a smooth core, a reinforcing layer, and a cover.

Type-B Liquidtight Flexible Nonmetallic Conduit

	⅜" DIA. CONDUIT	½" DIA. CONDUIT	¾" DIA. CONDUIT
14 AWG	5	9	15
12 AWG	4	7	12
10 AWG	3	5	9

Type-B liquidtight flexible nonmetallic conduit (LFNC-B) has a core with built-in reinforcement.

Electrical Metallic Tubing

	½" DIA. CONDUIT	¾" DIA. CONDUIT
14 AWG	8	15
12 AWG	6	11
10 AWG	5	8

Electrical metallic tubing (EMT) is a thin-walled metal pipe.

Rigid Nonmetallic Conduit

	½" DIA. CONDUIT	¾" DIA. CONDUIT
14 AWG	6	11
12 AWG	5	9
10 AWG	3	6

Rigid nonmetallic conduit (RNC) is PVC conduit.

Electrical Nonmetallic Tubing

	½" DIA. CONDUIT	¾" DIA. CONDUIT
14 AWG	7	13
12 AWG	5	10
10 AWG	4	7

Electrical nonmetallic tubing (ENT) is flexible, corrugated PVC.

ELECTRICAL BOXES

Wiring projects usually begin with installing boxes. Wiring splices and wire connections to fixtures or devices must be made inside a code-approved electrical box. (Some fixtures, such as fluorescent and recessed lights, have self-contained electrical boxes approved by most building departments.)

Plastic or metal?
Check with your building department to see whether plastic boxes are acceptable. Some municipalities require metal boxes, which are more expensive but usually no more trouble to install. Use weathertight boxes for outdoor work (pages 262–263).

In older systems that use conduit or the sheathing of armored cable as a grounding path, the boxes must be metal because they are part of the grounding system (page 28). Homes with NM or MC cable use green-insulated or bare copper wires for grounding and don't require metal boxes. However some local codes call for metal boxes, which provide stronger bonds for the grounding wires (page 43).

Remodel and new-work boxes
A remodel box has fittings that secure it to a finished wall. See page 20 for various types and how to install them. Remodel boxes all have internal clamps that clasp the cable to the box.

New-work boxes install quickly into framing that has not been covered with drywall or plaster (page 168). To install most types, position the box so the front edge extends beyond the framing far enough to be flush with the finished wall surface. New-work boxes usually have nailing brackets attached.

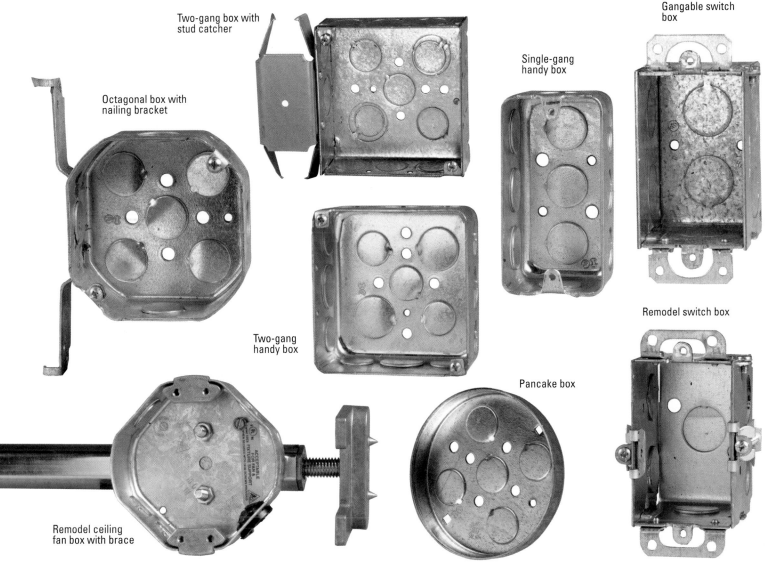

Two-gang box with stud catcher

Gangable switch box

Single-gang handy box

Octagonal box with nailing bracket

Two-gang handy box

Pancake box

Remodel switch box

Remodel ceiling fan box with brace

ELECTRICAL BOXES *(continued)*

Number of gangs

A single-gang box has space and screw holes for one switch or receptacle; a two-gang box is designed for two devices, and so on. Gangable metal boxes can be partly dismantled and joined to form a box of as many gangs as needed.

Adapter rings

A box may be installed with its front edge flush with the wall or ceiling. Or the box may be installed ½ inch behind the wall, in which case an adapter ring, also called a "mud ring," is installed onto the front edge of the box. Use a 4×4-inch box and a single-gang mud ring when installing a 240-volt receptacle (pages 184–185) so there is room for the wiring.

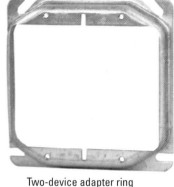

Two-device adapter ring

Single-gang box

Ceiling remodel box

New-work ceiling box

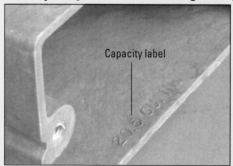

Remodel box with wings

Two-gang box

STANLEY

Pro Tip: Buy boxes that are big enough

Capacity label

Always buy as big a box as fits the available space. Usually the cubic-inch capacity of electrical boxes is marked in the box.
To calculate box capacity use these figures: A 14-gauge wire counts as 2 cubic inches; a 12-gauge wire is 2.25 cubic inches. Count the fixture or device as two wires, all bare ground wires together as one, and all clamps as one (see chart, opposite page). The box above contains eight 12-gauge "wires"—two blacks, two whites, one receptacle, three grounds, and two clamps—a total of 18 cubic inches.

How Many Wires?

Placing too many wires into an electrical box is difficult, dangerous, and against the National Electrical Code. To avoid possible shorts and overheating due to tightly packed wires, the code limits the number of wires you can put into an electrical box. Wires aren't the only things that count as wires, however.

The switch box shown has a total of eight "wires"—one for each of the four insulated wires, two for the switch, one for all of the bare ground wires, and one for the cable clamps. The jumper wire does not count as a conductor.
Referring to the chart "Number of Conductors Allowed in a Wiring Box", below right, you'd need a 3×2×3 ½ -inch device box if you were wiring with 12-gauge wire.

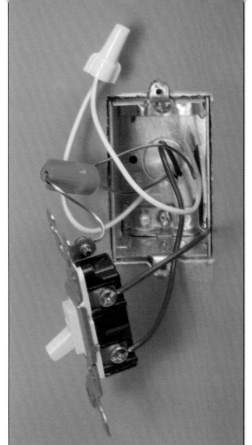

When two or more switches or outlets occur together, you can join gangable boxes together to make a single box. To join the boxes loosen the screws to remove the sides, join the boxes, and screw them together at the tops and bottoms.

Counting Wires in Electrical Boxes

Item	Counts as
Each insulated wire	1 wire
All cable clamps combined	1 wire
Each support for light or other fixture	1 wire
All uninsulated wires combined	1 wire
Each switch, outlet, or other device	2 wires
Jumper wire	0 wires

Number of Conductors Allowed in a Wiring Box

		Wire Size			
Box Size	Type of Box	14	12	10	8
(4 × 1¼)	round/octagonal	6	5	5	5
(4 × 1½)	round/octagonal	7	6	6	5
(4 × 2⅛)	round/octagonal	10	9	8	7
(4 × 1¼)	square	10	9	8	6
(4 × 1½)	square	12	10	9	7
(4 × 2⅛)	square	17	15	13	10
(4¹¹⁄₁₆ × 1¼)	square	12	11	10	8
(4¹¹⁄₁₆ × 1½)	square	14	13	11	9
(4¹¹⁄₁₆ × 2⅛)	square	21	18	16	14
(3 × 2 × 1½)	device	3	3	3	2
(3 × 2 × 2)	device	5	4	4	3
(3 × 2 × 2¼)	device	5	4	4	3
(3 × 2 × 2½)	device	6	5	5	4
(3 × 2 × 2¾)	device	7	6	5	4
(3 × 2 × 3½)	device	9	8	7	6
(4 × 2⅛ × 1½)	device	5	4	4	3
(4 × 2⅛ × 1⅞)	device	6	5	5	4
(4 × 2⅛ × 2⅛)	device	7	6	5	4

FASTENERS AND CLAMPS

In addition to cable and boxes, supplies for electrical wiring include tape, staples, or straps to secure cable to framing members, and clamps that secure the cables to boxes.

Light fixtures usually come with all the necessary hardware for fastening to the ceiling box. If you have old boxes, you may need to buy extra hardware.

Cable fasteners

Codes require that all exposed cable be tightly stapled to the wall, ceiling, or a framing member. Also use staples when running cable in unfinished framing. For NM cable buy plastic-insulated staples that are the right size for the cable.

To anchor metal conduit hammer in drive straps every few feet. For PVC conduit or armored cable, use one- or two-hole straps; make sure they fit snugly around the cable or conduit.

Avoid black drywall (or all-purpose) screws because they break easily. Wood screws cost more but are more reliable.

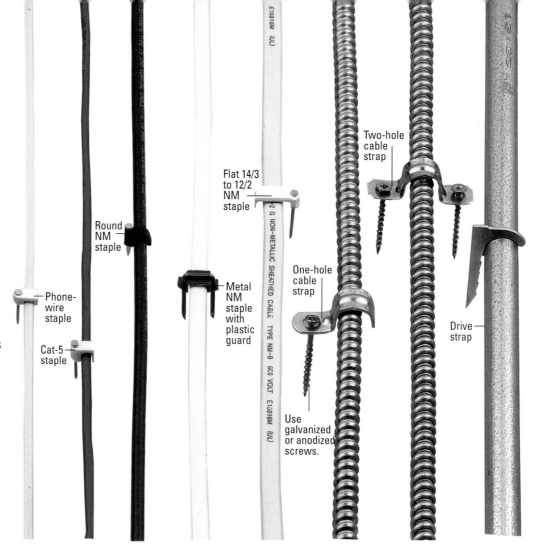

Phone-wire staple

Cat-5 staple

Round NM staple

Metal NM staple with plastic guard

Flat 14/3 to 12/2 NM staple

Use galvanized or anodized screws.

One-hole cable strap

Two-hole cable strap

Drive strap

Clamp types

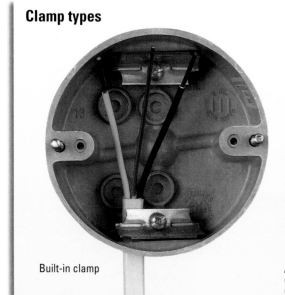

Built-in clamp

Armored cable clamp

NM cable clamp

New-work plastic boxes have holes with plastic flaps that grab NM cable. With this type of box, you must staple the cable to a framing member near the box (page 159). Use these only in unfinished framing. When installing a remodel box or when installing a box that is exposed, the cable or conduit must be firmly clamped directly to the box.

A cable clamp comes in two parts: the clamp and the locknut. An NM cable clamp holds the cable using a strap with two screws; an armored cable clamp holds the cable using a single setscrew.

For instructions on how to clamp cable to a box, see page 159.

WIRE NUTS

In old installations wire splices often were covered with thick electrician's tape. That is not only a slow way to cover a splice but also a code violation. Cover every splice with an approved wire nut.

Assemble a collection of various-size nuts so you are ready for any splice. Wire nuts are color-coded according to size. The colors and sizes may vary according to manufacturer. Read the packaging to make sure the nuts you buy fit over your splices. The most common arrangement is like this:

■ The smallest wire nuts—which usually come with light fixtures—are often white, ivory, or blue. If these have plastic rather than metal threads inside, throw them away and get orange connectors with metal threads for a secure connection.
■ Orange nuts are the next size up and can handle splices of up to two #14 wires.
■ Midsize yellow wire nuts are the most common. Use them for splices as small as two #14s or as large as three #12s.

■ Red connectors are usually the largest wire nuts and can handle a splice of up to four #12s.
■ Green wire nuts are used for ground wires. They have a hole in the top, which allows one ground wire to poke through and run directly to a device or box.
■ Gray twister wire nuts are designed to be all-purpose—they can handle the smallest to the largest splices. However they are bulky and expensive.
■ B-cap wire nuts are slim, which makes them useful if a box is crowded with wires.

Two #16 stranded wires

Two #14 solid wires

Two #14 solid grounding wires

Three #12 wires

Four #12 wires

All-purpose twister wire nuts

Space-saving B-cap wire nuts

STANLEY® PRO TIP

Use high-quality tape

Professional-quality electrician's tape costs more than bargain-bin tape, but it sticks better and is easier to work with.

You should cut pieces of tape rather than ripping them off the roll; the rippled ends of torn-off pieces do not stick well. Cutting with a utility knife is often awkward and time-consuming, so buy tape in a dispenser—just unroll the tape and pull it down to make a clean cut.

Grounding pigtail

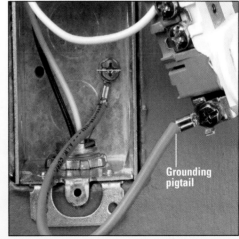

Grounding pigtail

If codes require attaching grounds to metal boxes, grounding pigtails save time and work. If your boxes do not already have green-tinted grounding screws, buy some that fit into the threaded holes in the boxes.

CHECKING YOUR ELECTRICAL SYSTEM

Electrical work is straightforward and you can repair or alter the system in your home safely and easily by following simple rules. Before you start a project, become familiar with the basics of electricity and household electrical circuits. Review electrical safety. Survey your home's electrical system and understand it before you begin any project. If you are wary of any aspect of the project, review the appropriate parts of this book to find answers.

This chapter introduces some principles of home electrical systems to help you become familiar with the wiring in your home. The chapter begins with an overview of residential wiring. It also shows you what to look for when you inspect your system and how to work safely.

The knowledge you need
In this chapter you'll learn:
- How to test for power and make sure power is off
- How circuits work and which parts of your house are protected by each fuse or circuit breaker in the service panel
- How switches and receptacles work
- How your total system is grounded
- How each electrical box is grounded
- How a ground fault circuit interrupter (GFCI) works and how to test one
- How to determine the purpose and function of any wire you may encounter.

A surface inspection
Most electrical problems are easy to spot once you know what to look for. You can spot many problems without removing a cover plate or fixture. The inspection described in this chapter helps you find and correct dangerous situations and electrical code violations that are found in many homes.

Getting more information
This book covers the common situations encountered in home wiring. If your house has some unusual installations, seek additional advice. You might find help at a home center or hardware store. Or call your local building department and schedule an appointment with an electrical inspector. Or you may decide to hire a professional electrician to inspect your home's electrical system and recommend necessary work to correct any problems.

Take time to evaluate the overall safety of your household electrical system.

CHAPTER PREVIEW

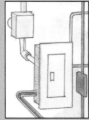
Understanding circuits
page 26

How circuits are grounded and polarized
page 28

The house ground
page 29

Service entrance and meter
page 30

Surface inspection
page 32

Knob-and-tube wiring
This older system uses two separate wires that are routed through porcelain knobs and tubes. It is not unsafe as long as the wires are undisturbed. However it does not provide a ground path.

Armored cable
Two or more insulated wires, and perhaps a ground wire, are encased in flexible metal sheathing.

NM cable
Nonmetallic (NM) cable contains two or more insulated conductors and a bare ground wire wrapped in plastic outer sheathing.

Various types of cable may be intermixed in the electrical system of an older home that has been remodeled several times. Vintage knob-and-tube wiring, NM cable, and armored cable enter the same electrical box in the house wiring shown above.

Service panels
page 36

Opening boxes
page 38

Inspecting boxes
page 40

Junction boxes and subpanels
page 42

Grounding
page 43

Difficult wiring configurations
page 45

UNDERSTANDING CIRCUITS

Electricity moves through any metal conductor, such as a wire or the metal contacts and other components inside a switch or receptacle. Electrical current must move in a loop, or circuit. If the circuit is broken at any point, the flow of power stops.

From power grid to service panel
Power comes to your home through the power company's transmission and distribution lines, passes through a meter, and enters the service panel.

In the service panel the power energizes two strips of metal called hot bus bars. Circuit breakers or fuses attach to the hot bus bars. Power must pass through a breaker or fuse before it leaves the service panel and goes into the house through a branch circuit.

Each branch circuit supplies power to a number of outlets. An outlet is any place where power leaves the wires to provide service. Devices (receptacles and switches), ceiling lights and fans, and appliances (such as a water heater or a dishwasher) are the most common outlets.

Circuit wiring
Power leaves the service panel via a hot (energized) wire—one with insulation that is black, red, or a color other than green or white—and returns to the panel through a neutral wire—one with white insulation. Another wire, bare or with green insulation, provides the ground.

The neutral and ground wires connect to the separate neutral bus bar in the service panel. That bus bar is connected to the neutral line from the power line.

The thicker the wire, the more electrical current it can safely carry. If too much current passes through a wire, the wire overheats, the insulation can fail, and a fire or shock could result. The service panel (often called the fuse box or breaker box) provides protection against this possibility.

Breakers and fuses
A breaker or fuse is a safety device. When it senses that its circuit is drawing too much power, it automatically shuts off. A breaker "trips" and can be reset; a fuse "blows" and must be replaced. Both devices keep wires from overheating.

Volts
Volts are the amount of force exerted by the power source. Household wiring carries 120 volts. (Actually voltage varies constantly but stays within an acceptable range, from 115 to 125 volts.)

Most outlets supply 120 volts, which is provided by one hot wire bringing the power to the outlet and one neutral wire carrying it back to the service panel. Some heavy-duty appliances, such as large air conditioners, electric ranges, and electric water heaters, use 240 volts, supplied by two 120-volt hot wires with one neutral wire.

Amps and watts
Though the force pushing current through all wires is the same—120 volts—fixtures and appliances use different amounts of power. Amperes (amps) measure the amount of electrical flow. Wattage (watts), the amount of power an electrical device consumes, is calculated by multiplying the voltage times the amperage.

Circuits are designed to carry a specific maximum electrical flow, usually 15 or 20 amps for 120-volt household circuits. Wires for a 20-amp circuit are thicker than those for a 15-amp.

When a circuit breaker trips or a fuse blows, it is a sign that the circuit is overloaded. The only solution is to remove some electrical load from the circuit. If you have a toaster, waffle iron, electric skillet, and other appliances running on the same circuit, plug some into another circuit.

Terms you may hear inspectors and electricians use

Device refers to any electrical receptacle or switch.

Feeder refers to an incoming hot wire. On a ground fault circuit interrupter (GFCI) receptacle, the word "line" refers to the incoming feeder and neutral wires.

Conductor is basically another word for a wire.

Outlet is any place where electricity leaves the wiring to be used, including fixtures, receptacles, and appliances.

Receptacle is a device with holes, into which you can insert a plug to deliver power to an appliance, power tool, or lamp.

Service panels
Panels have varying styles of covers and different styles of breakers. See pages 36–37 for more information.

Bus bars
For more about bus bars and the connections inside service panels, see pages 278–279.

Avoid overloads
For more about how to avoid overloading household circuits, see page 80.

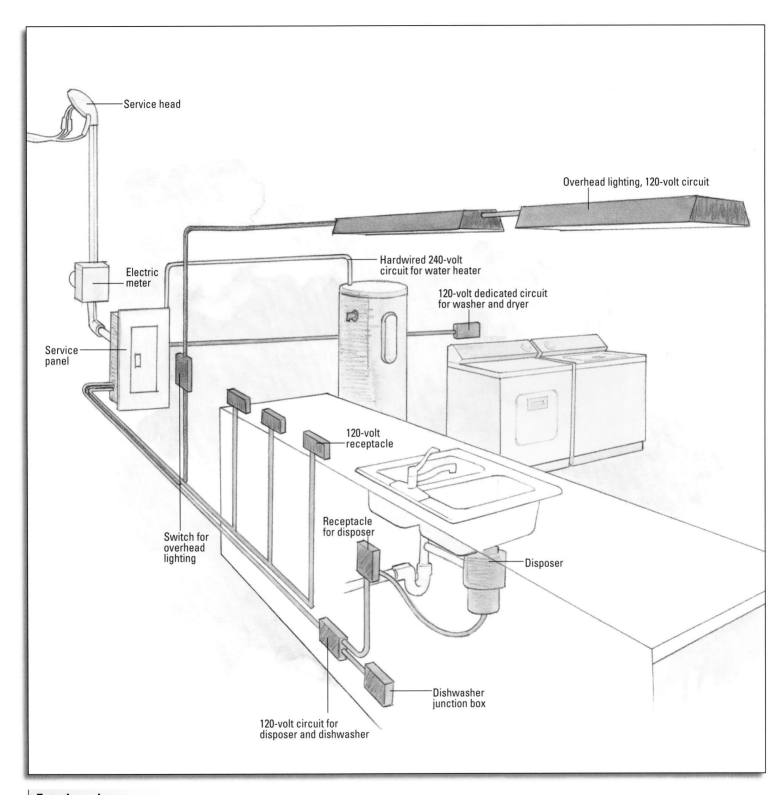

Service head

Overhead lighting, 120-volt circuit

Electric meter

Hardwired 240-volt circuit for water heater

120-volt dedicated circuit for washer and dryer

Service panel

120-volt receptacle

Switch for overhead lighting

Receptacle for disposer

Disposer

Dishwasher junction box

120-volt circuit for disposer and dishwasher

Entering a home
See pages 30–31 for details on the ways electrical lines enter your home.

HOW CIRCUITS ARE GROUNDED AND POLARIZED

If an electrical system works correctly, power travels safely through insulated wires to fixtures and appliances. However if a receptacle is damaged or a wire comes loose, power may flow to unwanted places such as a metal electrical box or the metal housing of an appliance. Because the human body is a fairly good conductor of electricity, a person touching these objects receives a painful shock. Grounding and polarization reduce this danger.

You can quickly find out whether a receptacle is grounded and polarized by using a receptacle analyzer (page 32).

Grounding

Electricity always travels the path of least resistance, either in a circuit back to its place of origin or toward the earth. A grounded electrical system provides an alternate path for the power to follow in case something goes wrong.

Many homes built before World War II have 120-volt circuits with only two wires, 240-volt circuits with only three wires, and no metal sheathing or conduit to act as a ground. These homes are not grounded, and receptacles in them should have only two slot-shaped holes.

Most modern homes are grounded. They have a third (or fourth) wire, usually bare copper or green insulated, called a ground wire; or their wires may run through metal conduit or flexible metal sheathing that can be used as a path for ground. A ground wire or metal sheathing carries misguided electricity harmlessly to the earth. Receptacles in these homes should have a third, rounded hole, which connects to the ground wire or sheathing.

Polarization

Most receptacles—grounded or ungrounded—have one slot that is longer than the other, so that a plug that has one prong wider than the other can be inserted only one way. These receptacles and plugs are polarized.

If a polarized receptacle is wired correctly, the narrow slot connects to the hot wire (delivering power to the receptacle) and the wide slot connects to the neutral wire (carrying power back to the service panel). When you plug a light or appliance into the receptacle, its switch controls the hot wire. If the receptacle or plug is not polarized or if a receptacle is wired incorrectly, the switch controls the neutral wire. This means that power is still present in the wires inside the light or appliance when you turn it off, posing a safety hazard.

120-Volt Light Circuit

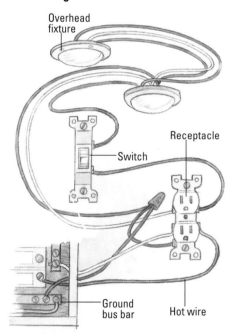

Overhead fixture

Receptacle

Switch

Ground bus bar

Hot wire

Any circuit that includes lights should be protected by a 15-amp breaker or fuse. (A light fixture's wires are thin and may burn up before they trip a 20-amp breaker.)

120-Volt Receptacle Circuit

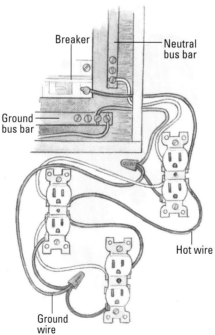

Breaker

Neutral bus bar

Ground bus bar

Hot wire

Ground wire

A receptacle circuit may be 15- or 20-amp. Black (hot) wires carry power to the receptacles, and white (neutral) wires lead back to the service panel.

Armored cable
Some codes do not allow use of armored cable as a ground. Check before you install.

240-Volt Circuit

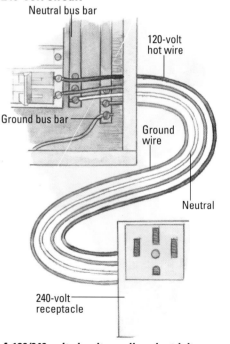

Neutral bus bar

120-volt hot wire

Ground bus bar

Ground wire

Neutral

240-volt receptacle

A 120/240-volt circuit supplies electricity to a heavy user of power such as an electric range or dryer. Two hot wires bring power, and one neutral wire leads back to the service panel. Current codes call for a fourth ground wire.

THE HOUSE GROUND

Ground wires for individual branch circuits (or metal sheathing that acts as a ground) lead back to the neutral or ground bus bar of the service panel. The service panel itself must be connected to the earth so that the entire electrical system is safely grounded.

Usually a service panel is grounded by a thick wire—bare copper or green insulated—leading to a ground rod or to a cold-water pipe. Follow the ground wire from the service panel to find how it is attached to the earth.

Ground rod
A copper ground rod is driven at least 8 feet into the ground. Its top may be visible, or it may be sunk beneath the ground. The service panel ground wire must be firmly attached to the ground rod, either with a special toothed clamp or by welding. Recent building codes often call for two or more ground rods for added security.

Cold-water pipe
The service panel ground wire may lead to a cold-water pipe, which is connected to supply pipes that lead deep underground. The connection must be firmly clamped. Hot water pipes are not acceptable for grounds because they run only to the water heater, not into the earth.

Other methods
In rocky areas, where it is difficult to drive a ground rod 8 feet down, a grounding plate may be used. This thick piece of metal is buried underneath a footing or foundation. Or a ground wire may connect to a metal reinforcing rod embedded in a house's concrete foundation.

If you have any doubts about your home's grounding—and especially if a receptacle analyzer shows that the receptacles are not grounded—have a professional electrician inspect your home.

Ground rod: Many ground lines are clamped to an 8-foot-long copper rod driven into the ground. The connection may be above ground (shown) or a few inches beneath.

Cold-water pipes: Because municipal water pipes are buried, a firm connection to a cold water pipe forms an effective ground.

WHAT IF...
Your house is ungrounded?

If your home's receptacles have only two holes or if a receptacle analyzer indicates they are ungrounded, don't panic—people have lived with ungrounded homes for decades. However grounding considerably improves a home's safety and is well worth adding.

If you want to ground an entire system, you have to call in a pro to rewire the entire home—an expensive job. If you want to ground only one receptacle, you can ask an electrician to run an individual ground wire from the receptacle to a cold-water pipe.

Here's a simpler solution: Install ground fault circuit interrupter (GFCI) receptacles. These offer protection similar to grounding. Installed correctly a single GFCI can protect all the receptacles on a circuit. (For more on GFCIs see page 32.)

STANLEY PRO TIP
Add a meter jumper

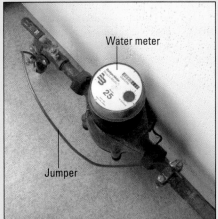

If your house ground connects to a cold-water pipe, the pipe must connect directly to municipal pipes underground. A newer water meter or a water filter may have nonmetal parts and break the connection. Clamp a copper jumper cable to either side of any such obstruction to complete the connection.

SERVICE ENTRANCE AND METER

A power company generates electrical power and sends it to your neighborhood through overhead or underground wires. Transformers, located on utility poles or on the ground, reduce the voltage before electricity enters a home.

Power arrives at most homes via two insulated hot wires, each carrying 120 volts, plus a bare neutral wire. Homes built before World War II may have only one hot wire, which limits service possibilities. It should be upgraded; contact your local power company.

A service entrance consists of the wires leading from the transformer to the house (overhead wires are sometimes referred to as a service drop), the point of attachment for those wires to the house (the service head), the meter, and the wires leading from the meter to the service panel (commonly called the breaker box or fuse box).

The power company is usually responsible for the wires up to the utility splices or to the service head. A professional electrician installs the wires after the service head, as well as the meter and service panel.

With an underground service entrance, the power company brings power all the way to the meter base (see opposite page).

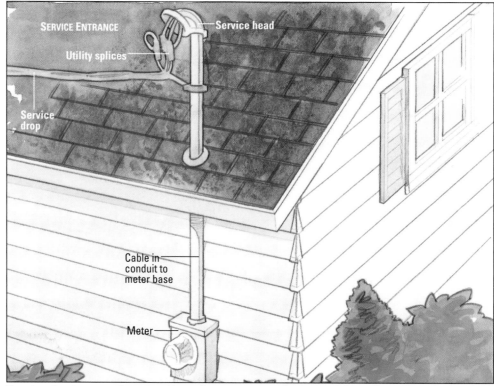

Overhead entrance wires should not droop lower than 12 feet from the ground at any point and should be clear of branches, which can damage the insulation. The point of attachment and the utility splices (below left) must be firm. Conduit should protect the wires leading to the meter base.

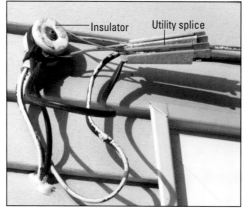

On older homes the point of attachment may be a porcelain insulator, securely screwed into a framing member within the wall. Call the power company if the insulator is cracked or loose.

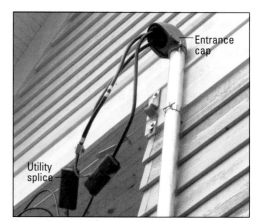

A service head (or masthead) has an entrance cap with insulated openings to keep the wires dry. Older entrance caps have goosenecks that point down so rainwater doesn't enter. On either, check that the wire insulation is not frayed near the opening and that the pipes are firmly anchored.

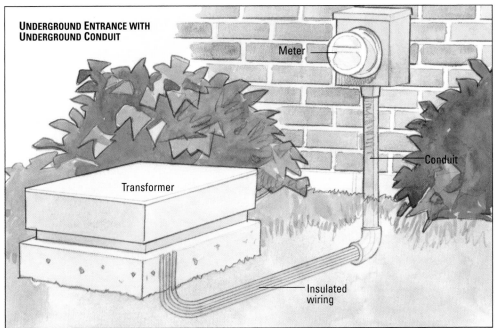

UNDERGROUND ENTRANCE WITH UNDERGROUND CONDUIT

Meter

Conduit

Transformer

Insulated wiring

An underground entrance begins with a transformer, usually sitting on a concrete pad. Three insulated wires, buried 3 or 4 feet underground, run to the house. These wires may be encased in conduit. When they reach the house, they extend up through metal or PVC conduit to reach the meter. In some locales the meter may be placed away from the house, near the transformer. Find out where the underground wires are located to avoid accidentally nicking them with a shovel. Call your local utility company to mark the locations before you start digging.

Read your meter: Even if the power company doesn't require you to read your meter, you can compare numbers at the beginning and end of each billing cycle to keep track of electrical usage. To read a dial meter, write down the digit that each dial is pointing to, working from left to right.

From the meter base to the service panel

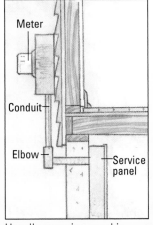

Meter

Conduit

Elbow

Service panel

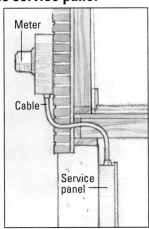

Meter

Cable

Service panel

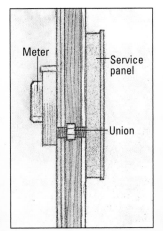

Meter

Service panel

Union

Usually a service panel is located as near as possible to the meter. In warm climates the service panel may be on

the outside of the house. The meter and panel are usually connected in one of the three ways shown above.

Cable traveling from the meter to the panel may be exposed, or encased in conduit.

SURFACE INSPECTION

Even if your electrical system has been trouble-free for decades, it may not be completely safe. On the next four pages, you'll learn how to spot shortcomings often found in household electrical systems.

To perform this inspection you need a receptacle analyzer and a flashlight. You won't have to remove any cover plates or open any boxes, but be prepared to move furniture to uncover every outlet.

In addition to living areas, check out-of-the-way places such as garages, basements, attics, utility rooms, or crawlspaces. There you may find exposed cables and electrical boxes, which help you better understand your wiring.

Testing receptacles

Receptacle analyzer

Grounded and polarized: Begin an inspection by plugging a receptacle analyzer into each outlet of every 120-volt receptacle in your home. The analyzer quickly tells whether receptacles are grounded and polarized. If only one or two receptacles lack grounding or polarizing, examine the wiring in each more closely. (See pages 40–42. To wire outlets correctly see pages 106–107.) If all or most receptacles test as ungrounded, make sure the house ground wire is connected (page 29). If you cannot determine why the test indicates there is no ground, call a professional electrician.

Test button

GFCI: A GFCI receptacle offers effective protection against shock, but it can wear out and lose its ability to work properly. Test the device once a month by pushing the test button. Doing so should shut off power. If it doesn't, replace the GFCI (page 108).

Mounting screw

Short slot

Two-slot receptacles: The box still may be grounded, even if the receptacle lacks a grounding hole. Poke one probe of a voltage tester into the short slot and touch the other to the mounting screw (scrape off any paint first). If the tester glows, you can install a grounded receptacle (pages 106–107).

Checking receptacles for damage

Crack

Cracks: A cracked receptacle may work just fine, but don't take a chance. The contacts on the inside could be damaged, creating sparking and shorts. Replace the receptacle (pages 106–107).

Missing plate: A cover plate is not just for show; it protects you from the live wires that lie just an inch or so behind the wall's surface. Install cover plates wherever they are missing.

Problems with switches

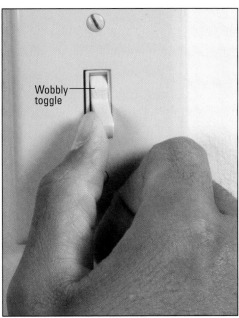

Wobbly toggle

Loose switch: If a toggle feels loose or wobbly, **shut off power to the circuit,** remove the cover plate, and tighten its mounting screws. If it still wobbles replace the switch (pages 92–97).

SAFETY FIRST
Protecting kids from shocks

Protective insert

Twist opening

Receptacles are located at a tempting height for babies and toddlers. Protect them by pushing plastic inserts into each outlet.

For more secure protection purchase a special cover plate with outlet covers that must be twisted before a plug can be inserted, or buy a receptacle with sliding protective covers.

Missing knob

Missing knob: A dimmer switch missing its knob or lever is more than just an eyesore and an inconvenience; it is easily damaged. Replace the knob or install a new dimmer.

Dangerous cords and plugs

Overload: This tangle of cords plugged into one receptacle places it and its circuit at risk of overloading. The cords also create a tripping hazard. A safer alternative: Install an additional receptacle or two, using surface-mounted raceway components (pages 110–112).

Cracked plug: A cord plug protects your fingers from dangerous amounts of electricity. If a plug is damaged in any way, replace it (pages 60–61).

Cracked plug body

Taped cord: A repair like this is not only unsightly; it's dangerous. Tape, even if wound tightly and neatly, can come loose, tempting youngsters to unwrap it. Replace the cord (pages 64–65).

Risky wires and cables

Loose cable: All exposed cable should be securely anchored to minimize the risk of accidentally snagging it. Anchor the cable using staples or straps (page 22). Never hang anything on exposed electrical cable.

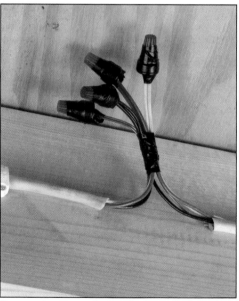

Exposed splices: Safety codes strictly forbid wire splices outside approved electrical boxes. Exposed splices like this may come loose if bumped, causing shock or fire. Have an electrician install a junction box.

No cable clamp: A cable entering a metal box must be held firmly with an approved clamp. A loose cable like this is easily damaged by the metal box's edges. Install a clamp like the one shown on page 41.

Light fixture problems

Bare bulb: An illuminated lightbulb is hot enough to ignite nearby clothing or cardboard, and it is easily broken. Install a protective globe fixture (pages 118–119).

Loose fixtures: Sometimes a ceiling fan or a heavy chandelier will come loose and fall from the ceiling. Check that your fan is securely mounted to a fan-rated box (pages 128–129).

Old wiring: Old knob-and-tube wiring like this is safe if it was properly installed and is not damaged. Check that the insulation is not cracked and take steps to ensure that the wiring does not get bumped.

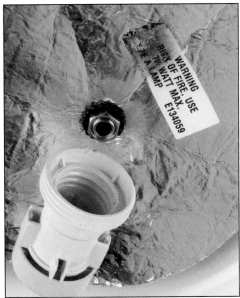

Overheating: When you remove a light fixture's cover to change a bulb, check for evidence of overheating. If you see a brown spot or if the wire insulation has become brittle, replace the fixture (pages 118–119).

Wrong wattage: Heed the sticker telling you how much wattage a light fixture can handle. If you use bulbs of higher wattage, the fixture will overheat.

SERVICE PANELS

If your home has undergone remodeling, new circuits might have been added to the service panel. Even if the panel was properly installed, mistakes may have been made in later wiring. Here's how to safely remove the cover of a service panel and inspect for damage or incorrect wiring.

Shut off power

Before removing a cover, **shut off the main breaker or pull the main fuse** (pages 6–7). This will de-energize everything in the panel except the thick wires that come from the outside. Those are still live, so stay away from them. Wear rubber-sole shoes and stand on a dry surface, just in case you accidentally touch a live wire.

Check the obvious

A service panel must be kept dry, clean, and undisturbed. If you see dampness or signs of rust, find out how water is getting in and seal any cracks or holes. If the panel is badly dented or if rust is extensive, have an electrician inspect it.

Clean away any dust, dirt, and construction debris inside the service panel. They pose a fire hazard.

Wire problems

The wires in a service panel should run in an orderly manner around the perimeter of the panel. They should be clear of bus bars and breakers.

Carefully inspect for nicked or cracked wire insulation. If the damage is minor to just a few wires, you may be able to fix it yourself. See pages 73–75 to learn how to repair damaged wires. Call in a pro if the damage is extensive.

One wire should connect to each circuit breaker or fuse, although sometimes two wires are allowed. If you see more than two wires on a connection, call a professional.

Shut off power
See pages 6–7 for how to access and shut off power in a service panel.

Opening the panel

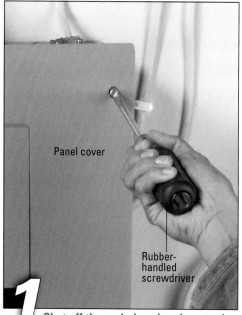

1 **Shut off the main breaker.** Locate the cover screws; placement varies according to manufacturer. Unscrew each and set them where they won't get lost.

Panel cover

Rubber-handled screwdriver

2 Grasp the cover at the bottom and gently pull outward. Lift up to unhook the cover at the top and remove the cover.

REMOVE THE COVER
Opening panels with two covers

Some panels have two covers. Remove the outer cover to access all the breakers and the inner cover to access the wires.

1 Remove the mounting screws. You may have to remove a mounting screw below the cover. Lift the outer cover up and out.

2 The inner cover has mounting screws attached to tabs. Unscrew them, then pull the inner cover off.

Inspecting the panel

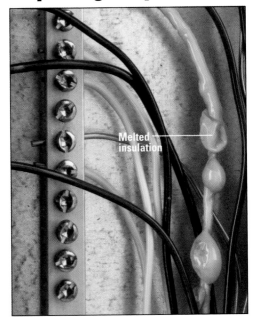

Overheated wires: Look for signs of overheating. If you spot a wire with melted insulation, check to see whether the circuit breaker or fuse that protects it is the correct amperage. If you find obvious signs of fire, such as a charred bus bar or housing, call a professional electrician for evaluation.

Wires too close: If any wire comes close to an electrical connection, move the wire to the side if possible. Don't push too hard or you may disconnect it. If things seem hopelessly tangled, call in a pro.

Wrong amperage: Check the wire gauge. If it is not printed on the wire's insulation, compare the wire with a known gauge—a #14 wire is thinner and belongs on a 15-amp circuit; a #12 wire is thicker for a 20-amp circuit (page 15). If a breaker's amperage is too high for its circuit's wire, call a pro.

(page 15)

SAFETY FIRST
Correct amperage of fuses

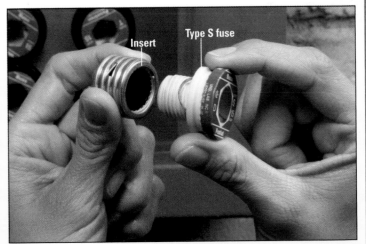

Likely overload: If you find a 30-amp fuse on a typical household circuit, it likely was installed by someone who got tired of changing 20- or 15-amp fuses on an overloaded circuit. This is very unsafe. Only circuits wired with 10-gauge or thicker wire should have a 30-amp fuse.

Inserts for safety: To make it impossible to install an incorrectly sized fuse, use Type S fuses. The fuses are supplied with inserts that screw into the panel. When the insert is in place, only the correct fuse fits.

OPENING BOXES

Some homeowners fear the power that lurks behind a receptacle cover plate or light fixture. Others dive in with reckless abandon. These pages chart a middle course, preparing you to work with both confidence and caution.

Shut off power to the circuit first (pages 6–7). Perform an initial test for power (pages 48–49). Test a receptacle by inserting the prongs of a voltage tester into the slots of one outlet, then the other. Test a switch or light fixture by flipping on the switch. Even if the initial test indicates no power, there still might be power in the box. Use a voltage tester to double-check inside the box (Step 2).

Removal tips
When removing screws grasp a rubber-grip screwdriver only by the rubber handle. Stand on a fiberglass or wood ladder (not aluminum) when removing an overhead light fixture.

Cover plates are cheap, so don't hesitate to replace one that is ugly or damaged.

If your light fixture installation has hardware different from what is shown, see pages 118–121 for mounting options.

PRESTART CHECKLIST

☐ **TIME**
1 minute to open a switch or receptacle; several minutes to remove a fixture

☐ **TOOLS**
Rubber-grip #1 slot and phillips screwdrivers, voltage tester

☐ **PREP**
Spread an old dish towel or small drop cloth to catch debris when you remove receptacle cover plates. Use a sturdy fiberglass ladder for reaching ceiling fixtures.

Receptacle and switch boxes

1 Shut off power and test for power. Use a small-tipped (#1) slot screwdriver to remove cover plate mounting screws. If the cover plate does not come off easily, pry it gently from the wall. If it has been painted over, cut lightly around its perimeter with a utility knife.

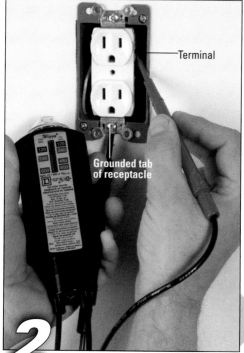

Terminal

Grounded tab of receptacle

2 Test again for power—there may be live wires in the electrical box that do not connect to the device or fixture. Touch voltage tester probes to all possible wire combinations. If you have a metal box, also test by touching one probe to the box and the other probe to each wire.

STANLEY PRO TIP: **What the wire colors mean**

Wire insulation colors have straightforward meanings: A black wire is hot, bringing power from the service panel to the box; a white wire is neutral, carrying power back to the panel; and a bare or green-insulated wire is the ground. Other colored wires—red is the most common—also carry power. (See pages 26–28 for more on circuits.) However it is not unusual to find amateur wiring with the colors mixed up. If you suspect this is true in your house, call in a pro.

If you have old wires that all look black or gray, it may not be obvious which are hot and which are neutral. If your metal boxes are grounded, remove wire nuts and touch one probe of a voltage tester to the box. Touch the other probe to each wire in turn. The tester glows when you touch a hot wire. If the wiring is in a receptacle box, plug in a receptacle analyzer. It indicates a fault if the hot wire has been improperly connected to the silver terminal of the receptacle.

Stay safe
A voltage tester is an essential tool for electrical work. Buy one and use it.

Opening a fixture

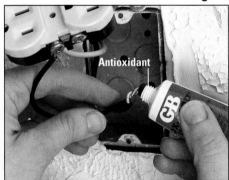

3 Unscrew the screws holding the device to the box; they come out of the holes in the box but may remain attached to the device by little pieces of plastic or cardboard. Carefully grab the device by its plastic parts only and gently pull it out. Inspect the wiring and the box.

1 **Shut off power.** Position a ladder so you can reach and see all around the light fixture. With your fingers loosen but do not remove at least two of the setscrews that hold the glass shade or globe. If a screw is rusted, you may need a screwdriver or pliers to turn it. Remove the glass shade or globe.

2 Find the screws that hold the fixture to the ceiling box (usually there are two). Unscrew them, supporting the fixture with your other hand. Gently pull the fixture down. If the fixture is heavy, support it with a coat hanger or stiff wire attached to the box while you inspect the box and wiring.

WHAT IF ...
Your house has aluminum wiring?

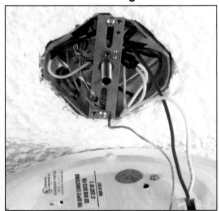

Antioxidant

Some houses built in the early 1970s have aluminum wiring. It is dull silver in color, thicker than copper wiring, and often has "AL" printed on its insulation.

Aluminum wiring expands and contracts with changing temperatures. Over time it often works loose from terminals. Wherever aluminum contacts a copper terminal or wire, it eventually oxidizes, creating a bad connection. For these reasons aluminum was banned from electrical systems a few years after builders started using it.

Don't panic if you find aluminum wiring in your house. Rewiring a house with copper is probably not necessary. Instead make sure that all the switches and receptacles are labeled CO/ALR, meaning it is safe to wire them with aluminum. Wherever you must splice an aluminum wire with a copper lead (for example when you install a light fixture), squirt a bit of antioxidant onto the connection before attaching the wire nut. Antioxidant and CO/ALR devices are available at home centers or electrical suppliers.

CEILING BOX
Center-mount ceiling fixture

Some light fixtures mount with a nut and a single-threaded nipple (small pipe). Support the fixture with one hand and unscrew the nut. Then slide the fixture down and out.

INSPECTING BOXES

Once you've removed a cover plate or light fixture, it takes only a few seconds to check the wiring inside for damage or unsafe connections.

Shut off power and test to see that power is off before you touch any wires. Use rubber-grip tools. Often you need to gently pull the device out of the box to inspect it.

Always assume that the wires are hot, even though you have de-energized the circuit. Touch only wire nuts or wire insulation—never bare wires.

Before you replace the devices in their boxes, wrap the terminal connections with electrical tape if local codes allow. The added protection helps hold wires in place and keeps terminal screws from touching the sides of a metal box.

STANLEY PRO TIP

Check the GFCI wiring

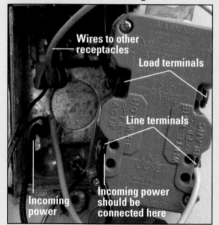

A ground fault circuit interrupter (GFCI) protects you from shock, but only if it is wired correctly. The wires coming from the power source must connect to the terminals labeled "line." These wires test hot when disconnected from the device when the circuit is live. The wires leading out to other receptacles must connect to the "load" terminals (page 109).

Check for incorrect wiring

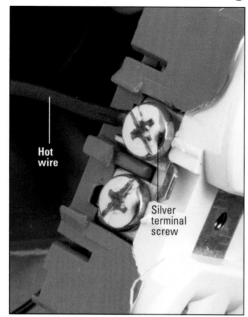

Reversed connections: The black or colored wire (hot) must be connected to a terminal with a brass-colored screw; the white wire (neutral) to the terminal with the silver screw. If the wires are reversed, the receptacle supplies power but is not polarized (page 28). Connect the wires to the correct terminals.

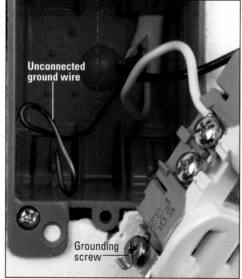

No ground: A receptacle that is not grounded delivers power but lacks an important safety feature. Connect the ground wire to the receptacle's ground screw and test with a receptacle analyzer. For other grounding methods see pages 43–44.

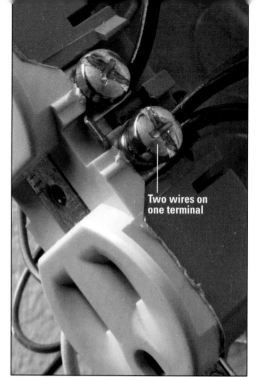

Too many wires: It is against building safety code to connect two or more wires to a single terminal because they can easily come loose. Splice the two wires into a pigtail and connect the pigtail to the terminal (page 53).

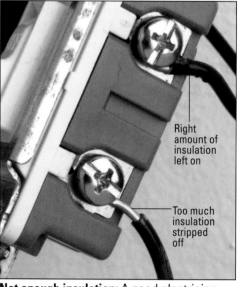

Not enough insulation: A good electrician covers as much bare wire as possible. The bottom wire has too much insulation stripped, making it unsafe. Cover it with tape. Better yet, cut, restrip, and reconnect the wire (page 74).

Check for damaged wire

Exposed bare wire: Even new wiring may have nicks and cuts in the insulation, leaving bare wire dangerously exposed. Wrap a small nick tightly with electrician's tape.

Cracked insulation: Older insulation or insulation behind an inadequately shielded fixture may become brittle and easily cracked. Cover it with heat-shrink tubing (page 74).

Box problems

Loose box: A loose box can lead to damaged wires and a faulty connection. If the box is next to a stud, remove the cover and pull out the device. Drill a hole into the side of the box and secure it to the stud with a screw. Otherwise replace it with a remodel box that fastens to the drywall.

NICKS AND CUTS
Protecting wires in armored cable

Armored cable should have plastic bushings installed wherever wires enter a box. Armored cable's sheathing has sharp edges, which can gouge insulation. If bushings are not already in place, buy some and install them. Do this whether you see damaged insulation or not, to protect the wires from any sharp edges. Slip a bushing around the wires, then slide it down into the sheathing.

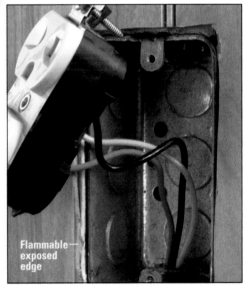

Recessed box: Codes call for all boxes to be nearly flush with the surrounding wall surface so wires are enclosed. Paneling on a wall may result in an improperly recessed box, which poses a fire danger. Install a box extender (page 74).

JUNCTION BOXES AND SUBPANELS

In addition to a service panel, switches, receptacles, and light fixtures, most houses have junction boxes. These metal or plastic electrical boxes enclose spliced wires. No electrical splice or connection should exist outside an approved electrical box.

Where to find junction boxes

You find junction boxes in utility areas such as a garage or basement. Less commonly they are located in living areas. A junction box is covered with a blank cover plate held in place with screws, which can be removed to inspect the box. Most junction boxes are about 4 inches square.

Subpanels expand service

A subpanel holds not only wires but also circuit breakers or fuses. It expands service—for instance when an addition is built and new circuits are added. Open and inspect a subpanel the same way you would a service panel (pages 36–37).

A subpanel connects to the main service panel by a cable. A double-pole circuit breaker or a large fuse in the service panel controls power to the subpanel. To de-energize the subpanel shut off the double-pole breaker or remove the fuse in the main panel that supplies power to the panel.

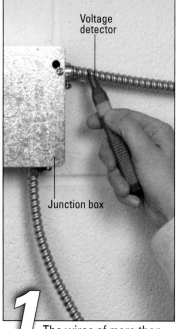

1 The wires of more than one circuit are often in the same junction box. **Shut off power at the service panel** (pages 6–7), then use a voltage detector (page 48) to test each cable in the box, as well as the box itself.

Voltage detector

Junction box

2 In a utility area a blank cover probably is metal; in a living area you may find a plastic cover. Loosen or remove the screws and remove the cover.

Junction box cover

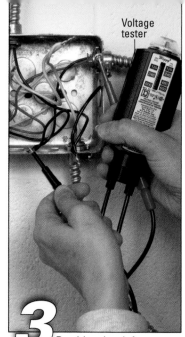

3 Double-check for power using a voltage tester (page 48) on all the wires.

Voltage tester

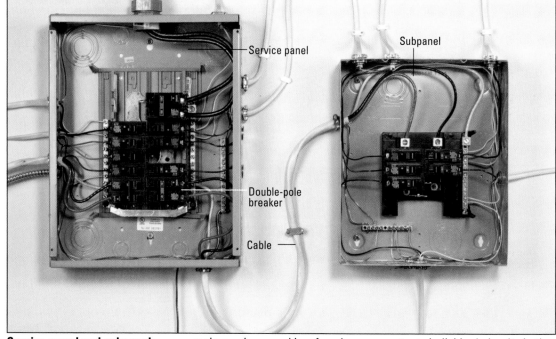

Service panel

Double-pole breaker

Cable

Subpanel

Service panel and subpanel: In a typical setup a 30-amp or larger double-pole breaker in the service panel feeds power to the subpanel through a cable. If the main service panel is a fuse box, a fuse block containing cartridge fuses supplies power to the subpanel. The subpanel is wired much like the main panel and protects individual circuits in the same way. (See pages 36–37 to remove covers.)

GROUNDING

Building codes have changed over the years and differ from region to region. As a result grounding methods can vary widely. You may find any of the configurations shown here in your home.

No matter the method it's important that the ground circuit provides an unbroken path to the earth (pages 28–29). Ground wires must be firmly connected at all points. If conduit or sheathing is used as a ground path, connections must be tight. A receptacle analyzer (page 32) tells you whether your receptacles are grounded.

METAL BOXES
Other grounding methods

Grounding clip

Armored cable connector

In a system with metal boxes, the pigtail method shown at the top of the middle column is considered the most secure. Other methods also work well if installed correctly—one is a grounding clip that clamps the ground wire to the box.

If a house is wired with armored cable or conduit (page 16), often there is no ground wire. The cable connector joins the metal sheathing or conduit to the box to provide the path for ground.

In boxes

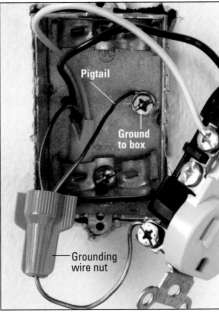

Pigtail

Ground to box

Grounding wire nut

Metal boxes: In this arrangement both the receptacle and metal box are grounded. Ground wires are spliced together and attached with a pigtail to the box and receptacle. The grounding wire nut shown has a hole in its top that makes installing a pigtail easier.

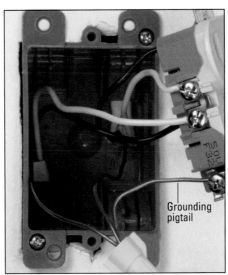

Grounding pigtail

Plastic boxes: Where plastic boxes are used, a ground wire typically connects to the receptacle only. Here, where wiring runs through this box to another box, a grounding pigtail connects to the device.

In fixtures and switches

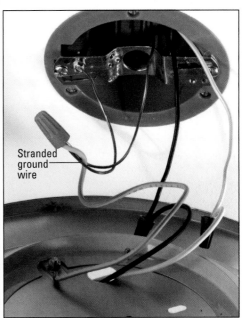

Stranded ground wire

Old fixtures: Many older ceiling fixtures are not grounded. Recent codes, however, call for grounding. Connect the fixture's ground lead (usually a stranded wire) to the strap on a metal box or to a ground wire.

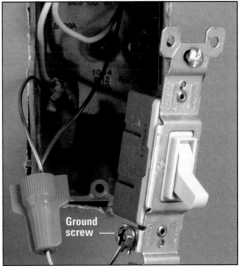

Ground screw

Old switches: Most older switches are not grounded; many switches do not even have a ground screw. Recent codes call for switches to be grounded. Replace an older switch with a newer one that has a ground screw and connect it to a ground wire.

GROUNDING (continued)

From a safety standpoint the most important part of an electrical circuit is the ground you stand on. Like lightning domestic electricity travels toward the biggest uncharged surface: the ground. Because the consequences are potentially fatal if the electricity flows through you on its way there, wiring systems provide electrons a path of less resistance—the ground wire. Here's how it works.

Normally electricity flows from the generator through the breaker or fuse box and through a black wire to, say a drill you're using to fix something. The electricity runs through the drill motor, and because it has to go somewhere, it runs through a white wire back to its favorite place—the ground.

All works fine until one day the black wire comes loose, electrifying the metal case while you're using the drill. The white wire is still connected, but to the motor, not to the case. Unless there's a separate path running to ground, you become the path of least resistance. A shock is a certainty, and electrocution a good possibility.

The ground wire, which is attached to the case, provides a separate path that runs through the entire electrical system and back to the ground.

Electricity wants to travel to the ground. If a black wire somehow comes into contact with the metal case of an electrical device, often the user is the path of least resistance.

When a tool has a ground wire, the wire becomes the path of least resistance, protecting the user from shock and possible electrocution.

DIFFICULT WIRING CONFIGURATIONS

Usually wiring is easy to figure out: A hot wire, a neutral wire, and a ground wire attach to a device or fixture. Sometimes, however, you may find configurations that aren't as clear.

■ **Two cables in a switch box:** Switch wiring may involve two cables entering the box or only one (page 90).

■ **Through wires:** If wires travel through a box but are not connected to a device or fixture, they may belong to another circuit.

■ **Three-way switch:** A switch with three terminals (and three wires connected to it) is a three-way switch (page 94).

■ **Unusual colors:** Some homes have color-coded circuits. For instance one circuit may have a brown hot wire, while another circuit has a purple hot wire. You find this only in houses with conduit.

■ **Aluminum wire:** Silver-color wires with "AL" printed on the insulation are aluminum wires (page 39).

■ **Three-wire cable:** Electricians sometimes use three-wire cable (with a black, red, white, and ground) to carry power for two different circuits. The black wire is attached to one circuit; the red wire to another. The white and ground serve both.

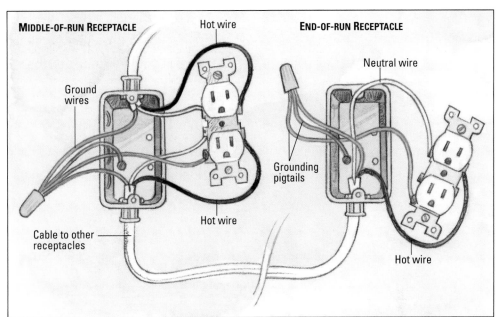

If two cables enter a receptacle box, the receptacle is in the middle of a wiring run. Power goes out of the box to other receptacles or fixtures. Usually the two blacks connect to the two brass terminals and the two whites connect to the two silver terminals. Sometimes pigtails are used.

If only one cable enters a receptacle box, the receptacle is at the end of the run, meaning that it is the last receptacle on the circuit. Wiring is simple: black to the brass terminal and white to the silver terminal.

WHAT IF...
Two switches share a box?

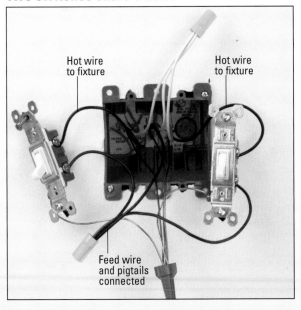

Hot wire to fixture

Hot wire to fixture

Feed wire and pigtails connected

When two switches share a box and are on the same circuit, they may share a single hot wire. The feed wire (the one that brings power into the box) connects to two pigtails, one to serve each switch. Each switch has another hot wire, leading to its light fixture.

How a split receptacle works

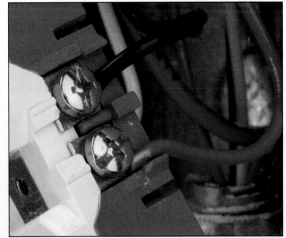

If the tab that joins the two brass terminals has been broken off and two hot wires connect to the brass terminals, the receptacle is split. Each outlet may be on a separate circuit, or one of the outlets is controlled by a wall switch while the other is always hot.

BASIC TECHNIQUES

A clear understanding of how an electrical system works is valuable knowledge when you start doing electrical work. Equally important to know are the techniques required to make safe and secure electrical connections. The skills you need to complete your own projects—cutting and stripping wire and making connections—are the same ones professional electricians use every day. You don't need to be as fast as a pro, but your work can and should be as safe and reliable.

Why good technique matters
If wires are spliced or connected to fixtures or devices haphazardly, the circuit may function for a while. But there is a good chance a wire will work its way loose, creating a dangerous condition.

Wiring correctly is relatively easy. It takes only an hour or two to learn how to make splices and connections just as solid as those made by professionals. In most cases using the right technique is faster and easier than doing something the wrong way. Looping a wire around a terminal screw clockwise (page 53) keeps it from sliding out from under the screw head as you tighten the screw, for example.

Use the right tools
Before beginning electrical work gather the basic set of tools described on pages 12–13. These tools are designed for wiring and give better results than general tools. If you try to strip wires using a knife instead of a stripper, you probably will nick the copper and weaken the wire. Twisting wires together using a pair of household slip-joint pliers is difficult, and the loose connection might come apart. Lineman's pliers help you join wires to make professional-quality connections easily.

Safety while working
Electrical work is safe if you always follow the most important safety measure: **Shut off power** and test to make sure power is off (page 48) before you start the project. Review the safety tips on page 5 before beginning any wiring project.

Proper splices and connections are the key to safe and reliable electrical installations.

CHAPTER PREVIEW

Testing
page 48

Stripping and splicing wire
page 50

Joining wire to a terminal
page 52

Mapping and indexing circuits
page 54

Lay a small drop cloth (an old towel works well) on the floor or countertop beneath the electrical box you are working on. It catches debris and protects surfaces from scratches. Complete a repair by wrapping terminal connections and wire nuts with electrician's tape for an extra measure of protection, where codes allow.

Screwdriver

Side cutters

Wire strippers

Long-nose pliers

TESTING

Electricians keep their testers handy at all times—a practice worth imitating. Make it a habit to test for the presence of power before beginning any work.

In addition to a receptacle analyzer (page 32), a do-it-yourselfer needs a voltage tester to see if the power is on and a continuity tester to check for broken connections or disconnected wires.

Good testing habits

Testers are easy to operate. Always work methodically to ensure reliable results from your tests.

■ Be sure to make contact with the metal parts you are testing. Pressing hard isn't necessary, but the probe must make direct contact with metal, not plastic insulation or electrician's tape.

■ Insert the voltage tester probes at least an inch into the receptacle being tested.

■ If a wire or screw is painted, use a rubber-grip screwdriver to scrape some paint off before touching it with a probe.

Voltage detector

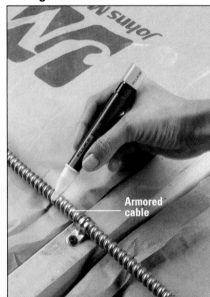

A voltage detector senses power through insulation and metal or plastic boxes.

Just hold it on or near a cable, wire, or electrical box and press the detector's button; it lights or buzzes to signal the presence of current.

Test for power

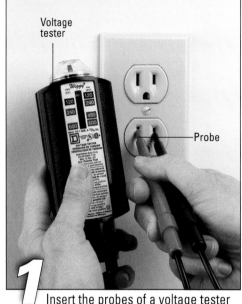

Voltage tester

Probe

1 Insert the probes of a voltage tester into the two slots of a receptacle to test for power. The light glows or the needle moves if electrical current is present.

2 Once you have opened a box, test again to be sure there is no current. Hold one probe to each screw terminal on either side of the receptacle, where wires are connected. Also touch each wire.

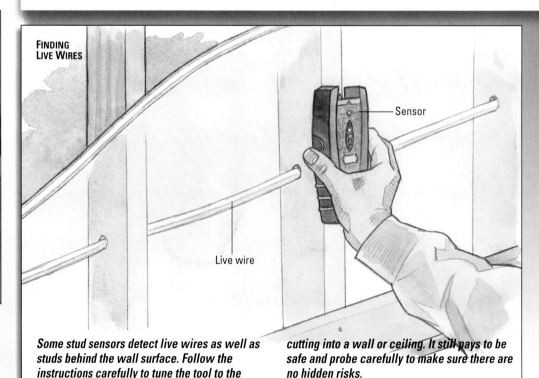

FINDING LIVE WIRES

Armored cable

Sensor

Live wire

Some stud sensors detect live wires as well as studs behind the wall surface. Follow the instructions carefully to tune the tool to the thickness of the wall. Use a sensor before *cutting into a wall or ceiling. It still pays to be safe and probe carefully to make sure there are no hidden risks.*

Test for continuity

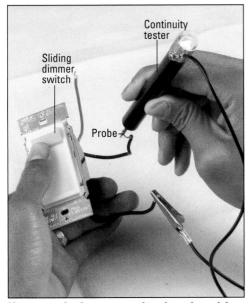

Use a continuity tester only when the wiring is disconnected from power. To test a switch attach the alligator clip to one terminal and hold the probe against the other terminal. If the tester glows when the switch is on and does not glow when it is off, the switch is OK.

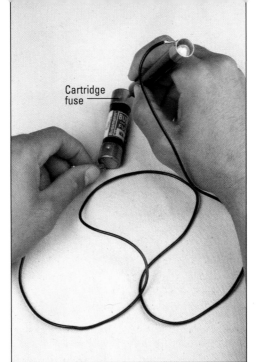

To test a cartridge fuse, hold the alligator clip against one end and the probe against the other. If the tester does not glow, replace the fuse.

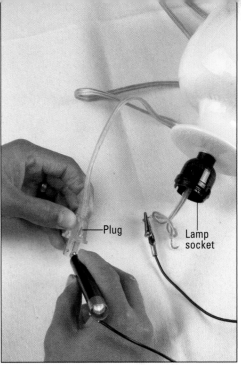

To test lamp wiring attach the alligator clip to one end of a wire and touch the probe to the other end. If the tester does not glow, the wire is broken at some point.

STANLEY Pro Tip

Test the tester

Testers can malfunction. To make sure one is working properly, always test the tester. Each time you get a reading of no power when using a voltage tester, insert the probes into a receptacle you know is hot. The tester should glow, confirming that it is functioning properly.

Avoid cheap testers

You may be tempted to buy an inexpensive tester with a neon bulb. These bulbs can fail and are easily damaged. A reliable tester is well worth a little extra money.

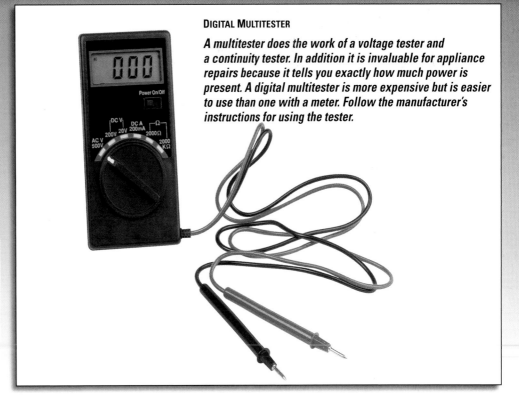

DIGITAL MULTITESTER

A multitester does the work of a voltage tester and a continuity tester. In addition it is invaluable for appliance repairs because it tells you exactly how much power is present. A digital multitester is more expensive but is easier to use than one with a meter. Follow the manufacturer's instructions for using the tester.

STRIPPING AND SPLICING WIRE

Before making an electrical connection, you must strip the insulation from the end of a wire. This is a simple process, but it's important to do it right so you don't damage the copper wire. Use a stripper instead of a knife or wire cutter.

It takes a few minutes' practice to learn how to make firm splices. The right tool is essential: Nothing does the job like a pair of lineman's pliers.

Always take a few moments to check your work. Check the bare wire after you strip it to make sure it is not gouged. After splicing wires and adding the correct size wire nut, tug on the wires to make sure they are securely joined.

Both tools do a good job stripping wire, but the long-nose strippers get into tight places more easily.

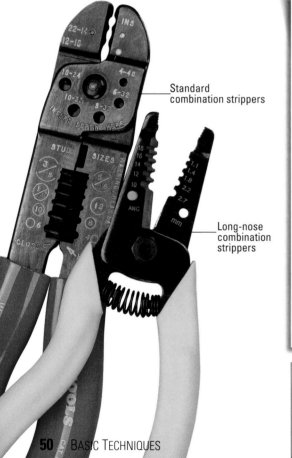

Standard combination strippers

Long-nose combination strippers

Stripping wire

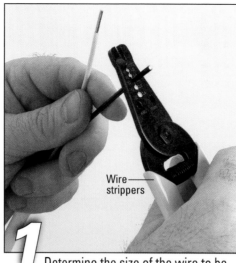

Wire strippers

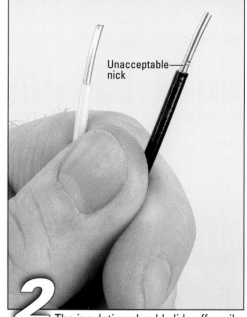

Unacceptable nick

1 Determine the size of the wire to be stripped (page 15). Open the strippers, insert the wire into the correct notch, and squeeze the stripper shut. Give a slight twist, then slide the insulation off.

2 The insulation should slide off easily, with no more than a slight mark on the wire. If you have to pull hard or the stripper leaves a nick or scrapes the wire, check that you are using the right hole. If the problem persists buy a new stripper.

Working with cord

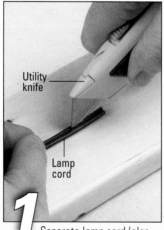

Utility knife

Lamp cord

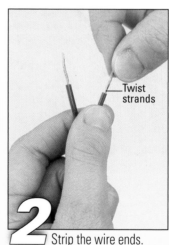

Twist strands

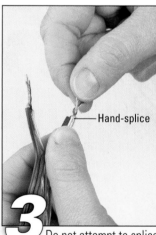

Hand-splice

1 Separate lamp cord (also known as zip cord) before stripping. Poke the tip of a utility knife between the two wires. Pull the cord to split it.

2 Strip the wire ends. With your fingers twist the exposed strands clockwise until tight.

3 Do not attempt to splice cord wire using lineman's pliers; it's too easy to break strands. Instead twist the wires together clockwise by hand and add a wire nut.

How much insulation should be stripped?
If you are joining the wire to a terminal, remove about ¾ inch. If you are splicing a wire to another wire, remove about 1 inch.

Splicing wire

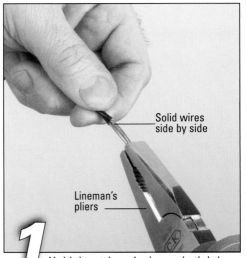

Solid wires side by side

Lineman's pliers

1 Hold the stripped wire ends tightly next to each other. Grip both ends with lineman's pliers. Twist clockwise with the pliers until you feel more resistance, then stop. Twisting too hard could break a wire. Practice on scrap wire before you start a project.

2 Cut the tails off the tip of the splice with diagonal cutters or lineman's pliers. This makes it easy to push the splice into a wire nut and ensures that both wires are held firmly together. Trim so that about ¾ inch of spliced wire remains.

Spliced, trimmed wire

Wire nut

3 Choose a wire nut to fit the size and number of wires you have spliced (page 23). Push the spliced wires in, then twist the nut clockwise to tighten. Tug on the wires to make sure the connection is tight, then wrap the bottom of the nut with electrician's tape.

WHAT IF…
Solid wire joins to stranded wire?

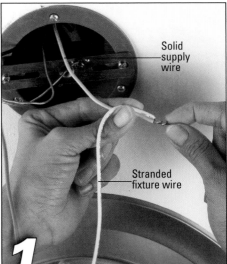

Solid supply wire

Stranded fixture wire

1 Light fixtures typically have stranded wires that connect to solid feed wires. Strip ¼ inch of insulation from each wire. Using your fingers twist the stranded wire tightly around the solid wire, leaving about ⅛ inch of stranded wire extending beyond the end of the solid wire.

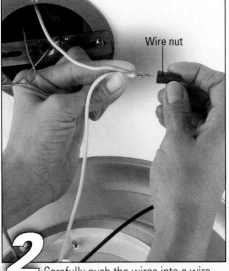

Wire nut

2 Carefully push the wires into a wire nut so that the protruding tip of the stranded wire goes as far as possible into the nut. Twist the nut clockwise until tight. Tug on the stranded wire to check the connection. Wrap the bottom of the nut with electrician's tape.

STANLEY PRO TIP

Twist three or more wires at once

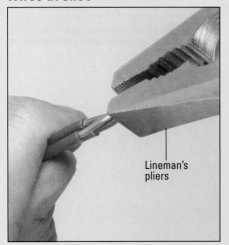

Lineman's pliers

When splicing more than two wires, it's tempting to splice two and then twist the third to the splice. Don't—the wires might break. Instead grab all three (or four) wires at the same time with your lineman's pliers and twist. It may take you a few attempts to master this technique.

JOINING WIRE TO A TERMINAL

Joining a wire to a terminal screw is a simple procedure. But it's worth a few minutes and a little practice to learn how to make a secure connection. Terminal connections come under a lot of stress when devices such as switches or receptacles are pushed into boxes, and a poor connection can come loose.

Wrap the wire almost all the way around the screw before tightening it. Make sure to wrap the wire clockwise around the terminal screw so that as the screw tightens it pulls the loop in.

In an ideal connection all the wire under the screw head is stripped and no more. (Page 40 shows how stripping too much insulation leads to an unsafe situation.)

Most homeowners use long-nose pliers to bend a loop in the wire (see steps at right), but if you plan to install a number of devices, consider purchasing a wire-bending screwdriver.

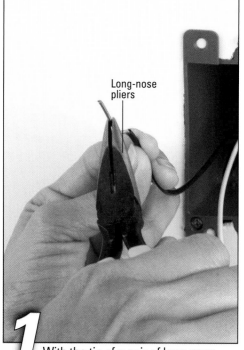

Long-nose pliers

1 With the tip of a pair of long-nose pliers, grab the bare wire just past the insulation. Twist to the left. Slide the pliers up a little and bend to the right.

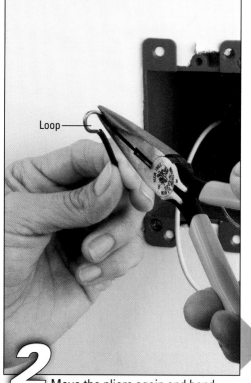

Loop

2 Move the pliers again and bend again to the right. This should form a partial circle with an opening wide enough to fit over the threads of a terminal screw.

WIRE-BENDING SCREWDRIVER
A perfect loop every time

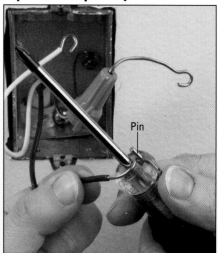

Pin

This handy tool makes it easy to form perfect loops in wire ends. Just slip the wire between the screwdriver shaft and the pin and twist.

SAFETY FIRST
Avoid push-in connections

Most switches and receptacles have connection holes on the backs that accept stripped wire ends. Using them saves a little time, but the resulting connection is not as secure as one made to a terminal screw.

STANLEY PRO TIP

Save time by bending with long-nose strippers

Some strippers are shaped so their tips act much like long-nose pliers. This allows you to strip and bend without changing tools. You also can use them to squeeze the wire around the terminal (Step 3).

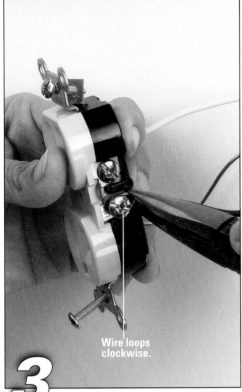

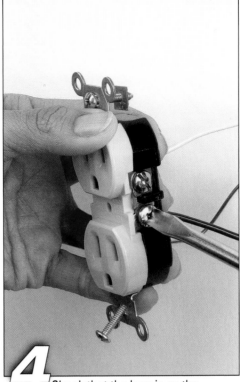

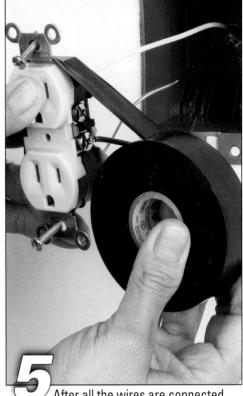

3 Loosen the terminal screw until it becomes hard to turn. Slip the looped wire end over the screw threads. Grab the wire on either side of the screw with long-nose pliers and tighten it around the screw.

Wire loops clockwise.

4 Check that the loop is on the terminal screw clockwise. Tug to make sure the wire cannot come loose. Tighten the terminal screw until the wire is snug between the screw head and the terminal surface.

5 After all the wires are connected, wrap electrician's tape tightly around the device to cover the terminal screws. (Some inspectors prefer that the tape be left off so they can look at the connections.)

WHAT IF...
The job calls for an unusual connection?

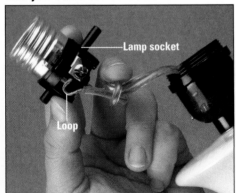

Loop

Lamp socket

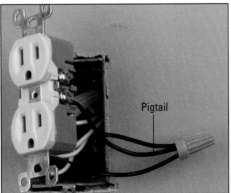

Pigtail

Setscrew

Stranded wire To join a stranded wire to a terminal, strip the wire end and twist the strands together (page 50). Use your fingers to form a loop. Wrap the bare wire clockwise around the terminal screw. You may need to push the wire into place as you tighten the screw to make sure no strands slip out.

Two wires, one terminal Never attach two wires to a single terminal. Instead make a pigtail. Cut a piece of wire about 6 inches long and strip both ends. Splice one end to the two wires you need to connect and attach the other end to the terminal.

Setscrew terminals In service panels, 240-volt receptacles, and other high-voltage connections, you find setscrew terminals. Loosen the setscrew, push the stripped wire end into the terminal hole, and tighten the setscrew.

MAPPING AND INDEXING CIRCUITS

Somewhere inside the service panel—usually on the door—there should be an index that shows what circuit breaker or fuse serves which areas of the house. The index helps you shut off power to the correct circuit before working on it.

Codes require service panels to be indexed, but installers sometimes don't bother to trace down each circuit. If there is no index, make one. To complete the index work systematically to identify the circuit for every electrical outlet in the house. Be prepared to find some odd combinations. In older homes a single circuit may travel through several floors. Or you may find an entire circuit serving only a couple of receptacles. Avoid attaching family members' names to the index; they might change rooms. Use more permanent directional designations like "east bedroom" or "front hall."

Indexing is easiest when working with a helper who can turn circuits on and off while you test the lights, receptacles, and appliances.

1 Make a rough sketch of each room in the house, showing the location of all electrical outlets—lights, receptacles, and hardwired appliances. Don't forget the basement, hallways, attic, garage, and outdoor electrical service.

2 Flip on all the lights in the house. Assign a circuit number to each fuse or breaker in the service panel. Shut off one breaker or unscrew one fuse.

WORKING WITH A HELPER
Communication methods

If two people are working, the one stationed at the service panel must let the other know which circuit is off. Once the roamer has finished testing outlets, tell the other person to flip the breaker back on and a new one off.

If the house is small, just shouting back and forth can work. In a larger home use cell phones or walkie-talkies.

If you are working alone, follow this process: Go into every room and flip on all the light switches and lamps. Then shut off all the circuits except one and look for the lights that are on. To tell from a distance whether a receptacle is on or off, plug in a radio and turn it up loud. Once you know the general area covered by a circuit, test all the receptacles systematically.

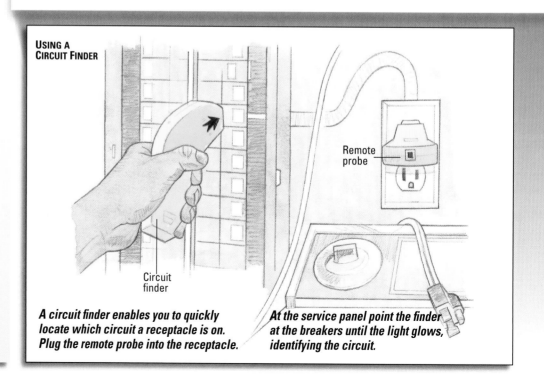

USING A CIRCUIT FINDER

Circuit finder

Remote probe

A circuit finder enables you to quickly locate which circuit a receptacle is on. Plug the remote probe into the receptacle.

At the service panel point the finder at the breakers until the light glows, identifying the circuit.

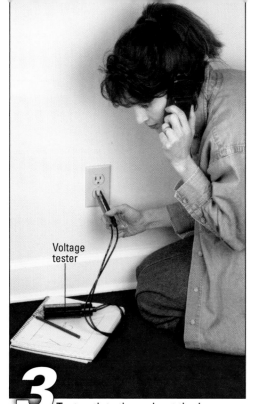

3 Test outlets throughout the house. Note lights that have turned off. Open the refrigerator door so you can see whether the interior light is on. Turn on appliances and test each outlet in each receptacle.

Voltage tester

4 When you encounter an outlet that has been turned off, mark the circuit number on that room's sketch. After you have tested all outlets, restore power to the circuit you just tested and shut off the next circuit. Work systematically.

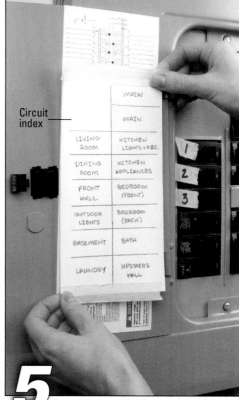

5 Transfer your findings in chart form to a piece of paper that fits the panel door. For clarity position the circuit numbers near the actual fuses or breakers.

Circuit index

	MAIN
	MAIN
LIVING ROOM	KITCHEN LIGHTS + REC.
DINING ROOM	KITCHEN APPLIANCES
FRONT HALL	BEDROOM (FRONT)
OUTDOOR LIGHTS	BEDROOM (BACK)
BASEMENT	BATH
LAUNDRY	UPSTAIRS HALL

Situations to watch out for

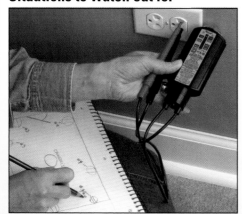

Same receptacle, different circuits The two outlets of a receptacle may be connected to different circuits (page 45). Always check both outlets and mark the drawing accordingly.

Low-voltage circuits Don't forget low-voltage power devices such as doorbells. The thermostat is especially important. Crank it all the way up or down so that the heat or air-conditioning stays on during the test.

Appliances Test all appliances, such as the garbage disposer, by turning them on. Electric ranges, air-conditioners, and water heaters should each be controlled by separate 240-volt circuits.

REPAIRS

It may not be worth your while to repair an inexpensive lamp or a small appliance. But if the piece is valuable—for economic or sentimental reasons—you can give it new life with just a little work. The basic tools and techniques presented in the preceding chapters equipped you to make most of the repairs needed around a home.

Finding and solving problems

Any electrical repair project begins with safety. Before dismantling a lamp or appliance, unplug it. Shut off power to the circuit before working on a light fixture.

To diagnose a problem you often use a continuity tester (page 49). It tells you whether there is a break (i.e., a lack of continuity) along the length of a wire, or whether the contacts of an electrical device have broken. It can help you isolate and identify the problem: a bad plug, cord, socket, or switch.

Lamps, which plug in, and light fixtures, which are permanently connected to household circuits, are wired in much the same way. Most parts, such as sockets and cords, are widely available at reasonable cost. Repair techniques are largely a matter of common sense: Pull the new cord through the lamp to replace the old cord, or replace a faulty socket with a new one of the same type. Wire new components the same way as the old ones.

For best results work away from distraction. Try to finish a repair in one sitting, so you can remember where all the parts should go.

Chronic problems

This chapter also demonstrates easy and safe solutions for a circuit that chronically overloads. It shows how to repair damaged wire inside an electrical box. In addition you'll learn how to solve problems with door chimes and thermostats.

CHAPTER PREVIEW

Changing lightbulbs
page 58

Energy-saving lights
page 59

Plugs and cord switches
page 60

Lamp sockets and switches
page 62

Rewiring a lamp
page 64

Fluorescents
page 66

Bulbs, starters, ballasts, and electronic ballasts
page 68

Halogen lights
page 70

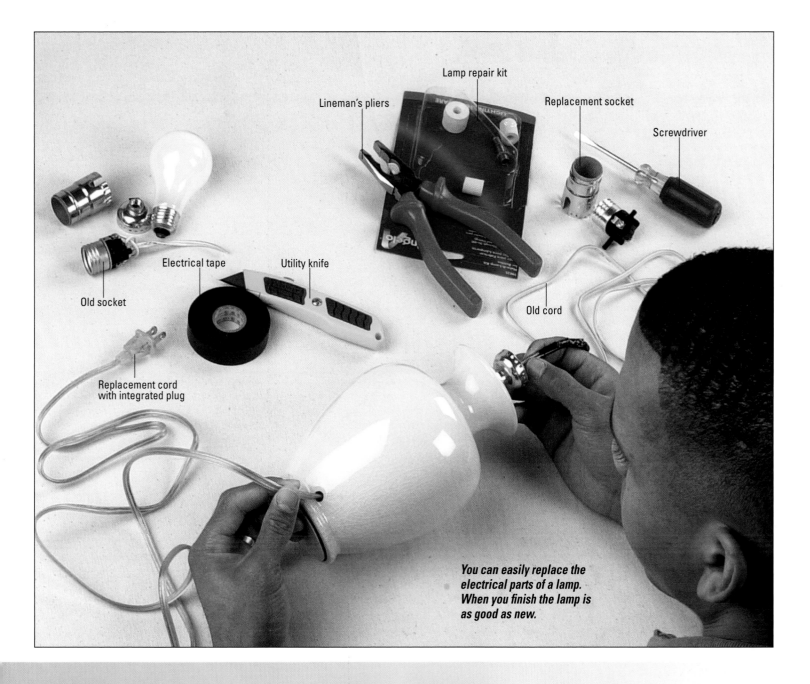

Lamp repair kit

Lineman's pliers

Replacement socket

Screwdriver

Electrical tape

Utility knife

Old socket

Old cord

Replacement cord
with integrated plug

You can easily replace the electrical parts of a lamp. When you finish the lamp is as good as new.

Chandelier repairs
page 71

Repairing wiring in boxes
page 73

New dryer cord
page 76

Repairing a door chime
page 77

When a circuit overloads
page 80

Low-voltage thermostats
page 81

Digital thermostats
page 82

Replacing a thermostat for an electric baseboard heater
page 84

CHANGING LIGHTBULBS

If you have to change the bulb in a fixture more than once every few months, buying a long-life bulb saves you both hassle and money. If a light fixture or lamp is brighter than necessary, install bulbs of lower wattage or replace the switch with a dimmer (page 98).

If a light stops glowing altogether, chances are you simply need to replace the bulb. If a bulb doesn't glow unless you screw it in hard or if the bulb flickers, the problem may be the socket or wiring, not the bulb; see pages 62–63 for the remedy.

Get the wattage right
Heed the warning sticker on the fixture that tells how much wattage it can handle. Installing a bulb of too-high wattage overheats the fixture, causing bulbs to burn out quickly, damaging the fixture and the ceiling material, and creating a potential fire hazard. If you need more light than the fixture can deliver, replace the fixture with one that can take more or larger bulbs.

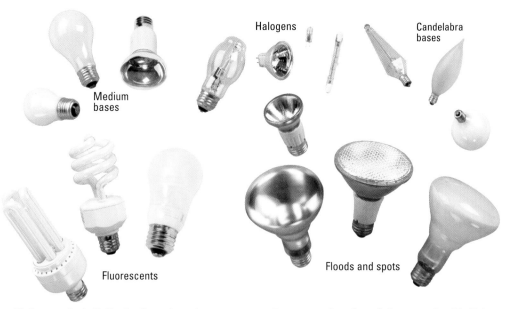

Medium bases · Halogens · Candelabra bases · Fluorescents · Floods and spots

Make sure the bulb fits the fixture's socket; several sizes exist. To improve energy efficiency in standard incandescent fixtures, buy a screw-in compact fluorescent; several shapes and sizes are available. Halogen bulbs deliver concentrated beams suited to accent and task lighting.

For recessed canister lights use a flood bulb for general illumination and a reflector bulb (also called a directional flood) for a spotlight effect.

Low-voltage halogen fixtures and lamps call for either single- or double-ended bulbs. For information on fluorescent tubes, see page 66.

SAFETY FIRST
Handle halogens with care

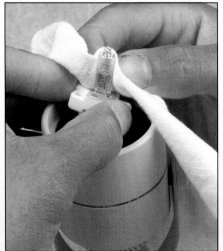

Halogen bulbs get very hot and they're sensitive to oils—just touching one with fingers can greatly shorten a bulb's life. So let a bulb cool, then handle it with a clean cloth or light gloves.

STANLEY PRO TIP: Removing a broken bulb

Changing a lightbulb is no joking matter if the glass has broken. **Make sure the power is off.** Rather than handling it with fingers, gently push a raw potato onto the shards and twist.

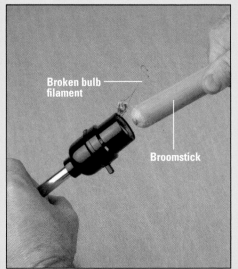

Broken bulb filament

Broomstick

If most of the glass is gone from a broken bulb, insert a broomstick into the bulb's socket and twist it out.

ENERGY-SAVING LIGHTS

Thomas Edison's invention of the incandescent light bulb revolutionized life and held sway for more than 100 years. But as costs of electricity rose and global warming became an issue, the search started for more energy-efficient ways to produce light. Two of the answers—compact fluorescents (CFL) and cold cathode fluorescents (CCFL)—are existing types of bulbs used in new ways. Another answer—the light-emitting diode (LED)—has appeared in everything from computer screens to auto brake lights. But only with the recent development of diodes that gave off white light have LEDs been developed as light sources.

Because each bulb produces light differently, the light varies from bulb to bulb. Not all white light is the same—the white we associate with an incandescent isn't pure white. It's rich in yellow, giving it a warm feeling that was lacking in early compact fluorescents. And where some bulbs shine light throughout the room, others shine light in only one direction, making them better suited in desk lamps than as general lighting. Bulbs are constantly improving, so check the shelves of your hardware or home center regularly for new developments that can save you energy and money.

LIGHT-EMITTING DIODES

Light-emitting diodes— the same solid-state lights used on some computer screens—are expensive but are also very promising. The LED emits a focused beam, and a 2.5-watt LED bulb can light up a small area as well as a 50-watt incandescent. The difference is that the LED lights up only the small area, while incandescent would light up the rest of the room. This makes LEDs well suited for reading lights, task lights, and even flashlights. There are some general lighting LED bulbs, which are actually hundreds of LEDs in an array pointed in different directions. As a result general lighting LEDs are only slightly better than incandescents when lighting a room, and only about a third as effective as CFLS. Current research, however, is producing bulbs in the laboratory that are six inches square and more efficient than fluorescents.

COMPACT FLUORESCENT LIGHTS

Compact fluorescent lights, which give off light when a gas inside them is electrically charged, have always been more efficient than standard incandescent bulbs. But the first improvement you could take into your living room was the compact fluorescent light (CFL), which screws into a standard socket. Using from one-third to one-fourth the wattage, a CFL can put out as much light as an incandescent. A CFL also lasts longer—anywhere from 6,000 to 15,000 hours, compared with the 750 hours of an incandescent bulb. Early bulbs were slow to start, flickered, and gave off cold, white light. New bulbs match the color given off by an incandescent, light instantly, and the flickering problem has been solved. Some bulbs are dimmable, and you can now get 3-way compact fluorescents.

COLD CATHODE FLUORESCENT LIGHTS

Screw-in cold cathode fluorescent lights (CCFLs) are even more efficient than CFLs. Conventional fluorescents heat up a coil of wire, called a cathode, that emits electrons, which initially charge the tube. Unfortunately for the energy conscious, power runs to the cathode the whole time the light is lit. Cold cathode tubes, on the other hand, operate at a higher voltage, which overcomes the need to heat the cathode. A CCFL produces as much light as an incandescent bulb while using about one-sixth the wattage. CCFLs last 18,000 to 25,000 hours. Typically the 8-foot tubes used in commercial lighting are cold cathode and are both efficient and bright. The compact screw-in models aren't quite as effective yet. At 8 watts the most powerful bulb produces as much light as a 45-watt incandescent.

PLUGS AND CORD SWITCHES

If a lamp cord and plug are brittle or damaged, rewire the lamp with a new cord that has an integrated plug. If the plug has a cracked body or loose prongs but the cord is in good shape, install one of the replacement plugs shown here.

Cord maintenance

Always grasp the plug when you pull a plug out of a receptacle. If you tug on the cord, you may loosen or break wiring connections in the plug. Organize and run your cords to minimize tripping hazards.

PRESTART CHECKLIST

☐ **TIME**
About 10 minutes

☐ **TOOLS**
Phillips screwdriver, cutting pliers, utility knife, wire strippers, long-nose pliers

☐ **SKILLS**
Cutting and twisting stranded wire; attaching stranded wire to terminals

☐ **PREP**
A suitable work surface

☐ **MATERIALS**
Replacement plug, cord switch

Flat lamp plugs

Terminal

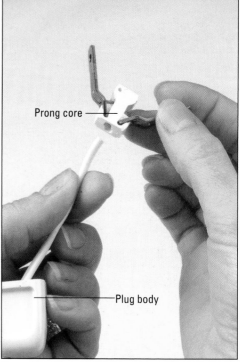

Prong core

Plug body

Screw terminals: To replace a plug snip the cord near the old plug, divide the cord, and strip ¾ inch of insulation from the end of each wire. Slip the wires through the replacement plug and connect them to the terminals. Tug to check the connections and make sure there are no loose strands.

Snap-together plug: To add a squeeze-type replacement plug, snip off the old plug and feed the cord through the new plug body. Place the prongs over the cord and push the cord completely into the prong core. Squeeze the prongs tight. Slide the body up and snap it onto the core.

Neutral and hot wires

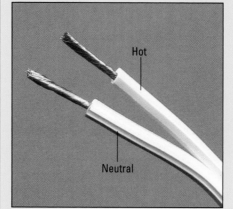

Hot

Neutral

The neutral wire connects to the shell of a lamp socket (the silver screw); the hot wire goes to the contact in the center or the switch (the brass terminal). The smooth side of the cord is the hot wire, while ridges or ribs on the insulation mark the neutral.

REPLACEMENT PLUG OPTIONS

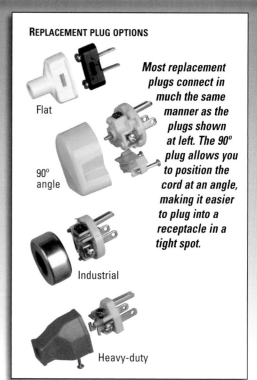

Flat

90° angle

Industrial

Heavy-duty

Most replacement plugs connect in much the same manner as the plugs shown at left. The 90° plug allows you to position the cord at an angle, making it easier to plug into a receptacle in a tight spot.

Appliance plugs

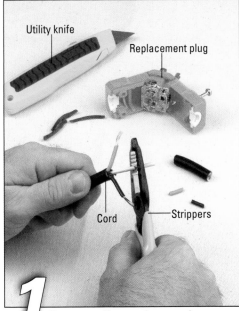

Utility knife
Replacement plug
Cord
Strippers

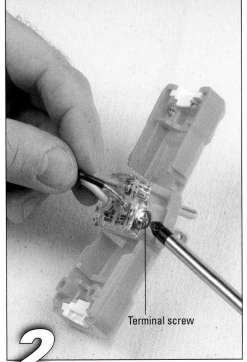

Terminal screw

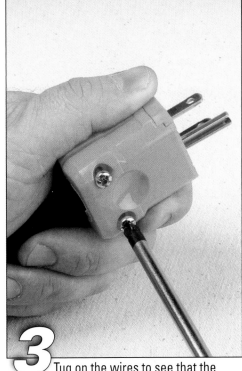

1 For an appliance choose a heavy-duty plug with a grounding prong. Working carefully with a knife to avoid cutting into wire insulation, strip about 2 inches of sheathing from the end of the cord. Strip about ¾ inch from the ends of each wire and twist the wire strands tight (page 50).

2 Slide the replacement plug's body onto the cord. Connect the wires to each of the terminals—black to hot (the narrower prong), green to ground (the round prong), and white to neutral (the wide prong).

3 Tug on the wires to see that the connections are firm and make sure there are no loose strands. Assemble the plug body and tighten the screws.

Rotary cord switches

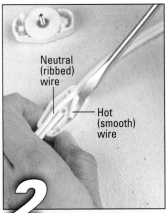

Neutral (ribbed) wire
Hot (smooth) wire

1 If a lamp switch is hard to reach, install a cord switch. To install a rotary cord switch, cut through the hot (smooth) wire, leaving the neutral (ribbed) wire intact. Separate the wires about ¾ inch on each side of the cut.

2 Without stripping the ends push the wires into the body of the switch as shown. When you screw the two parts of the body together, prongs on the switch contacts will pierce the hot wire to make contact.

Rocker cord switches

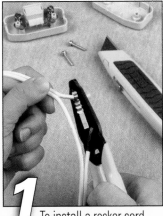

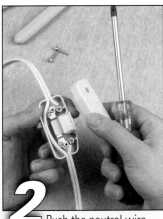

1 To install a rocker cord switch, snip the hot (smooth) cord without damaging the neutral (ribbed) cord. Separate the wires about 1 inch on each side of the cut. Strip about ¾ inch from the cut ends and twist the strands tight (page 50).

2 Push the neutral wire into the switch's groove. Connect the stripped ends to the switch's terminals (page 53). Snap the top part of the switch over the wires and tighten the screws.

LAMP SOCKETS AND SWITCHES

If a lamp flickers or doesn't come on even after you've changed the bulb, check the cord (especially near the plug) for breakage. If you see no damage, unplug the lamp and examine the socket. The problem may be in the wire connections to it (Step 3).

The socket shown is the most common. Other types are made of plastic or porcelain and attach to the lamp or light fixture with screws or a nut and bolt. Take the old socket to a hardware store or home center for a replacement that fits.

PRESTART CHECKLIST

☐ **TIME**
About 20 minutes (not including shopping) to test and replace a socket

☐ **TOOLS**
Screwdriver, continuity tester, perhaps strippers and lineman's pliers

☐ **SKILLS**
Fastening wire to a terminal; testing for voltage

☐ **PREP**
Unplug the lamp

☐ **MATERIALS**
Replacement socket, switch

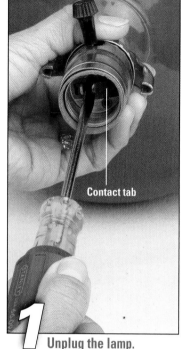

1 **Unplug the lamp.** Before you replace a socket, pry up the contact tab with a screwdriver to make stronger contact with the bulb's base. If a contact tab is rusty, scrape it clean with a screwdriver. Plug it in again and test the lamp.

Contact tab

2 If the problem is not solved, **unplug the lamp** and remove the socket. Unscrew the small screw near the contact tab. Squeeze the socket shell and pull it out. (If the shell reads PRESS, put your thumb there when you squeeze.)

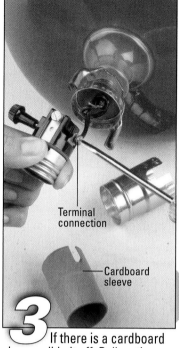

3 If there is a cardboard sleeve, slide it off. Pull up the socket and examine the terminal connections. If you cannot fix the problem by tightening a terminal screw, loosen the screws, remove the wires, and remove and test the socket.

Terminal connection

Cardboard sleeve

TEST THE SOCKET
Check for faulty connections

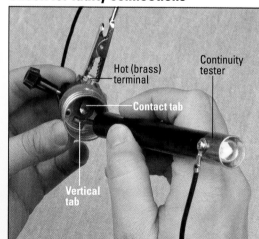

Hot (brass) terminal

Continuity tester

Contact tab

Vertical tab

If the socket has a switch, attach the clip to the hot (brass) terminal and touch the probe to the vertical tab or the contact tab. The tester should glow with the switch on and not glow with the switch off. If this does not occur, replace the socket.

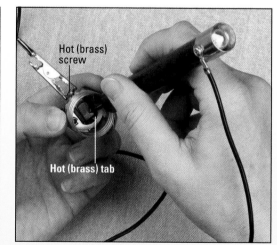

Hot (brass) screw

Hot (brass) tab

If the socket does not have a switch, attach the clip to the hot (brass) screw and touch the probe to the brass tab, as shown. Then clip onto the neutral (silver) screw and touch the probe to the threads. If the tester does not glow in either test, replace the socket.

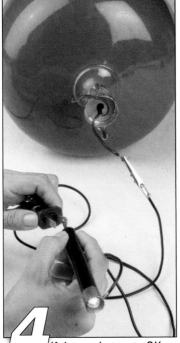

4 If the socket tests OK, or if you replace the socket and that does not solve the problem, test the wires for continuity. If there is a break in continuity, rewire the lamp (pages 64–65).

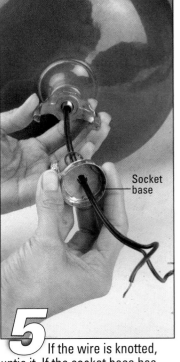

Socket base

5 If the wire is knotted, untie it. If the socket base has a setscrew, loosen it. Unscrew and remove the socket base. Purchase a new socket that matches the old one.

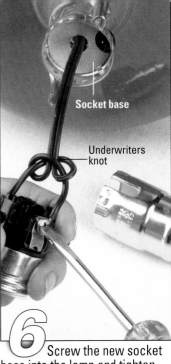

Socket base

Underwriters knot

6 Screw the new socket base into the lamp and tighten the setscrew. Tie the cord in an Underwriters knot so it won't pull out. Twist the wire strands tight with your fingers and connect them to the terminals.

7 Slide on the cardboard sleeve (if there is one) and the socket shell. Push down to snap the shell onto the base.

WHAT IF...
A switch needs replacing on a lamp or ceiling fan?

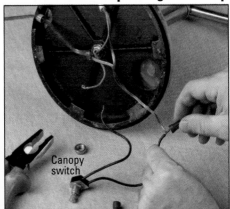

Canopy switch

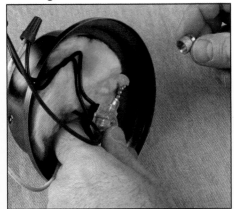

The little switches on a lamp or fixture—called canopy switches—can fail, but they are easy to replace. To replace a canopy switch on a lamp, you may have to remove a metal or cloth cover on the bottom of the lamp base. Unscrew the nut, detach the wires, and replace the switch.

A pull-chain switch on a ceiling light or fan mounts in the same way as a lamp switch. To replace one, **shut off power to the circuit** and remove the fixture's canopy (page 39). Replace the switch as described at left.

Fixture and lamp switch options

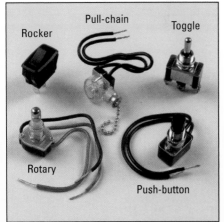

Rocker Pull-chain Toggle

Rotary

Push-button

You can replace one type of canopy switch with another—a toggle with a rotary switch for example. The hole for the switch shank is usually a standard size. A switch that mounts differently, such as a rectangular rocker switch, requires modifying the fixture.

REWIRING A LAMP

If the socket and the plug are ruled out as the cause of a lamp malfunction, then wiring must be the culprit. No matter what shape or size the lamp, the wiring is essentially the same: A cord runs from the plug to the socket. A multisocket lamp contains a sort of junction box, where the main cord is spliced to shorter cords that lead to individual sockets.

It is rarely a good idea to replace only part of a cord: The splice is unsightly, and the cord could be damaged elsewhere in the lamp. It's usually not much more work to replace the entire lamp cord.

To divide, strip, and fasten cord wires to terminals, see pages 50–53.

PRESTART CHECKLIST

□ **TIME**
About 1 hour to rewire a simple lamp

□ **TOOLS**
Continuity tester, lineman's pliers, strippers, screwdriver

□ **SKILLS**
Stripping wires and connecting them to terminals

□ **PREP**
Unplug lamp, remove bulb, and place lamp on a work surface.

□ **MATERIALS**
Lamp cord with molded plug or a rewire kit containing a cord, electrician's tape

Table or floor lamp

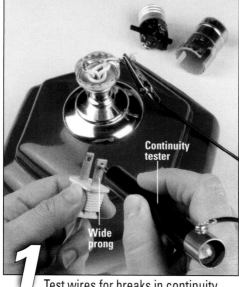

1 Test wires for breaks in continuity. Attach a tester clip to the stripped end of the neutral (ribbed) wire and touch the probe to the wide prong of the plug at the other end. Repeat for the narrow prong and the hot (smooth) wire. If the tester does not glow for both, replace the cord.

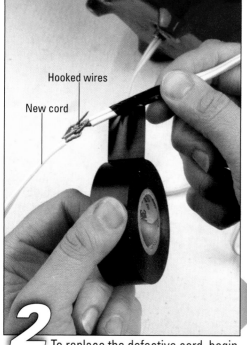

2 To replace the defective cord, begin by cutting the old cord. Strip about 1 inch off the ends of the old and new cord wires. Form hooks on all four wire ends and splice the old to the new in a splice that is thin enough to slide through the lamp. Wrap tightly and smoothly with electrician's tape.

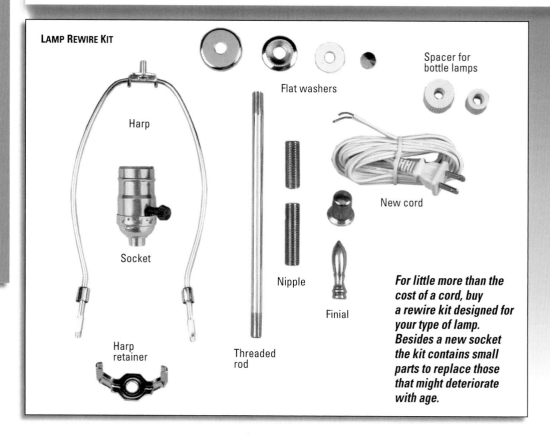

LAMP REWIRE KIT

Harp

Socket

Harp retainer

Flat washers

Spacer for bottle lamps

Nipple

Threaded rod

Finial

New cord

For little more than the cost of a cord, buy a rewire kit designed for your type of lamp. Besides a new socket the kit contains small parts to replace those that might deteriorate with age.

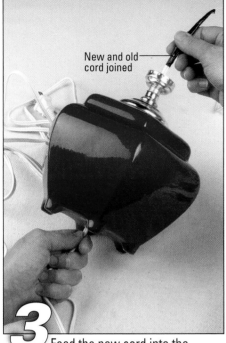

New and old cord joined

3 Feed the new cord into the base of the lamp while pulling the old cord through the top. Keep pulling until the new cord emerges. If rewiring a floor lamp, have a helper feed the cord into the base. Separate the cords and discard the old one.

Desk lamp

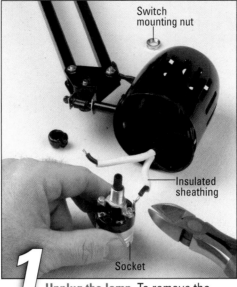

Switch mounting nut

Insulated sheathing

Socket

1 **Unplug the lamp.** To remove the socket from a desk lamp, you may need to remove the nut from the twist switch or unscrew a mounting screw located near the contact tab (page 62). Pull the socket out and disconnect the wires from the terminals.

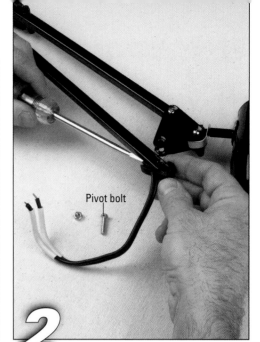

Pivot bolt

2 Splice the new cord to the old and pull it through, as in Steps 2 and 3 at left. Pulling may be complicated if the lamp has pivot points; it may require removing a nut and bolt to feed the wire through.

WHAT IF…
A lamp has two sockets?

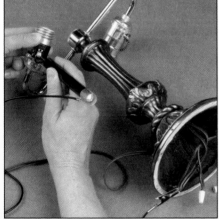

If one socket on a multisocket lamp fails to light, test the socket. If that is not the problem, open the junction box cover and pull out the wires. Test the wires leading from the socket to the junction box for continuity (Step 1 on page 64). If all the sockets fail to light, test the cord leading from the plug to the junction box.

STANLEY PRO TIP: **Halogen lamps**

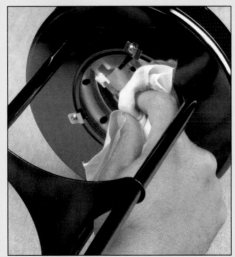

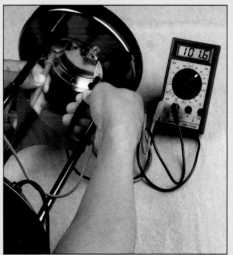

A halogen bulb gets very hot and may burn out if the lamp gets bumped while it is lit. Remove a bulb carefully, using a cloth, and find an exact replacement. If that does not solve the problem, test the socket.

Test the socket with a multitester (page 49). If the reading is lower or higher than the lamp's rating, check the fuse in the lamp for proper amperage. Then test the wires for continuity. If these tests do not reveal a problem, the transformer is probably bad; replace the lamp.

FLUORESCENTS

A new fluorescent fixture is inexpensive and easy to install (pages 120–121), so replacing rather than repairing is often the better option. Before you do, however, quickly check the components in this order: the tube, the starter (if any), the sockets, and the ballast.

Very old fluorescents have both a heavy ballast and a starter. More recent models have rapid-start ballasts and no starter. The latest models have electronic ballasts, which are nearly maintenance-free.

Fluorescent fixtures are often flimsy. Check that sockets are firmly seated and not cracked. Tubes should fit snugly between the sockets.

An old, delayed-start fluorescent flickers a few times before coming on as the starter delivers a burst of energy to get the tube going. A newer, rapid-start fixture has a ballast that supplies extra power when turned on so the light comes on immediately. A circular fluorescent differs from a straight tube only in shape.

Troubleshooting fluorescents

When faced with the following problems, work your way through the solutions one by one until the light functions.

Does not light
Twist a tube to tighten it or replace the tube. If there is a starter, replace it. Replace a damaged socket. Replace the ballast or the fixture.

Tube is blackened
If only one end is black, turn the tube around. Replace the tube if both ends are black.

Flickers or takes a long time to light
Tighten, turn around, or replace a tube. If there is a starter, replace it. Replace the ballast or the fixture.

Hums and/or seeps black gunk
Don't touch the seepage with your fingers. Wear gloves. Tighten the screw securing the ballast. Replace a leaking ballast or the fixture.

Tubes

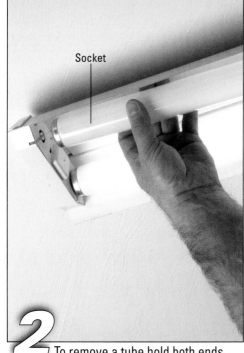

Rotate tube.

1 If a tube is black at both ends, replace it (Step 2). If it flickers or does not come on, try rotating it in the socket until it seats firmly or until the light comes on.

Socket

2 To remove a tube hold both ends and rotate until you feel it come loose at one end. Guide the pins out of the socket. To install a new tube, insert pins into one socket and guide the pins into the other socket. Rotate the tube a quarter-turn until you feel it seat or until it lights.

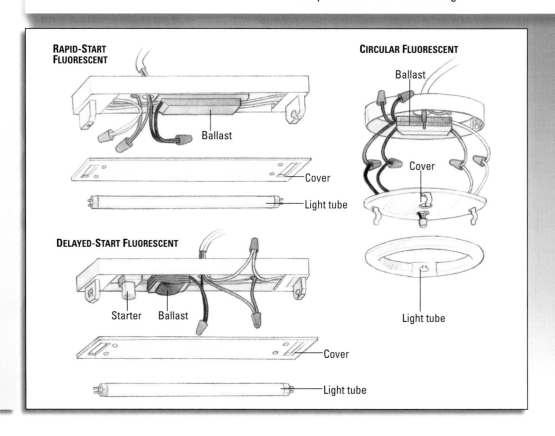

RAPID-START FLUORESCENT

Ballast

Cover

Light tube

DELAYED-START FLUORESCENT

Starter   Ballast

Cover

Light tube

CIRCULAR FLUORESCENT

Ballast

Cover

Light tube

Starters

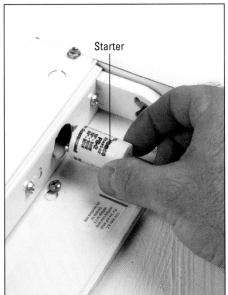

Starter

If a fixture has a starter, replace it every time you replace a tube. Be sure to buy a starter with the same serial numbers as the old one. If a tube is slow to light, tighten the starter. If that does not solve the problem, replace the starter. If the light still doesn't work, the ballast is to blame.

Sockets

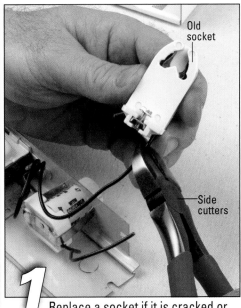

Old socket

Side cutters

1 Replace a socket if it is cracked or does not hold the tube firmly. Some sockets just slide out, while others are held in place by a screw. If you cannot remove the wires, cut them near the socket.

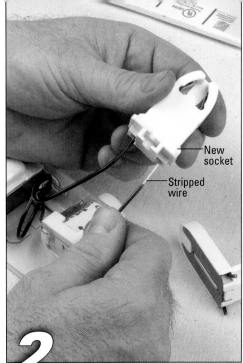

New socket

Stripped wire

2 Buy a replacement to match the old socket. Strip ¾ inch of insulation from each wire end and push the wire end into the hole of the new socket. Push the new socket firmly into the fixture.

BALLAST
Install an exact replacement

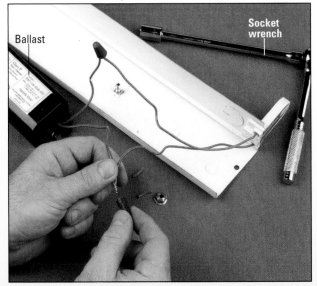

Socket wrench

Ballast

If all other fixes fail, the ballast is the problem. (See the troubleshooting box on page 66.) A replacement ballast may cost about the same as a new fixture, but it may be a bit less work to install a ballast than replace the fixture. **Shut off power to the light.** Tag the wires for future reference. Disconnect wires, if possible, or cut them. Remove the ballast and buy an exact replacement, wiring it just as the old ballast was wired.

STANLEY Pro Tip
Guard tubes from damage

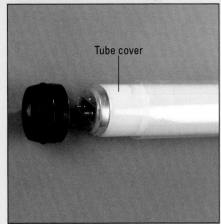

Tube cover

Fluorescent tubes break easily and are sensitive to cold. If your fixture doesn't have a cover and the tubes might get bumped, protect them with a clear plastic sleeve. Covers also can help if the fixture is slow to start in the cold.

BULBS, STARTERS, BALLASTS, AND ELECTRONIC BALLASTS

A fluorescent bulb glows because the electricity running through it excites a gas, which causes the coating on the inside of the tube to glow. In most modern fluorescent lights, starting the bulb requires a high voltage; keeping the bulb bright and from burning out requires rapidly limiting the current flowing in the tube. All of this is the job of the ballast.

Before starting some fluorescent tubes, the ballast sends low voltage to filaments at each end of the lamp, preheating them. The heated filaments give off electrons that charge the inside of the tube. The heat this creates also helps vaporize a small amount of mercury in the tube. Once the mercury is vaporized and the tube is charged, the ballast switches gears and pumps higher voltage into the tube. This is the arc voltage—the power that travels from one

end of the bulb to the other, energizing the mercury vapor and causing it to give off ultraviolet light. This excites the coating in the tube to make visible light.

As the electrons flow through the gas, they knock other electrons loose, and the gas becomes a better conductor. (Conductors have lots of free electrons, enabling them to carry other electrons—electricity—from one place to another.) If the ballast didn't limit the amount of power available at this point, the tube would burn out.

In the early days of fluorescent lights, a heat-sensitive switch, called a starter, controlled the change from the startup voltage to operating voltage. These small, thumb-size canisters contained a heat source and a metal strip that bent when warmed. As it bent the strip moved from one contact to another, changing the amount of

electricity that went to the ballast. Later designs removed the need for the starter.

Traditional ballasts are essentially transformers—wires wrapped around an iron core—that change line current to the necessary voltage. The magnetic field created by the core acts as a governor to slow changes in current, keeping the bulb from receiving too much power.

A traditional ballast is too large to fit inside a compact fluorescent. The ballast in a compact fluorescent is a solid-state control built into the base of the bulb. In addition to being smaller, this ballast improves on the traditional ballast by reducing bulb flicker. Line current changes direction every 60 seconds, causing a slight flicker in fluorescent bulbs. An electronic ballast increases the current to 400 cycles per second, resulting in a more constant light.

PRESTART CHECKLIST

☐ **TIME**
About 30 minutes to remove and replace the ballast

☐ **TOOLS**
Screwdriver, wire cutters, socket set or wrench

☐ **SKILLS**
Cutting and connecting wire; unscrewing or unbolting ballast

☐ **PREP**
Remove light tubes

☐ **MATERIALS**
New ballast that matches existing ballast, wire nuts

Early fluorescent fixtures had a starter (far right) that acted as a switch that lowered the power once the bulb warmed up.

Later bulb and ballast designs (bottom) eliminated the need for a starter.

Compact fluorescents (right) have a solid-state ballast in the base so that the bulb will fit in a traditional lamp socket.

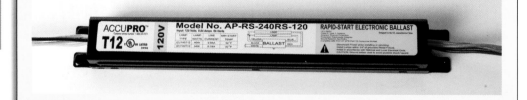

Replacing a ballast

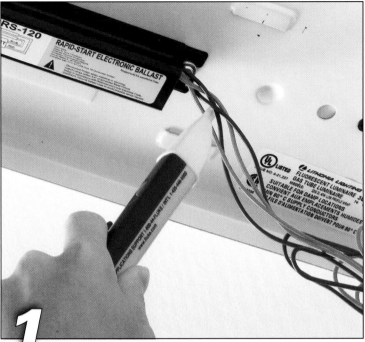

1 **Turn off the power at the breaker.** Remove the bulbs and cover plate. Test with a voltage tester to make sure the power is off. If it isn't, turn off the correct breaker.

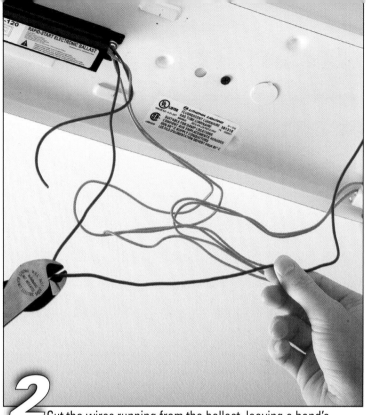

2 Cut the wires running from the ballast, leaving a hand's length of wire on the section that remains.

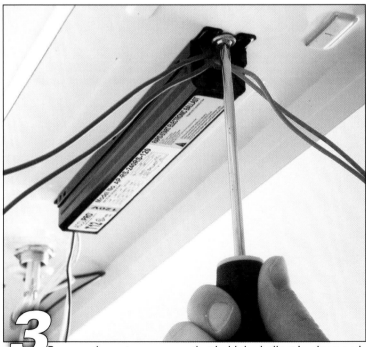

3 Remove the nuts or screws that hold the ballast in place and remove the ballast. Take it to a lighting supply or home center and buy an exact replacement.

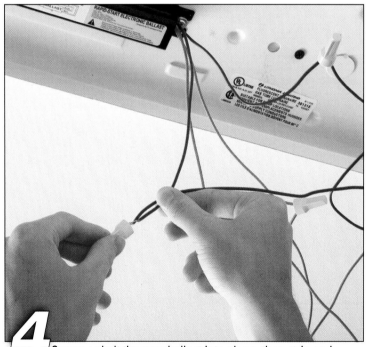

4 Screw or bolt the new ballast into place, then strip and connect the wires.

HALOGEN LIGHTS

Despite their appearance and the white-hot light they produce, halogen lights are closely related to standard incandescent lights. Both are encased in gas-filled glass envelopes and have tungsten filaments that glow to create light.

In standard incandescents the gas is argon, which keeps the filament from going up in a flash of light, as it would if exposed to oxygen. In normal operation the tungsten gets so hot that it vaporizes. It's a slow process, but when the filament becomes too thin, the bulb fails.

In halogen bulbs the gas in the bulb is one of the gases in the halogen family—iodine and chlorine are halogens. As the filament in the bulb vaporizes with use, halogens redeposit the tungsten on the filament. This lengthens bulb life from about 750 hours to 2,000 to 6,000 hours. Recycling tungsten within the bulb only occurs at high temperatures, so the bulbs burn both hot and very white. To withstand the high temperatures, the casing around the light is usually quartz, which can deteriorate from oil and dirt, causing the lamp to burn out.

Low-voltage halogens

While halogen bulbs aren't much more efficient than standard incandescent bulbs, the light they produce is far brighter when focused in a small area. A good halogen desk light runs on 20 watts; a standard desk light with a traditional incandescent needs a 60-watt bulb.

Originally low-wattage, highly focused halogen bulbs were developed for cars and planes, which run on lower-voltage power supplies. Track lights, desk lights, and other low-wattage halogen fixtures continue in the tradition, in part because operating at low voltage means the bulb filament can be shorter, the bulb smaller, and the light easier to focus.

A standard feature of low-voltage halogen fixtures is a transformer that reduces line voltage (120 volts) to a lower voltage, usually 12 volts. Frequently halogen desk lights have the transformer in the base; low-voltage halogen track lights often have a built-in transformer that reduces the voltage. This lets you run the track at 120 volts and mix and match lights. A 120-volt incandescent can sit right next to a 12-volt halogen, with both operating at the proper voltage.

Line-voltage halogens

Line-voltage halogen lights typically operate between 45 to 500 watts. The lower end of the scale is found on line-voltage track lights, the higher end is found in spotlights. Although these bulbs sometimes are used for general lighting, what's true of low-voltage lights is true of line-voltage. With one exception halogens are about as efficient as regular lights and not nearly as efficient as fluorescent lights.

The exception: bulbs coated with a material that reflects infrared light (heat) back into the bulb. Up to 90 percent of the energy radiated by halogens is heat. Reflecting infrared light back into the bulb helps heat the tungsten filament. As a result the temperature necessary for efficient operation is maintained with less electrical input.

Halogen spotlights, technically called parabolic aluminized reflector (PAR) lights, benefit particularly from this coating, called IR coating. Some studies rate the efficiency of a halogen IR PAR at 65 percent higher than a standard incandescent spot. Similar savings are found with single-ended (T-4) tube halogens and double-ended, high-wattage quartz tube (T-3) lamps.

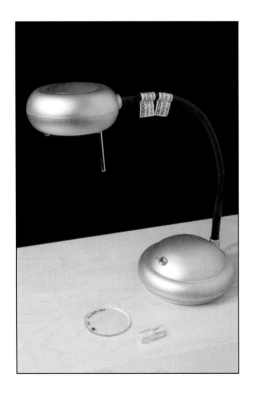

Dimmers and bulb life

Halogen lights run on standard dimmers. If you use a dimmer, occasionally run the bulb at full to deposit spent tungsten back onto the filament and extend the bulb's life.

Smoke alarm

Don't panic if a halogen bulb smokes the first time you use it. Many halogen bulbs have a protective coating that burns off the first time you light it.

SAFETY FIRST
Shield the bulb: halogen safety

Leave the glass shield and wire cage, if any, on a halogen light fixture. It protects you from touching the bulb accidentally and keeps flammable material away from the bulb. The shield also protects on the rare occasions when the bulbs explode.

CHANDELIER REPAIRS

Older chandeliers often need repair. Many were manufactured with little regard to the heat the bulbs produce, and larger bulbs than recommended have often been installed. Years of overheating makes the wire insulation brittle. A typical fixture has cord running through tubes to the bulb sockets, allowing several opportunities for malfunctions.

Because sockets and the wires attached to them are near a hot bulb and often enclosed, they deteriorate. If all the lights do not work, the stem wire probably needs to be replaced (Step 4, page 72). If some wiring needs replaced, consider rewiring the entire fixture—it won't take much longer.

If only one light fails to come on, try pulling up the contact tab inside the socket (page 62). Vacuum dust from the socket. If the bulb still does not light, remove the socket and test it (Step 2).

PRESTART CHECKLIST

☐ **TIME**
About 3 hours to dismantle, test, and run new wires in a chandelier

☐ **TOOLS**
Phillips screwdriver, voltage tester, continuity tester, wire strippers, long-nose pliers

☐ **SKILLS**
Testing for power and continuity, stripping and connecting wires

☐ **PREP**
Line up a helper to assist with removing the fixture. Lay a drop cloth onto a work surface to cushion the fixture as you work on it.

☐ **MATERIALS**
Cord wire, electrician's tape

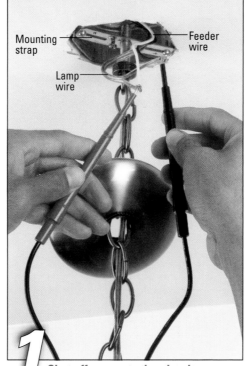

Mounting strap, **Feeder wire**, **Lamp wire**

1 **Shut off power to the circuit** (in addition to flipping off the light switch). Support the chandelier. Loosen the screws or screw collar holding the canopy in place and slide it down. Pull the wires apart, restore the power temporarily, and test for power (page 48). Shut off the power again.

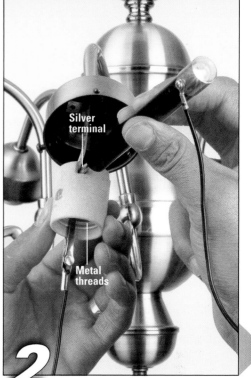

Silver terminal, **Metal threads**

2 Attach a continuity tester clip to the metal threads inside the socket and touch the neutral (silver) terminal with the probe. Then clip onto the brass screw and touch the probe to the contact tab inside the socket. If the tester light does not come on for both tests, replace the socket (page 63).

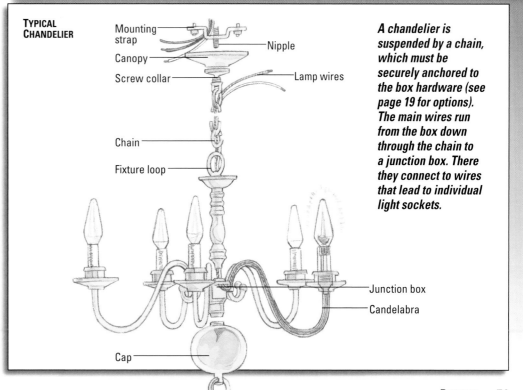

TYPICAL CHANDELIER

Mounting strap, Nipple, Canopy, Screw collar, Lamp wires, Chain, Fixture loop, Junction box, Candelabra, Cap

A chandelier is suspended by a chain, which must be securely anchored to the box hardware (see page 19 for options). The main wires run from the box down through the chain to a junction box. There they connect to wires that lead to individual light sockets.

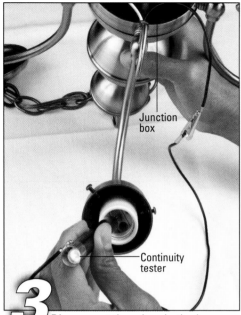
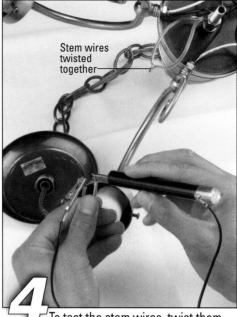
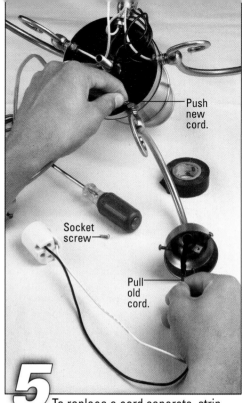

Junction box

Continuity tester

Stem wires twisted together

Push new cord.

Socket screw

Pull old cord.

3 Disconnect the wires in the box, remove the chandelier, and place it on a work surface. Open the chandelier's junction box and pull out the wires. Test both the neutral (ribbed) and hot (smooth) wires for continuity.

4 To test the stem wires, twist them together at the junction box. At the other end attach a continuity tester clip to one wire and touch the probe to the other wire. If the tester does not glow, replace the stem wires.

5 To replace a cord separate, strip, and splice the old cord to the new (pages 64–65. Pull the old wire through until the new wire appears.

STANLEY PRO TIP: **Accessing and pulling chandelier wires**

A chandelier's junction box is located in the center of the fixture. To open it remove the nut at the bottom. Inside you find a tight mass of wires. Space may be at a premium, so after rewiring, cut the wires as short as you can. Use the smallest wire nuts possible.

Some chandelier junction boxes are crammed tightly with wires. To figure out where a socket wire ends up in the junction box, tug the wires at the socket end and feel the wires at the other end.

Chandelier tubes may be narrow. Join the new cord (using lamp cord, which can withstand heat) to the old with a tight splice (page 64); a bulky splice may stick. If you still have trouble pulling wires through an old fixture, there may be corrosion in the tubes. Try blowing through the tubes and run a single wire through the tubes to remove any obstructions.

REPAIRING WIRING IN BOXES

A loose wall box can strain wiring. Secure the box with mounting brackets or by fastening it to adjacent framing with a screw or two.

Wire insulation in a box—especially a ceiling fixture box, which gets very hot—deteriorates more quickly than wiring inside a wall or ceiling. So even if the wires you see are damaged, the wiring hidden in your walls is probably OK.

Wire repair tips

■ If bare wire shows below a wire nut, remove the nut, snip the bare wire to shorten it slightly, and reinstall the nut. If the insulation is nicked, wrap electrician's tape tightly around the damaged area. If wiring is generally brittle and cracked, cover the affected wire with heat-shrinkable tubing.

■ If a wire's insulation is nicked near the point where it enters a box, it may be difficult to reach the damaged area with tape. Try slipping on a red plastic armored cable bushing (page 41).

■ Whenever you untangle a wire splice or disconnect a wire from a terminal, you rebend a wire and thereby weaken it. If you have enough wire, snip off the old loop and start again.

PRESTART CHECKLIST

☐ **TIME**
About 30 minutes to repair a box and wrap four to six damaged wires

☐ **TOOLS**
Voltage tester, heat gun, utility knife, side cutters, lineman's pliers

☐ **SKILLS**
Splicing wires; applying tubing

☐ **MATERIALS**
Mounting brackets, electrician's tape, heat-shrinkable tubing

1 Turn off power and test for power in the box. Rather than disconnecting a device and repairing the wire ends, save time by simply cutting the wires just behind the terminals. Then strip and reconnect. Make sure remaining wires are long enough—6 to 8 inches—before you cut.

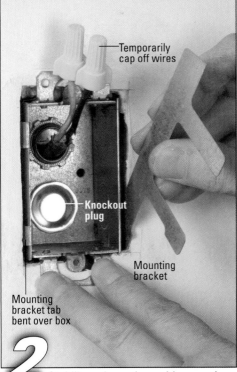

Temporarily cap off wires

Knockout plug

Mounting bracket

Mounting bracket tab bent over box

2 Stabilize a loose box with mounting brackets. On each side of the box, slip the bracket between the box and the wall material. Slide it down so both ends are behind the wall and bend the tabs into the box (or fasten it with screws). Replace missing knockouts with snap-in plugs.

Evaluating old wire and cable

Old Romex

Knob-and-tube wiring

Friction tape splice

Old Romex or knob-and-tube wiring may have cloth insulation that deteriorates with age. Clothlike friction tape may cover splices, particularly with knob-and-tube wiring. As long as the insulation is sound and the splice is covered, the wiring is safe. If a tape-covered splice is unraveling, remove the tape and twist on a wire nut or retape it.

Old wiring may be so dirty that you cannot tell hot (black) wires from neutral (formerly white) wires. It is important to find out—if you connect the neutral wire rather than the hot wire to a switch, power is always present in the box, even when the switch is off. With the power off, gently clean portions of old insulation using a cloth dampened with alcohol or soapy water until you can tell which wire has white insulation.

Fixing wires in a ceiling box

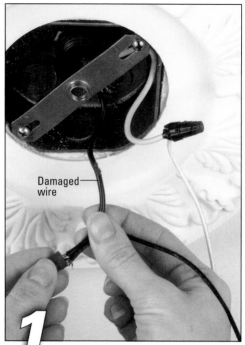

1 **Shut off power to the circuit.**
Gently pull the wires out and unscrew the wire nuts. If you find thick tape instead of a wire nut, slice it with a knife, taking care not to damage the wire beneath.

Damaged wire

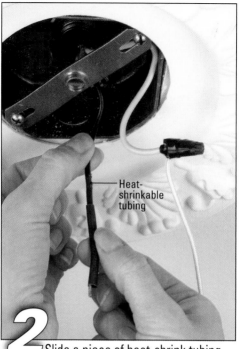

2 Slide a piece of heat-shrink tubing over the wire as far as it goes. Cut off the tubing to expose the stripped wire end.

Heat-shrinkable tubing

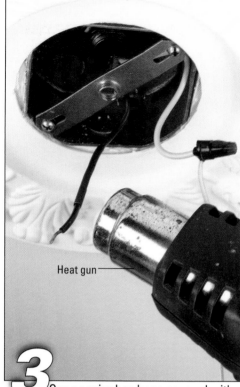

3 Once a wire has been covered with heat-shrinkable tubing, direct a heat gun at the wire until the tubing has shrunk tightly onto the wire.

Heat gun

WHAT IF...
A box is set back?

Codes require that a box be tightly enclosed to prevent an electrical fire from spreading. If a box's front edge is not flush with the wall or ceiling surface around it, slip in a metal or plastic box extender, available in various sizes.

STANLEY PRO TIP: **Clip and restrip**

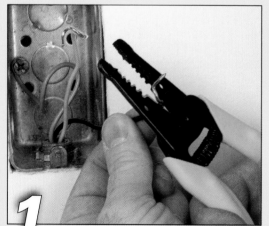

1 Wire that has been bent a few times is liable to break. So whenever you install a device or fixture, cut off the previously stripped portion of the wires.

2 Strip the wire ends (page 50), removing a ¾-inch piece of insulation if you loop and attach the wire to a terminal, or a 1-inch piece if you splice with a wire nut (pages 51–53).

Grounding an old receptacle

Knockout slug

1 If you have an old system with ungrounded receptacles and want to ground one receptacle, **shut off power to the circuit,** test for power, and pull out the receptacle. Pry out a knockout slug and then twist it back and forth to remove it.

New ground wire

Fish tape

2 Use the techniques shown on page 43 to make a pathway for a ground wire. Use one or two fish tapes to run a #12 green-insulated wire from the box to the service panel or to a cold-water pipe.

Grounding clamp

Cold-water pipe

3 Connect the wire to the ground screw of the receptacle. Connect the other end to a cold-water pipe (not a hot water pipe) with a special grounding clamp.

Test a two-hole receptacle for grounding

If your system has two-hole receptacles, it is probably an ungrounded system. To make sure **shut off power,** pull out a receptacle, and restore power. Insert one probe of a voltage tester into the hot (shorter) slot of the receptacle and touch the other probe to the metal box. If the tester doesn't light, the system is not grounded. However if it lights the box is grounded; you can install a three-hole (grounded) receptacle and run a ground wire from the receptacle grounding terminal to a grounding screw in the box. Test the new receptacle for ground using a receptacle analyzer (page 32).

Tricks for replacing cable

If you find a wire with brittle insulation inside a box, the wiring hidden inside your walls is probably still in good condition. However if you find brittle insulation in several boxes, call a professional electrician for an evaluation; the wiring in your house, or some of it, may need to be replaced.

Rewiring a house is usually a job for professionals, but if you work systematically and with your building department's approval, you may attempt it. The safest way is to pull and replace one cable at a time.

Running cable and connecting wires is probably less than half the work of a rewiring job. What takes longer is cutting into walls and ceilings to gain access to run the cable, then patching and painting afterwards.

Start by replacing exposed cable (for example, in a basement or attic). Refer to pages 174–177 for methods of running cable through walls.

In some cases you may be able to pull cable through a wall or ceiling without damaging it. Once you've discovered where a cable leads (for example between two receptacles), disconnect the cable at both ends. At one end tightly tape the new cable to the old cable, making the splice as thin as possible so it can run through tight holes. Pull on the other end, and if you're lucky, the new cable comes through. In most cases, however, there are tight turns or the cable is stapled to the framing, so this technique does not work. You have to cut into the wall or ceiling.

NEW DRYER CORD

Older, 240-volt electric dryer receptacles have three prongs, attaching to three wires—two hot leads and one neutral. New codes require a four-prong receptacle, which connects to two hot wires, a neutral, and a ground wire.

If a dryer cord does not match the receptacle, hire a pro to change the receptacle or change the cord yourself. The following steps show how to change from a three-wire to a four-wire cord. (Do not change from a four-wire to a three-wire. You will eliminate the ground wire, which offers extra protection against shock.)

PRESTART CHECKLIST

☐ **TIME**
About 1 hour to remove the old cord and install a new one

☐ **TOOLS**
Screwdriver, drill, and perhaps strippers

☐ **SKILLS**
Drilling a hole into metal; attaching wires to terminals

☐ **MATERIALS**
A new dryer cord and a grounding screw with a head large enough to capture the cord's ground wire

Old cord

New cord

1 Purchase a cord with a plug that fits the receptacle. See that the cord amperage rating matches the receptacle. **Unplug the dryer before beginning work.**

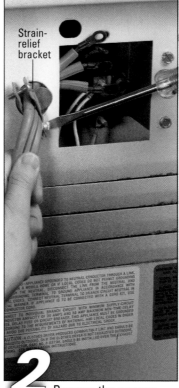

Strain-relief bracket

2 Remove the access panel at the back of the dryer. Loosen the screws to the strain-relief bracket and remove the old wires. Connect the black, red, and white wires from the new cord to the same terminals.

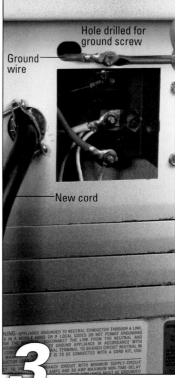

Hole drilled for ground screw

Ground wire

New cord

3 On the dryer's metal housing, drill a hole slightly smaller than the diameter of the screw shank. Feed the grounding screw through the ground-wire connector and finish tightening the screw.

STANLEY PRO TIP

Testing a 240-volt receptacle

Voltage tester

If a 240-volt receptacle delivers no power or only partial power to an appliance, check the service panel to make sure power is on. Then carefully make a live test: Insert one probe of a voltage tester into the neutral slot. Insert the other probe into one hot slot then the other; you should get a reading of 120 volts in each position. Insert one probe into each hot slot; the reading should be 240 volts. If you get different results, have a pro install a new receptacle.

SAFETY FIRST
240 volts pack a wallop

A shock from 120-volt wiring is startling but probably will not harm an adult. However a shock from 240 volts is more dangerous. Even inserting a plug requires caution. To be safe **shut off power to the circuit,** insert the plug into the receptacle, then turn the power back on.

REPAIRING A DOOR CHIME

If a chime or bell does not sound when you push the button, follow the steps shown on these pages: Check the button first, then the chime, then the transformer.

All these components are easily repaired or replaced. However if the wiring is damaged inside walls, replacing it can be very difficult.

Power for a doorbell is supplied by a transformer, usually attached to a metal electrical box in some out-of-the-way location such as a basement, crawlspace, garage, or inside a cabinet. Work carefully—other components, such as thermostats, might have similar-looking transformers. Follow the wires to be sure.

Doorbell wires may be color-coded, but there is no predicting what color goes to which button. Often all the wires are the same color.

Because the bell circuit operates on low voltage, you do not need to turn off power while testing the button or chime. However, the transformer is connected to 120 volts. Shut off power before removing or replacing the transformer.

PRESTART CHECKLIST

☐ **TIME**
About 2 hours to diagnose and repair most problems, not including time spent buying the new part

☐ **TOOLS**
Screwdriver, brush, strippers, multitester, vacuum cleaner

☐ **SKILLS**
Stripping wires, attaching wires to terminals, using multitester

☐ **MATERIALS**
Short length of wire, steel wool or fine sandpaper, perhaps new button, chime, or transformer

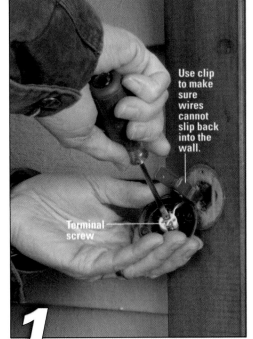

Use clip to make sure wires cannot slip back into the wall.

Terminal screw

1 Detach the button from the wall. If the mounting screws are not visible, you may need to snap off a cover to reach them. To remove a small, round button, pry it out with a screwdriver. Clean away any debris. Make sure wires are not broken. Tighten terminal screws.

Spark

2 If that does not solve the problem, detach the wires from the terminals. Hold each wire by its insulation and touch the bare wires together. If you get a tiny spark and the chime sounds, replace the button. If you get a spark and the chime does not sound, test the chime (Step 4). If there is no spark, check the transformer (Step 5).

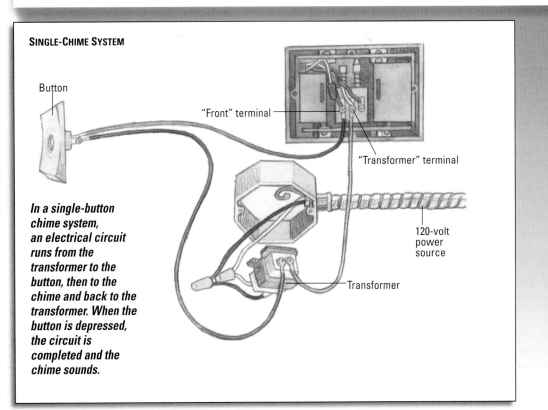

SINGLE-CHIME SYSTEM

Button

"Front" terminal

"Transformer" terminal

120-volt power source

Transformer

In a single-button chime system, an electrical circuit runs from the transformer to the button, then to the chime and back to the transformer. When the button is depressed, the circuit is completed and the chime sounds.

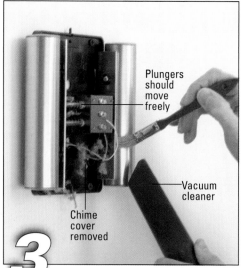

Plungers should move freely

Vacuum cleaner

Chime cover removed

Multitester

Transformer

3 If a chime does not sound or has a muffled sound, remove the cover and clean any dust or gunk. Make sure the wires are firmly connected to the terminal screws. If there is corrosion on the connections, detach and clean the wires and terminals with steel wool or fine sandpaper.

4 Set a multitester to a low AC reading and touch the probes to "front" and "trans" terminals, then to "rear" and "trans." If you get a reading that is close to the chime's voltage rating, power is entering the chime. That indicates the chime mechanism is not functioning and the chime needs replacing.

5 If there is no power at the chime, test the transformer. Remove the thin wires. Touch the probes of the multitester to both terminals. If the reading is more than 2 volts below the transformer's output rating, replace the transformer.

Wireless options

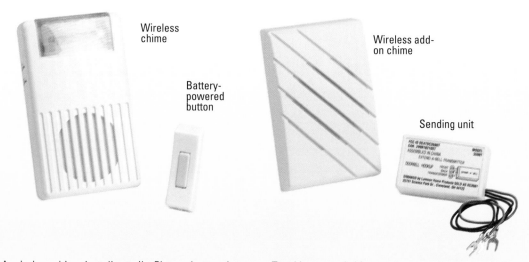

Wireless chime

Battery-powered button

Wireless add-on chime

Sending unit

A wireless chime installs easily. Place a battery into the button and attach the button to the outside of the house. Mount the chime, following the manufacturer's instructions and plug it into an electrical receptacle.

To add a second chime to your system, buy a wireless add-on chime. Place the sending unit inside the existing chime and connect its wires to the terminals. Mount the chime and plug it in.

CHIME NEEDS REPLACING
Find a new chime with the same voltage rating

Before removing a chime tag the wires so you know where to reconnect them. Loosen the terminal screws and remove the wires. Remove the mounting screws. Pull the chime out, carefully threading the wires through the hole in the chime.

Purchase a new chime of the same voltage rating as the transformer. (Usually the voltage rating is printed on the chime unit.) To prevent having to paint the wall, make sure the chime housing covers the old chime's mounting area. Slip the wires through the opening in the housing, mount it to the wall, and connect the wires.

6 Before you replace a transformer, make sure power is reaching it. If the transformer is attached to a receptacle box, insert the tester probes into the receptacle slots. If the transformer is attached to a junction box, carefully remove the cover and test the wires (page 48). **Remember, these are 120-volt wires.**

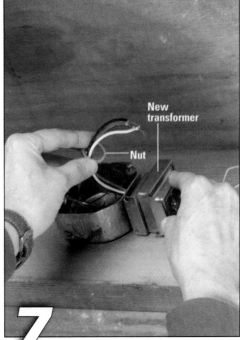

7 If the transformer doesn't work, buy a new one with the same voltage rating. **Shut off power** to the circuit. Open the box and disconnect the transformer wires. Remove the nut that clamps the transformer to the box and pull out the transformer. Wire and clamp the new transformer.

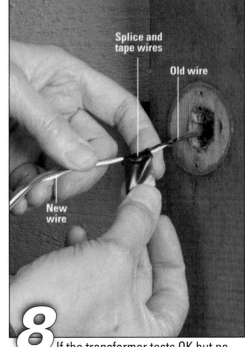

8 If the transformer tests OK but no power reaches the chime or a button, the wiring is damaged. You may be able to attach new wire to the old and pull the new wire through. If you can't rewire install a wireless chime (page 78).

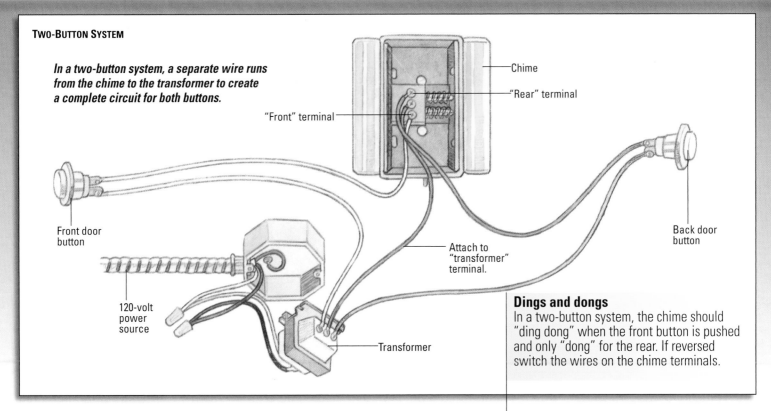

TWO-BUTTON SYSTEM

In a two-button system, a separate wire runs from the chime to the transformer to create a complete circuit for both buttons.

Chime

"Rear" terminal

"Front" terminal

Front door button

120-volt power source

Attach to "transformer" terminal.

Transformer

Back door button

Dings and dongs
In a two-button system, the chime should "ding dong" when the front button is pushed and only "dong" for the rear. If reversed switch the wires on the chime terminals.

WHEN A CIRCUIT OVERLOADS

Many homes have a similar problem: When you run the toaster and the microwave at the same time or use a blow dryer while the bathroom fan is on, a circuit overloads, causing a fuse to blow or a breaker to trip.

One solution is to install a new circuit with new receptacles—a messy, expensive job. But there is a simpler solution: Plug that toaster or blow dryer into a receptacle powered by another circuit.

If you have a detailed index of your circuits (pages 54–55), it's easy to find alternative receptacles. If none is nearby use an extension cord option, shown below, or hire a pro to install a new circuit.

1 List the items on the problem circuit. Using your circuit index determine which items you can move to another circuit to relieve overloading. In this example moving any of the three items works. Make sure the change doesn't overload the other circuit.

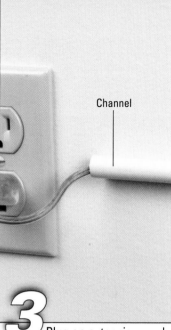

2 Make sure you have the correct size breaker or fuse for the circuit. A circuit using #12 wire can be on a 20-amp breaker or fuse; a circuit using #14 wire must be on a 15-amp (page 15).

3 Plug an extension cord into a receptacle powered by a different circuit (one that is not already overloaded). If none is nearby consider running an extension cord through a wall-mounted channel.

How much can a circuit handle?

The higher the amperage of a circuit, the more power it can handle. To figure out how many watts a circuit can take, multiply volts by amps. A circuit's safe capacity is only 80 percent of its total capacity. So a 120-volt, 15-amp circuit has a total capacity of 1,800 watts (120 × 15 = 1800). A safe capacity for that circuit is 1,440 watts.

Extension cord options

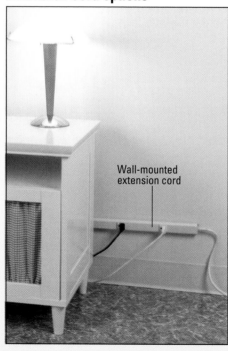

Wall-mounted extension cord

Various solutions are available to extend a circuit's reach without running new cable through walls. One option is a wallmounted extension cord, which has one or two outlets per running foot. Raceway wiring is another option (pages 110–111), but it involves a little more work to install. Both are somewhat unsightly, but you can often hide them behind furnishings.

WHAT IF...
A fuse blows?

If the metal strip is broken or melted but the window is clear, the fuse has blown because the circuit has overloaded—too much power was used at once (pages 26–27, 148–149). If the window is blackened, a short circuit is the culprit. Check the circuit's wiring for loose or damaged wiring (pages 40–41).

Overload

Short

LOW-VOLTAGE THERMOSTATS

A thermostat senses when the air temperature moves above or below the desired level and switches the heating or cooling system on or off.

If a thermostat is attached to an electrical box and has standard house wires connected to it, it is a line-voltage unit. If it malfunctions **shut off power** to the circuit, remove it, and take it to a dealer for a replacement.

A low-voltage thermostat like the one shown here receives power from a transformer, much like that for a door chime. Typically the transformer is located on or near the heating or cooling unit. Replace the transformer if it does not deliver power (pages 78–79). In a standard setup two wires control the heater and two control the air-conditioner. If there are more wires, consult a heating and cooling pro.

PRESTART CHECKLIST

☐ **TIME**
Less than 1 hour for most repairs

☐ **TOOLS**
Screwdriver, soft brush, strippers

☐ **SKILLS**
Stripping wire, making connections

☐ **MATERIALS**
Short length of thin-gauge wire, perhaps a replacement thermostat or transformer

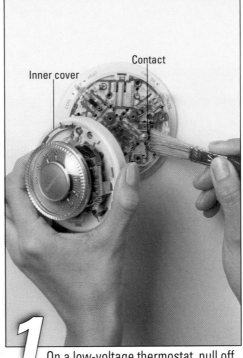

Inner cover *Contact*

1 On a low-voltage thermostat, pull off the outer cover and loosen screws to remove the inner cover. Clean away dust with a soft brush. Gently lift the control lever and clean the contact beneath it. Replace the covers and test.

2 If it still doesn't work, test for power. Strip the ends of a short wire and touch the terminals marked W and R. If they spark and the heating unit comes on, the thermostat is broken and should be replaced. If nothing happens check the transformer (page 78).

WHAT IF...
The room temperature is far different from the setting?

A thermostat that sends the wrong signal to the heating unit or air-conditioner may just be out of plumb. Use a string with a small weight near the two alignment marks. If they do not line up, loosen the mounting screws and twist the thermostat.

PRO TIP
Installing a new thermostat

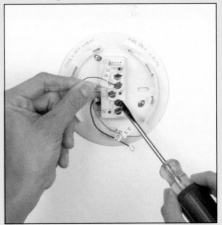

When replacing a thermostat, tag the wires before you remove the old unit. Make sure the new thermostat is plumb (see box at left) and drive mounting screws. Attach the wires, inner cover, and outer cover.

DIGITAL THERMOSTATS

A programmable digital thermostat is one of the simplest ways to cut back on energy use. If the house is empty or everyone is asleep, it doesn't need to be kept at the usual temperature. You can save up to 20 percent in heating costs just by lowering your thermostat 5 degrees at night and 10 degrees during the day. Similar savings apply to cooling too.

A programmable thermostat will do this automatically. It doesn't make mistakes and it doesn't forget. Depending on the model you buy, a programmable thermostat can be set to run your furnace and air-conditioning at several settings throughout the day, and the settings can vary from day to day. A heat program, for example, might set the heat at 65 degrees 30 minutes before you wake up and turn it back down to 55 when you leave for work. The setting could go up just before you come home and drop to 60 at bedtime.

A programmable thermostat is easy to use and install.

1 Remove the cover from the old thermostat. The cover usually snaps off, but if your cover doesn't come off easily, look for and remove screws that may hold it in place.

2 Disconnect the wires. The wires are usually color coded, with some of the wires controlling the cooling system (if any) and the others controlling the heat. If the wires aren't color coded, label them with tape, marking the tape with the letter of the terminal the wire attaches to.

PRESTART CHECKLIST

☐ **TIME**
About 15 minutes

☐ **TOOLS**
Screwdriver, drill, hammer

☐ **SKILLS**
Stripping wire, drilling holes

☐ **MATERIALS**
Programmable thermostat

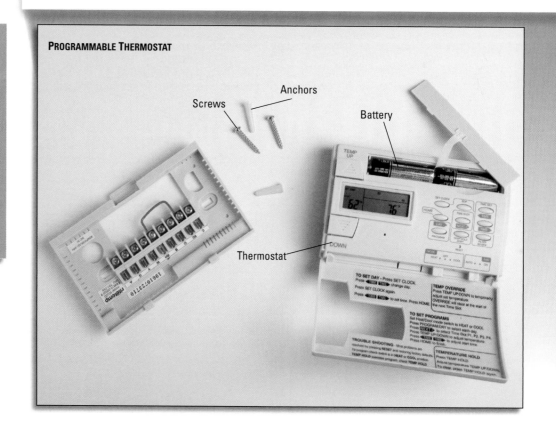

PROGRAMMABLE THERMOSTAT

Screws   Anchors   Battery   Thermostat

3 Remove the thermostat from the wall. Screws hold the back of the thermostat to the wall. Find and remove them.

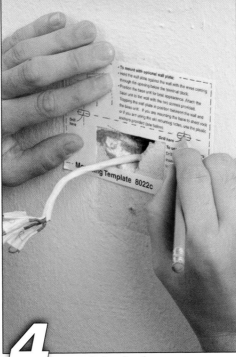

4 Lay out holes for the new thermostat. Use the template that comes with the new thermostat to mark the hole locations on the wall. Drill the holes using the bit size the manufacturer recommends.

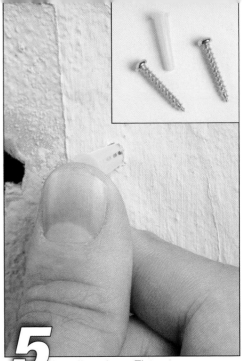

5 Install anchors. The new screws go into plastic anchors that come with the thermostat and mount into the wall to keep the screws from pulling out. Insert the anchors into the holes you drilled and tap them in with a hammer.

6 Screw the new backplate to the wall. Hang the thermostat on the wall using the screws that come with it.

7 Wire the base. Connect the wires to the terminals, matching the color of the wire to the labels by each terminal.

8 Attach the body. Place batteries into the thermostat and snap the body of the thermostat over the backplate. Follow the manufacturer's instructions to program.

REPLACING A THERMOSTAT FOR AN ELECTRIC BASEBOARD HEATER

Line-voltage thermostats operate at either 120 or 240 volts and control gable vent fans, electric baseboard heaters, and similar appliances. Replacing them is different but no harder than replacing a furnace thermostat. There is one important—and potentially dangerous—difference between the two, however. A conventional low-voltage thermostat operates at 24 volts. An electric baseboard heater may operate at 240 volts. Always **make sure the power is off** when working on either type of thermostat, but be doubly cautious with a line-voltage thermostat.

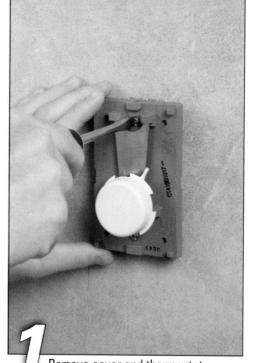

1 Remove cover and thermostat. **Turn off power to the circuit.** Take the cover off the thermostat and remove the screws that attach it to the junction box. Without touching any of the wires, lift the thermostat away from the box.

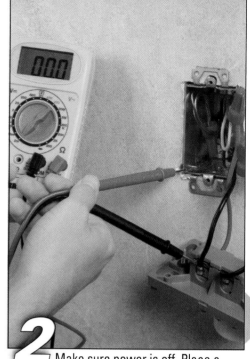

2 Make sure power is off. Place a circuit tester or multimeter across the ground wire and each of the other wires in turn to make sure there is no voltage flowing in the lines. If the ground wire is attached to a metal junction box, you can substitute the box for the ground wire when testing.

PRESTART CHECKLIST

☐ **TIME**
About 1 hour to cut off power; double check, remove, test, and if necessary replace the thermostat

☐ **TOOLS**
Multimeter or circuit tester and continuity tester, screwdriver

☐ **SKILLS**
Connecting wires

☐ **PREP**
Find breakers controlling circuit; turn off power and check to make sure

☐ **MATERIALS**
Line-voltage thermostat, wire nuts

Programmable high-voltage thermostats

Because electric heat is one of the most expensive ways to heat your home, you can cut your heating bills significantly by installing a programmable thermostat, like this one, which automatically turns down the heat when it isn't needed. Make sure you buy a high-voltage thermostat designed for electric baseboard heat. Thermostats for electric-baseboard heaters operate at the same voltage as the heater—usually 240 volts. Low-voltage thermostats designed for gas, oil, or heat pumps won't work and are extremely dangerous on a high-voltage system.

3 Label the wires as you disconnect them. Mark which wires go to the terminals labeled "line" and which go to the ones labeled "load."

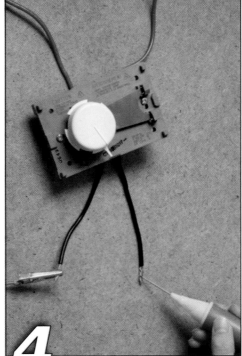

4 Test the thermostat. Attach one lead of a continuity tester to one "line" wire and the other lead to the "load" wire on the same side. Turn the dial from high to low. If the thermostat is good, the tester remains lit in both positions. Repeat on the other set. If the light goes out, replace the thermostat.

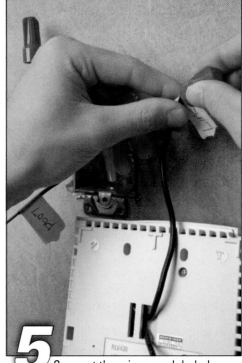

5 Connect the wires you labeled "line" to the line wires on the thermostat.

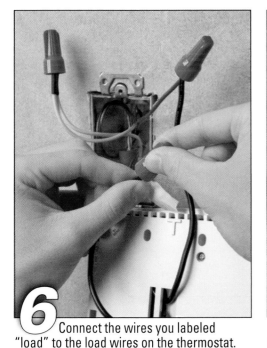

6 Connect the wires you labeled "load" to the load wires on the thermostat.

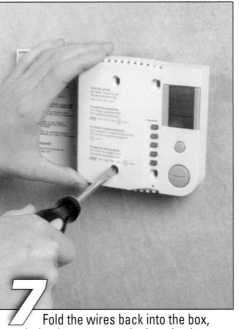

7 Fold the wires back into the box, attach the thermostat to the junction box, and reposition the cover.

Gable fan thermostats

Attic gable fans are controlled by a line-voltage thermostat, which can be replaced if it fails. **Turn off the power and check to make sure it's off.** Disconnect the wires, labeling them as you go. The white wire from the power supply connects with the white fan wire. One of the black thermostat wires connects to the black line from the power supply. The other black thermostat wire connects to the fan. Connect the ground wire to the ground screw in the thermostat, pigtailing it to the fan ground wire, if there is one.

SWITCHES & RECEPTACLES

It's not unusual for a switch to be flipped on and off tens of thousands of times before it malfunctions. When a switch does finally wear out, replacing it is a simple job. Or you may want to replace a simple toggle switch with a dimmer.

This chapter shows how to replace common residential switches and presents other switches that meet the needs of special situations. These handy devices, such as dimmers and motion-sensor switches, are just as easy to install as standard switches.

Receptacles have no moving parts and can last even longer than switches, provided they are not abused. Replacing one is just as easy as putting in a switch.

Always turn the power off and test a receptacle for power before you remove the cover plate. Once the box is open, test again for power (page 48). See pages 38–39 to learn how to safely open boxes to access a switch or receptacle.

Use the tools and skills shown in the previous chapters. To complete these projects you should be able to strip wire insulation, splice wires, and connect wire ends to terminals.

Working in a box
Wires inside a box may be short, and space may be tight. To make working in the box easier, pull out the device and straighten the wires. Take your time.

A mistake could force you to cut a wire for a second or third time, making it even shorter. If you do need to lengthen a wire, use a pigtail (page 93).

After you have pulled a device out of a box, examine the wiring before you loosen terminal screws. If you do not understand the wiring, you may find it explained on pages 26 or 45. If the wiring is complicated, tag each wire with a piece of tape as you unhook it that tells you where the wire should be reattached. Take digital photos of the wiring as you work for reference. Work methodically to ensure a safe and successful installation. Call in a professional if you are still confused.

Replacing and upgrading switches and receptacles call for just a few simple skills.

CHAPTER PREVIEW

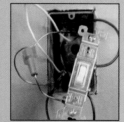
Switch wiring
page 90

Testing switches
page 91

Single-pole switches
page 92

Three-way switches
page 94

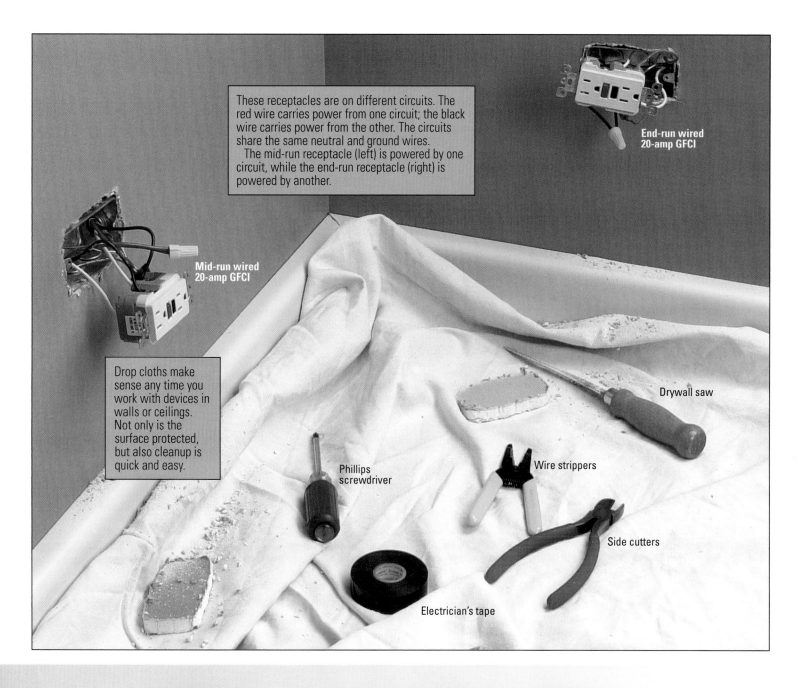

These receptacles are on different circuits. The red wire carries power from one circuit; the black wire carries power from the other. The circuits share the same neutral and ground wires.

The mid-run receptacle (left) is powered by one circuit, while the end-run receptacle (right) is powered by another.

End-run wired 20-amp GFCI

Mid-run wired 20-amp GFCI

Drop cloths make sense any time you work with devices in walls or ceilings. Not only is the surface protected, but also cleanup is quick and easy.

Phillips screwdriver

Wire strippers

Drywall saw

Side cutters

Electrician's tape

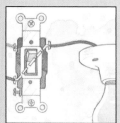

Four-way switches
page 96

Special-duty switches
page 100

Testing a receptacle
page 105

Replacing a receptacle
page 106

Install a GFCI
page 108

Raceway wiring
page 110

PROBLEMS WITH COVER PLATES

Cover plates are the last lines of defense between human hands and live wires. A cracked (or ugly) plate is easy to replace, and it only takes a few minutes to straighten a device that is out of plumb. (Use a torpedo level if you don't want to eyeball it.)

Cover plates are available in many styles and can be made of plastic, wood, metal, glass, or ceramic. Cost varies according to style and material, but even a plain, inexpensive plate can be easily dressed up.

One option is paint. With the cover plate installed, use a roller that is slightly damp with paint, so paint does not seep into the receptacle slots.

It is also possible to wrap a cover plate with wallpaper or a small art reproduction.

PRESTART CHECKLIST

☐ **TIME**
About 10 minutes to adjust or replace a cover plate

☐ **TOOLS**
Screwdriver with a small slot head, phillips screwdriver, drill, level

☐ **PREP**
Lay a towel or small drop cloth on the surface below the device.

☐ **MATERIALS**
Have on hand plenty of receptacle and switch cover plates—they're inexpensive.

1 If a cover plate is crooked or doesn't cover the wall completely, note in which direction it needs to move. **Shut off power to the circuit** and remove the plate. (A receptacle is shown here, but this will also work with switchplates.)

Phillips screwdriver

2 Loosen the screws that hold the device to the box. Slide the device until it is plumb, tighten the screws, and reposition the cover plate. (If you have a small level, hold it firmly against the side of the device to check its alignment.)

OVERSIZE PLATES

If a standard-size cover plate cannot cover damage to a wall, a slightly oversize plate may do the trick.

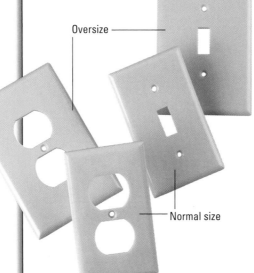

Oversize

Normal size

WHAT IF...
A box needs straightening?

Occasionally a box may be so out of plumb that you cannot straighten the device. To straighten it **shut off the power** and pull the device off to the side. Drill a hole into the side of the box and drive a drywall screw through the hole into a nearby stud. Be careful not to nick any wires.

SWITCHES

*T*urn a switch on and it completes the circuit, letting electricity flow through it. Turn it off and the circuit is broken; the switch creates a gap that stops the flow.

Essential switches
The most common household switch, a single-pole, has two terminals and simply turns power on or off.

A three-way switch has three terminals; a four-way has four. These control a light from two or three locations, such as in a stairwell, at either end of a hallway, or in a large room with more than one entrance.

A dimmer switch controls a light's intensity. Usually you can replace any single-pole switch with a dimmer. However for a fan or fluorescent light, buy a special switch rated to control those devices.

Special switches
In addition to the familiar toggle and rotary switches, specialty switches can do everything from turning on when you walk into a room to varying the speed of whole-house fans. Other special-duty switches can be time-programmed or let you know whether a remote light is on or off. Decorative switches include styles that rock, turn, or slide rather than toggle.

A **single-pole** switch has two terminals and a toggle labeled ON and OFF. Always connect two hot wires to it, not two neutrals.

A **three-way** switch has three terminals, and its toggle is not marked on or off. (See page 94 for wiring instructions.)

A **four-way** switch is similar to a three-way, except it has four terminals and controls three lights.

A **rotary dimmer** switch is the most common type. Some styles look like toggle switches. (See page 99 for instructions to install a dimmer switch.)

A **sliding dimmer** with an on/off toggle turns the light back on to the brightness you had set the last time it was on.

If you don't like the look of big knobs and sliders, a **dimmer switch** with a small slider next to the toggle is almost invisible.

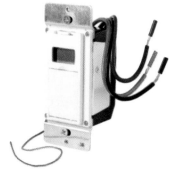

A **programmable timer and switch** can be preset to turn the lights on and off on an automatic schedule. If you need light immediately, just press the button, and the lights come on regardless of the program.

A **wall-control dimmer** not only controls and dims several lights, it also can be programmed to turn on a combination of lights at given brightness with the touch of a button.

An **occupancy switch** saves energy. Its built-in motion detector turns the light on when someone enters the room and leaves it on for a predetermined time.

SWITCH WIRING

The way a light switch is wired depends on whether the power comes into the light box or the switch box first. If power comes into the switch box first, the neutral white line from the service panel and the white line that leads to the light are spliced together. The hot black wire from the power source travels through the switch and from there to the light. Flipping the switch interrupts the flow of electricity to the light, turning it off and on.

If the line carrying power comes into the light box first, the circuit must still be wired so the switch interrupts the black line. The white wire from the service panel is wired to one side of the light. The black wire is spliced to a black wire in a cable that runs to the switch. That cable's white wire is also connected to the switch and runs back to and is connected to the light. Flipping the switch interrupts the flow of electricity, and the switch does its job.

Because the white wire from the switch to the light is now a hot wire, it must be marked to show it is hot. Wrap a piece of black electrician's tape around it at both ends or color the end black with a marker to show that it carries power.

Power through switch

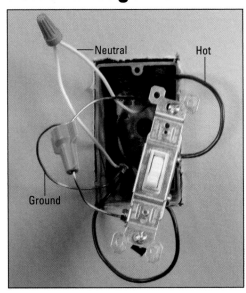

Neutral — — Hot

Ground

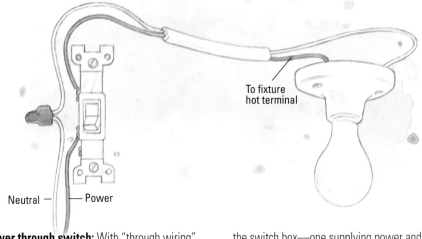

To fixture hot terminal

Neutral — — Power

Power through switch: With "through wiring" power enters the switch box. The feed wire (the hot wire coming from the service panel) runs to the switch before it goes to the fixture. Two cables enter the switch box—one supplying power and one going to the fixture. The neutral wires are spliced, and a black wire connects to each switch terminal. Ground wires are not shown.

End-line switch

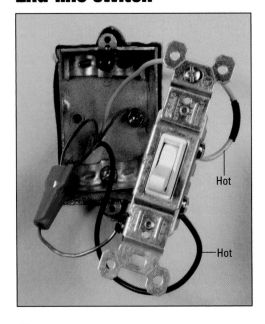

Hot

Hot

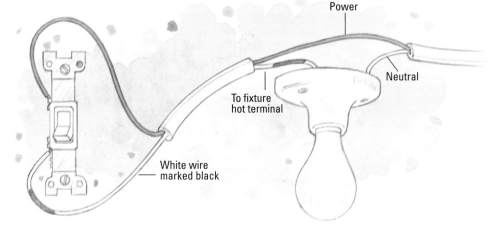

Power

Neutral

To fixture hot terminal

White wire marked black

End-line switch: If power goes to the fixture first and then to the switch, you have "end-line" wiring. Only one cable enters the switch box, coming from the fixture. Here the white wire to the switch is marked black to indicate that it is hot. Ground wires are not shown.

TESTING SWITCHES

If a circuit fails it's simple to test a single-pole switch and see whether the switch is at fault. Testing a circuit with a three- or four-way switch, however, is more complicated. You must determine which switch, if any, is bad. No matter what kind of switch you test, you use a continuity tester and a bit of logic. You have to remove the switches to test them, so make sure you **turn the power off first.** Mark the wires as you remove them so you know how to rewire the switch.

PRESTART CHECKLIST

☐ **TIME**
About 10 minutes for a single-pole switch; up to 1 hour to test three four-way switches

☐ **TOOLS**
Screwdriver, continuity tester

☐ **SKILLS**
Reading a continuity tester

☐ **PREP**
Turn off the power, take out the switches, and mark the wires so you know how to reconnect the switches.

☐ **MATERIALS**
Replacement switch if necessary

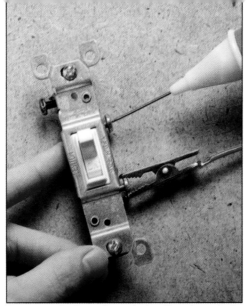

To test a **single-pole switch,** clip one end of a continuity tester to one of the terminals and touch the probe to the other. If the switch is good, the continuity detector should turn off and on as you flip the switch.

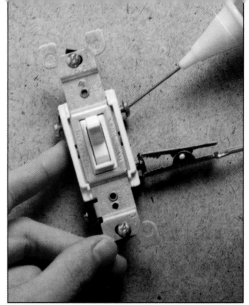

Test a **three-way switch** by clipping the tester to the common terminal, which is a different color from the two traveler terminals. Attach the probe to one of the travelers. If the switch is good, the light goes on and off when you flip the switch. Attach the probe to the other traveler—if the switch is good, the light turns on when the switch is in the position opposite the one that turned it on during the first test. It should go off and on as you flip the switch.

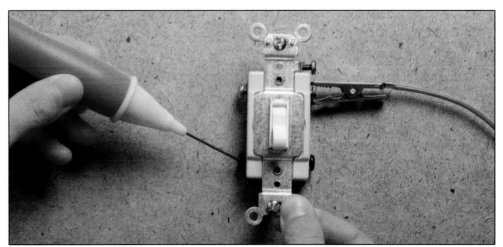

A **four-way switch** has four terminals and two toggle positions. One toggle position connects one pair of terminals; the other position connects the other pair. Usually the pairs of terminals are at the top and bottom of the switch housing rather than on the same side. You can find the pairs by trial and error for testing if the switch is not marked. Start by clipping the tester to one terminal and attaching the probe to any of the others.

If the tester fails to light, flip the switch. If it still doesn't light, move the probe to each of the remaining screws until you find a pair of screws that turn on the light.

Repeat on the other pair of terminals. If the switch is good, flipping the toggle turns on the test light when it is connected to these terminals. The continuity tester should light for only one pair of terminals at a time.

SINGLE-POLE SWITCHES

A single-pole switch is the most common switch for residential wiring. It turns one thing on or off, whether it's a light, an outlet, a fan, or some other device. A single-pole switch is easy to recognize—there are only two terminal screws. (New switches also have a green ground screw, required by code.) The switch is always wired so that it interrupts a hot wire rather than a neutral wire, ensuring that when the switch is in the off position, the power flow is stopped. A switch can be physically located either somewhere between the breaker box and device it controls or somewhere after the device it controls. You can tell by looking at the box where in the circuit the switch is located.

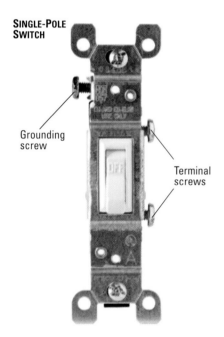

SINGLE-POLE SWITCH

Grounding screw

Terminal screws

A single-pole switch controls a single device and can function as anything from a light switch to a furnace cut-off switch. It has two terminals and a ground. The switch interrupts the hot black wire feeding the device. Power comes in on one side of the switch but won't go on to feed the device unless the switch is in the ON position.

Recognizing an end-of-run circuit

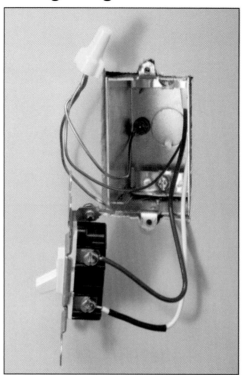

If a switch box has only one cable coming into it, it is at the end of the circuit—an "end-of-run switch. The cable supplying power from the breaker box runs directly to the box holding the device the switch controls—typically a light. Instead of going to the light, however, the power connects to a black wire in a second cable. The black wire carries the power to the switch, and the white wire in the cable carries the power back to one side of the light. The other side of the light connects to the white wire that travels back to the breaker box, completing the circuit. Because the white wire carries power whenever the switch is on, it's tagged with a piece of black tape in each box to show that it's potentially hot.

Recognizing a middle-of-run circuit

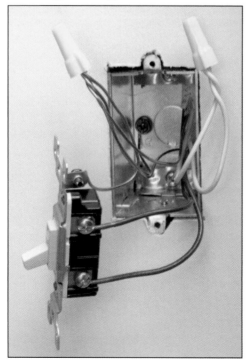

A "middle-of-run" switch is in a box with two cables. One of the cables comes in from the breaker box to supply power. The other cable travels to the device the switch controls. The hot black wire from the breaker box connects to one of the terminals on the switch—it doesn't matter which one.

The black wire in the cable leading to the controlled device connects to the other terminal. When the switch is on, power flows from the breaker box through the switch and to the load through the black wires. A white wire connected to the load carries the power back to the switch box, where it is spliced to the white that travels back to the breaker box.

REPLACING SINGLE-POLE SWITCHES

If a switch fails to turn on or if its toggle feels loose, replace it.

A single-pole switch is the most common type of switch. It has two terminals (not counting the ground), and its toggle is marked with ON and OFF. If three wires attach to a switch (not counting the ground), it's a three-way switch (page 94).

Replace a single-pole switch with an exact match or install a dimmer or special switch (pages 98–101).

PRESTART CHECKLIST

☐ **TIME**
About 20 minutes to replace a single-pole switch

☐ **TOOLS**
Screwdriver, strippers, side cutters, long-nose pliers, voltage tester

☐ **SKILLS**
Stripping wires and fastening them to a terminal

☐ **PREP**
Lay a towel or small drop cloth on the surface below the switch

Voltage tester

1 **Shut off power to the circuit** so that the switch cannot turn the light on. Remove the cover plate. Unscrew and pull out the switch gently. Test to make sure there is no power in the box.

2 Check the wires and terminals. If the wire ends are nicked, kinked, or deformed, cut and restrip. Otherwise loosen the terminal screws and disconnect the wires.

3 Form loops with wire ends, wrap clockwise around terminals, and tighten screws. Wrap the device with electrician's tape to cover terminal screws and any bare wire. Reinstall the switch and cover plate.

REFRESHER COURSE
Cut and restrip wire ends

1 To make sure a wire doesn't break after being bent several times, cut off the bare end using a stripper or side cutters.

2 Place the wire in the proper size hole on the strippers, give a slight twist, and slide the insulation off. Bend the wire into a loop.

Ensure grounding
If your system has metal boxes and no ground wire so that sheathing acts as the ground (page 43), remove the little cardboard or plastic washers from screws to make a firm contact between the device and the box.

Pigtail short wires

If the feed wires in the box aren't long enough to easily connect a device, don't try to pull more slack into the box— you might damage the wires. Instead make a pigtail— a 6-inch-long wire stripped at both ends (page 53). Splice one end to the wire and connect the other end to the terminal.

THREE-WAY SWITCHES

A three-way switch is recognizable by its three terminals plus ground screw. Three-ways are used in pairs to control a single device. Either switch can turn the device on and off, regardless of the position of the other switch. The most common application is a light in a stairway that's controlled by a three-way switch at the bottom of the stairs and a second three-way at the top.

Two of the terminals are called "traveler" terminals. A traveler wire runs between a traveler terminal on each switch. A second traveler wire runs between the other two traveler terminals. The remaining terminal on each switch is the common terminal. One common connects to the power source; the other connects to the hot lead on the light.

Flipping the switch back and forth determines which traveler wire carries the current. For a more complete explanation, see "How Three-Ways Work" on page 195.

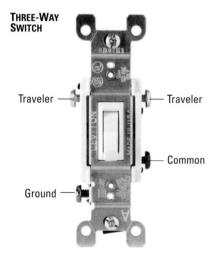

THREE-WAY SWITCH

Traveler — — Traveler

— Common

Ground —

A three-way switch has three terminals plus a ground. The two traveler terminals connect to wires that run back and forth between the switches. The common terminal on one switch connects to the device the switch controls. The common on the other switch connects to the power source. Flipping the switches determines whether a traveler delivers power from the common terminal of one switch to the other.

Three-way switch at the end of the run

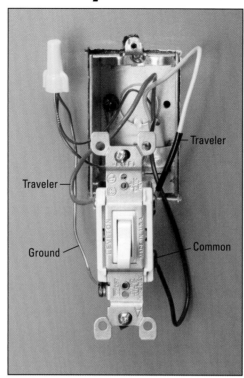

— Traveler

Traveler —

Ground — — Common

A three-way switch with a single three-wire cable coming into the box is at the last position in a circuit or at the "end of a run." The black leads back to the power source. It connects to the common terminal and provides power to the circuit. The red and white (marked with black) traveler wires connect to the traveler terminals on the other three-way switch. The black wire on that switch connects to the light or whatever device the switches control. The white wire is marked with a piece of black tape to indicate it can sometimes be hot.

Three-way switch in the middle of the run

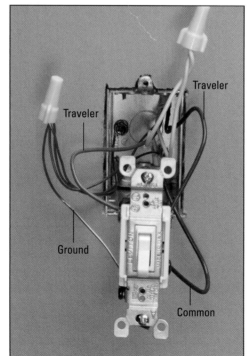

— Traveler

Traveler —

Ground —

Common —

A three-way switch in the middle of a run has two cables entering the box—one with two wires, the other with three. The black wire from the two-wire cable connects to the common terminal. It leads back to the power source from one switch and to the device the switches control from the other switch. The white wires are joined together. The remaining wires are the travelers, which run between the traveler terminals on the two switches.

REPLACING THREE-WAY SWITCHES

If a switch does not have "On" and "Off" marked on its toggle and has three terminals (not counting the ground), it is a three-way switch. A pair of three-way switches can control the same fixture by flipping the toggle on either switch.

If one or both of a pair of three-ways fails to control the light, replace the faulty switch or switches. If the toggle is wobbly, replace the switch.

If you keep track of which wire goes where, replacing a three-way is not much more difficult than replacing a single-pole switch (page 93). If you forget to tag the wires, however, the proper connections can be difficult to figure out.

PRESTART CHECKLIST

☐ **TIME**
About 25 minutes if you remember to tag the wires; possibly longer if you forget

☐ **TOOLS**
Screwdriver, side cutters, voltage tester, strippers, long-nose pliers

☐ **SKILLS**
Stripping wires and joining them to terminals

☐ **PREP**
Lay a towel or small drop cloth on the surface below the switch

☐ **MATERIALS**
One or two three-way switches, wire and wire nuts for pigtails, electrician's tape

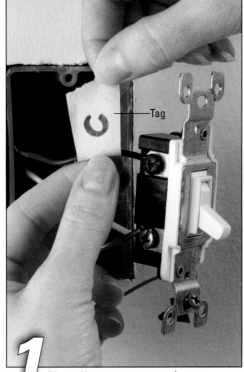

Tag

1 **Shut off power,** remove the cover plate, pull out the switch, and test for power (page 48). A three-way switch has a common terminal that's a different color than the two traveler terminals. Tag the wire that connects to the common terminal.

Ground wire

2 Cut and restrip wire ends (page 74) and form them into loops. Connect the ground wire. Connect the tagged wire to the common terminal and the other two wires to the traveler terminals. (It doesn't matter which wire goes to which traveler terminal.)

STANLEY PRO TIP

If you forget to tag wires

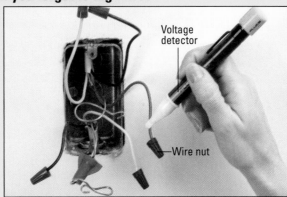

Voltage detector

Wire nut

Determine the switch's position in the circuit (opposite page). Inspect the other switch in the circuit to identify which wires are the travelers. **Shut off power,** place a wire nut on the end of each wire, and restore power. Check wires with a voltage detector; if flipping the other switch makes a wire hot or not, it is a traveler. A wire that is always hot or never hot goes to the switch common terminal.

WHAT IF...
It's a four-way switch?

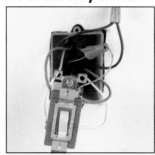

If three or more switches control the same fixture, two are three-ways and the others are four-way switches. A four-way has four terminals (plus a ground). Two wires connect to input terminals and two to output terminals. Before you remove the switch tag each wire. Without tags, it could take a pro to sort them out.

FOUR-WAY SWITCHES

To understand how a four-way switch works, you need to understand how a three-way switch works. In fact a four-way circuit is nothing more than two three-way switches with one or more four-way switches in between.

So a quick review of three-way switches is in order. The illustration "Three-way switches" shows how power, represented by a yellow line, travels through the circuit. When the toggle on the first switch is down, power travels through the switch, down to the black wire, and into the second switch. If the toggle on the second switch is up, the power is shunted to the light. If you flip the first switch, power is shunted into the second switch via the red wire, which for the time being at least, is a dead end. The light goes out and stays out until you flip the second switch down, connecting the red wire with the common terminal that leads to the light.

Identifying terminals on a four-way switch

When you remove a four-way switch, look at it carefully before you take off the wires. The pairs of terminals will be marked in one way or another. One pair may have copper-colored screws; the other pair may be silver-colored. One pair may be labeled "IN," and the other labeled "OUT" or not labeled at all. The important thing is that both terminals in a pair must connect to the same three-way switch. Find the pairs in the existing switch and label them with pieces of tape as "Pair 1" and "Pair 2." Look for the markings identifying pairs on the new switch and attach the wires accordingly.

Three-way switches

If you want to control the light with an additional switch, you'll put a four-way switch between the two three-ways. A four-way switch has four terminals, arranged as two pairs. The pairs can be connected to each other in one of two ways, as shown in the switch schematic, depending on the position of the toggle.

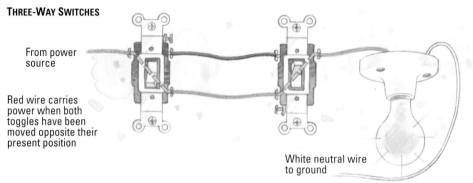

THREE-WAY SWITCHES

From power source

Red wire carries power when both toggles have been moved opposite their present position

White neutral wire to ground

Four-way switches

The four-way switch is wired as shown below. In the upper part of the diagram, power comes in through the common terminal and is routed down to the yellow path by the first switch. Power travels along the path to the four-way switch, which routes it to the other side of the switch and from there into the last switch and to the light.

Flipping the four-way switch, as shown in the lower part of the diagram, directs power to the path which is not connected to the light, turning it off. Flipping any switch can make or break a power path to the light.

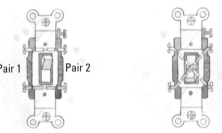

HOW A FOUR-WAY SWITCH WORKS

Pair 1   Pair 2

Power can travel directly from one pair of terminals to the other

Power can criss-cross from one pair of terminals to the other

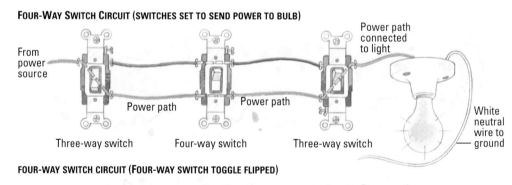

FOUR-WAY SWITCH CIRCUIT (SWITCHES SET TO SEND POWER TO BULB)

From power source

Power path connected to light

Power path

Power path

White neutral wire to ground

Three-way switch   Four-way switch   Three-way switch

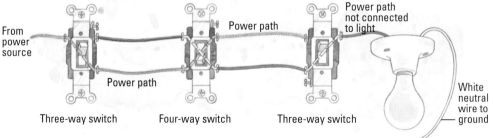

FOUR-WAY SWITCH CIRCUIT (FOUR-WAY SWITCH TOGGLE FLIPPED)

From power source

Power path not connected to light

Power path

Power path

White neutral wire to ground

Three-way switch   Four-way switch   Three-way switch

REPLACING FOUR-WAY SWITCHES

When a four-way circuit fails, the problem can be in any one of the three switches. Finding the culprit is a process of elimination. You'll turn off the power, remove the switchplates, and look to see which switches are three-way (they'll have three terminals in addition to the ground) and which is four way (four terminals in addition to the ground.) Once you know which is which, you test one three-way, then the other. If both of them are good, the problem is almost certainly in the four-way switch. You can test it, as described in "Testing Switches," page 91, to make sure the problem isn't in the wiring, or you can bet on the near certainty that the problem is the switch and simply replace it.

Always label the wires before you disconnect them, so you'll know which wire goes where when it's time to reassemble the circuit.

PRESTART CHECKLIST

☐ **TIME**
About 1 hour

☐ **TOOLS**
Continuity tester, phillips and slot screwdrivers; cutting pliers, long nose pliers, stripper

☐ **SKILLS**
Testing a switch

☐ **PREP**
Turn off the power

☐ **MATERIALS**
Replacement switch (type depends on results of testing)

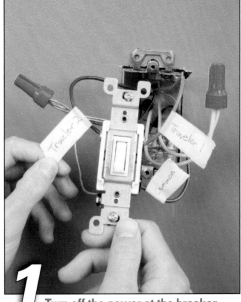

1 **Turn off the power at the breaker box**. Pull one of the three-way switches out of its switch box. Label the wires with pieces of tape so that you'll be able to reconnect them easily.

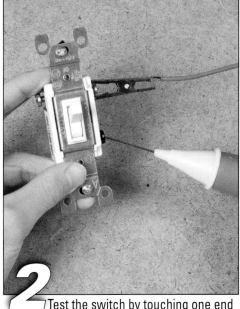

2 Test the switch by touching one end of a continuity tester to the common terminal, which will be a different color from the two traveler terminals. When the other end of the tester is on either one of the travelers, flipping the switch will turn the tester light on and off. The switch is good if the position that turns the light on when the probe is on one traveler turns the light off when the probe is on the other traveler.

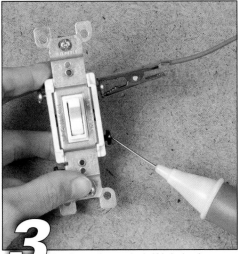

3 Replace the switch if it is bad, turn the power back on, and see if all the switches work properly. If not **turn the power back off** and test the second three-way switch, replacing it if needed. Restore the power and try all the switches again.

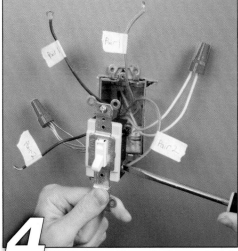

4 If both three-way switches are good and the circuit still doesn't work, the problem is most likely the four-way switch. Label the wires carefully before removing them—it is virtually impossible to get them on the right terminals if you don't. Test as described on page 91 and replace if necessary. If all three switches are good and the circuit still doesn't work right, the problem is in the wiring. Call an electrician.

REPLACING A DIMMER

Replacing a dimmer is much like replacing any other switch. If you keep track of the wires and label them as you take out the old dimmer, wiring the new dimmer is straightforward.

Dimmers controlling incandescent lights are like any other switch: They can either control the circuit singly or in combination with another switch. If a dimmer controls a light by itself, it's a single-pole dimmer. If it and another switch control the same fixture, the switch is a three-way switch and the dimmer is a three-way dimmer. Fluorescent light fixtures and fans require special dimmers.

When you're replacing a dimmer you should know exactly what it controls—incandescent bulbs totaling 300 watts for instance. If you are unsure take the old dimmer with you and ask a knowledgeable salesperson for help.

PRESTART CHECKLIST

☐ **TIME**
About 20 minutes to replace or install a new dimmer switch

☐ **TOOLS**
Screwdriver, side cutters, voltage tester, lineman's pliers, strippers

☐ **SKILLS**
Stripping and splicing wire

☐ **PREP**
Lay a towel or small drop cloth on the surface below the switch.

☐ **MATERIALS**
Dimmer switch, wire for pigtails, wire nuts (they may come with the switch), electrician's tape

1 **Turn off the power** at the fuse or breaker box. Unscrew the screws holding the faceplace to the wall. If the dimmer has a knob on it, pull the knob off first.

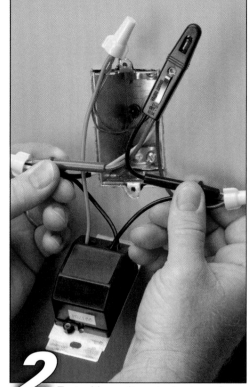

2 Test with a voltage tester to make sure there is no power in the circuit. If there is power remove fuses or flip breakers back at the box until the circuit is dead. Remove the old dimmer.

Dimmer in a one-switch circuit

On a one-switch circuit: If the dimmer is the only switch controlling the light, the dimmer has one green and two black wires or a green, a black, and a red. Connect the green wire to a pigtail that grounds the box and to the green or bare wire entering the box. If both wires are black, connect each to one of the remaining unconnected wires. If the wires are red and black, check the directions. One needs to connect to the hot wire, the other to the light.

Dimmer in a two-switch circuit

If the dimmer and a three-way switch control the circuit, the dimmer has a common wire that is most likely black. The two travelers are the same color as each other, usually red. If there's any confusion check the directions that come with the dimmer. Then check to see which wire in the switch box is hot, as described in "If you forget to tag wires," page 95. Connect the hot wire to the common wire. Connect the ground to ground and connect the remaining two dimmer wires to the remaining unconnected wires.

INSTALL A DIMMER SWITCH

You can replace a switch for any incandescent light with a dimmer.

■ Fans and fluorescent lights use special dimmers.

■ You can replace one of the three-way switches in a circuit with a three-way dimmer.

■ A dimmer can control line-voltage halogen lights. A dimmer won't work with low-voltage halogens.

■ A dimmer switch rated for 600 watts can handle most ceiling lights. For a chandelier, add up the wattage of all the bulbs; you may need a dimmer with a higher rating.

PRESTART CHECKLIST

☐ **TIME**
About 20 minutes to replace an on–off switch with a dimmer

☐ **TOOLS**
Screwdriver, side cutters, voltage tester, lineman's pliers, strippers

☐ **SKILLS**
Stripping and splicing wire

☐ **PREP**
Lay a towel or small drop cloth on the surface below the switch.

☐ **MATERIALS**
Dimmer switch, wire for pigtails, wire nuts (they may come with the switch), electrician's tape

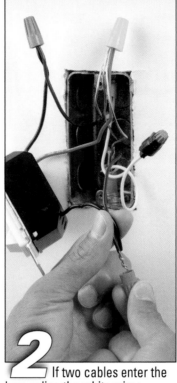

1 **Shut off power to the circuit.** Remove the cover plate, pull the switch out, and test to make sure there is no power (page 48). Loosen the terminal screws and remove the wires. Cut and restrip the wires.

2 If two cables enter the box, splice the white wires together. Splice each black lead to a black wire on the dimmer. Connect the grounds.

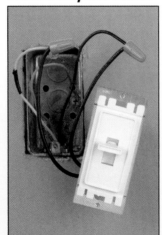

3 Fold the wires back as you push the dimmer into the box. The dimmer is bulkier than a regular switch, so the box may be crowded.

WHAT IF...
There's only one cable?

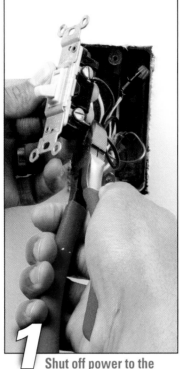

If only one cable enters the box, splice one lead to the black wire and one lead to the white wire (which should be marked with black).

How a dimmer works

Dimmers are often inaccurately called rheostats, the name for variable resistors sometimes used to dim theater lights. A rheostat has a movable contact that slides along an energized resistance coil to tap power for the light. As resistance increases, power to the light decreases, dimming it. High resistance generates heat and wastes energy.

Solid-state dimmers rely on electronic switching rather than resistance. AC current changes direction 60 times a second, and solid-state dimmers suppress the power for a fraction of each cycle to dim the light. The longer the shutdown, the dimmer the light. Even a long shutdown is so short, you can't detect any flicker. Only minimal power is consumed, generating much less heat. Solid-state dimmers are 99 percent efficient—they use about 1 watt to control a 100-watt bulb.

SPECIAL-DUTY SWITCHES

A switch that controls a device by some means other than flipping a toggle can be a useful improvement. Installing one usually is no more complicated than installing a standard switch.

Examine a switch carefully before buying it. Some special-duty switches are three-ways (page 94) and can be installed only if you have two cables entering the switch box. (See Pro Tip on opposite page.)

Installing a special switch is similar to installing a dimmer (page 99). **Shut off power to the circuit before removing the switch.** Connect the switch's ground wire to the house ground. To be sure that wires don't break after being rebent, cut and restrip all wire ends before you connect them to the new switch (page 74).

PRESTART CHECKLIST

☐ **TIME**
About 25 minutes to remove an existing switch and install a special switch

☐ **TOOLS**
Screwdriver, side cutters, strippers, lineman's pliers

☐ **SKILLS**
Stripping and splicing wire

☐ **PREP**
Lay a towel or small drop cloth on the surface below the switch.

☐ **MATERIALS**
Special-duty switch, wire nuts (they may come with the switch), electrician's tape

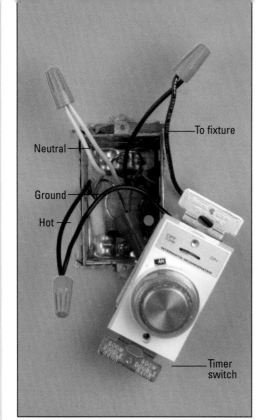

Neutral — Ground — Hot — To fixture — Timer switch

Timer switch: A timer switch turns lights on and off once a day. Most commonly it is used for outdoor lights. Connect the grounds and splice the neutral (white) wires to the white lead. Splice each black lead to a black wire.

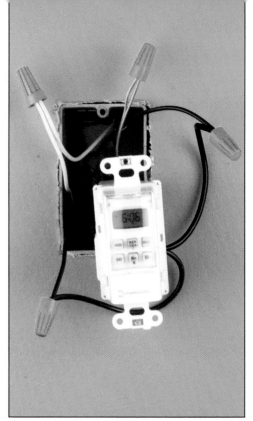

Programmable switch: Use a programmable switch to turn lights on and off more than once a day. It can fool a potential robber into thinking people are at home while they are away on vacation. Wire this switch just as you would a dimmer switch (page 98).

Remote-control switch

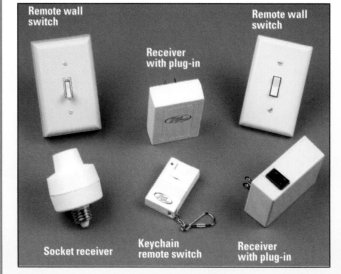

Remote wall switch — Receiver with plug-in — Remote wall switch — Socket receiver — Keychain remote switch — Receiver with plug-in

If you have a fixture controlled by a pull-chain switch and would rather have a wall switch, consider a remote-control device you can install without having to run cable through walls. To install one open the fixture and wire the receiving unit, following the manufacturer's instructions. Place a battery in the remote wall switch, which contains the transmitter. Mount it anywhere on the wall. You can also control the fixture with a keychain remote switch.

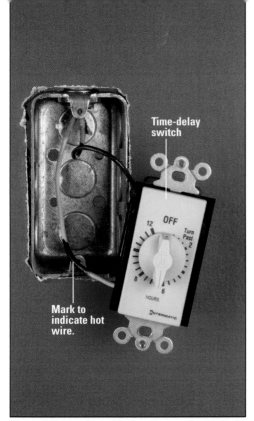

Time-delay switch

Mark to indicate hot wire.

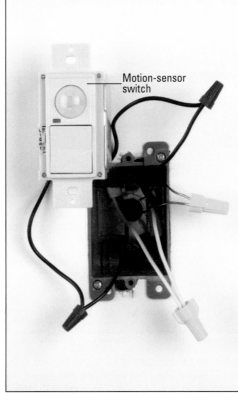

Motion-sensor switch

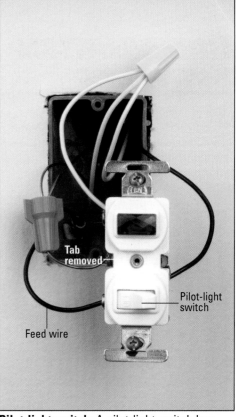

Tab removed

Pilot-light switch

Feed wire

Time-delay switch: With a time-delay switch, crank the dial to turn the fixture on and set it to turn off after a specified time. This is useful for fixtures that are risky or expensive to run—a bathroom vent fan or a space heater for instance. Wire it as you would a dimmer switch (page 98).

Motion-sensor switch: A motion-sensor switch turns a light on when it senses movement in the area, then turns the light off after a set time. (Some models allow you to determine how long the light stays on.) Wire it as you would a dimmer switch (page 98).

Pilot-light switch: A pilot-light switch has a small bulb that glows when the device, such as a fan, is turned on. Connect the white wires to the silver terminal (you may need a pigtail) and connect the grounds. Attach the feed wire to the brass terminal without a connecting tab and connect the other black wire to the other brass terminal.

STANLEY PRO TIP

Some switches need two cables in the box

There are two ways to wire a switch: Through-switch wiring brings power into the switch box, then out to the fixture. End-line wiring brings power to the fixture. In that circuit a single cable runs from the fixture to the switch box; the white wire should be marked black. If a switch has more than two terminals, it can be installed only if two cables enter the box.

OTHER SWITCHES

Plug-in timer

Hour electronic timer switch

Touch-control dimmer

Browse the electrical department of a home center to find even more special-duty switches. A plug-in timer (left) turns a floor or table lamp on and off at set times. A 20-amp hour timer switch (center) lets you run an attic fan or pool filter motor for 2, 4, 8, or 12 hours. A touch-control dimmer (right) turns the light up, down, on, or off with the tap of a finger.

COMBINATION SWITCHES

These devices combine two functions. Correctly installed they are just as safe as two individual switches.

Combination switches are always installed with through-switch wiring and never with end-line wiring. That means two or three cables entering the box (page 45).

Shut off power to the circuit before removing the old switch. To be sure that rebent wires do not break, cut and restrip the wire ends before you connect them.

Your choice in combination switches was once limited to a switch and a receptacle or switch and a switch. These days, the possibilities are endless: Remote controls, switch and dimmer, fan and light controls to name a few. The switches shown on page 103 are some of what you'll find. Any of these switches may be available in several styles.

PRESTART CHECKLIST

☐ **TIME**
About 30 minutes to remove an old combination switch and replace it

☐ **TOOLS**
Screwdriver, side cutters, strippers, long-nose pliers

☐ **SKILLS**
Stripping wire, connecting wire to terminals

☐ **PREP**
Lay a towel or small drop cloth on the surface below the switch.

☐ **MATERIALS**
Combination switch, electrician's tape, wire for pigtails

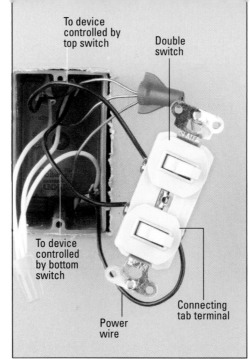

Double switch: Squeeze two switches into the space of one. Three cables enter the box: one brings power, the other two run to separate fixtures. Connect the grounds and splice all the neutral (white) wires together. Attach the feed wire to a terminal with the connecting tab. Connect the other two black wires to terminals on the side with no tab.

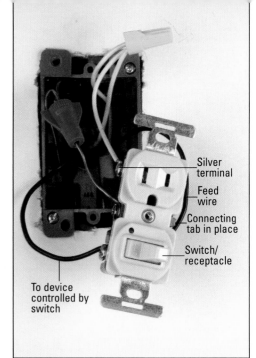

Unswitched plug: To make the plug always hot (not controlled by the switch) on a switch/receptacle, splice a pigtail to all the neutral (white) wires and connect the pigtail to the silver terminal. Connect the power wire to the brass terminal with the connecting tab. Splice the grounds. Attach the black wire from the switched fixture to the brass terminal with no connecting tab.

WHAT IF...
A switch controls a receptacle?

To have the switch control a middle-of-run receptacle, connect the grounds. Make a white pigtail and connect it to a chrome terminal on the side of the device that doesn't have a connecting tab. Splice all the white wires together. Attach the black feed wire to the brass terminal that is not attached to the connecting tab. Attach the outgoing black wire to one of the black terminal screws next to the connecting tab.

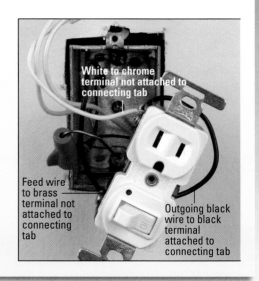

Feed wire
This is the wire (usually black or red) that brings power into the box.

Grounding
For information on connecting ground wires, see page 43.

Toggle switch with dimmer.
This switch lets you set the light level with a slider to one side of the on/off switch so that you can turn the light on to exactly the same level each time. You can also adjust the brightness at any time with the slider.

Remote fan control and light switch. When you replace a light with a ceiling fan, the old switch will still turn the fan off and on. To control speed and light levels without significant rewiring, however, you can use a remote switch. A wall-mounted remote looks like a normal switch but lets you adjust both fan speed and light level without rewiring.

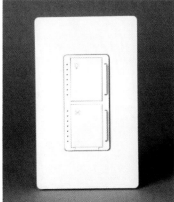

Fan control, dimmer, and module. This hardwired switch lets you adjust up to four fans and their lights from a single switch. Replace the existing switch and attach a module to each fan. The switch and module allow you to adjust fan speed and dim lights without having to run new wires from the fan to the switch.

Combination switch with GFCI.
This is a variation of the old switch/receptacle combination. Because GFCIs don't work if they're switched on and off, the switch on these units is meant to control other things, such as lights or exhaust fans in areas that require a GFCI. The switches are available in a wide variety of styles, including a device with two switches and a GFCI.

Motion detector with adjustable photocell and time delay.
Walk into a room and the light automatically turns on when this switch is installed. It remains on for a length of time you select. When the time is up, the lights go out—as long as no one is moving in the room. A manual override lets you turn the light on and leave it on for as long as you like.

Triple switch. Sophisticated lighting schemes call for more switches. It's not unusual for a room to have two or three sets of lights each controlled by its own switch. A line of switches on the wall can detract from the room's style. Traditional double switches cut the space consumed in half, but triple switches are even better.

Single-pole with three-way switch. A combination switch like this is handy at places like the top of the stairs, where the single-pole switch can control a hall light, and the three-way works in conjunction with a downstairs switch to control the light above the stairs.

Switch with pilot. There are times when it helps to know that you really did flip the switch. Did you remember to turn off the garage light? Is the on-at-dusk light going to come on at dusk or did you accidentally flip the cutoff switch? Check the pilot light. If it's on so is the power.

RECEPTACLES

*T*he 120-volt duplex receptacle (a receptacle with two outlets) is the workhorse of any residential electrical system. Because household wiring has remained standardized almost from the time it was first introduced, you can plug even the oldest tools and appliances into a modern duplex receptacle.

Receptacles are easy to replace, so install new ones if your old receptacles are damaged, paint-encrusted, or simply ugly. (See page 106 for more on how to install them.) However do not replace an older, ungrounded receptacle with a three-hole receptacle unless you can be sure it is grounded. (See page 32 to test grounding.)

If the wires connecting to a receptacle are 12-gauge or thicker and the circuit is protected by a 20-amp breaker or fuse, you can safely install a 20-amp receptacle. Otherwise install a standard 15-amp receptacle. Amp ratings are printed or stamped on the side of the receptacle.

Some people prefer to mount the receptacle in the box with the ground hole on top; others prefer it on the bottom. In terms of safety it does not matter. For appearance be consistent.

Standard receptacles are fine for most purposes. But if a receptacle is to receive a lot of use or is in a high-traffic area— a busy hallway for example—purchase a spec-rated or commercial receptacle, which is stronger and more resistant to damage.

The most common electrical device in your home is probably a **grounded 15-amp, 120-volt receptacle.** It supplies adequate power for all but the most power-hungry appliances and tools.

If a receptacle's neutral slot (the longer one) has a horizontal leg, it is rated at 20 amps. Codes often call for **20-amp receptacles** in kitchens or workshops, where power use is heavy.

A **GFCI** (ground fault circuit interrupter) receptacle provides extra protection against shocks and is required by code in damp areas. (See page 108 for more about GFCIs.)

An **ungrounded receptacle** has two slots and no grounding hole. If one slot is longer than the other, the outlet is polarized.

240-volt receptacles

Appliances that use 240 volts are all rated for certain levels of amperage and have plugs configured to fit only one type of receptacle. Here are the common types:

A **dryer receptacle** supplies the heating element with 240 volts and the timer and buzzer with 120 volts. The receptacle shown requires four wires; older models use only three wires. (See page 76 for how to replace a dryer cord.)

An **electric range receptacle** provides 240 volts for the heating elements and 120 volts for the clock, timer, and light.

This single-outlet **air-conditioner receptacle** provides 240 volts only. Check your air-conditioner to make sure its amperage and plug configuration match the receptacle.

TESTING A RECEPTACLE

he voltage reading on a multitester or multimeter tells you if power is reaching an outlet. But properly used your multimeter also tells you whether the white and black wires are reversed, whether the receptacle is properly grounded, and which cable entering the box feeds power to the outlet. (If you don't have a multimeter, you can use a voltage detector in place of the voltmeter and a continuity tester in place of ohmmeter.)

If a problem arises usually you can diagnose it by running only one or two of these tests. There's no way of knowing which two you need, however, so it doesn't hurt to be familiar with all of them. Note that you conduct most of these tests with the power on, so work carefully. To be safe hold both meter probes in the same hand so that a shock doesn't pass through your body.

Set a multimeter to **measure voltage**. Insert a probe into each slot to measure the line voltage. A properly working outlet gives a reading of 110 to 120 volts. If there is no reading, check the wiring and the outlet.

A **properly grounded outlet** registers voltage when one probe of a voltage detector is inserted into the small outlet slot and the other probe is placed on the receptacle's center screw. If the light fails to light, the outlet is not properly grounded. Conduct a <u>polarity test.</u>

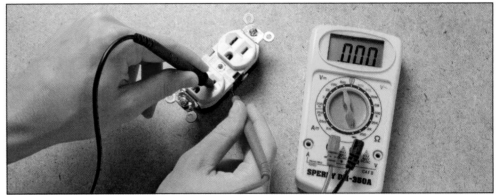

Test the outlet by **turning off the power** and removing the outlet entirely from the wiring. Set your multimeter to ohms and put a probe into one of the outlet slots and the other probe on the nearest terminal screw. The meter should indicate continuity. Test the remaining slot and terminal. Test the ground slot to the grounding terminal.

Testing to determine the hot cable

When two cables enter a box, one leads to the breaker or fuse box; the other carries power to other devices on the circuit. To determine which is the hot cable, **turn off the power,** disconnect the outlet, and place caps on all the wires except one black one. Turn the power back on, and touch a probe to the ground wire or the box and the other probe to the black wire. If you get a reading, it is the hot wire. If not it is the wire leading to the other devices. To double-check, turn off the power, move the cap from one black wire to the other, turn the power back on, and test the uncapped wire.

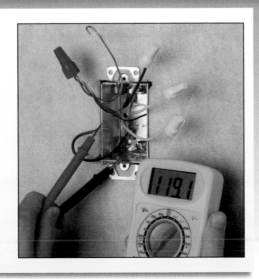

POLARITY TEST

Insert one probe into the large slot and the other against the screw (scrape off any paint to insure a good contact).

If the voltage detector lights, the hot and neutral wires are reversed. If the light doesn't light with the probe placed in either slot the wiring should be checked further.

REPLACING A RECEPTACLE

A new receptacle is inexpensive and easy to install, so don't hesitate to replace one that is cracked or caked with paint. If a receptacle fails to deliver power, **shut off power to the circuit,** pull the receptacle out, and make sure all the wires firmly connect to its terminals.

If you have to replace an outlet, it's a simple matter to replace a three-hole outlet with another three-hole outlet. Replacing a two-hole outlet may be another story, as two-hole outlets are no longer available. If there's a ground wire in the box, you can install a three-hole outlet. If there's no ground, however, it's against code to put in a three-hole outlet. Install a GFCI instead. Although it doesn't protect against a ground fault, its monitoring circuit gives you the same protection you get from a ground wire.

PRESTART CHECKLIST

☐ **TIME**
About 30 minutes to remove a receptacle and install a new one

☐ **TOOLS**
Screwdriver, side cutters, strippers, long-nose pliers

☐ **SKILLS**
Stripping wire, connecting wire to terminals

☐ **PREP**
Lay a towel or small drop cloth on the surface below the receptacle.

☐ **MATERIALS**
Receptacle, wire for pigtails, electrician's tape

Three-hole outlets

1 Replacing a three-hole outlet is simple. **Shut off power.** Remove the cover plate and the mounting screws and gently pull out the old receptacle (pages 38–39). Test for power. Loosen the terminal screws and remove the wires or use side cutters to cut the wires.

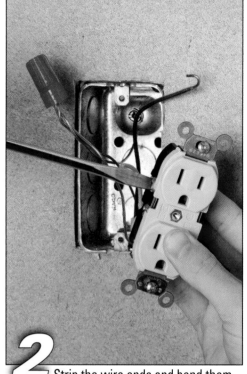

2 Strip the wire ends and bend them into loops. Connect the black or colored (hot) wire to the brass terminals and the neutral (white) wire to the silver terminals. Connect the ground wire, pigtailing it to any other ground wires in the box and to the box, if it is metal.

WHAT IF...
A receptacle is on two circuits?

Connecting tab

If a receptacle has more than two wires connected to it, look at the tab that connects the two hot (brass) terminals. If it is broken off, the receptacle is split, meaning either that it is on two circuits or that one half is switched. Break off the tab on the new receptacle and wire it like the old one.

Spec-rated receptacles

Most homeowners turn to the bargain bin for their receptacles. Those work just fine. But if a receptacle often gets bumped or if people yank on cords when pulling plugs out, consider upgrading to a spec-rated (commercial) receptacle.

Making connections
For tips on connecting wires to terminals see pages 52–53.

Two-hole outlets

1 If the outlet that needs to be replaced is a two-hole outlet, test for power and remove it from the box. If there is a ground wire—which is either green or bare—you can replace the outlet with a modern three-hole outlet.

2 Attach the ground wire to the green screw on the receptacle, pigtailing the wire to any other ground wires in the box and to the box, if it is metal. You may have to buy a green ground screw to attach the wire in the box.

3 Attach the white wire to the silver-colored screws and the black wire to the copper-colored screws.

WHAT IF...
There's no ground wire in the box?

If there's no ground wire in the box, replace a two-hole outlet with a GFCI. Attach the black and white wires as you would in a normal GFCI installation. There is no ground wire, so simply tighten the ground screw as far as it goes. The GFCI gives you the protection a ground wire does, but not full GFCI protection. Code requires you to place a sticker on the outlet indicating that the outlet is not GFCI protected. For more on installing GFCIs, see page 108.

Take a picture

When you open a box to remove a device and replace it, take a few digital photos from several angles. Get closeup pictures of the wires in the box, the terminals on the device, and the wire connections to the terminals. You can refer to the photos when you install the replacement device to make sure the connections don't get switched. And you can take a photo of the device to the store when you shop for a replacement if you don't want to remove the device first.

INSTALL A GFCI

Wiring for a GFCI depends on where it falls in the circuit and whether you want it to protect the other outlets.

Turn off the power and look into the box to see whether the receptacle is at the start, end, or in the middle of a run. If it is in the middle or at the start, it can protect other outlets. Consider any drawbacks to protecting outlets in the circuit after the GFCI. Do you risk cutting off power to a freezer if the GFCI trips, for instance?

This page shows wiring for protecting a single outlet. The following page shows wiring to protect a GFCI and all the outlets downstream.

PRESTART CHECKLIST

☐ **TIME**
About 25 minutes to remove a receptacle and install a GFCI

☐ **TOOLS**
Screwdriver, side cutters, strippers, lineman's pliers, voltage detector

☐ **SKILLS**
Stripping and splicing wire

☐ **PREP**
Lay a towel or small drop cloth on the surface below the receptacle.

☐ **MATERIALS**
GFCI receptacle, wire nuts, electrician's tape

1 **Turn off the power.** Test to make sure the power is off. Look inside the box to see where in the circuit the outlet falls. This box has two cables coming into it, making it a middle-of-run outlet. Disconnect the wires.

2 If you want GFCI protection only for the outlet you're installing and not the ones down the line, pigtail all the white wires together and connect the pigtail to the terminal labeled WHITE LINE.

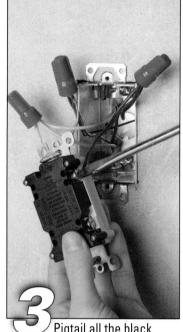

3 Pigtail all the black wires together and connect the pigtail to the terminal marked HOT LINE.

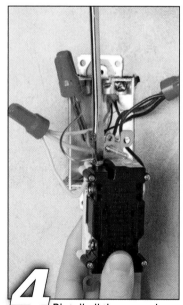

4 Pigtail all the ground wires together and connect the pigtail to the green ground screw. Wrap tape around the GFCI to cover the terminals. Attach it to the box and cover with a cover plate.

WHAT IF...
There is only one cable in the box?

If only one cable enters the box, the receptacle is at the end of the line. Connect the black wire to the BLACK LINE terminal and the white wire to the WHITE LINE terminal. Connect the ground wire to the ground screw, pigtailing it to the box if the box is metal.

STANLEY PRO TIP

Finding LINE and LOAD wires

To protect all the receptacles on a circuit, install a GFCI at the beginning of the circuit run. If you don't know which wires bring power into the box and which lead to other receptacles, remove the wires, spread them out so they do not touch each other, and cap with wire nuts. Restore power and use a voltage tester to find out which is the hot wire (page 105). Connect it and its neutral wire to the LINE terminals. Connect the other wires to the LOAD terminals.

GFCI protection for downstream outlets

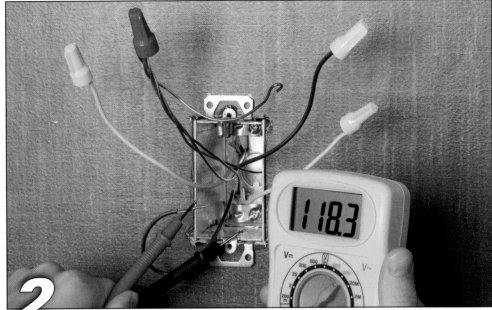

1 **Turn off the power.** Test to make sure the power is off. Look inside the box to see where in the circuit the outlet falls. This box has two cables coming into it, making it a middle-of-run outlet. Disconnect the wires.

2 If you want the GFCI to protect itself and the outlets downstream, find out which wires supply power (the line wires). Cap all the wires with wire nuts except one black one and turn the power back on. Place a meter across the black wire and the ground wire or metal box. If there's no reading it's a wire in the load cable; if it reads approximately 120 volts, it's a wire in the line cable. Double-check by repeating the test with the other black wire, turning the power off to move the wire nut and on to test the wire.

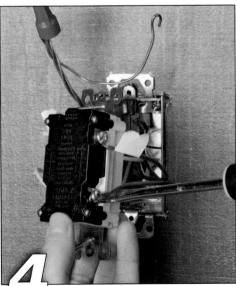

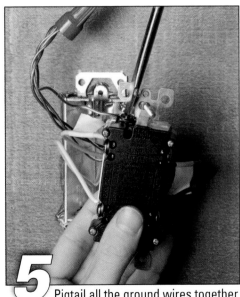

3 Connect the white line wire to the WHITE LINE terminal. Connect the other white wire to the WHITE LOAD terminal.

4 Connect the black line wire to the BLACK LINE terminal. Connect the other black wire to the BLACK LOAD terminal.

5 Pigtail all the ground wires together and connect the pigtail to the green ground screw on the GFCI. Wrap tape around the GFCI to cover the terminals. Attach it to the box and cover with a cover plate.

RACEWAY WIRING

If you need a new receptacle or a new light and switch, the usual procedure is to run cable inside walls. That is a complicated, messy job. In fact cutting and patching walls takes much more time than the wiring. Wall-mounted raceway wiring eliminates that trouble.

The drawback to raceway wiring is the unsightly channel mounted on the wall. In a living area, however, furnishings can hide raceway.

Planning the job
Choose plastic raceway (as shown here) or metal raceway, which can be painted. Have a salesperson help you assemble all the raceway parts you need: a starter box, channel, clips, cover plates, and elbows if you need to turn a corner. You need black, white, and green wire for the length of your run. Use 14-gauge wire for a 15-amp circuit and 12-gauge for a 20-amp circuit.

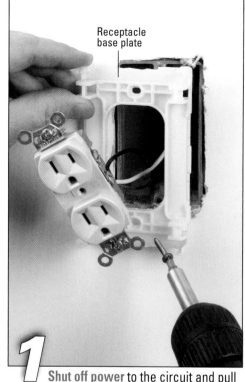

1 **Shut off power** to the circuit and pull out the existing receptacle (pages 38–39). Test for power. Screw the base plate to the electrical box.

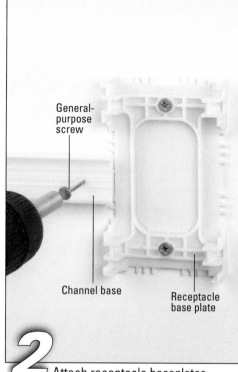

Receptacle base plate

General-purpose screw

Channel base

Receptacle base plate

2 Attach receptacle baseplates wherever you want a new receptacle. With a hacksaw cut pieces of channel to fit between the plates. Screw them to the wall. Where possible drive screws into studs for solid mounting; otherwise use plastic anchors to attach screws to wallboard.

PRESTART CHECKLIST

☐ **TIME**
About 3 hours to install two new receptacles

☐ **TOOLS**
Drill, screwdriver, level, rubber mallet, strippers, side cutters, hacksaw, lineman's pliers

☐ **SKILLS**
Stripping, splicing, and connecting wires to a terminal; cutting metal or plastic channel; driving screws into a wall

☐ **PREP**
Spread drop cloths on the floor

☐ **MATERIALS**
Raceway components, plastic anchors, wire nuts, electrician's tape, screws

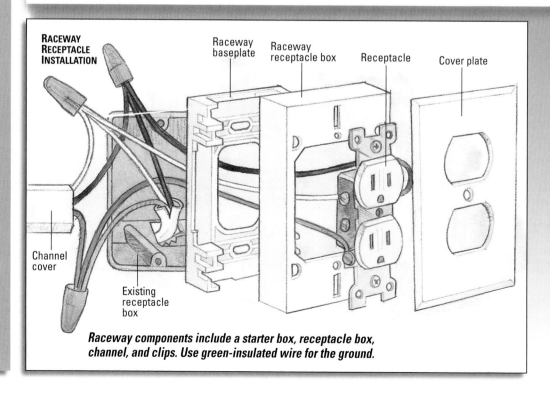

RACEWAY RECEPTACLE INSTALLATION

Raceway baseplate

Raceway receptacle box

Receptacle

Cover plate

Channel cover

Existing receptacle box

Raceway components include a starter box, receptacle box, channel, and clips. Use green-insulated wire for the ground.

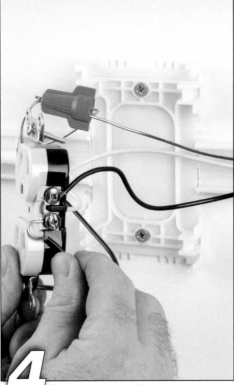

Channel clip

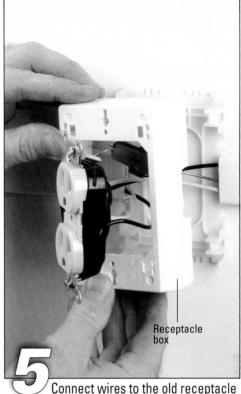

Receptacle box

3 Insert black, white, and green wires into the channels and secure them with the clips provided. Leave about 8 inches of wire at each receptacle box or starter box.

4 Connect wires to the new receptacles—black wires to brass terminals, white wires to silver terminals, and green wires to ground.

5 Connect wires to the old receptacle to supply power. Snap on the covers for the channel. Attach the covers for the new receptacle boxes and install cover plates.

Metal raceway

Metal components cost a bit more, but they withstand more abuse than plastic and they can be painted. Install the parts on the wall, then push wires through the channels.

Stripping and joining

For tips on stripping and joining wires, see pages 50–53.

SUPPLY POWER
Options for connecting to existing wires

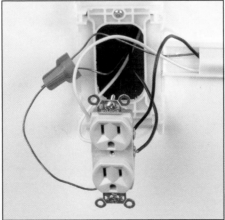

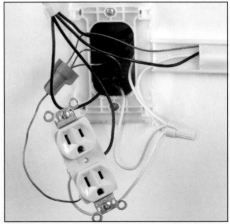

End-of-run: If the existing receptacle is at the end of a run (page 92), connect the raceway wiring to the two open terminals—black to the brass terminal, white to the silver terminal. Pigtail the ground (page 43).

Middle-of-run: If the existing receptacle is in the middle of a run (page 92), remove wires from two of the terminals and reconnect to terminals with pigtails, as shown.

Wiring metal raceways

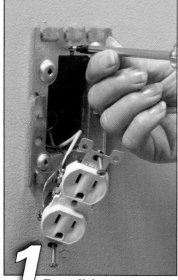

1 **Turn off the power** and test to make sure it is off. Take the cover off an outlet and pull out the receptacle. Screw a raceway starter box, which has a large opening in the back, over the box in the wall. Pull the receptacle out through the opening.

2 Position a flat elbow onto the end of the raceway channel and hold it over a stud. Have someone help you hold the channel in place, and level it. Mark where to cut the channel—when installed the channel extends into the box by about ⅜ inch. Cut the channel with a hacksaw.

3 Position the channel temporarily into place. Level it and trace along it. Find the studs with a stud finder and drill pilot holes into them for screws that hold the channel clips in place. Attach the clips.

4 Reposition the flat elbow back on. Tap the channel gently with a rubber mallet to snap it into place. Screw the elbow to the wall.

5 Cut a second length of channel, attach it with clips, and tap it into place with a rubber mallet.

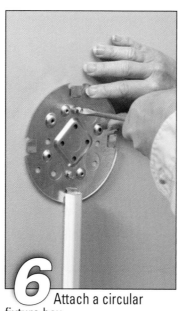

6 Attach a circular fixture box.

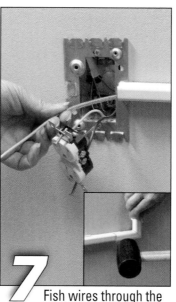

7 Fish wires through the channel and attach the covers over the elbow.

8 Hang the fixture and connect it into an outlet the same way you would when wiring a plastic raceway.

SURGE PROTECTION

Generally power is steady and constant. Your lights may flicker occasionally due to a drop in power that lasts less than a second. This is normal and does no damage. Less commonly the power coming into your house may suddenly increase or surge for an extremely short time. This can damage most electrical components and may harm a computer, modem, or other electronic equipment.

Telephone lines also may carry unwanted current surges. In fact surges damage modems more often than other items plugged into household receptacles.

A surge arrester senses any increase in voltage and directs it to the ground wire so it can flow harmlessly into the earth. Surge protection works only if your household electrical system is grounded (page 29).

For most homes all that's needed is a good-quality plug-in surge protector (also called an arrester or suppressor) or two. For your office choose a protector that includes a phone connection to safeguard the modem. If you have state-of-the-art audio/visual equipment, plug those components into a surge protector as well.

Lightning protection

In rural areas lightning sometimes can damage houses. The devices shown here do not protect your electrical system against a lightning strike. A local electrical contractor can help you determine whether you should install lightning protection.

A lightning strike on your house can cause a fire. For protection install a lightning rod mounted on the roof, fastened to a wire that runs into the ground. When lightning strikes the house, the rod directs much of the power into the earth.

If lightning strikes overhead power lines near your house, the burst of power could damage your service panel or house wires and fixtures. Surge arresters mounted in the service panel are designed to direct excess voltage to the house ground. Consult with contractors and your local building department to determine whether such a device could make your home safer.

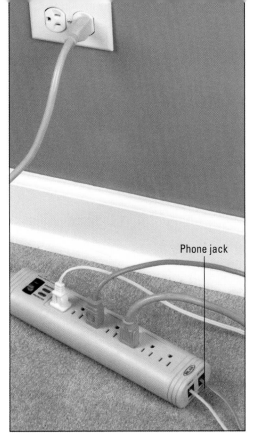

Phone jack

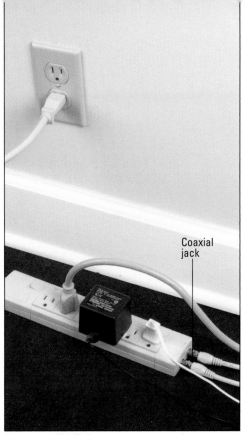

Coaxial jack

Simple protection: A simple power strip like this not only protects against surges but also makes it easy to organize your cords.

Protect a TV: This surge protector has a coaxial jack to protect a TV from a surge through the cable.

Whole-house surge protector

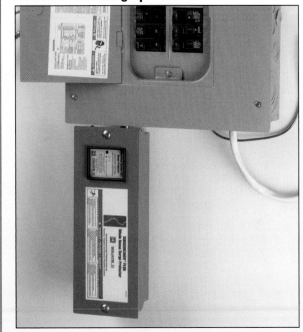

To protect all receptacles and lights from surges, have a whole-house surge protector installed. It is wired directly into the service panel. Fully protecting an electrical system from a direct lightning strike is not possible. However this device may keep your wires from harm since direct strikes usually do not cause lightning damage. A whole-house surge protector helps protect sensitive electronic equipment from damage due to a power surge traveling through local service lines.

LIGHTS & FANS

No matter how old your electrical system, it is always possible—and usually easy—to remove an old wall or ceiling fixture and install a new one. A new fixture can dramatically change the appearance of a room. You can replace a ceiling light with a plain light, a chandelier, track lighting, or even a ceiling fan. See pages 116–117 for more lighting options.

Mounting hardware
If your home was built after World War II, attaching a new fixture should be easy. Mounting hardware has changed little, and the new fixture should come with all the parts you need. Simply attach a strap to the ceiling box, and perhaps a center stud as well. Splice the wires, screw the fixture to the strap or the stud, and you are done.

If you have an older home, the old fastening hardware may not line up with the new fixture. Home centers carry adapters to solve this problem.

If the new fixture's canopy (the part that snugs up to the ceiling) is smaller than the old one, you may have to paint or patch the ceiling. A medallion (page 119) can hide the problem and save work.

Installing a ceiling fan or a heavy chandelier calls for removing the electrical box and installing a heavy-duty fan-rated box (pages 128–129).

Wiring a light or fan
Shut off power before removing an existing fixture. Test the box for power after removing the fixture (pages 9, 48). To ensure a conductive and long-lasting splice, cut and restrip old wire ends (page 74) before joining them to the stranded leads (pages 50–51) of new fixtures.

Wiring a light or fan is straightforward: Splice white lead to white wire, black to black, and connect the grounds. Installing a new fixture where there was none before is more involved and best left to a professional electrician or someone with experience running new cable. Running cable through walls is a time-consuming and complicated task.

Installing a new light fixture is an easy way to make a dramatic change in any room.

CHAPTER PREVIEW

Choosing lights
page 116

Installing flush-mounted lights
page 118

Installing fluorescents
page 120

Installing shop lights
page 122

Installing pendent lights
page 124

Wall lights are wired just like ceiling lights but the mounting hardware differs. A center stud or a swivel strap allows the light to be adjusted so it is plumb. Outdoor fixtures have foam or rubber gaskets to seal out moisture.

To avoid straining the wires, cut and bend a coat hanger to support the fixture while you attach the wires.

Replacing a light fixture is an easy upgrade that usually takes no more than 1 or 2 hours. A porch light is no exception. Shut off power. Work on a stable ladder if the fixture is out of reach.

Installing track lights
page 125

Installing a ceiling fan box
page 128

Attaching a ceiling fan
page 130

Adding under-cabinet lights
page 133

Installing undercabinet Xenon lights
page 135

Installing low-voltage track lights
page 137

Adding a porch light
page 139

Choosing Lights

A light fixture's packaging tells how high in wattage the bulb or bulbs can be. Installing bulbs of higher wattage damages the fixture, and the bulbs burn out quickly.

An existing light may seem adequate, but often a room benefits from a brighter light. Buy a new fixture that provides more light than the old one. Install bulbs of lower wattage if it turns out to be too bright.

In living and dining rooms, you may want bright light at some times and a mellow effect at other times. If so install a dimmer switch (page 99).

Canopies to cover

After removing an old fixture, measure its canopy—the part that attaches to the ceiling. If the new fixture has a smaller canopy, you have to paint and maybe patch the ceiling. Or you may purchase a medallion, a round decorative piece that covers up ceiling imperfections (page 119).

Pendent lights

The lower a light hangs the more attention it commands and the more focused its light becomes. Most pendent lights hang by chains; the lamp cord runs through the links to the fixture. Some modern versions have a decorative cable, and some run cord through a pipe. A pendent light may be a chandelier with many arms and bulbs, or it may have a single bulb surrounded by a shade or a globe.

Chandeliers have numerous bulbs, often encased in decorative glass. A chandelier that hangs over a dining room table should be a foot or so narrower than the table and hang about 3 feet above the table. Control a chandelier with a dimmer switch to achieve both brilliant and subdued effects.

If you don't like the look of newer-style chandeliers, seek out a dealer who specializes in refurbishing old fixtures. An older chandelier that is completely rewired is as reliable as a new unit.

A one-piece pendent light often is used in an entryway. Hang it in the center of the room at least 6½ feet from the floor, so people don't bump their heads.

A pendent light with a shade directs most of its light at a table or counter directly below, although it also can provide general

Lantern-shape pendent

Globe pendent

Chandelier

illumination if the shade is translucent. A small fixture can hang as low as 24 inches above a tabletop. Just make sure the bulb does not shine directly into people's eyes when they are seated at the table.

Flush-mounted lights

A flush-mounted light fastens against a ceiling or wall. A ceiling-hugging fixture in the middle of a room may be all that is needed to light a bedroom or small dining room. Wallmounted fixtures are ideal for lighting bathrooms, especially near a vanity mirror. Sconces are good in hallways.

Most flush-mounted fixtures use standard incandescent bulbs, but energy-saving fluorescents and halogens are available. A semiflush fixture hangs down a few inches and casts light upward at the ceiling for a more even distribution of light.

If you cannot find a light fixture that is pleasing and affordable, you can buy an inexpensive flush-mounted fixture and paint its canopy to match your ceiling color.

Over-mirror fixture

Swivel halogen lamp

Flush-mounted fixture

Semiflush-mounted fixture

Wall sconce

Decorative wall sconce

Two-light wall sconce

Sconces and other wallmounted fixtures install much like ceiling lights, except they mount on a wall. Such fixtures typically attach to a box using a strap and nipple (page 119) so they can be leveled easily.

If a sconce is to be mounted lower than 7 feet above the floor, purchase one that doesn't stick out too far from the wall. Some sconces shine upward and provide ambient lighting; others point out or down to illuminate stairs or subtly light a hallway.

Other types
Sleek fixtures that hang from wires or twist in whimsical shapes add a contemporary look. They use low-voltage halogen bulbs, which save energy but get very hot.

In addition to the lights shown here, consider fluorescent (pages 120–121) and track lighting (pages 125–127). To light inside or under a cabinet, see pages 133–134.

Recessed canisters need new cable
In some cases a recessed canister light can replace a single fixture. Typically, though, canisters are installed in a series. That means running new cable through walls and ceilings—an advanced procedure best left to the pros or experienced do-it-yourselfers.

Installing Flush-Mounted Lights

Replacing a ceiling fixture is simple. The old fixture's hardware often can be reused, and the new fixture usually comes with necessary hardware too.

Compare the wattage of the new fixture with the old one to be sure it provides the amount of light you want. Choose a fixture with a canopy large enough to cover any imperfections in the ceiling or use a medallion (page 119).

Wires in a ceiling box may contain cracked or brittle insulation due to overheating. See page 73 for repair advice. Ground the new fixture if possible. If it is being installed in a metal box, connect the fixture ground lead to the box and to the house ground wire. Check local building codes.

Prestart Checklist

□ **Time**
About 30 minutes to remove a fixture and install a replacement, as long as there are no problems with the hardware

□ **Tools**
Screwdriver, strippers, side cutters, voltage tester, ladder

□ **Skills**
Stripping wire, splicing stranded wire to solid wire

□ **Prep**
Spread a drop cloth on the floor below; set up a stable, nonconductive ladder

□ **Materials**
Replacement fixture, wire nuts (the ones that come with the fixture may be too small), electrician's tape

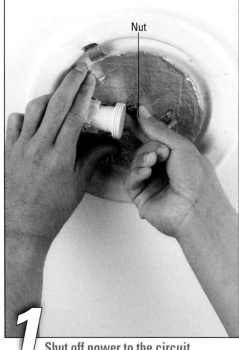

1 **Shut off power to the circuit.** Open the fixture (page 39). Remove the nut or screws holding the fixture to the box and pull the fixture down. Remove the wire nuts and **check for power in the box** (page 48). Pull the leads off the house wires and remove the fixture.

2 If the existing mounting hardware does not fit the new fixture or if it doesn't have a grounding screw, remove it and attach a new strap to the box.

STANLEY PRO TIP: **Attaching to older boxes**

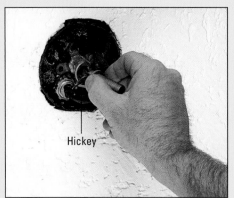

An older "pancake" box like this may have a ⅜-inch pipe running through the middle. To install a center-mount or pendant fixture, use a hickey, which has two sets of threads, one for the pipe attached to the pancake box and the other for a center stud. A hickey is helpful for wiring chandeliers because it has an opening through which a cord can run.

If the pipe protrudes too far, purchase a mounting strap with a hole large enough to accommodate the pipe. Or attach the strap off center by drilling pilot holes in the box and driving sheet metal screws through the slots in the strap and into the box. However make sure the fixture's canopy is large enough to cover the box.

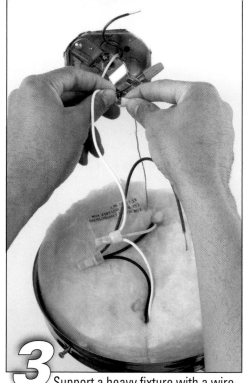

3 Support a heavy fixture with a wire coat hanger while you work (page 115). Connect the ground wire. Splice white lead to white wire and black to black. Wrap the wire nuts with electrician's tape.
The insulation may be in your way, but don't remove it; it's a safety feature.

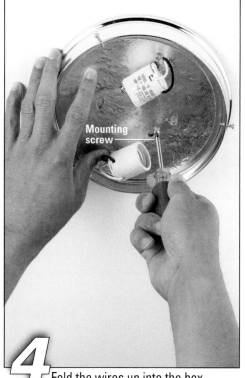

Mounting screw

4 Fold the wires up into the box. Start one mounting screw, then the other, then tighten them. If the fixture has keyhole-shape screw holes, attach the screws to the box; slip the fixture over the large holes. Rotate the canopy so the screws fit into the smaller slots and tighten the screws.

Setscrew

5 The setscrews that hold the globe may already be in the base or may have to be installed. Push the globe to raise the lip above all the setscrews, then hand-tighten all the setscrews evenly.

WHAT IF...
The new fixture's canopy doesn't cover the old hole?

If the new canopy is not large enough to cover up holes or unpainted portions of the ceiling—or simply to add a decorative touch—purchase a medallion. Hold it against the ceiling while you wire the fixture. Before tightening the canopy see that the medallion is centered.

WHAT IF...
The fixture has a center mounting hole?

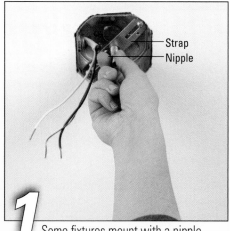

Strap
Nipple

1 Some fixtures mount with a nipple (short threaded pipe) and a nut in the center rather than two screws. Install a strap and screw in a nipple. If the nipple that comes with the fixture is too short or too long, purchase another one.

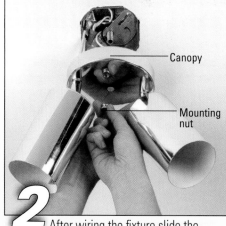

Canopy

Mounting nut

2 After wiring the fixture slide the canopy up so the nipple pokes down through the center hole. Screw on and tighten the mounting nut.

INSTALLING FLUORESCENTS

Fluorescent lighting is inexpensive to run, but the light from standard tubes is cold and industrial. Replace them with tubes labeled "warm" or "full spectrum," which produce light that is more suitable for a home. Adding a translucent cover diffuses the light and reduces the glare.

Replacing an incandescent fixture with a fluorescent one is relatively easy. A simpler solution if your goal is simply to save energy costs is to install a fluorescent bulb in an incandescent fixture (page 59).

An existing fluorescent light might have cable running directly into it with no electrical junction box. That's OK—usually the fixture's housing is considered adequate for protecting spliced wires.

Because some fluorescent fixtures are heavy and bulky, enlist a helper when removing or installing one.

PRESTART CHECKLIST

☐ **TIME**
About 1 hour to remove a fixture and install a new fluorescent

☐ **TOOLS**
Screwdriver, drill, strippers, side cutters, voltage tester, lineman's pliers, ladder

☐ **SKILLS**
Stripping and splicing wires, driving screws

☐ **PREP**
Spread a drop cloth on the floor beneath the light; set up a stable ladder

☐ **MATERIALS**
New fluorescent fixture, wire nuts, screws, electrician's tape

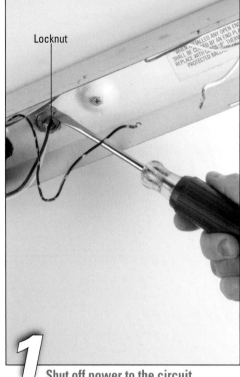

Locknut

1 **Shut off power to the circuit.** Remove the wire nuts and disconnect the house wires from the fixture wires. (Or snip and restrip them as shown on page 74.) Loosen and remove the locknut that holds the cable clamp to the fixture.

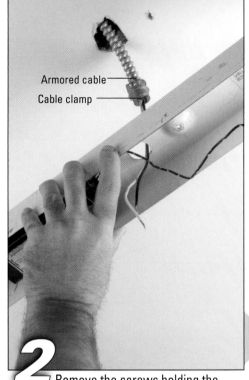

Armored cable
Cable clamp

2 Remove the screws holding the fixture in place—usually there are several driven into ceiling joists. Support the fixture as it comes loose and guide the wires out through the hole. Note the locations of the ceiling joists. Mark the new fixture to line up screws with joists.

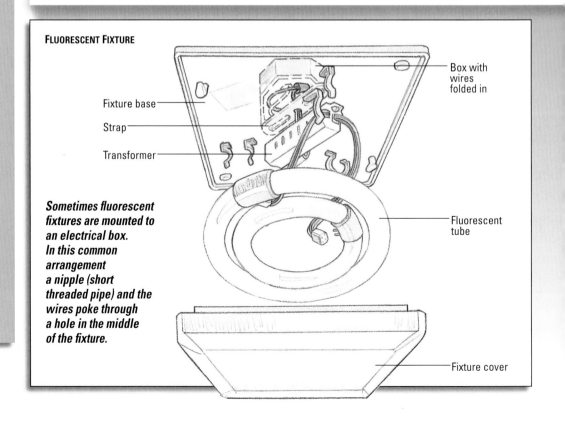

FLUORESCENT FIXTURE

Box with wires folded in

Fixture base

Strap

Transformer

Fluorescent tube

Sometimes fluorescent fixtures are mounted to an electrical box. In this common arrangement a nipple (short threaded pipe) and the wires poke through a hole in the middle of the fixture.

Fixture cover

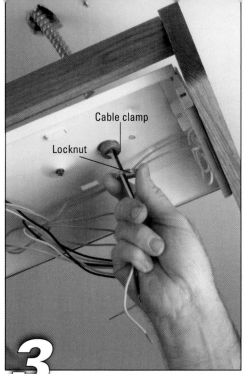

Cable clamp

Locknut

3 With a hammer and screwdriver, open a precut knockout hole in the top of the fixture, then twist off the piece with pliers. Thread the wires through the hole and attach the cable clamp to the fixture with a locknut.

4 Have a helper hold the fixture against the ceiling. Drive the mounting screws into joists.

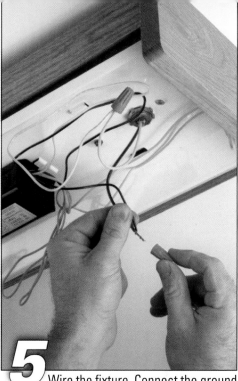

5 Wire the fixture. Connect the ground wires together and to a grounding screw on the fixture. Splice white fixture wire to white house wire and black to black. Install the fixture tubes and cover.

Circular fixture

A round fluorescent fixture usually mounts to a box. Thread the house wires through the hole in the middle and splice them to the fixture wires. Start driving both mounting screws into the electrical box, then tighten.

WHAT IF…
The defective fixture is in a suspended ceiling?

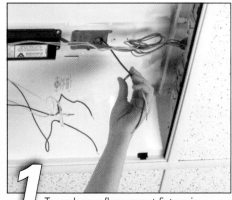

1 To replace a fluorescent fixture in a suspended ceiling, **shut off power to the circuit.** Remove the ceiling panels around the fixture. Remove the diffuser, disconnect the wires, unscrew the locknut, and pull out the cable (Steps 1 and 2, opposite). With a helper lift the old fixture out and set the new fixture into place in the ceiling frame.

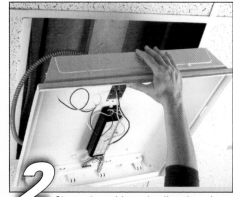

2 Clamp the cable and splice the wires, as in Steps 3 and 5 above. Replace the ceiling panels, install tubes, and slip on the diffuser.

INSTALLING SHOP LIGHTS

The most important—and confusing—step in installing shop lights is choosing the right fixture. You're likely to find several types of lights—strip lights, utility lights, wraparounds, T5, T8, and T12 lights. Fortunately it's not as hard as it looks.

The first three—strip, utility, and wraparound lights—are types of fixtures; the last three—T5, T8, and T12—are types of bulbs. And while some fixtures will handle more than one kind of bulb, most won't. Start by choosing the kind of bulb you want (and to make a long story short, T8 bulbs are energy efficient and start well in a cold shop.) Then choose the style of fixture (strip, utility, and wraparound are all suitable as shop lights.) Finally make sure the bulb you've chosen will fit the fixture and that the fixture has the right kind of ballast to power the bulb. The packaging usually will list the kind of bulbs a fixture can handle. If not ask for help.

Installing a wrap-around flourescent fixture

1 Choose a circuit controlled by a switch. **Turn off the power** at the breaker or fuse box and check to make sure the power is off. Remove the existing fixture and a knockout in the side of the box. Put a cable clamp in the new hole.

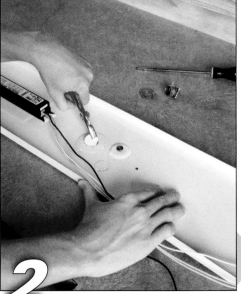

2 Punch out one of the knockouts on top of the light and put a cable clamp in the hole to protect the wires that will go through it, as required by code.

PRESTART CHECKLIST

☐ **TIME**
About 30 minutes

☐ **TOOLS**
Circuit tester, flathead screwdriver, phillips screwdriver, hammer, drill

☐ **SKILLS**
Installing a cable clamp, wiring, hanging a light

☐ **PREP**
Remove existing fixture.

☐ **MATERIALS**
Light fixture, bulbs, cable clamp, wire nuts, electrician's tape, cover for junction box

Choosing a fixture

Utility lights. Lights sold as utility lights are the most convenient lights to use in your shop. They come with a cord, a pull-string switch, and are completely assembled. You hang them from the ceiling—usually by chains that attach to each end of the light. If you've got an outlet handy, all you need to do is hang the light and plug it in.

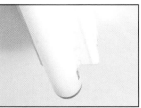

Strip lights. A strip light is about as simple as it gets. No reflector, no diffuser, no switch, no cord or plug. Strip lights cost considerably less than utility lights. Because they have no switch, cord, or plug, you should think of them the same way you think about putting in any other ceiling light. Take out the existing light (or run a circuit if necessary), hardwire the light, and hang it. You'll control it with the switch that's on the wall.

Wraparound lights. Wraparound lights are a type of strip light, the difference being that they have a plastic diffuser over the light. They're good over a workbench where you want lots of light but no glare. Like other strip lights they usually come without a cord or switch and are hardwired into the circuit.

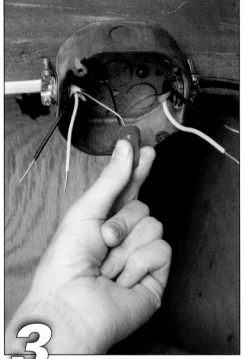

3 Put a cable long enough to reach the light in the clamp. Attach the ground from the new cable to the existing ground wire, and pigtail both to the ground screw in the box.

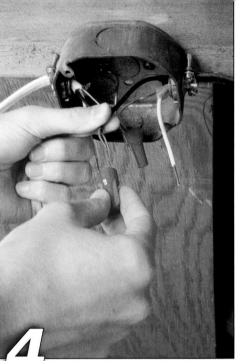

4 Attach the black wire from the new cable to the existing black wire. Put a piece of black tape around both white wires because they will be carrying power, and attach them to each other.

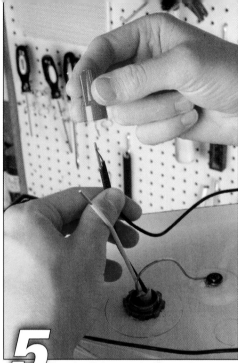

5 Put the light on a ladder or have someone hold it while you work. Attach the bare wire to the green screw. Connect the blacks to each other, and then connect the whites to each other.

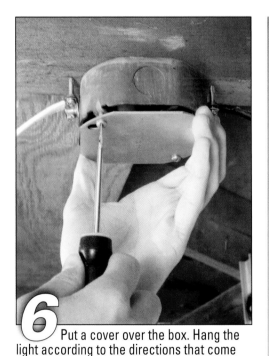

6 Put a cover over the box. Hang the light according to the directions that come with it.

Choosing a bulb

T12 bulbs are the oldest of the three common types of fluorescent bulbs. Generally speaking the least expensive fixture is designed for a T12. While the fixtures are a good deal, the bulbs are somewhat inefficient: What you save on the fixture, you will eventually pay for in electricity. More importantly the T12 is a warm weather bulb that needs to be at 60 degrees before it will start. In colder weather the light will flicker or appear as a dim spiral until the bulb heats up.

T8 bulbs and fixtures are slightly more expensive but will start instantly at temperatures below freezing. The exact starting temperature depends on the ballast, the part of the light that starts the bulb. Check the packaging to see what you're buying.

T5 and T5HO bulbs are easily recognized by their size. They're only about ⅝ inch in diameter. Because the smaller bulb puts out roughly the same amount of light as a T12 or T8, T5 bulbs appear to be brighter. T5HO are high output bulbs and actually are brighter—about twice as bright, so bright that looking at them is uncomfortable. Unless you have high ceilings, T5HO bulbs are a bad choice for workshops.

INSTALLING PENDENT LIGHTS

Replacing a ceiling fixture with a pendent light or chandelier is usually simple. Study the pendent's mounting system before you start the project.

To adjust the height of a fixture that hangs by a chain, remove or add links. On other types you may need to alter the length of the cord or cable.

A heavy fixture may require a fan-rated ceiling box (pages 128–129).

PRESTART CHECKLIST

☐ **TIME**
About 2 hours to remove an existing fixture and install a new pendent fixture

☐ **TOOLS**
Screwdriver, long-nose pliers, strippers, side cutters, lineman's pliers, voltage tester, nonconducting ladder

☐ **SKILLS**
Stripping wire, splicing stranded wire to solid wire

☐ **PREP**
Spread a drop cloth on the floor and set up a ladder.

☐ **MATERIALS**
New pendent fixture, wire nuts, electrician's tape

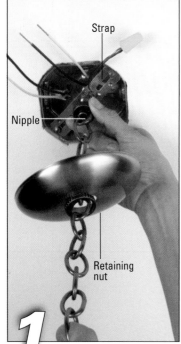

1 **Shut off power to the circuit** and remove the old fixture (page 39). Screw a nipple into a strap so the nipple hangs down about ¾ inch. Screw on the fixture's retaining nut.

2 Thread wires through the chain. Cut and strip the wire ends. Splice the ribbed wire to the house's white wire and the other wire to the black house wire. Connect the grounds.

3 Fold the wires into the box. Slide the canopy up against the ceiling and tighten the canopy nut.

STANLEY PRO TIP
All on board?

It's easy to get a pendent fixture installed only to find you've omitted a part. Work carefully and install parts in order. On a fixture with a chain, be sure to slide the canopy onto the chain, then thread the wires all the way through the chain and retaining nut before making electrical connections.

Get the height right
If people walk under a pendent light, it should be at least 6½ feet high.

WHAT IF...
The fixture has a downrod or retaining ring?

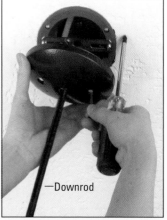

A pendent light with a solid downrod or a round cord typically attaches to the canopy with two nuts, one on either side of the canopy. The canopy attaches to the box with two screws.

Some lightweight pendent fixtures with chains do not attach directly to the box. A retaining ring secures the chain to the canopy, and the canopy attaches to the box.

INSTALLING TRACK LIGHTS

Track lighting offers plenty of options. You can install the track in various configurations (page 126). Lamps, available in many styles, can go anywhere on the track and point in any direction. You can intermix types of lights, some for general illumination and others to highlight work areas or spotlight art.

The track usually takes power from a light fixture box via a mounting plate. Sketch your planned installation and show the drawing to a salesperson, who can help you gather the track, mounting plate, lamps, and other fittings. A starter kit includes everything needed for a basic installation.

PRESTART CHECKLIST

☐ **TIME**
About 4 hours to remove an old fixture and install about 8 feet of track with one or two turns, as well as several lamps

☐ **TOOLS**
Screwdriver, tape measure, strippers, drill, side cutters, voltage tester, lineman's pliers, hacksaw, stud finder, nonconducting ladder

☐ **SKILLS**
Measuring accurately, driving screws into joists, stripping wire, splicing stranded wire to solid wire

☐ **PREP**
Spread a drop cloth on the floor and set up one or two ladders. A helper comes in handy when installing long pieces of track.

☐ **MATERIALS**
Parts for the track system (see illustration), plastic anchors, screws, wire nuts, electrician's tape

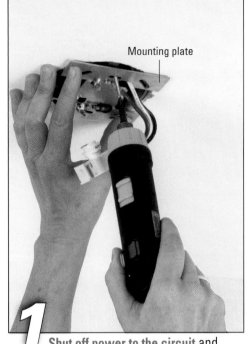

Mounting plate

1 **Shut off power to the circuit** and remove the existing light fixture (page 39). Splice the mounting plate leads to the house wires—green to ground, white to white, and black to black. Fold the wires up into the box. Screw the mounting plate snugly to the box.

2 If necessary cut pieces of track to length. To cut a track hold it firmly. If you use a vice, take care not to bend the metal. Cut with a hacksaw. Support the waste side of the piece when nearing the end of a cut so it does not fall and bend the track.

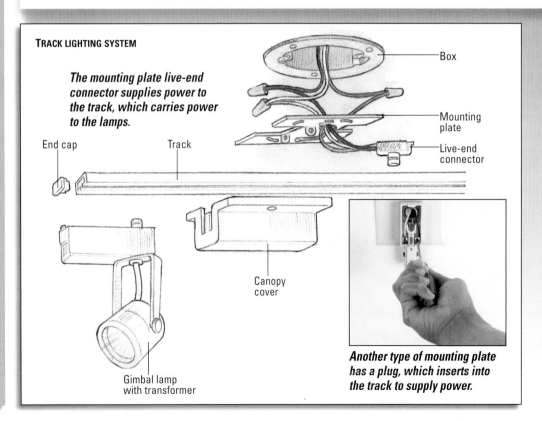

TRACK LIGHTING SYSTEM

The mounting plate live-end connector supplies power to the track, which carries power to the lamps.

Box

Mounting plate

Live-end connector

End cap

Track

Canopy cover

Gimbal lamp with transformer

Another type of mounting plate has a plug, which inserts into the track to supply power.

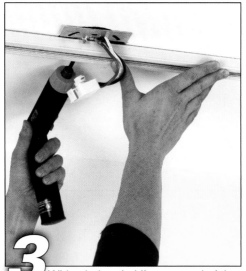

Track

3 With a helper holding one end of the track, push the track up against the mounting plate. Secure it by tightening the setscrews.

4 With a helper holding one end of the track, measure at two points along the track so it parallels the nearest wall. If the track configuration includes any 90-degree angles, use a framing square to mark a guideline.

5 Locate joists with a stud finder. Drive a screw into every joist the track crosses. If the track parallels the joists, drill holes every 16 inches, tap in plastic anchors, and drive screws into the anchors.

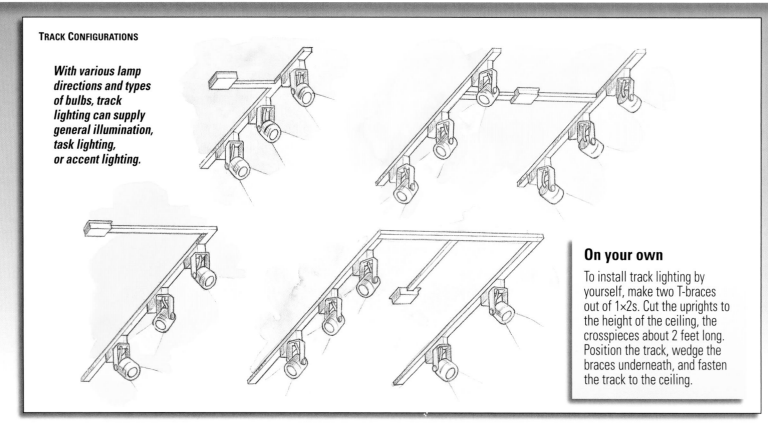

TRACK CONFIGURATIONS

With various lamp directions and types of bulbs, track lighting can supply general illumination, task lighting, or accent lighting.

On your own

To install track lighting by yourself, make two T-braces out of 1×2s. Cut the uprights to the height of the ceiling, the crosspieces about 2 feet long. Position the track, wedge the braces underneath, and fasten the track to the ceiling.

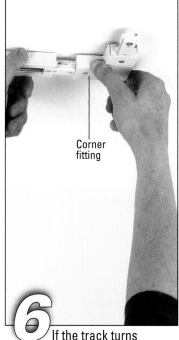

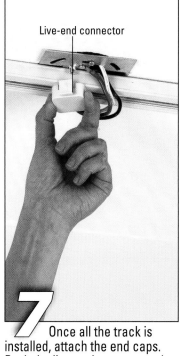

Live-end connector

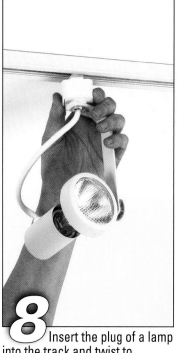

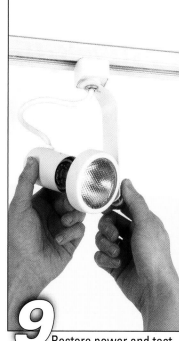

Corner fitting

6 If the track turns a corner, slide the fitting onto the track just installed. Slide the next piece onto the connector, measure to see that it parallels the nearest wall, and anchor it to the ceiling.

7 Once all the track is installed, attach the end caps. Push the live-end connector plug into the track; twist it to make contact with both contacts in the track. Attach the canopy cover.

8 Insert the plug of a lamp into the track and twist to tighten. To move a lamp along the track, loosen it first—do not force it while it is still attached.

9 Restore power and test. If a lamp does not function, remove it and twist it back on again. Once it functions adjust the lamp to direct the light where needed.

FITTINGS
Any shape you need

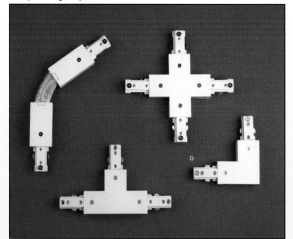

Track fittings allow you to form different shapes. A flexible fitting turns to most any angle. With each fitting you use, make sure the exposed ends of all the tracks have end caps, or the track will not energize.

AVAILABLE LAMPS

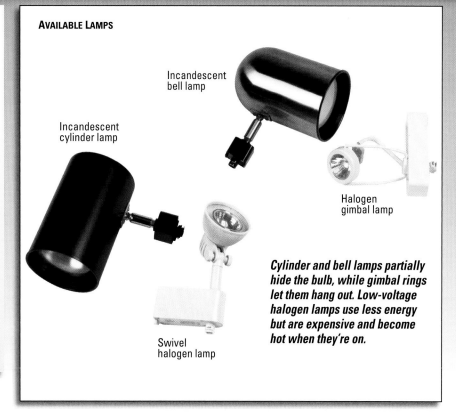

Incandescent bell lamp

Incandescent cylinder lamp

Halogen gimbal lamp

Swivel halogen lamp

Cylinder and bell lamps partially hide the bulb, while gimbal rings let them hang out. Low-voltage halogen lamps use less energy but are expensive and become hot when they're on.

INSTALLING A CEILING FAN BOX

Ceiling fans are heavy and they vibrate. A fan installed on a standard ceiling fixture box could come loose and perhaps crash to the floor.

The first step in adding a ceiling fan is to inspect the existing electrical box. **Shut off power to the circuit.** Test to confirm that the power is off and remove the existing ceiling fixture (page 39).

Most building codes require ceiling fans to be mounted onto special fan-rated boxes (opposite), which are made of metal or strong plastic and have deep-threaded holes for the mounting screws. The box must be mounted firmly, either by attaching it directly to a framing member or by using a fan-rated brace (Step 1, page 129).

Replacing a ceiling box is a messy job. Work carefully to avoid cutting through wires hidden in the ceiling.

PRESTART CHECKLIST

☐ **TIME**
About 2 hours to remove an old box and install a new one

☐ **TOOLS**
Ladder, screwdriver, hammer, drill, pry bar, utility knife, flashlight, wrench or groove-joint pliers, perhaps a reciprocating saw

☐ **SKILLS**
Cutting drywall, prying boxes out without damaging surrounding ceiling or wall

☐ **PREP**
Spread a drop cloth on the floor below; set up a ladder.

☐ **MATERIALS**
Fan-rated box, box brace

Remove old box

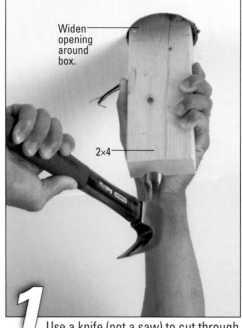

1 Use a knife (not a saw) to cut through the drywall or plaster all around the old box. The box should be attached to a joist with screws or two horizontally driven nails. Force the box loose by hammering a 2×4 into it.

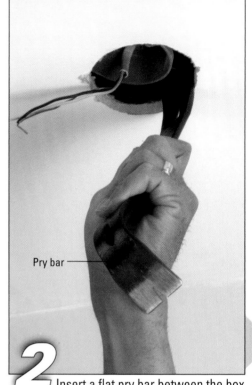

2 Insert a flat pry bar between the box and the joist. Pry the box away from the joist. You may need to pry out a staple anchoring the cable to the joist. Work carefully to avoid unnecessary damage to the ceiling.

WHAT IF...
There is another type of box in the ceiling?

Older pancake boxes mount with screws driven into a framing member. Remove the screws and pry out the box.

If a box is too firmly mounted to be knocked free, cut a hole into the ceiling just large enough so you can see the mounting nails and the cable. Carefully cut through the nails with a reciprocating saw.

3 Pry out the box's mounting nails and pull the box down from the ceiling. Disconnect the cable from the box. The box shown has a slot that the cable slides through; pry the tab and pull the cable out. If the box has a cable clamp, remove the locknut.

Poke the tab to release the cable.

Install a new box

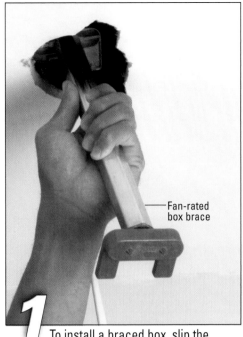

Fan-rated box brace

1 To install a braced box, slip the brace through the hole. Rotate the shaft of the brace clockwise until it touches a joist on either side and its legs rest on top of the drywall or plaster.

U-bolt

2 Tighten the brace with a wrench or groove-joint pliers. Attach the U-bolt to the brace and slide the box up through it. Tighten the nuts.

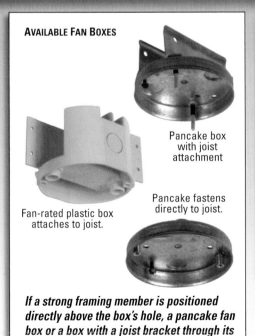

AVAILABLE FAN BOXES

Pancake box with joist attachment

Pancake fastens directly to joist.

Fan-rated plastic box attaches to joist.

If a strong framing member is positioned directly above the box's hole, a pancake fan box or a box with a joist bracket through its center may be the easiest to install.

WHAT IF...
You can work from above?

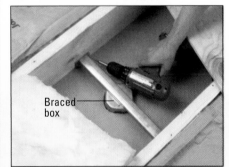

Braced box

If you can get at the attic space above the ceiling box, go there to disconnect the old box. Install a braced box.

Don't depend on plaster lath
If you have a plaster ceiling, make sure you attach a box to a joist—not the ⅜-inch-thick pieces of lath, which have very little strength.

Screw the fan bracket to a ceiling joist

Here's an option that eliminates the need for a new box. Screw the fan's mounting bracket (page 130) directly to a nearby joist. The plate will be off center, so you may need a medallion (page 119) to cover the hole.

ATTACHING A CEILING FAN

Although a ceiling fan is a complex fixture with lots of parts, each step of installation is fairly simple. The most challenging task is assembling the parts in the right order.

Make sure the ceiling box is fan-rated and firmly attached to framing (pages 128–129).

If there is three-wire cable (with black, white, red, and ground wires) from the fixture box to the switch box, you can install a standard fan/light switch (page 132).

With two-wire cable use one of the following means of controlling the fan and the light:

■ Let the wall switch control both the fan and the light; turn one or the other off using the fixture's pull-chain switches.

■ Install a fan with a built-in wireless remote control or add a wireless remote to the fan (opposite page).

■ Purchase a fan that has a special switch that controls fan and light functions through a two-wire cable. (These are expensive.)

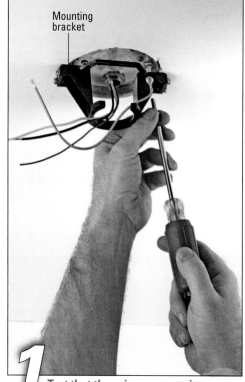

1 **Test that there is no power in the box.** Secure the fan mounting bracket to the ceiling fixture box with screws. If rubber washers are provided, be sure to install them between the bracket and the box.

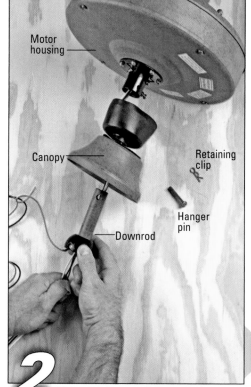

2 Slide the downrod through the canopy, slip on the yoke cover, and pull the wires through. Attach the downrod to the motor housing with the hanger pin and retaining clip.

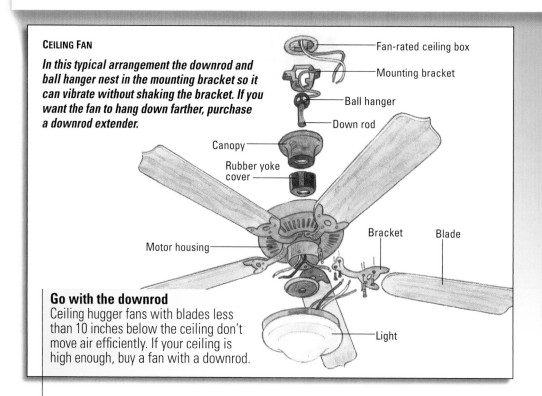

CEILING FAN

In this typical arrangement the downrod and ball hanger nest in the mounting bracket so it can vibrate without shaking the bracket. If you want the fan to hang down farther, purchase a downrod extender.

Go with the downrod
Ceiling hugger fans with blades less than 10 inches below the ceiling don't move air efficiently. If your ceiling is high enough, buy a fan with a downrod.

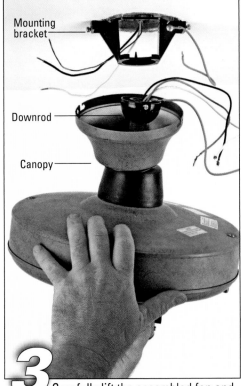

Mounting bracket

Downrod

Canopy

Fan blade

Fan bracket

Canopy setscrew

Cordless drill with phillips bit

3 Carefully lift the assembled fan and hook the ball-like end of the downrod into the mounting bracket. Avoid having wires getting caught between the brackets and the end of the downrod. This ball-and-socket arrangement lets the fan unit swing slightly.

4 Wire the fan. The black lead controls the motor and the blue or striped lead controls the light. If you have two-wire cable, splice both to the black house wire. Splice white lead to white wire and connect the grounds.

5 Fold the wires into the box. Push the canopy against the ceiling and secure it to the mounting bracket with the provided setscrews. Screw a fan bracket onto each fan blade. Attach each fan bracket to the underside of the motor. Make sure all the screws are tight.

Wireless remote control

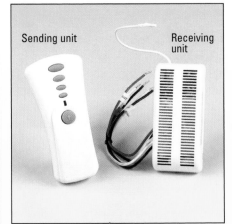

Sending unit

Receiving unit

A wireless remote-control fan/light switch controls both the fan and the light from anywhere in the room. It has two parts. Wire the receiving unit according to its instructions and tuck it inside the canopy. The sending unit is battery-powered.

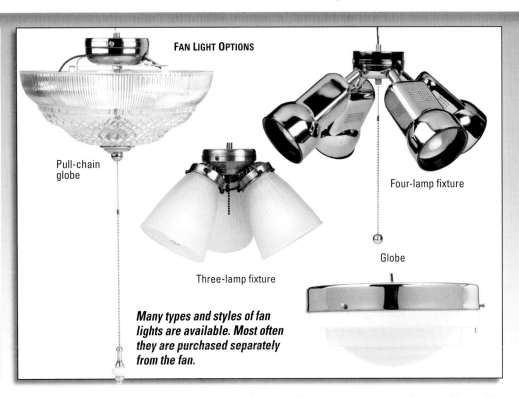

FAN LIGHT OPTIONS

Pull-chain globe

Three-lamp fixture

Four-lamp fixture

Globe

Many types and styles of fan lights are available. Most often they are purchased separately from the fan.

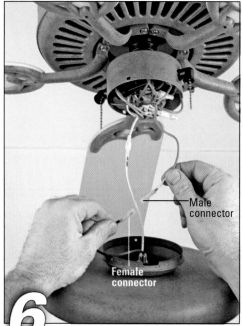

Male connector

Female connector

6 Remove the plate on the bottom of the fan and wire the light kit. The model shown above uses plug-together connectors. Some fans require that wires be spliced.

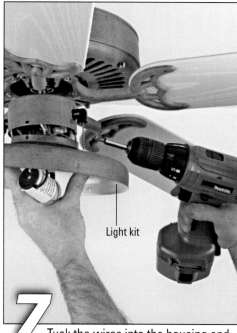

Light kit

7 Tuck the wires into the housing and push the light kit onto the fan. Tighten the screws to secure it. Install the lightbulb(s) and globe.

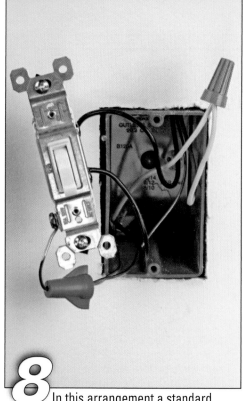

8 In this arrangement a standard single-pole switch turns the fan and the light on and off at the same time. To turn one or the other off, use the fan's pull-chain switch. Avoid installing a standard dimmer for a fan—it damages the fan.

FAN SWITCH OPTIONS

If you installed a fan only, with no light kit, a push-button fan control (left) operates the fan at different speeds.

With more expensive ceiling fans, switches are available that have separate controls for the fan and the light, though they require only two-wire cable.

Balancing the fan

If the fan wobbles as it runs, tighten the blade bracket screws. Measure from the ceiling to each blade; replace any warped blades. If that doesn't solve the problem, remove the blades and turn on the motor. If the fan wobbles without the blades, make sure the downrod is assembled correctly. If the fan still wobbles, purchase a fan balancing kit, which uses small weights on the blades to balance the fan. Finally the motor itself may be defective and need to be replaced.

WHAT IF...
There is three-wire cable?

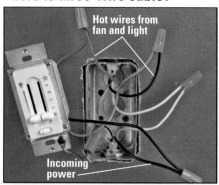

Hot wires from fan and light

Incoming power

A two-wire cable brings power to the switch and three-wire cable runs from the switch to the fixture box. Splice the black lead on the switch to the black incoming power wire. Splice the switch light lead to the hot wire from the lamp and the switch fan lead to the hot wire from the fan. Splice the white wires together and connect the grounds.

ADDING UNDERCABINET LIGHTS

The easiest way to light kitchen counterspace is to install low-voltage halogen lights under the wall cabinets. Halogens also help create a dramatic display area inside glass-fronted cabinets.

The most common type of halogen is called a puck light because of its shape, but other shapes are available. Buy a kit that includes lights, cord, a transformer, and a cord switch.

Halogens get very hot. Locate them out of children's reach or where they aren't accidentally touched. In areas where heat can build up—such as inside a cabinet—install bulbs of lower wattage.

Plan the locations of the lights and the plug-in unit and work out the least conspicuous route for the cord. Either staple the cord under a cabinet or shelf, or drill small holes and run the cord inside the cabinets and out of sight.

To control halogens from a wall switch, install a switch/receptacle (pages 188–189). To install permanent fluorescent lights, see pages 198–199.

1 Position each lighting unit as recommended by the manufacturer. Check that the mounting screws provided don't pierce through to the inside of the cabinet. Fasten each fixture in place.

Plug-in halogen light

Connecting cord

2 When all the fixtures are in place, run connecting wires between them; then connect the source line that runs from the lights to a receptacle. Some kits come with plugs already installed. Coil any excess wire and hide it near the back of the cabinet.

PRESTART CHECKLIST

☐ **TIME**
About 2 hours to install five or six halogens with transformer and switch

☐ **TOOLS**
Screwdriver, drill, strippers, long-nose pliers, hammer

☐ **SKILLS**
Drilling holes, driving screws

☐ **PREP**
Spread a towel or small drop cloth on the surface below.

☐ **MATERIALS**
Halogen light kit, including lights, a plug-in unit, transformer, cord, and switch

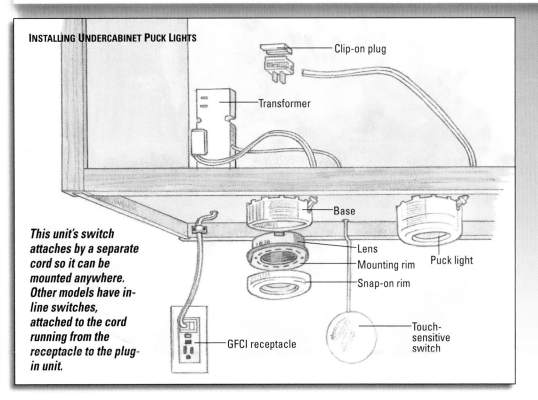

INSTALLING UNDERCABINET PUCK LIGHTS

Clip-on plug

Transformer

This unit's switch attaches by a separate cord so it can be mounted anywhere. Other models have in-line switches, attached to the cord running from the receptacle to the plug-in unit.

GFCI receptacle

Base

Lens

Mounting rim

Snap-on rim

Puck light

Touch-sensitive switch

ADDING UNDERCABINET LIGHTS *continued*

Plastic staple

3 Fasten the connecting cords to the underside of the cabinet. Use the staples provided with the kit or plastic-coated or round-topped staples. Don't use standard metal square-topped staples; they may cut the cord.

Halogen bulb

Switch

4 Slide back the lens covering. Holding the halogen bulb with a cloth, install it in the fixture. Replace the lens.

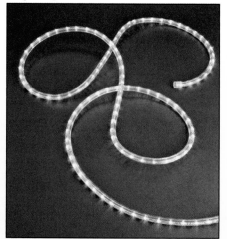

Adjustment handle

5 Plug in the main cord and turn the lights on with the switch. On the model shown above, the direction of the lamp adjusts by swiveling the lamp housing.

STANLEY PRO TIP: **Wiring a switch/receptacle**

Shut off the power. Remove the old receptacle. Connect the black wire to the brass terminal that does not have a connecting tab and connect the white wire to the silver terminal on the same side. Connect the ground. The switch turns the receptacle on and off.

If the receptacle is in the middle of the run, with two cables entering the box, splice the black wires and the white wires to pigtails. Connect the pigtails to the brass (black) and silver (white) terminals on the side that does not have a connecting tab. Connect the ground.

Rope lights

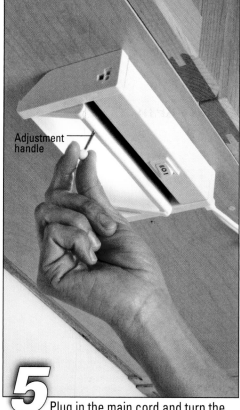

Rope lights are easy to install: Just staple them where you want, using the plastic staples supplied, and plug them in. Install an in-line cord switch (page 61) or plug the rope into a switched receptacle.

INSTALLING UNDERCABINET XENON LIGHTS

While an overhead light gives you the light you need to make it from the refrigerator to the stove, it may not be enough light to read a cookbook or chop vegetables. Small xenon lights installed under the upper cabinets provide task lighting on the counter. Installing them was once a major project, but newer under-the-counter lights are easy to install. There are several varieties, each slightly different.

Most kits include a number of lights, a transformer to power them, and a length of lamp cord to connect them. You can position the lights as close together or far apart as you want—just position the lights and transformer, then cut the wires to fit. Some transformers, like the one in the kit shown, are small enough to simply stick underneath the cabinet with double-face adhesive. Others need to be attached with screws. Like the lights, the transformer is wired only after it is in place.

PRESTART CHECKLIST

☐ **TIME**
About 30 minutes to install the light system

☐ **TOOLS**
Flathead screwdriver, phillips screwdriver, pliers, wire cutters, hammer, drill bits and drill

☐ **SKILLS**
Basic wiring, drilling holes

☐ **PREP**
The lights need to be near a 120-volt outlet.

☐ **MATERIALS**
Lighting kit

1 Lay out the position of the lights and transformer. Measure the distance between the two lights furthest from the transformer, and cut two wires to that length.

2 Strip the ends of the wires and put them in the wiring holes in one of the lights.

3 Install the bulb and reflector on the light. Assemble all the lights you will use.

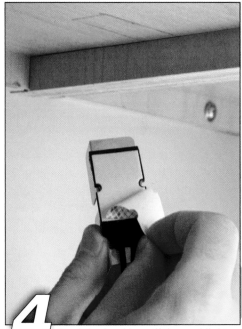

4 Peel the backing off the end light to expose the adhesive, and stick it in place. Install and wire the remaining lights the same way, working back to the transformer

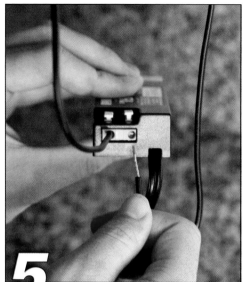

5 Put the wires from the closest light into the holes for them in the transformer. Pull off the adhesive protective paper, and attach the transformer to the cabinet.

6 Connect the plug to the wire. If you want, you can put an inline switch on the cord. Note the ribbed covering over one of the wires. Put the switch on the smooth-jacketed wire, which is the hot wire.

7 Plug the transformer into an outlet. If you didn't put in an inline switch, plug the transformer into a switched outlet.

STANLEY PRO TIP: **Low-tech depth gauge**

The screw and the hole for it should only go partway into the surface you're mounting the lights on. To make sure you don't drill all the way through the cabinet bottom, put a piece of tape on the drill bit. Place the tape on the bit so it brushes against the surface of the cabinet when the hole is the right depth.

SAFETY FIRST
Protect wires from damage

When routing and fastening cords, including low-voltage leads, always use insulated staples. A metal staple could damage the wire insulation and create a short circuit. An insulated staple minimizes the chance of a short circuit, even if the wire is damaged.

If you run cords for low-voltage lighting inside kitchen cabinets, place the cords where appliances or cookware stored in the cabinets won't damage them. Secure the cords to the cabinet along the back wall or inside top, if possible, so items won't sit on the wires or be dragged across them.

INSTALLING LOW-VOLTAGE TRACK LIGHTS

High-tech-looking Eurostyle lights are readily available at lighting stores and home centers. They appear complicated but are easy to install.

You can replace an existing light fixture with the type shown on these pages or buy a unit that simply plugs into a receptacle.

Low-voltage halogens save on energy use, but the bulbs get hot. Keep the lights out of the reach of children and away from combustible surfaces such as curtains.

The fixture shown uses a transformer that steps voltage down to 8 to 20 volts. However you hook it up to standard household wiring, so be sure to **shut off power** before working. To remove an existing light fixture, see page 39.

PRESTART CHECKLIST

☐ **TIME**
About 2 hours to remove a ceiling fixture and install a Eurostyle light

☐ **TOOLS**
Screwdriver, drill, voltage tester, stud finder, strippers, lineman's pliers, nonconducting ladder

☐ **SKILLS**
Attaching hardware with screws, stripping wire, splicing stranded wire to solid wire

☐ **PREP**
Spread a drop cloth on the floor.

☐ **MATERIALS**
New light fixture, wire nuts, electrician's tape

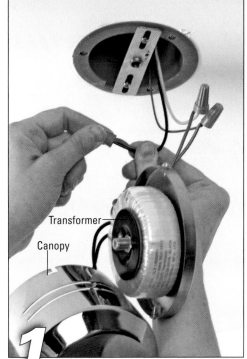

1 **Shut off power to the circuit.** Remove an existing light fixture (page 39) and splice the transformer leads to the house wires.

Transformer

Canopy

Rod holder

2 Measure carefully and try to position the rod holder under a joist. Attach the holder with screws long enough to reach through drywall or plaster and fasten at least ½ inch into the joist. Use plastic wall anchors if no joist is available.

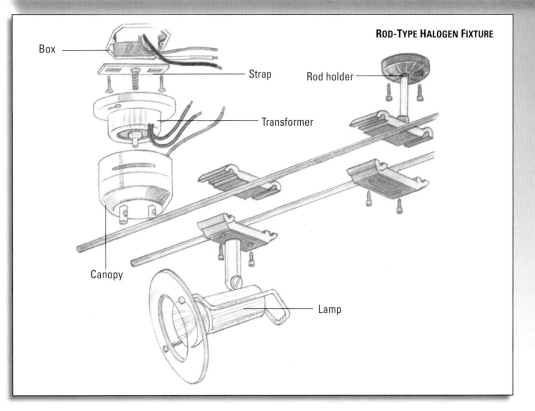

ROD-TYPE HALOGEN FIXTURE

Box

Strap

Rod holder

Transformer

Canopy

Lamp

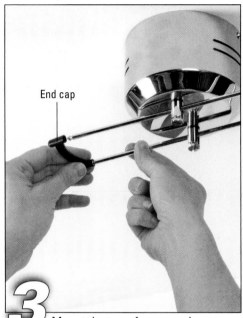

End cap

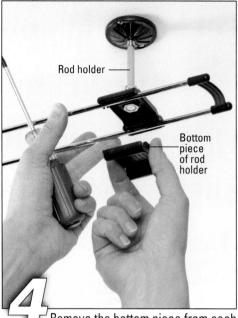

Rod holder

Bottom piece of rod holder

3 Mount the transformer and canopy to the ceiling box strap. Slide the rods through the canopy rod connectors. Slip an end cap onto each end of both rods.

4 Remove the bottom piece from each rod holder. Snap the rods into the grooves and reattach the holder bottom piece.

5 Attach the lamps to the rods, following the manufacturer's instructions. These attach with two-piece holders similar to the rod holders shown in Step 4. Position each lamp and tighten the screws.

Stylish options

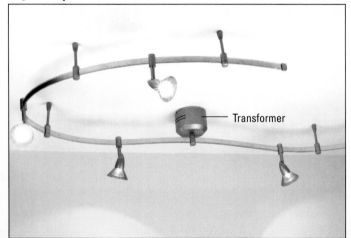

Transformer

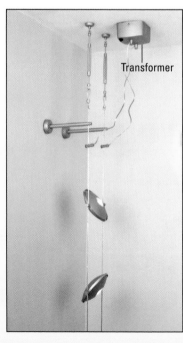

Transformer

With a track that can bend into curves, the halogen fixture above is as decorative as it is functional. The transformer mounts anywhere along the track, and the track can be cut to any length.

Lights straddle two vertical wires that deliver low-voltage current in another fixture style (right). Lights can slide up or down and rotate on an axis. The fixture can be installed horizontally.

REFRESHER COURSE
Switch/receptacle for plug-in transformers

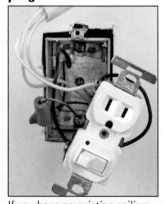

If you have no existing ceiling fixture, buy a unit that plugs into a receptacle. Page 102 shows how to replace a receptacle with a switched plug so you can control the light from a wall switch.

ADDING A PORCH LIGHT

Porch lights add safety, security, and style to an entryway. They illuminate steps and help you see callers before you open the door.

See pages 174–179 for how to run cable through finished walls. You need to supply power and install an interior switch (pages 190–193).

PRESTART CHECKLIST

☐ **TIME**
   About 6 hours to run cable, install fixture and a switch

☐ **TOOLS**
   Voltage tester, drill, ¼-inch bit, jigsaw, fish tape, drywall saw, screwdriver, strippers, long-nose pliers, lineman's pliers

☐ **SKILLS**
   Locating studs; cutting into siding; stripping, splicing, and connecting wires to terminals; installing boxes; running cable into boxes

☐ **MATERIALS**
   Fixture(s), outdoor box(es), two-wire cable, interior switch box, switch, electrician's tape, caulk, wire nuts, bent coat hanger

Installing the box and fixture

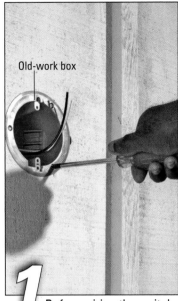

Old-work box

1 Before wiring the switch use a fish tape to pull the switch cable out through the fixture box opening. Strip 8 inches of sheathing and clamp the cable to the box. (For two lights run cable and install the second box. See page 193 for how to wire.) Install the box.

Strap

2 Strip the individual wires, removing about ¾ inch of insulation from each. Attach the mounting strap (typically provided with the light fixture) so the mounting bolts are positioned to hold the fixture.

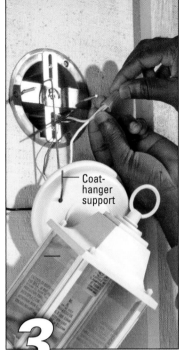

Coat-hanger support

3 Support the fixture with a wire coat hanger. Connect the ground. Splice white lead to white wire and black to black. Fold the wires into the box and install the fixture onto the mounting bolts. Caulk around the base. Wire the switch, install a bulb, and test.

CUTTING A HOLE FOR THE BOX OPENING

1 Using a ¼-inch bit, drill a finder hole and use a bent wire to check that the box is not positioned over or too near a stud. (If it is not possible to move the box, cut the opening and chisel out the stud.)

2 Check for any pipes or cables in the wall. If clear, trace the outline of the box on the siding. Use a jigsaw to cut an opening for the box.

REFRESHER COURSE
Installing a programmable switch

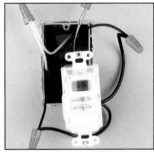

For convenience and security wire porch lights with a programmable switch. Set them to go on at dusk and off at bedtime. For added security program the lights to stay on until dawn. Such switches have override options for turning the light on and off at will.

PLANNING NEW ELECTRICAL SERVICE

Anytime you install new cable—whether adding one receptacle or wiring a remodeled kitchen—you add new service to your system. This may increase the demand on circuits or require new circuits, and calls for careful planning.

Put your plans on paper
The first step is to make rough drawings that depict the lighting and electrical service you want to achieve. Pages 142–145 show typical electrical systems for a kitchen, a bathroom, and a utility room. Installations vary; these pages serve as a guide to help calculate how many circuits of which amperages are needed. Start planning cable runs that can be routed with minimal damage to the walls.

Next determine whether your existing service can support new electrical lines. You may be able to connect to existing circuits. If not you need to add a circuit or two to your existing service panel or install a subpanel or service panel. Pages 148–151 guide you through those calculations.

Why codes count
The importance of building safety codes can't be overemphasized. First, codes protect everyone in your home from shock and fire. Second, they provide common ground for everyone who works on electrical systems. When someone else works on your home's wiring after you, he or she can understand the system.

Check local codes
Pages 146–147 describe requirements throughout much of the U.S. However code requirements can vary, so contact your local building department when planning a project. Have the department review your rough drawings and finished plans. See pages 154–155 for tips on drawing plans that an inspector can read easily. Follow the department's instructions and schedule inspections if needed. Start work only after you are sure the plan is approved.

Adding new service calls for carefully assessing demand and making detailed project plans.

CHAPTER PREVIEW

Wiring a kitchen
page 142

Wiring a bathroom
page 144

Wiring utility rooms
page 145

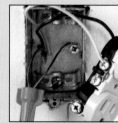

Code compliance
page 146

Jobs that involve running new cable typically require a building permit.

Post your work permit in a highly visible location.

Once you have presented acceptable plans to your building department, you receive a work permit. Follow the inspection schedule and instructions to the letter.

Loading circuits for safety
page 148

Checking out your basic service
page 150

Electricity from the sun
page 152

Drawing plans
page 154

WIRING A KITCHEN

Electrical services abound in modern kitchens: lights on the ceiling; lights in, on, and under cabinets; counter receptacles with the capacity to run six or seven appliances at once; and separate circuits for appliances, including the refrigerator, dishwasher, and microwave. A medium-size kitchen may require six, seven, or more circuits.

Types of lighting
General lighting (or ambient lighting) is usually provided by ceiling-mounted fixtures. Consider fluorescent fixtures with daylight tubes and opaque lenses to disperse the light. Or install a series of recessed canister lights or incandescent fixtures.

If you use a track fixture for general lighting, shown here, you get better illumination if you run several tracks around the room rather than having a single track in the middle. That way the light comes from several different directions.

Cove lighting mounts on top of wall cabinets and points upward, providing general lighting and creating a halo effect.

Area lighting focuses on a certain spot while also providing some general illumination. A recessed canister light equipped with a spotlight bulb, for instance, may shine down on the sink. Be sure to position it so the person doing dishes does not cast a shadow over the work area.

Pendent shade lights, as shown, are ideal area lights placed over a dining table or a counter. Position them over the center of the table or counter and adjust the heights so they do not shine into people's eyes.

Task lighting directs a beam of light at a work surface. The position of task lighting is critical: It must be in front of the worker to eliminate shadows but it must not shine into the worker's eyes. Fortunately a perfect location is available in almost every kitchen: the underside of wall cabinets. Undercabinet lights are available as fluorescent or low-voltage halogen fixtures.

Accent lighting spotlights an object such as a wallhanging. As shown small lights inside a glass-doored cabinet draw attention to a collection of fine china and crystal.

You can put in a grow light pointed at decorative or culinary plants. A typical grow light cannot supply plants with all the light they need, but it can be a supplement.

Light switches
Think carefully about the location of switches. If you position four or five next to each other, people may be confused about what switch controls which light. Where possible position switches near their lights.

Be sure that you can turn on lights easily, no matter which door or entryway you use. Often the most convenient arrangement is to use three-way switches so that a single light or series of lights can be controlled by two different switches (pages 194–197).

Typically the lights in a kitchen are on a single 15-amp circuit.

Receptacles
Codes often require a separate circuit for a refrigerator. A microwave oven may need its own circuit too, depending on its size and power.

Most codes require two circuits for countertop receptacles. In some areas the receptacles must be ground fault circuit interrupters (GFCIs) (page 183) and must be on 20-amp alternating circuits. In other areas the required arrangement is to have two 15-amp circuits with non-GFCI receptacles wired with split circuits so the two plugs are connected to two different circuits (page 187). Check local codes.

Appliances
An electric range, cooktop, or oven must be wired to a dedicated 240-volt circuit (page 184). Other appliances are 120-volt.

An undersink receptacle for the garbage disposer may be split so that one plug is switched and the other is always hot (page 188), allowing you to plug in a garbage disposer and a hot-water dispenser. Or the disposer may be hardwired into a switched box. Usually the switch is placed on the wall near the sink.

A dishwasher may have its own circuit, or it may be on the same circuit as the garbage disposer. A range hood (pages 215–217) typically is hardwired.

Oversink canister light

Cove lighting

Grow light

Switch for garbage disposer

Wire for dishwasher and disposer under the sink.

Track lighting

Inside-cabinet light

Pendent light

Light for desk area

Undercabinet lights

20-amp GFCI

Receptacle for appliances used on island

This kitchen combines ambient track and cove lighting, area lighting from a canister light over the sink and pendent light, and task lighting from undercabinet halogens and fluorescents. Halogens placed inside a cabinet provide accent lighting.

WIRING A BATHROOM

Even a relatively large bathroom tends to be damp. Light fixtures must be watertight, ventilation must be effective, and the receptacles should be ground fault circuit interrupters.

Circuits
The lights and fan must be on a different circuit from the receptacle(s). Some codes require that bathrooms have their own circuits; others permit bathrooms to share circuits with receptacles or lights in other rooms. In some locales all bathroom wiring—including the lights—must be GFCI-protected (pages 183 and 279).

The vent fan
To satisfy codes and for your comfort, a bathroom needs a fan that effectively pulls moist air out and sends it outside. Pages 220–223 show how to install one. Some local codes require that the fan always comes on when the light is on; others allow you to put the fan on its own switch.

Usually there is a vent/light fixture in the middle of the ceiling, which may be controlled by one or two switches. Some fixtures also include a heating unit or a nightlight. A bathroom heater—whether it is a separate unit or a part of a fan/light—may use so much electricity that it requires its own circuit.

Lights
In addition to a light or fan/light in the middle of the ceiling, plan to position lights over the sink, where they can shine on a person standing at the mirror. A strip of lights above the mirror is a common arrangement, but most people find that two lights, one on each side of the mirror, illuminate a face more clearly. A mirror light's switch may be by the entry door or near the sink.

A tub or shower does not need to be brightly lit, but people shouldn't have to shower in the dark. Install a recessed canister light with a waterproof lens made for shower areas.

Receptacles
Install at least one 20-amp GFCI receptacle within a foot or so of the sink. Position the receptacle so a cord does not have to drape over the sink when someone is using a blow-dryer.

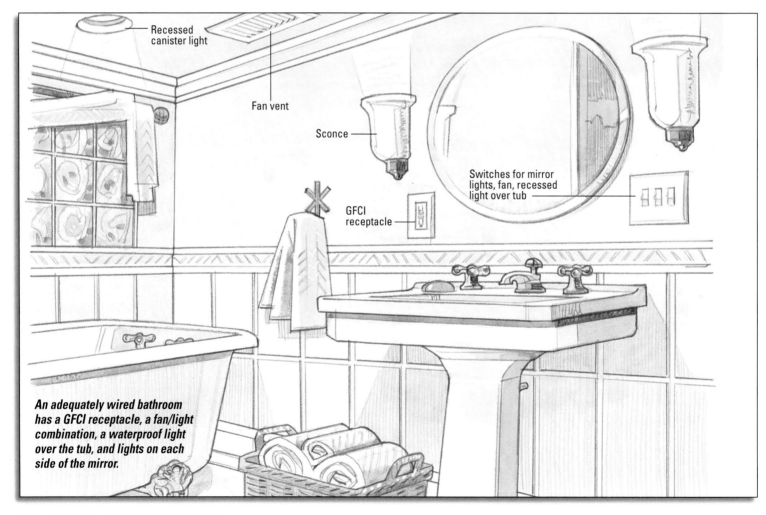

An adequately wired bathroom has a GFCI receptacle, a fan/light combination, a waterproof light over the tub, and lights on each side of the mirror.

Recessed canister light

Fan vent

Sconce

GFCI receptacle

Switches for mirror lights, fan, recessed light over tub

WIRING UTILITY ROOMS

Work areas tend to be informal, with unfinished walls and exposed framing. Unfortunately the wiring is sometimes just as informal, with exposed cable, overloaded receptacles, missing cover plates, and a tangle of extension cords.

Safe utility wiring

Attach all boxes firmly and staple or strap cables so they are taut and out of harm's way. Although some codes allow it, exposed NM cable is unsafe in an area where people work. Replace it with armored cable or conduit (pages 160–164).

Make sure there are enough receptacles placed conveniently to avoid the need for long extension cords or cube taps. If the area is damp, install GFCIs.

Wiring a workshop

People wield tools and move large pieces of lumber, so take special care in placing the receptacles. In a large shop with serious power tools, add up the amperages to see whether one or two dedicated circuits are needed (page 80). Position a receptacle near each stationary power tool such as a tablesaw or drill press. Scatter plenty of other receptacles so you can plug in hand power tools without using extension cords.

Provide plenty of overhead lighting. Large fluorescent fixtures do the trick easily and inexpensively. Install lenses to cover the tubes to prevent breakage. For work that requires close scrutiny, plug in desk lamps.

Wiring a laundry room

Codes are very specific about laundry room requirements. Use common sense when positioning receptacles so cords are well away from the folding table.

If the dryer is electric, you need a separate 120/240-volt receptacle (pages 154–155). If the dryer is gas, it can plug into a receptacle on the same circuit as the washer. An extra receptacle ensures that you don't have to reach back and unplug the washer or dryer when you need power.

The receptacles in a laundry room must be on a dedicated 20-amp circuit. Lights can share a circuit with lights in another room.

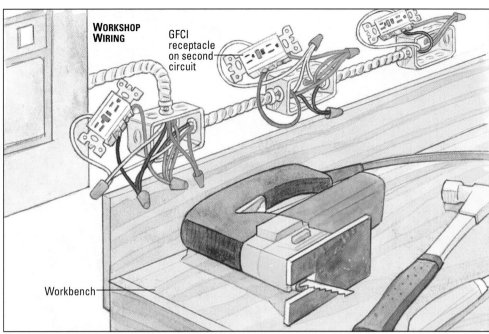

These GFCI receptacles, spaced about a foot apart, are on two circuits (page 186) so there is little chance of overloading.

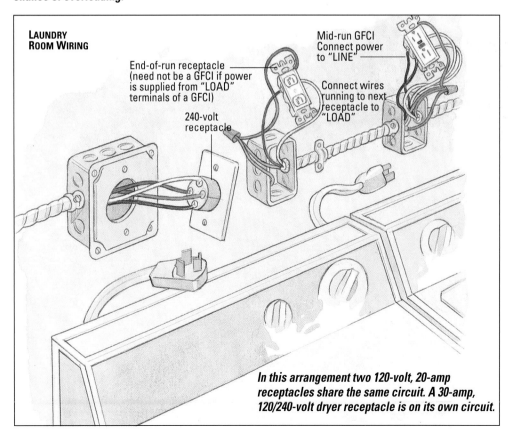

In this arrangement two 120-volt, 20-amp receptacles share the same circuit. A 30-amp, 120/240-volt dryer receptacle is on its own circuit.

CODE COMPLIANCE

If you're replacing an existing fixture, switch, or receptacle, there's usually no need to contact the building department. But when you run new electrical cable for new service, whether wiring several circuits or adding just one receptacle, be sure to work with a building inspector and comply with all local codes.

National and local codes

Professional electricians often refer to the National Electrical Code (NEC), a massive volume that describes national codes for residential and commercial wiring. You don't need to buy this book, but you may need to refer to a library copy from time to time.

Local building departments often modify the NEC, and you must satisfy those local codes. It's not unusual for adjacent towns to have very different codes; for instance one may allow plastic boxes while another requires metal boxes.

This section presents many of the most important code requirements. However it is not exhaustive. **Have a local inspector approve your wiring plans before you begin work.**

If existing wiring does not meet local codes, chances are that your building department will not require you to change the wiring.

Usually only the new work must be up to code. However if the old wiring is unsafe, you should change it. Extensive remodeling also may require you to bring the entire house up to current codes.

Loading and grounding circuits

Any plan, however simple or complex, must start with two considerations. First make sure the new service doesn't overload a circuit. Pages 148–149 explain how.

Second see that all receptacles and appliances are safely grounded. Local codes probably require that switches and light fixtures also be grounded. Grounding protects against shock in case a wire comes loose or an appliance or device malfunctions. Check using a receptacle analyzer (page 32).

All receptacles and appliances must attach to a ground wire (or metal sheathing) that runs to the service panel. The most common methods of grounding are shown below. Check with local codes to determine the approved method.

A thick ground wire should emerge from the service panel and clamp tightly to a cold-water pipe or grounding rods driven into the ground outside the house.

Common code requirements

Here are some of the most common general requirements for home electrical systems. Keep in mind that local building departments may have different demands.

■ **Boxes:** Plastic electrical boxes are common throughout much of the United States and Canada; some localities require metal boxes. Buy large boxes so wires aren't cramped (page 20). Attach them firmly to a framing member whenever possible or use remodel boxes that clamp to the wall surface (pages 172–173).

■ **Receptacles, fixtures, and appliances:** New receptacles and appliances must be grounded. Fixtures and appliances should be approved by Underwriters Laboratories (UL).

■ **Cable:** Nonmetallic (NM) cable is the easiest to run and is accepted by most building departments. Wherever cable is exposed rather than hidden behind drywall or plaster, armored cable or conduit may be required. See the chapter "Installing Cable & Boxes" for the correct ways to install cable so it is protected.

■ **Circuits:** Most 120-volt household circuits are 15 amps, and all lights must be on 15-amp circuits. In kitchens and utility areas, 20-amp circuits may be required. To make sure your circuits aren't overloaded, see pages 148–149.

■ **Wire size:** Use 14-gauge wire for 15-amp circuits and 12-gauge wire for 20-amp circuits. Cable runs longer than 500 feet may need larger wire. Consult your building department.

■ **Service panels:** As long as you do not need to add a new circuit, your service panel, even if it is an old fuse box, is probably sufficient. If you add circuits you may need to upgrade the panel or add a subpanel (pages 280–281). Check with an inspector or professional electrician.

REFRESHER COURSE
Grounding methods

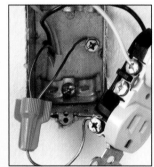

If the box is plastic, connect the ground wire to the receptacle only. For a middle-of-run receptacle (shown), splice the ground wires together and connect to the receptacle with a pigtail.

With a metal box attach ground wires to both the receptacle and to the box using a grounding screw. Use a pigtail and a grounding wire nut.

Systems that use armored cable or metal conduit may have no grounding wire. The sheathing or conduit provides the path for ground, so it must be connected firmly at all points.

Working with the electrical inspector

Filing for a permit and working with an electrical inspector may seem unnecessary, but the inspection process ensures safe and reliable electrical service. Most inspectors know their business; pay attention and follow their instructions to the letter. You will benefit from the sound advice.

■ **Find out if your building department requires a licensed electrician** to perform new electrical installations. Some departments require a homeowner to pass a written or oral test before doing certain types of work.

■ **Make a rough sketch and materials list** for the project before you start drawing plans; then find out as much as possible about local codes. Find out what kind of cable and boxes are required. Are there any specific requirements for the room you plan to wire? The building department may have pamphlets answering your questions, or an inspector may be able to answer them over the phone.

■ **The inspector's job is not to help you plan but to inspect.** An inspector may be willing to offer advice, but don't ask, "What should I do?" Instead propose a plan using the information in this chapter and present it for feedback.

■ **Draw up professional-looking plans** (pages 154–155) as well as a complete list of materials. Make an appointment with the inspector to go over your plans. Listen attentively and take notes. Be polite and respectful, but don't be afraid to ask questions if you don't understand.

■ **Schedule inspections.** There probably will be two: one for the rough wiring and one for the finished job. Don't call the inspector in until the required work is completely finished—inspectors hate having to come back for a reinspection. Above all do not cover up any wiring until the inspector has signed off on it. If you install drywall before the rough electrical inspection, you may have to tear it off.

Electrical codes room by room

Some codes apply to the entire house; others apply to specific rooms. Here are some general guidelines. Local codes may vary. These requirements usually apply only to new installations—older wiring does not have to comply as long as it is safe. These requirements make good sense and are not overly strict. Wiring that does not meet these standards would be either awkward or unsafe.

Bedrooms, living room, dining room

Every room must have a wall switch located near the entry door that controls either a ceiling fixture or a switched receptacle. All ceiling fixtures must be controlled by a wall switch and not by a pull chain. Receptacles must be no more than 12 feet apart, and there must be at least one on each wall. If a section of wall between two doors is wider than 2 feet, it must have a receptacle. Light fixtures must be on 15-amp circuits. Usually receptacles are allowed to share a circuit with lights. But a heavy electrical user, such as a window air-conditioner or a home theater, may need to be on a dedicated circuit.

Hallways and stairways

All stairways must have a light fixture controlled by three-way switches at the bottom and top of the stairs. Hallways may also need a light controlled by three-way switches. A hallway longer than 10 feet must have at least one receptacle.

Closets

There should be at least one overhead light, controlled by a wall switch rather than a pull chain. The light must have a globe rather than a bare bulb; a bulb can get hot enough to ignite clothing, stacked blankets, or storage boxes.

Attached garage

There must be at least one receptacle—not counting receptacles used for laundry or other utilities. There should be an overhead light (in addition to a light that is part of a garage door opener) controlled by at least one wall switch.

Kitchen

Here things can get pretty complicated; see pages 142–143. Many codes call for two 20-amp small appliance circuits controlling GFCI receptacles placed above countertops. Other codes call for 15-amp split-circuit receptacles. The refrigerator, microwave, garbage disposer, and dishwasher may need to be on separate circuits. The lights should be on a separate 15-amp circuit.

Bathroom

Codes require that all receptacles be GFCI-protected. Any light fixture should have a sealed globe or lens to shut out moisture. A fan/light/heater may draw enough power to require its own circuit.

Outdoors

Standard-voltage wiring requires either waterproof underground feed (UF) cable or conduit or both. The depth at which the cable must be buried varies by local codes. Special waterproof fittings and covers are called for. For low-voltage lighting standards are less strict; usually no permit is needed.

LOADING CIRCUITS FOR SAFETY

*W*hen adding only a few receptacles, lights, or a small appliance, tap into an existing circuit. Tap power from a nearby receptacle, junction box, switch box, or ceiling fixture box (pages 166–167) and run cable to the new electrical box. First make sure that you don't overload the circuit.

Indexing circuits

An index telling which electrical loads— lights, receptacles, and appliances—are on each circuit should be posted on the inside of a service panel door. However this index may not be accurate. Whenever evaluating a circuit **test to make sure which electrical loads are on what circuit.**

If there is no index, make one. Shut off one circuit and test to see which lights, receptacles, and appliances have turned off. Write down the results. Repeat for all the circuits until you have covered all electrical loads. Draw up the index and tape it to the service panel.

Indexing circuits is easier with two people: One stands at the service panel while the other tests plugs, lights, and appliances and notes the findings. Walkie-talkies or cell phones ease communication (pages 54–55).

Figuring the total load

Once you've identified all the loads on a circuit, total the wattage. If the wattage is not printed on an item's label, there should be an amperage rating (amps). Multiply the amps times voltage to get the wattage. For example a 4-amp, 120-volt tool consumes 480 watts (4×120=480).

Add the wattage of all the bulbs in each fixture. For each receptacle include the appliances or tools usually plugged into it. Include hardwired appliances such as a dishwasher. Once you've totaled all the electrical loads on a circuit, determine if adding new services overloads the circuit. The box (above right) shows how to make this calculation. If no convenient circuit has enough available capacity, install a new circuit (pages 278–279).

Major appliances, such as electric ranges and dryers, are on dedicated 240-volt circuits. Only one user connects to each circuit.

Calculating safe capacity for a circuit

To find the capacity of a circuit, multiply amps times volts (usually 120). Most local codes demand that all the users on a circuit must not add up to more than 80 percent of total capacity. This 80-percent figure is the circuit's "safe capacity."

15-amp circuit
Total capacity: 1,800 watts
Safe capacity: 1,440 watts (12 amps)

20-amp circuit
Total capacity: 2,400 watts
Safe capacity: 1,920 watts (16 amps)

30-amp circuit
Total capacity: 3,600 watts
Safe capacity: 2,880 watts (24 amps)

REFRESHER COURSE
Home electrical circuits

Power from the utility company enters the service panel, where it divides into individual branch circuits, each supplying power to specific lights, receptacles, or appliances. In each circuit a black or colored hot wire carries power to the user, and a white neutral wire completes the circuit by carrying power back to the service panel.

Some household electrical systems are orderly, with each circuit covering a clearly defined area. Others are helter-skelter— a single circuit may travel across the house or up two floors. Disorganized wiring is not necessarily unsafe, but it may take extra time to figure out what's going on when you add new service or track down a problem.

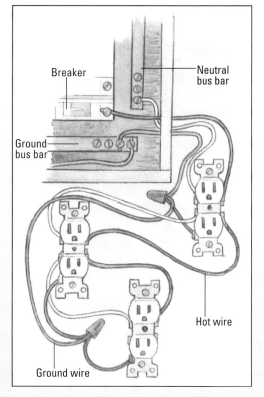

Breaker

Neutral bus bar

Ground bus bar

Hot wire

Ground wire

Appliances and tools that need special attention

To find how many watts a 120-volt appliance or tool consumes, look at its nameplate. If it shows only the amperage, multiply that times 120 to find watts. For example an 11-amp tablesaw uses 1,320 watts (11×120=1,320). Here are some typical wattages; yours may vary considerably. (All 240-volt appliances should be on dedicated circuits, so you never need to figure whether they can fit in a circuit.)

Television, 100–350 watts

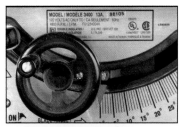
Tablesaw, 800–1,500 watts

Window air conditioner, 500–1,500 watts

Electric range, 8,000–12,000 watts

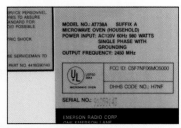
Microwave, 600–1,500 watts

Dishwasher, 1,000–1,500 watts

Garbage disposer, 400–850 watts

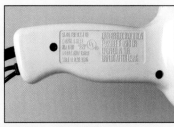
Hair dryer, 500–1,500 watts

Refrigerator, 200–700 watts

REFRESHER COURSE
Relieving an overloaded circuit

If a circuit often blows a fuse or trips a breaker, too many appliances, lights, and tools are sharing it. List the wattage ratings of all the users on the circuit. Add the numbers; the total probably exceeds the safe capacity.

The solution may be as simple as plugging an appliance into a nearby receptacle that is on another circuit. If that is not possible, install a wallmounted extension cord (center) or a cord in a protective channel (right) so you can plug the device into a receptacle on another circuit.

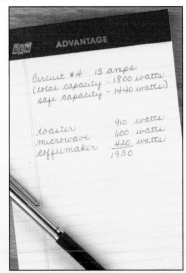

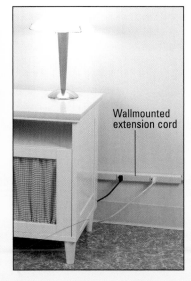
Wallmounted extension cord

Wallmounted channel

CHECKING OUT YOUR BASIC SERVICE

Installing a new circuit is not difficult. First make sure your service panel can handle the extra load. A service panel with too many circuits is dangerous.

Fuse boxes rarely have space for new circuits. If you have a fuse box and need new service, replace the fuse box with a new service panel or install a subpanel (pages 280–281).

If you see an available slot in a breaker box, either an open space or a knockout that can be removed, chances are you can simply install a new breaker there and run cable to it. If there is no open space, local codes may allow you to replace a single breaker with a tandem breaker, which supplies power to two circuits (page 278).

Make sure you do not overload your service panel. A panel's total amperage is printed near or on the main circuit breaker, which controls all the circuits in the panel. Most breaker boxes are 100, 150, or 200 amps. Add the amperages of all the individual breakers in the box. The total may be more than twice the total amperage of the box. For example a 100-amp service panel may have circuit breakers that add up to more than 200 amps. This is normal.

Take your total amperages and the name of the service panel manufacturer with you to meet with the inspector to ask about adding another circuit. Or compute your home's power needs using the information at right.

Evaluating a home's total loads

A 60-amp service is probably inadequate for a modern home. A 100-amp service is good for a home of less than 3,000 square feet that does not have central air-conditioning or electric heat. A home larger than 2,000 square feet that has central air-conditioning or electric heat probably needs a 200-amp service.

1. Calculate your total needs. First multiply the square footage of all the living areas times three watts. This is the total lighting and receptacle needs.

2. Add 1500 watts for each kitchen small-appliance circuit and laundry room circuit.

3. Add the wattages for all appliances that are on their own circuits, such as an electric dryer, water heater, or range; or a window air-conditioner. (Check the nameplates and remember that watts = volts times amps.)

4. Add the three numbers. Figure the first 10,000 watts at 100 percent and the remaining watts at 40 percent.

5. Add the wattage of either the heating unit or the central air-conditioner—whichever is greater.

6. Divide this figure by 230. This figure tells how many amps a home needs.

Example

Here's a sample calculation for a 2,000-square-foot home with central air:

1. 2,000 square feet × 3 =	6,000 watts
2. Two kitchen small-appliance circuits plus a laundry-room circuit: 3 × 1,500 =	4,500 watts
3. Water heater: 5,000 watts Dishwasher: 1,200 watts Electric dryer: 5,500 watts =	11,700 watts
	22,200 watts
4. First 10,000 at 100 percent =	10,000 watts
Remaining 12,200 at 40 percent =	4,880 watts
Subtotal =	**14,880 watts**
5. Central air =	4,000 watts
Total =	**18,800 watts**
6. Total divided by 230 =	÷ 230
(100-amp service will be enough for this home.)	**82 amps**

REFRESHER COURSE
Inspecting a service panel

A service panel should be located where adults can get to it easily but children can't. Any exposed cables leading to it should be firmly attached to the wall and clamped tightly to knockout holes in the panel. If there are any open holes, cover them with a knockout plug (available at hardware stores).

If a 14-gauge wire is connected to a 20-amp circuit breaker or fuse, replace the breaker or fuse with one that is 15 amps to prevent the wire from overheating. In most cases a 20-amp fuse or breaker should connect to a 12-gauge wire; a 30-amp fuse or breaker should connect to a 10-gauge wire.

Wires should run in a fairly orderly way around the perimeter of the panel. If you find a hopeless tangle, call in an electrician for an evaluation. Also call in a pro if you find melted or nicked wire insulation, any signs of fire, or extensive rust.

In an older home there's a good chance that new wiring has been added to a service panel. It may have been done by a pro but could be amateur work too. So check all the connections.

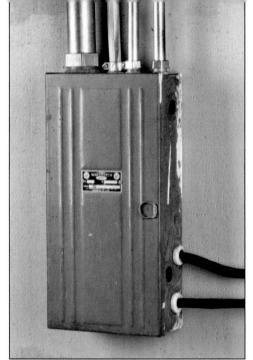

Small fuse box: A 60-amp fuse box may be found in an older home that has not had its wiring upgraded. It can supply power to only one 240-volt appliance and is probably inadequate for a home of 1,200 square feet or more.

Medium-size service: A 100-amp service panel provides enough power for a medium-size home, even if it has several 240-volt appliances and central air-conditioning (opposite page).

Large capacity: Many newer homes and some older large homes have a 150- or 200-amp service panel. Unless the home is a mansion, there is virtually no way to overload it.

STANLEY PRO TIP: **Making a room in a service panel**

Knockout tab

Tandem breaker

If a service panel has an unused slot for a circuit breaker, installing a new breaker is easy. Poke and twist out the knockout tab and install the new breaker (pages 278–279).

If there is no open space, codes may permit you to replace a single breaker with a tandem breaker, which supplies two circuits while taking up only one space. Ask an inspector.

Add capacity with a subpanel

Subpanel

If you can't fit new breakers into the service panel, either hire a pro to install a new service panel or add a subpanel. Pages 280–281 show you how to do this.

ELECTRICITY FROM THE SUN

Photovoltaics—solar cells—are a clean way to get free electricity from the sun. The contradiction of photovoltaics is that while you really can get something for nothing, it costs you initially.

A photovoltaic (PV) system on your roof or in your backyard produces pollution-free power at no cost. But once you factor in the cost of buying the solar cells and installing a system, the cost of "free" rises. The final cost depends on the type of solar cell (they vary in cost and efficiency), tax incentives you may receive, whether you can sell excess power to the electric company, and how much the sun shines.

The heart of a PV system is the array of solar cells, which may be rigid panels (most efficient) or thin flexible sheets (least efficient). Some double as roof shingles—less efficient, but the cost is reduced by what roofing would cost. It might take about 1,500 square feet of PV shingles to provide enough power for a house. Only 500 square feet of more efficient—but more expensive—rigid panels might provide the same power.

Photovoltaic cells

Types of photovotaic panels

Three basic types of solar cells are used in home photovoltaic systems.

Monocrystalline silicon panels are single large sheets of silicon, with metal strips laid across to collect electricity. They are the most expensive solar cells but also the most efficient, converting 15 to 18 percent of the available solar energy into electricity. They are often but not always the most cost-efficient.

Polycrystalline silicon panels are made from a block of silicon cut into a series of smaller cells. They are less expensive but are only 12 to 14 percent efficient.

Thin film panels are made of a thin layer of noncrystalline silicon, which can be sprayed on a variety of backings. They are inexpensive to manufacture and can be used in a variety of ways: Thin film panels are the basis for both photovoltaic shingles and photovoltaic windows. With their versatility and lower price come a drawback—they are only 5 to 6 percent efficient.

Group III-V technologies, panels made of materials found in Group III and Group V of the periodic table, reach 25 percent efficiency. But their high price limits them to aerospace applications.

Type of installations

In the northern hemisphere solar panels always face south because there is always at least some sun in the southern sky. The angle of the sun varies in summer and winter, and some systems adjust for the change. Others mount the array at an angle equal to the system's latitude, an angle which, on average, gives the most power. Still other systems are simply placed in a convenient location, with the hope that savings during installation offset the cost of inefficiency. Here are some ways to install solar arrays:

Building integrated photovoltaics (BIPV). These building materials have thin-film photovoltaic surfaces built in. They produce electricity while doubling as an integral part of the building. The most common BIPVs are shingles and windows.

Rack structures. Cells are mounted in a panel angled toward the sun for maximum efficiency year-round. They can be mounted on the roof or on the ground.

Flat mounting. Flat-mounted arrays are mounted on a south-facing roof. Gable roofs may approach the ideal angle of rack structures. On a flat roof efficiency drops.

Pole mounting. Similar to rack mounting pole mounting strategically places cells in areas where sunlight is patchy because of trees, terrain, or buildings.

Tracking structures. Tracking structures follow the sun, getting maximum efficiency out of the cells mounted in them.

Solar cells produce direct current, but houses run on alternating current. An inverter will change DC to AC. An inverter is neither complex nor expensive.

Once the sun stops shining, solar cells stop producing power. You can go solar during the day and use power from the electrical utility at night. If you're in one of 35 states that allow it, you can sell excess solar electricity to the power company during the day and buy power at night. Away from utility lines, as in the case of a remote cabin, batteries can store PV power collected during the day for use at night.

Installing a photovoltaic system is not a do-it-yourself project. The wiring is sophisticated, and you may tie into the power company's lines. Siting is crucial to the efficiency of a system.

Solar systems can last 20 to 30 years with a warranty for perhaps 5 years, if the system is professionally installed. The warranty is one of the standards by which you should judge a system. Given equal costs, efficiency, and experience, choose the system with the best warranty.

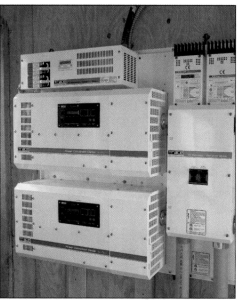

Photovoltaic cells (left and below left) convert sunlight to electricity during sunny days. Controls (above) convert the direct current from the cells to alternating current for household use and connect the home to the utility grid to draw power when the cells are inactive.

What does it cost?

A five-kilowatt system capable of powering the average home costs from $30,000 to $40,000 and has a life expectancy of 20–30 years. Before incentives this works out to about 25 cents per kilowatt-hour, double to quadruple what most utilities charge.

Incentives can reduce some of the cost. Among the incentives are one-time grants that pay back part of your initial investment. They're often paid at $4 or $5 per kilowatt, or $20,000–$25,000 on a five-kilowatt system. Some states offer tax incentives, and you may make money selling power back to the electric company. You can take a federal income tax interest deduction if you finance the system through a second mortgage.

Costs, incentives, and economic feasibility of a PV system can vary widely:

■ A California study found that after savings and grants, a system providing about two-thirds of a California household's power would cost about $6 a month.

■ A study in New York found that a system large enough to power an entire house there would pay for itself in eight to nine years.

■ In Philadelphia half the cost of a $20,000 system providing 70 percent of a household's power is returned in rebates. The system would make about $100 a year above the cost of added electricity. But at $100 a year, paying the $10,000 balance would take 100 years.

You can determine what is available to you through the Database of State Incentives for Renewables and Efficiency (DSIRE) at www.dsireusa.org. Click on the state you live in to see a list of available incentives.

DRAWING PLANS

Carefully drawn plans help show the building inspector that you've thought through your project. And spending an extra hour or two with pencil and paper helps you spot potential problems before you begin tearing into walls, saving you time and expense in the long run.

A drawing must include the locations and types of fixtures, switches, receptacles, hardwired appliances, and cables. On an attached sheet provide a list of materials.

Drawing plans

Get a pad of graph paper, a straightedge, a compass, and several colored pencils if you are installing several circuits. Make a scale drawing of the room, including features such as counters and cabinets.

First make a rough drawing. Use the symbols shown below or get a list of symbols from your local building department. Make a quick freehand drawing, using colored pencils to indicate each circuit. Are the switches in convenient locations? Are all the circuits correctly loaded (pages 148–149)? Do you have enough receptacles, and are they easy to reach? Once you've made your final decisions, draw a neat, final version of the plan.

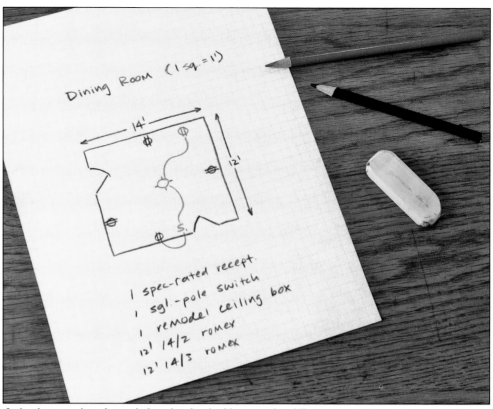

A simple extension of an existing circuit—in this example adding a receptacle and a switched light fixture—is easy to draw. Don't take the task lightly: Use the correct symbols and make the drawing clear and neat.

Electrical symbols

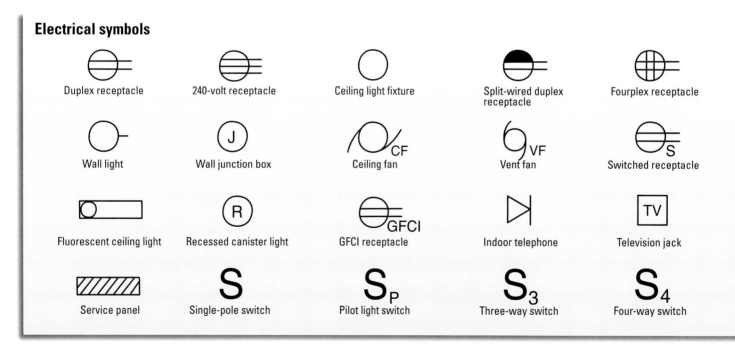

Duplex receptacle	240-volt receptacle	Ceiling light fixture	Split-wired duplex receptacle	Fourplex receptacle
Wall light	Wall junction box	Ceiling fan	Vent fan	Switched receptacle
Fluorescent ceiling light	Recessed canister light	GFCI receptacle	Indoor telephone	Television jack
Service panel	Single-pole switch	Pilot light switch	Three-way switch	Four-way switch

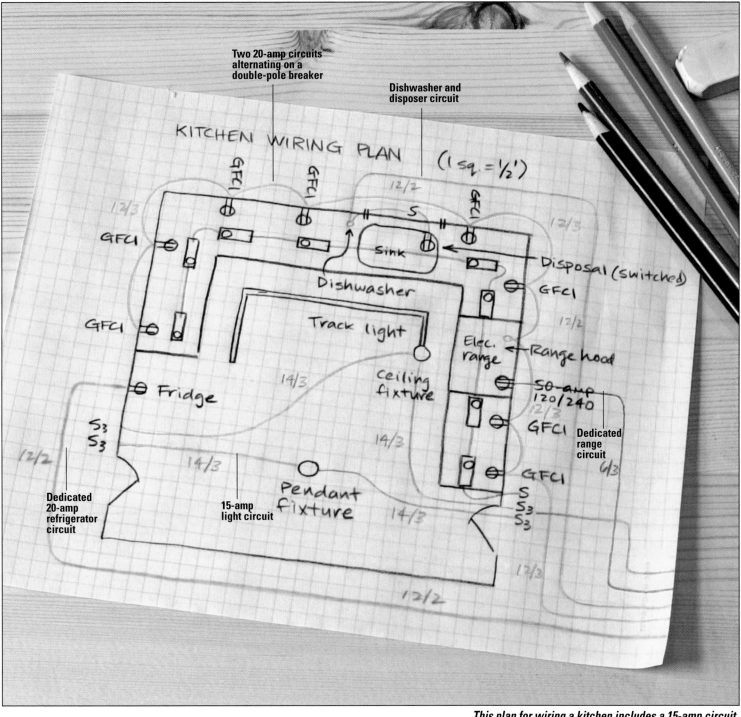

Two 20-amp circuits alternating on a double-pole breaker

Dishwasher and disposer circuit

KITCHEN WIRING PLAN (1 sq. = ½')

GFCI
GFCI
GFCI
12/3
12/2
12/3
GFCI
S
Sink
GFCI
Disposal (switched)
GFCI
Dishwasher
12/2
Track light
Elec. range
Range hood
GFCI
14/3
ceiling fixture
50-amp 120/240
12/3
GFCI
Dedicated range circuit
Fridge
S₃
S₃
14/3
GFCI
S
S₃
S₃
12/2
14/3
14/3
6/3
Dedicated 20-amp refrigerator circuit
Pendant fixture
15-amp light circuit
14/3
12/3
12/2

This plan for wiring a kitchen includes a 15-amp circuit for lights, some controlled by three-way switches. A 20-amp refrigerator circuit has been added, as well as two 20-amp small-appliance circuits and a 20-amp circuit for the dishwasher and garbage disposer. The range has its own circuit.

Safe capacity
To make sure the planned circuits aren't overloaded, check page 148 for how to calculate safe capacity.

Photocopy the floor plan
For complex projects draw your floor plan, then make several photocopies. This allows you to sketch out several trial plans.

INSTALLING CABLE & BOXES

In a typical wiring project, installing cable and boxes can take four or five times as long as making the wiring connections. It's important to plan cable runs and box placement carefully.

Getting the right materials

All the materials you plan to install need the approval of your local building department. Local electrical codes determine the type of cable you need, as well as whether the boxes should be plastic or metal. Buy boxes that are as large as possible or consult pages 20–21 to make sure your boxes are large enough for the wires they hold.

Cable, boxes, receptacles, and switches are not expensive, and you can return them if you do not use them. So buy more than you think you need to save trips back to the home center. Purchase plenty of the little items needed for a project too—straps or staples, nail guards, electrician's tape, and wire nuts of several sizes.

Plan your work

Be sure you understand exactly how each installation is to be wired. Consult the specific projects described in this book. Follow them from start to finish. Draw a plan and make a materials list. Have your local building department approve them. Buy all the materials you need and store them in an uncluttered space so you can easily get at what you need when you need it.

The order of work

Determine how to connect to power (pages 166–167). When working in exposed framing (in a new addition or if the drywall or plaster has been removed), first install the boxes, then drill holes and run the cable (pages 168–171).

If you are working in finished walls and ceilings, first cut holes for the boxes (page 172). Run the cable through a basement or attic or fish it through the walls (pages 174–177). Then install the boxes (page 173).

Here's how to install the backbone of a new circuit—boxes to hold devices and cable to carry power.

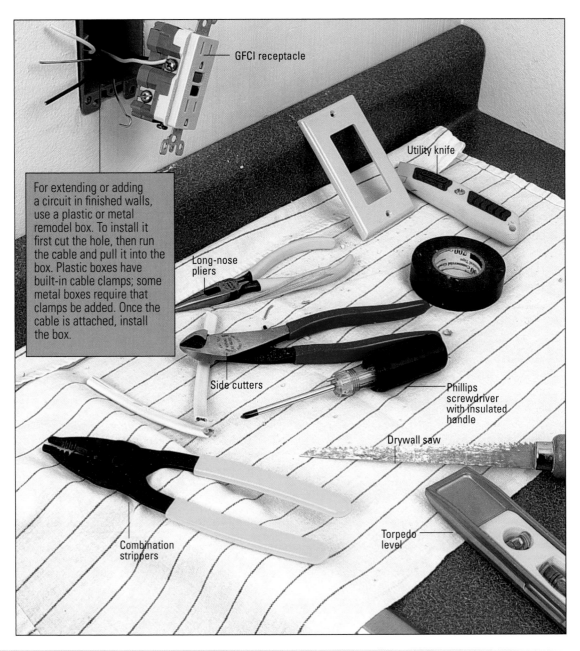

GFCI receptacle

Utility knife

For extending or adding a circuit in finished walls, use a plastic or metal remodel box. To install it first cut the hole, then run the cable and pull it into the box. Plastic boxes have built-in cable clamps; some metal boxes require that clamps be added. Once the cable is attached, install the box.

Long-nose pliers

Side cutters

Phillips screwdriver with insulated handle

Drywall saw

Combination strippers

Torpedo level

To attach a new receptacle or switch, start by removing sheathing from cable (page 158) and strip wire ends—1 inch for a splice or ¾ inch for a terminal connection—using a pair of combination strippers. Poke the stripped wires into the box and clamp the cable. If you need to splice two or more wires, hold them side by side, grab their ends with a pair of lineman's pliers, and twist them together to form a uniform spiral. Snip off the end and twist on a wire nut of the correct size (page 23). To connect a wire to a terminal, use long-nose pliers or a wire-bending screwdriver to form a clockwise loop in the wire end. Slip the loop over a loosened terminal screw, squeeze the wire tight to the screw threads, and tighten the screw.

Grabbing power
page 166

Installing boxes in framing
page 168

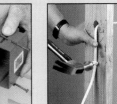

Running cable in framing
page 169

Working with metal studs
page 171

Installing boxes in finished walls
page 172

Running cable through finished rooms
page 174

Patching walls
page 178

STRIPPING AND CLAMPING NM CABLE

Nonmetallic (NM) cable is easy to work with and inexpensive, so it's not surprising that it is the most common type of cable used in household wiring.

NM cable is sold in lengths of 25, 50, or 100 feet, or more. When in doubt buy the larger package—it doesn't cost much more and it may come in handy later.

NM's plastic sheathing does not protect the wires much, so keep it out of harm's way. If the cable might get wet, install UF (underground feed) cable, which encases wires in molded plastic. Wherever cable is exposed—in a garage or basement— many local codes call for armored cable or conduit (pages 160–164).

Codes call for running NM through the center of studs so drywall nails cannot damage it. If the cable is 1¼ inches or less from the edge of a framing member, install a protective nailing plate (page 170). Some codes require metal plates even if the cable is in the center of a stud.

Take care not to damage wire insulation when working with NM cable. Slit the sheathing right down the middle using a sharp utility knife. To avoid slicing the wire insulation, don't cut too deep. Or use the sheathing stripper shown below.

When cutting cable to length, leave yourself an extra foot or two. If you make a mistake while stripping, you can recut the cable and try again.

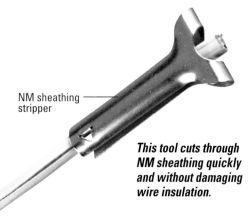

NM sheathing stripper

This tool cuts through NM sheathing quickly and without damaging wire insulation.

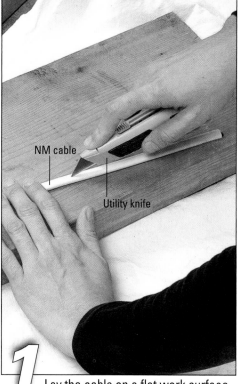

NM cable

Utility knife

1 Lay the cable on a flat work surface such as a small sheet of plywood. Starting 8–10 inches from the end, insert the tip of a utility knife blade into the center of the cable, pushing just hard enough to cut through the sheathing.

Pierce sheathing without nicking wires

2 Slice the sheathing, exerting even pressure. You feel the tip of the knife rubbing against the bare ground wire as you slice. With practice you can cut evenly and quickly without damaging wire insulation.

WHAT IF... You have three-wire cable?

NM cable that holds three wires (plus the ground) is round rather than flat. If you cut through the sheathing too deeply, you hit insulated wire rather than the ground wire. Practice cutting through the sheathing. Always examine the wires for damage after removing the sheathing.

REFRESHER COURSE Grounding NM cable

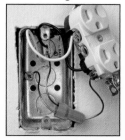

If the box is metal, code requires it to be grounded. The surest method is to connect both the device and the box to the ground wire using pigtails.

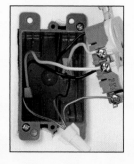

If the box is plastic, simply connect the ground wire to the device's grounding terminal.

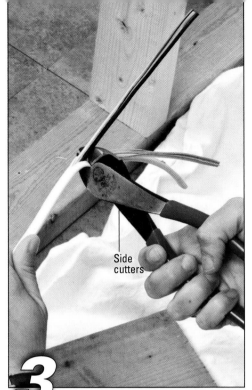

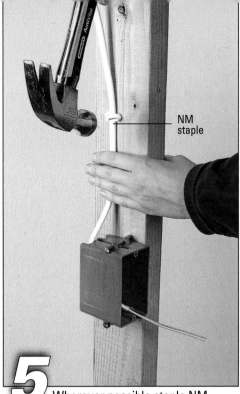

3 Pull back the plastic sheathing, as well as the paper that wraps the wires, exposing 8–12 inches of wire. Snip back the sheathing and paper with side cutters. If you use a utility knife, cut away from the wires to avoid cutting or nicking the insulation.

Side cutters

4 Insert the wires into the box. With this type of plastic box, push the wires through a hole, which has a tab that grabs the cable. Check that about ½ inch of sheathing is visible inside the box. Other types of boxes use other clamping methods.

5 Wherever possible staple NM cable firmly to a framing member, out of reach of nails. Staple cable within 8 inches of the box and every 2–4 feet along the run of the cable. Check your local building codes.

NM staple

OTHER CLAMPING METHODS

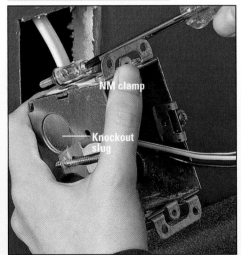

NM clamp

Knockout slug

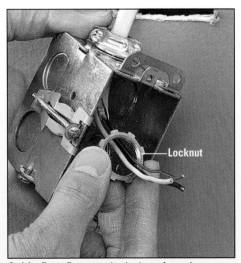

Locknut

Clamp on box: Remove a knockout slug from a metal box and fasten an NM clamp in the hole. Insert the clamp and tighten the locknut. Insert the cable through the clamp; tighten the screws.

Cable first: Remove the locknut from the cable clamp and fasten the clamp to the cable. Then insert the cable with clamp body into the box, slide on the locknut, and tighten it.

Built-in clamps: Some boxes have built-in clamps. Slide the cable behind the clamp and tighten the screw.

ARMORED CABLE

Some municipalities require either armored cable or conduit (pages 162–164) rather than NM. Even if your local codes do not demand it, you may choose to install armored cable for added safety, especially wherever cable is exposed.

Pluses and minuses
The coiled metal sheathing that wraps armored cable protects its wires from puncture by nails, unless a nail hits it dead-center. (Even conduit cannot offer absolute protection against a direct hit.) You may want to run armored cable behind moldings where it comes near nails (pages 174–175). Armored cable costs more than NM, takes longer to strip and clamp, and can't make tight turns. With some practice you can install armored cable nearly as quickly as NM cable.

BX cable has no ground wire (opposite, bottom right), is common in older homes, and is still available in some areas. Local code may limit use of BX to no more than 6 feet; then ground wire must be used. MC cable has a green-insulated ground wire, used like the bare ground wire in NM cable.

REFRESHER COURSE
Grounding MC cable

MC cable has a ground wire. Attach it the same way you would the ground wire in NM cable (page 158), except strip the green insulation first.

1 Bend the cable about 10 inches from its end and squeeze with your hand until the coils of the armor come apart. If you can't do this by hand, use pliers or employ one of the other cutting methods shown below.

2 Firmly grip the cable on each side of the cut and twist until the split-apart armor coil pops out, away from the wires. Use two pairs of pliers if you can't do this by hand.

OTHER CUTTING METHODS

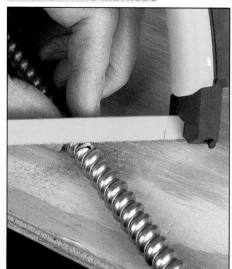

You can cut the cable with a **hacksaw.** Cut through just one of the coils and no more, so you won't damage any wires. Then twist and pull off the waste piece.

An **armored-cable cutter** cuts at just the right depth. Adjust it for the size of cable, slip in the cable, and turn the crank.

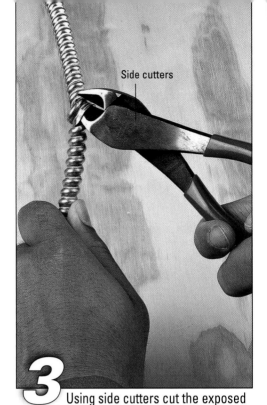

Side cutters

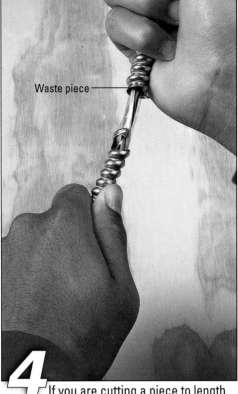

Waste piece

Bonding strip

3 Using side cutters cut the exposed coil of sheathing. You may have to grab the coil with the side cutters and work it back and forth to open and make the cut.

4 If you are cutting a piece to length, slide back the sheathing and cut through the wires. Otherwise slide the waste piece off and throw it away.

5 Cut off any sharp points of sheathing using side cutters. Remove the paper wrapping and any thin plastic strips. If the cable is BX it has a thin metal bonding strip. Cut it to about 2 inches.

STANLEY PRO TIP: **Clamping armored cable**

Bushing

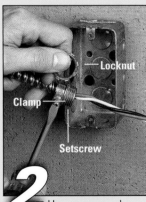

Locknut
Clamp
Setscrew

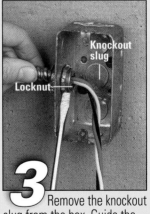

Knockout slug
Locknut

1 If the cable did not come with a bag of antishort bushings, purchase some. Slip a bushing over the wires and slide it into the sheathing so it protects wires from the cut end of the armor.

2 Use an armored-cable clamp, which has a single setscrew. Remove the locknut and slide the clamp over the wires and onto the bushing. Then tighten the setscrew to secure the clamp to the cable.

3 Remove the knockout slug from the box. Guide the wires and the clamp through the hole. Slip the locknut over the wires and screw it onto the clamp. Tighten the nut by levering it with a screwdriver or tapping it with a screwdriver and hammer.

BX CABLE WITH A BONDING STRIP

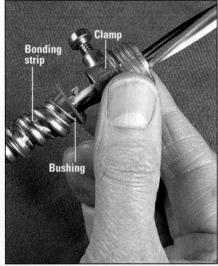

Clamp
Bonding strip
Bushing

The metal sheathing of BX cable acts as the ground; a thin metal bonding strip helps ensure a conductive connection. Before putting on a cable clamp, wrap 2 inches of the bonding strip around the sheathing.

METAL CONDUIT

onduit offers superior protection and safety for wires. Even if local codes permit NM or armored cable in a basement, garage, attic, or crawlspace, consider installing conduit to protect wiring.

Choosing conduit

Metal conduit comes in several thicknesses. For most interior home installations, EMT (also called thinwall) is strong enough. Outdoors use intermediate metal conduit (IMC) or PVC conduit (page 164). PVC is sometimes used indoors too.

Metal conduit may serve as the path for grounding, or local codes may require you to run a green-insulated ground wire. If you use PVC pipe, you definitely need a ground wire, either green-insulated or bare copper. **If there is no ground wire, make sure all the metal conduit connections are firm; a loose joint could break the ground path.**

Conduit fittings

A conduit bender, used by professional electricians, is a fairly expensive tool that takes time to master. Unless you are running lots of metal conduit, save time by buying prebent fittings. A coupling joins two pieces of conduit end to end. A sweep makes a slow turn, allowing wires to slide easily. A pulling elbow makes a sharper turn.

The setscrew fittings shown here are commonly used with EMT conduit; they provide joints that are firm but not waterproof. For weathertight joints use IMC conduit and compression fittings (page 263).

Flexible metal conduit

Flexible metal conduit, also called Greenfield, is like armored cable without the wires. It's not cheap, so typically it is used only in places where it would be difficult to run conduit.

When installing a hardwired appliance, such as an electric water heater or cooktop (page 277), buy an electrical whip, a section of armored cable with the correct fittings for attachment to that appliance.

Torpedo level · Offset fitting · Handy box

1 Anchor metal boxes to the wall with screws. For exposed wiring use handy boxes, which have rounded edges and metal covers. An offset fitting allows the conduit to run tight up against the wall.

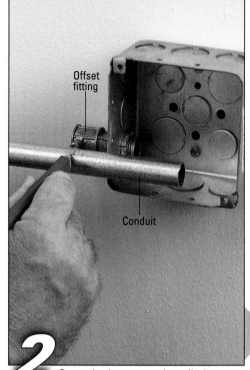

Offset fitting · Conduit

2 Once the boxes are installed, measure the conduit for cutting. The surest method is to hold a piece in place and mark it, rather than using a tape measure. Remember that the conduit slides about an inch into each fitting.

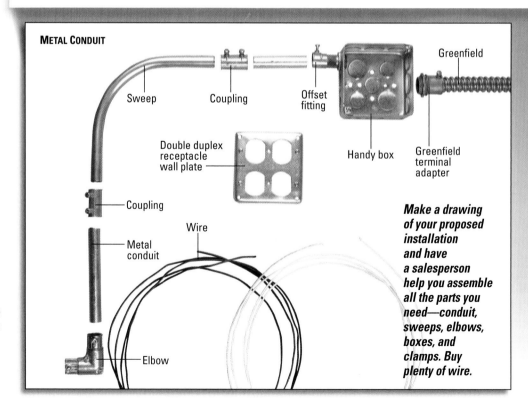

METAL CONDUIT

Sweep · Coupling · Offset fitting · Greenfield · Double duplex receptacle wall plate · Handy box · Greenfield terminal adapter · Coupling · Metal conduit · Wire · Elbow

Make a drawing of your proposed installation and have a salesperson help you assemble all the parts you need—conduit, sweeps, elbows, boxes, and clamps. Buy plenty of wire.

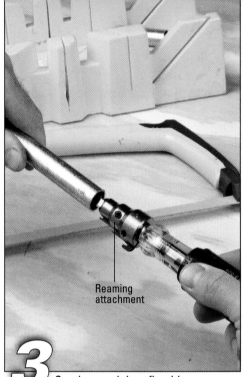

Offset fitting

Setscrew

One-hole strap

Reaming attachment

3 Cut the conduit to fit with a hacksaw. Do not use a tubing cutter, which creates sharp edges inside the conduit that could damage wire insulation. Remove the burrs inside and out with a conduit-reaming attachment on a screwdriver.

4 Slide the conduit all the way into a fitting and tighten the setscrew. Test to make sure the connection is tight. (If you are not installing a ground wire, these connections are critical for grounding.)

5 Anchor the conduit with a one- or two-hole strap at least every 6 feet and within 2 feet of each box. The larger the conduit, the closer the straps need to be. Check with local codes. Screws should be driven into joists or studs, not just drywall.

Conduit that's large enough

Make sure the wires have ample room inside the conduit to slide through easily. Codes have detailed rules regarding conduit size, but generally ½-inch conduit is large enough for five or fewer wires; ¾-inch conduit is used for more than five wires. When in doubt or if you might run more wire in the future, buy the larger size—it doesn't cost much more.

Anchoring conduit

Anchor conduit with one- or two-hole straps every 6 feet and within 2 feet of each box.

A pulling elbow every fourth turn

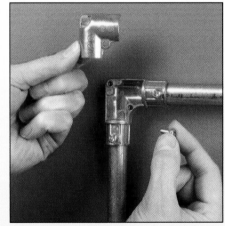

With every turn it gets harder for the wires to slide through a conduit. If the conduit makes more than three turns before entering a box, install a pulling elbow. Never make a splice here, just use it as an access point when pulling wires.

STANLEY PRO TIP
Anchoring to masonry

To attach boxes and straps to concrete, block, or brick, buy masonry screws and the correct masonry bit. Level the box and drill pilot holes.

Drive a masonry screw into the pilot hole, being careful not to overtighten it. The combination of proper hole and screw provides a much more secure attachment than a plastic anchor.

PVC CONDUIT

Plastic conduit is nearly as durable as metal conduit, and it costs less. Some local codes permit it for exposed indoor wiring as well as for outdoor installations.

When installing PVC connect four or five pieces in a dry run, then dismantle and glue the pieces together. When making a turn take care that the elbow or sweep faces in exactly the correct direction when you glue it. Once the glue sets there's no way to make adjustments. Work in a well-ventilated area when using PVC primer and cement; the fumes are powerful and dangerous.

Consult your local codes for the correct PVC cement. You may be required to apply purple-colored primer to every piece before you apply the cement. **Green-insulated ground wire always should run through PVC conduit.**

Backsaw
Miter box

1 Install PVC boxes, then measure and mark the conduit for a cut. Cut with a backsaw and miter box, or a hacksaw, or a circular saw equipped with a plywood blade.

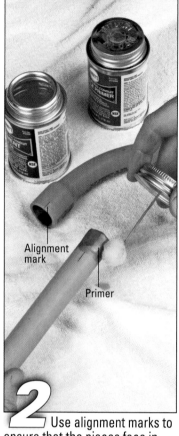

Alignment mark
Primer

2 Use alignment marks to ensure that the pieces face in the correct direction. Apply PVC primer (if needed) and cement to the outside of the conduit and to the inside of the fitting.

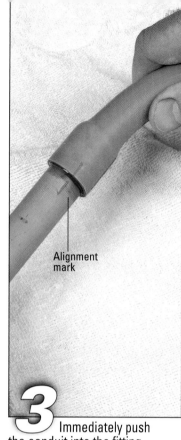

Alignment mark

3 Immediately push the conduit into the fitting, twisting slightly to align the marks. Hold the pieces together for about 10 seconds; wipe away excess cement.

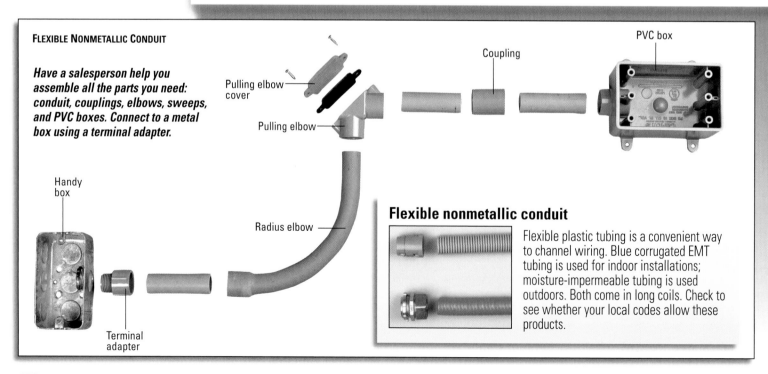

FLEXIBLE NONMETALLIC CONDUIT

Have a salesperson help you assemble all the parts you need: conduit, couplings, elbows, sweeps, and PVC boxes. Connect to a metal box using a terminal adapter.

PVC box
Coupling
Pulling elbow cover
Pulling elbow
Handy box
Radius elbow
Terminal adapter

Flexible nonmetallic conduit

Flexible plastic tubing is a convenient way to channel wiring. Blue corrugated EMT tubing is used for indoor installations; moisture-impermeable tubing is used outdoors. Both come in long coils. Check to see whether your local codes allow these products.

PULLING WIRES THROUGH CONDUIT

If wires travel less than 6 feet through conduit and make only one or two turns, you may be able to simply push them through. For longer runs use a fish tape.

If wires become kinked while you work, they get stuck. Have a helper feed the wire carefully from one end of the conduit while you pull at the other end. If you work alone precut the wires (leave yourself an extra 2 feet or so) and unroll them so they can slide smoothly through the conduit.

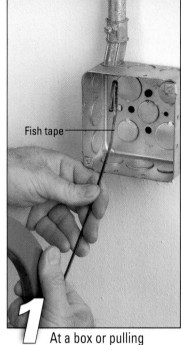

Fish tape

1 At a box or pulling elbow, push the fish tape into the conduit and thread it back to the point of entry.

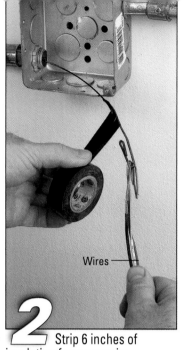

Wires

2 Strip 6 inches of insulation from one wire, 8 inches from another wire, 10 inches from a third wire, and so on. Fold the wires over the fish tape, as shown, and wrap tightly with electrician's tape.

3 Pull smoothly, using long strokes to avoid stopping and starting. If the wires get stuck, back up a foot or so and start again.

TEAM UP TO PULL WIRE THROUGH CONDUIT

Loop and tape wires to fish tape.

Conduit

Wires

Fish tape

Pull wires from box to box. If there are more than three turns between boxes, use a pulling elbow (page 163).

STANLEY PRO TIP

Pulling lubricant

If the pulling gets tough, try squirting some pulling lubricant onto the wires. Don't use soap, detergent, oil, or grease, which can damage wire insulation.

GRABBING POWER

When planning new electrical service, begin by deciding where you can tap into power. If you are adding a couple of receptacles or lights, it is usually easiest to grab power from a nearby receptacle or junction box. First, however, make sure the new service doesn't overload the circuit (pages 148–149).

If nearby boxes are on circuits that do not have enough available wattage for the new service, try a box farther away. If no circuit is usable or if the new service needs its own circuit, run cable all the way to the service panel and connect to a new circuit breaker (pages 278–279).

If you need to run cable through walls and ceilings to get at power, see pages 172–179.

PRESTART CHECKLIST

☐ **TIME**
About 2 hours to connect new cable to an existing receptacle or junction box (not including cutting a pathway for the cable and patching walls)

☐ **TOOLS**
Voltage tester, drill, pry bar, saw, close-work hacksaw or reciprocating saw, hammer, screwdriver, strippers, long-nose pliers, lineman's pliers

☐ **SKILLS**
Stripping wire and connecting wire to terminals, running cable through walls, prying and cutting nails

☐ **PREP**
Spread a drop cloth or towel on the floor. Run cable to the box from which you grab power.

☐ **MATERIALS**
New cable, wire nuts, electrician's tape, cable clamps, remodel box

1 To grab power from a receptacle, make a load list to verify that there is room on the circuit for new service. **Shut off power to the circuit and test that power is not present.** Disconnect the receptacle.

2 If the box is inside a wall, cut a hole into the wall to get at the box or pull the box out. Pry with a flat pry bar, then remove the nails or cut through them with a close-work hacksaw or reciprocating saw.

Grabbing power from a junction box and switch

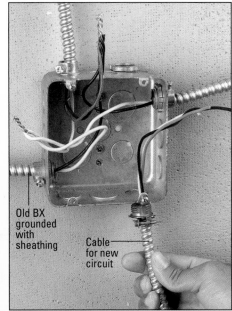

To grab power from a junction box, **shut off power,** remove wire nuts, and splice the new wires. You may need to cover the resulting splices with larger wire nuts.

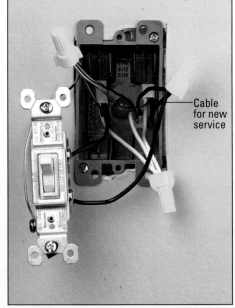

You can grab power from a switch box only if power enters the box (rather than going to the fixture) and two cables are present. Connect with pigtails as shown.

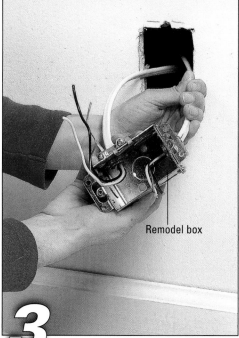

Remodel box

3 Pull out the box carefully—the cable may be stapled to a stud. Disconnect the cable(s) from the old box. Choose a remodel box to fit the hole (pages 19–20). Clamp the old and new cables to the remodel box.

4 Push the remodel box back into place and clamp it to the wall.

5 If the new receptacle is at the end of the run (with only one cable entering the box), simply connect the new wires to the proper terminals and connect the grounds.

STANLEY PRO TIP

Wire into the old box

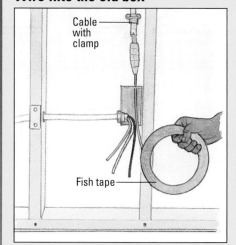

Cable with clamp

Fish tape

You may be able to avoid removing the old box. Pry out a knockout slug and run a fish tape up through the hole. Attach the tape to cable that has been stripped and has a clamp attached (with the locknut removed). Pull the wires through, seat the clamp, and screw on the locknut.

WHAT IF...
You grab power from a mid-run receptacle?

If two cables enter the box, the receptacle is in the middle of a run. Splice the wires and connect to terminals with pigtails as shown. The purpose of pigtails is to avoid multiple connections to one terminal screw where they could easily short or come loose. Make pigtails by removing the sheathing from about 8 inches of NM cable. Strip about ¾ inch for each end of the black and white wires and attach them as shown.

Pigtail

Pigtail

Code issues

Cable must be clamped to a box or stapled to a stud within 8 inches of the box. NM cable is the easiest to run, but some localities require armored cable or conduit. Some localities require metal rather than plastic boxes.

INSTALLING BOXES IN FRAMING

Wiring is easier before the walls and ceilings become covered with drywall or plaster (pages 172–179).

Buy switch and receptacle boxes that meet local codes and are large enough for the wires they hold (page 20). It's easy to underestimate, so buy extra supplies. At the same time you install boxes, attach fans, lights, or other fixtures that need to be hardwired.

Local codes specify where cable should run and at what height to place receptacles and switch boxes. Check codes before you begin.

PRESTART CHECKLIST

☐ **TIME**
About 1 hour to install eight boxes

☐ **TOOLS**
Hammer, tape measure, drill, screwdriver

☐ **SKILLS**
Measuring, driving nails

☐ **PREP**
Expose framing, remove obstructions in the room, make and follow a written plan that plots the location of each box.

☐ **MATERIALS**
New-work electrical boxes, 1¼-inch wood screws (not drywall screws)

1 Receptacle boxes typically sit 12 inches up from the floor. Measure with a tape measure or set your hammer upright on the floor and rest the box on top of the handle.

2 The front edge of the box must be flush with the finished wall surface, usually ½-inch-thick drywall. Some boxes have depth gauges. You can use a scrap of drywall to position the box.

3 Drive the box's nails into the stud or joist. If the box attaches with a flange, drive screws or nails to anchor the box (below).

Using a mud ring

Adapter rings, also called mud rings, are typically ½ inch or ⅝ inch thick. Choose a ring that matches the thickness of the drywall or paneling you install. Attach the box flush with the front edge of the framing member, then add the ring.

STANLEY PRO TIP

Mounting a ceiling light fixture box

Decide where you want a ceiling light fixture to go (usually the center of a room). Attach a flanged box directly to a ceiling joist (left). For more precise placement install a box attached to a hanger bar; the box slides along the bar. Note: A hanger bar cannot support a ceiling fan; you must use a fan-rated box (page 129).

RUNNING CABLE IN FRAMING

Nonmetallic (NM) cable is acceptable under most building codes; check local requirements. To run armored cable you may need to drill larger holes. Turning corners is more difficult.

If a wayward nail pierces NM cable, the result could be disastrous. Place holes in the framing out of reach of drywall nails and attach protective plates at every hole.

PRESTART CHECKLIST

☐ **TIME**
About 3 hours to run cable and attach to seven or eight wall or ceiling boxes

☐ **TOOLS**
Drill, ¾-inch spade bits, screwdriver, strippers, lineman's pliers, hammer, tape measure, level

☐ **SKILLS**
Drilling, stripping cable sheathing and wire insulation, attaching staples

☐ **PREP**
Double-check that all the boxes are correctly positioned; clear the room of all obstructions.

☐ **MATERIALS**
Correct cable (page 15), staples appropriate to cable type, nailing plates

1 Use a tape measure and level to mark holes in a straight line about 12 inches above the boxes. With a sharp spade bit, drill a ¾-inch hole through the center of each stud.

2 Uncoil cable carefully from the box to prevent kinks. Pull the cable through the holes. The cable should be fairly straight but not taut.

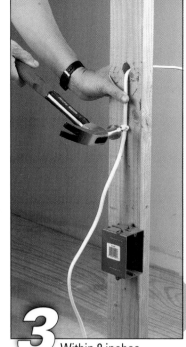

3 Within 8 inches of a plastic box or 12 inches of a metal box, anchor the cable in the middle of the stud with a staple. Drive staples every 2 feet where cable runs along a framing member.

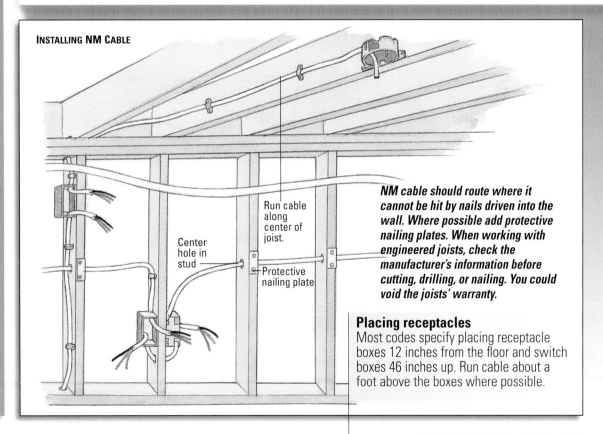

INSTALLING NM CABLE

Run cable along center of joist.

Center hole in stud

Protective nailing plate

NM cable should route where it cannot be hit by nails driven into the wall. Where possible add protective nailing plates. When working with engineered joists, check the manufacturer's information before cutting, drilling, or nailing. You could void the joists' warranty.

Placing receptacles
Most codes specify placing receptacle boxes 12 inches from the floor and switch boxes 46 inches up. Run cable about a foot above the boxes where possible.

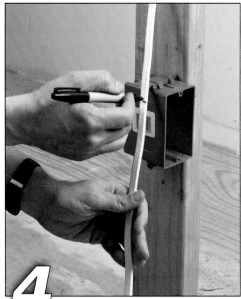

4 Mark where you will strip sheathing and cut the cable. About ½ inch of sheathing should enter the box, and the wires inside the box should be 8–12 inches long. (You can always trim them later.)

5 With a hammer and screwdriver, open the knockout. On some plastic boxes you remove the knockout entirely. For the one shown crack open one end of the tab so it can grab the cable. A metal box may have a built-in clamp, or you may have to add a clamp before sliding in the cable.

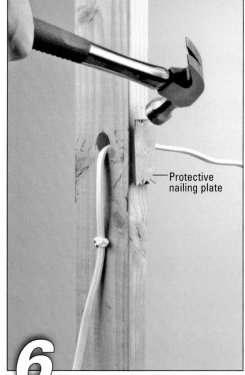

Protective nailing plate

6 Wherever a nail might accidentally pierce the cable, attach a protective nailing plate. Tap the plate into place. Attach a plate on both sides of the stud if needed.

STANLEY PRO TIP: **Turning a corner**

Corner framing

1 When you reach a corner, drill a hole into each stud. Bend the cable into an L shape.

Lineman's pliers

2 Poke the cable through the first hole and wiggle it into the next hole. When the cable starts to stick out the second hole, grab it with pliers and pull.

WHAT IF...
You have a lot of holes to drill?

A standard ⅜-inch drill may overheat after drilling four or five holes. If you have many holes to bore, rent a ½-inch right-angle drill. When using it hold on tightly and brace yourself; it has high torque and can twist around, possibly causing an injury.

WORKING WITH METAL STUDS

Metal studs save money and are easy to install. Metal studs have precut holes designed to accommodate electrical and plumbing lines. When running NM cable through metal framing, inspect the holes to be sure there are no rough or sharp edges that could damage insulation. Always use the special bushings (Step 2) designed to protect wiring.

PRESTART CHECKLIST

☐ **TIME**
About 3 hours to run cable and attach to seven or eight wall or ceiling boxes

☐ **TOOLS**
Screwdriver, tin snips, strippers, variable-speed drill, lineman's pliers, nonconducting ladder

☐ **SKILLS**
Installing metal framing, stripping cable sheathing and wire insulation, attaching bushings

☐ **PREP**
Assemble metal framing.

☐ **MATERIALS**
Bushings, cable, boxes for metal studs

1 Cut metal studs and channels with tin snips. Slide the studs into channels at the bottom and top of the wall. Drive a self-piercing screw into each joint.

Stud

Channel

Bushing

2 Where the cable runs through a stud, snap a protective bushing into place. These come in two pieces that press together.

3 Run the cable through the protective bushings. Pull the cable the same way you would pull it through holes in wood framing members.

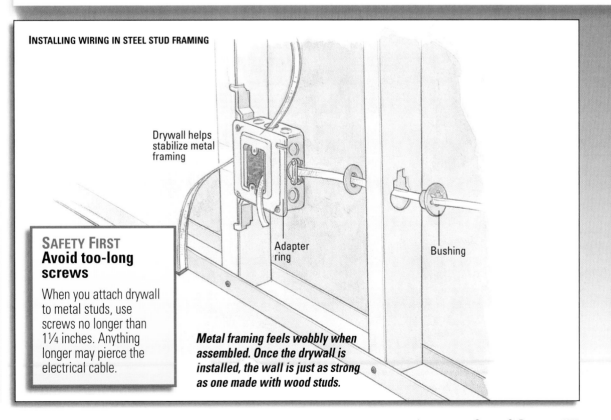

INSTALLING WIRING IN STEEL STUD FRAMING

Drywall helps stabilize metal framing

Adapter ring

Bushing

SAFETY FIRST
Avoid too-long screws

When you attach drywall to metal studs, use screws no longer than 1¼ inches. Anything longer may pierce the electrical cable.

Metal framing feels wobbly when assembled. Once the drywall is installed, the wall is just as strong as one made with wood studs.

INSTALLING BOXES IN FINISHED WALLS

Running cable through walls covered with drywall or plaster is difficult. Plan the job carefully before starting.

Remodel boxes (also called cut-in or old-work boxes) clamp to the drywall or plaster rather than attach to a framing member, making the work easier. However they are only as strong as the wall surface to which they are clamped. If the drywall or plaster is damaged, cut a larger hole and install a box that attaches directly to a stud or joist. Select boxes that meet local codes (pages 19–20). For a ceiling fan or a heavy light fixture, buy a fixture box that attaches to a fan-rated brace.

Before cutting a hole use a stud finder to make sure no joist or stud is in the way.

PRESTART CHECKLIST

☐ **TIME**
About 15 minutes to cut a hole and install a remodel box (not including cutting a pathway for the cable and patching walls)

☐ **TOOLS**
Stud finder, torpedo level, utility knife, screwdriver, hammer, drill, drywall saw (or rotary cutter or jigsaw)

☐ **SKILLS**
Measuring and cutting drywall

☐ **PREP**
Carefully plan the routes for the cables and the locations for the boxes (pages 142–145). Spread a drop cloth or large towel on the floor below.

☐ **MATERIALS**
Remodel boxes acceptable under local code, cable clamps, if needed

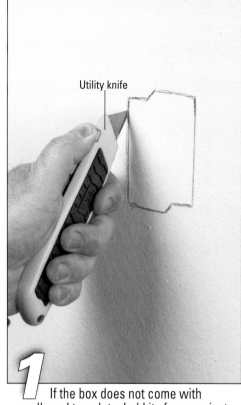

Utility knife

1 If the box does not come with a cardboard template, hold its face against the wall, use a torpedo level to make sure it is straight, and trace it. With a utility knife cut the line deeply enough to cut through the drywall paper.

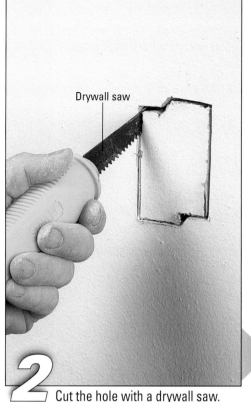

Drywall saw

2 Cut the hole with a drywall saw. Cut to the inside of the knife cut to prevent fraying the paper. Test to make sure the box fits in the hole.

WHAT IF...
The wall is made of plaster and lath?

Take your time cutting a lath-and-plaster wall—it's easy to damage the surrounding area. Most plaster is attached to ⅜-inch-thick wood lath, which cuts fairly easily if it does not vibrate. If it does vibrate as you saw, sections of plaster can loosen from the lath. It is difficult to make a neat hole in plaster and lath, so have patching plaster on hand. If plaster is attached to metal lath, cut all the way through the plaster with a knife and then cut the metal lath with side cutters.

Make several passes with a sharp knife. Drill starter holes at each corner and then cut with a jigsaw. Press the saw firmly against the wall to minimize lath vibration.

Alternatively use a rotary cutter equipped with a plaster-cutting bit. Practice first because it is hard to control.

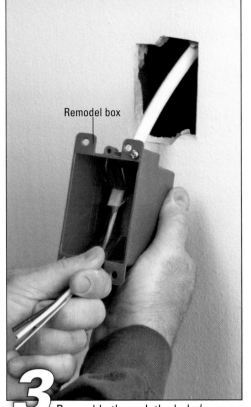

Remodel box

3 Run cable through the hole (pages 174–177). Strip 8–12 inches of sheathing and run the cable into the box. Whichever clamping method the box uses, ½ inch of sheathing should show inside the box. Tug to make sure the cable clamps tightly.

4 Push the box into the hole. If it fits tightly do not force it or you may damage the drywall. If needed use a utility knife to enlarge the hole.

5 This type of box has wings that extend outward when you start to drive the screw, then grasp the back of the drywall as the screw is tightened. Tighten the screw until you feel resistance and the box is firmly attached.

STANLEY PRO TIP
The old-fashioned way

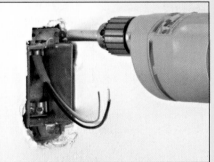

To install a box in a lath-and-plaster wall, cut the hole and remove ¾ inch of plaster above and below the hole. Loosen the setscrews and adjust the depth of the box's plaster ears so the box is flush with the wall surface. Insert the box, drill pilot holes (lath cracks easily), and drive screws through the ears into the lath.

Other remodel-box options

The round plastic ceiling box (left) has "wings" that rotate out and behind the wall surface. One metal box (center) has a flange that springs outward when the box is inserted; tightening a screw brings the flange forward. A variation on this has side clamps that move out and toward the front as screws are tightened. Yet another type (right) uses separate mounting brackets that slide in after the box is inserted and bend over the sides of the box to lock it in place.

RUNNING CABLE THROUGH FINISHED ROOMS

When running new electrical service through finished rooms, plan carefully to minimize damage to walls and ceilings. You sometimes can run cable through a basement or attic into a finished wall or ceiling. Removing a large section of drywall often results in less work than repairing many smaller holes.

Begin with a drawing of the room showing stud and joist locations. Use a stud finder to locate them. Find the easiest routes for cables and establish box locations. Moving a box may make a run easier.

Once you have a plan, cut the holes for the remodel boxes (pages 172–173), run the cable, and install the boxes. Connect the cable to a power source (pages 166–167).

Behind base molding

Base molding — Wood scrap — Pry bar — Base shoe

1 Pry away the base shoe (if any) and the base molding. Use a flat pry bar; place a scrap of wood under the bar to avoid damaging the wall.

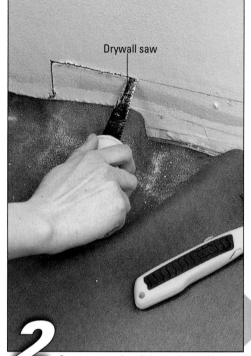

Drywall saw

2 Cut out a strip of drywall or plaster to reveal the bottom plate and studs. If possible cut low enough so you can replace the base molding to cover your work. If the molding is less than 3 inches wide, see the tip on page 175.

PRESTART CHECKLIST

☐ **TIME**
About 4 to 6 hours to run cable through a wall and a ceiling

☐ **TOOLS**
Stud finder, fish tapes, strippers, screwdriver, hammer, drill, fishing drill bit, pry bar, drywall saw or jigsaw

☐ **SKILLS**
Measuring, cutting through drywall or plaster, using fish tapes

☐ **PREP**
Spread a drop cloth on the floor of the room and cut holes for the remodel boxes.

☐ **MATERIALS**
Electrical cable, protective nailing plates, electrician's tape

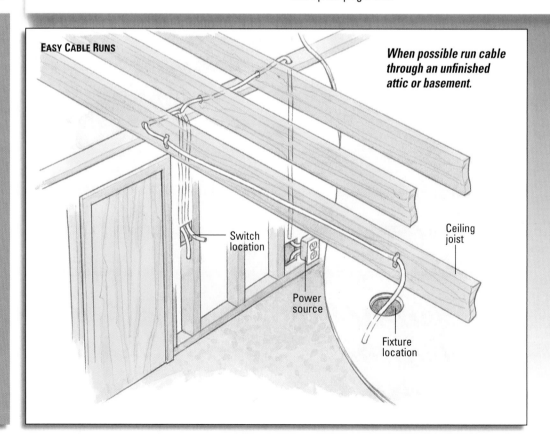

EASY CABLE RUNS

When possible run cable through an unfinished attic or basement.

Switch location — Power source — Fixture location — Ceiling joist

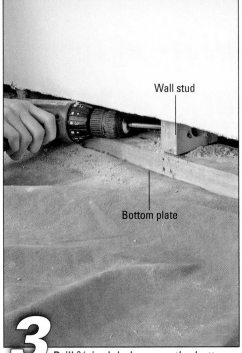

Wall stud

Bottom plate

3 Drill ¾-inch holes near the bottoms of studs. You may hit a nail or two with the drill bit, so have extra drill bits on hand to replace damaged or dull ones.

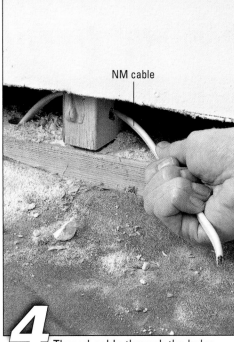

NM cable

4 Thread cable through the holes and pull it fairly tight. Once the cable is run, install a nailing plate to protect each hole.

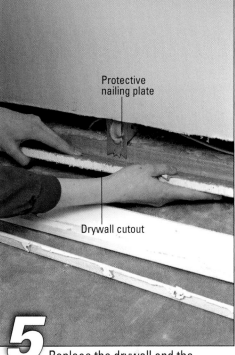

Protective nailing plate

Drywall cutout

5 Replace the drywall and the molding. (If the wall is plaster, shim out the bottom plate so the molding can sit flat.) You may need to attach the drywall with adhesive and reposition some nails to avoid hitting the protective plates.

Run cable behind a door casing

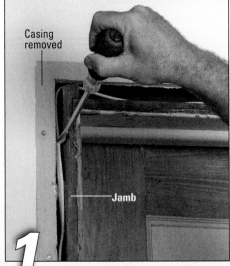

Casing removed

Jamb

1 Pry off the casing. Thread the cable through the gap between the jamb and framing. If the jamb is tight against a stud, drill a hole so you can run cable through the wall. Door frames are attached to a double stud, so the hole should be 3 inches deep.

Protective nailing plate

Jamb

2 Install a protective plate wherever a nail might pierce the cable. Use a chisel to cut a notch for the plate in the jamb so the casing sits against the jamb.

STANLEY PRO TIP

Add base cap when the base is not wide enough

If you need to cut a hole too high for the base molding to cover, replace the old molding with a wider base or install a base cap to add width to the base molding.

Through a basement

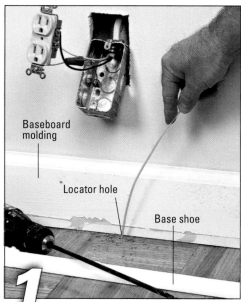

Baseboard molding

Locator hole

Base shoe

1 If the basement is unfinished, remove the base shoe and drill a locator hole. Poke a wire down through the hole.

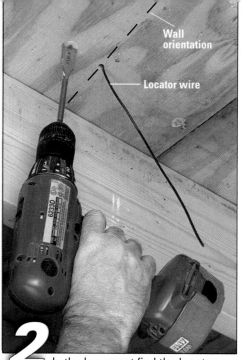

Wall orientation

Locator wire

2 In the basement find the locator wire. Measure the thickness of the baseboard and wall covering plus half the width of the wall plate. Mark a center to drill up through the middle of the bottom plate.

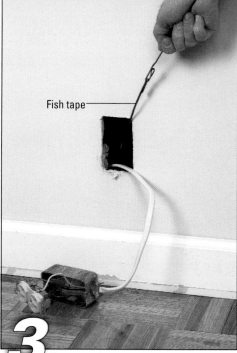

Fish tape

3 Remove the box and push a fish tape up through the basement hole. Hook the tape and pull it up. If the box is difficult to remove, punch out a knockout slug and feed a fish tape down through the knockout to hook the fish tape from the basement. Pull it up through the hole in the box.

STANLEY PRO TIP: **Fishing into the attic**

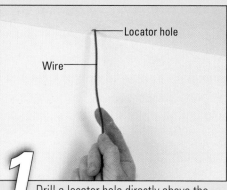

Locator hole

Wire

1 Drill a locator hole directly above the hole or box in the wall. Poke a wire through the hole. The wire may have to push through fiberglass or loose-fill insulation.

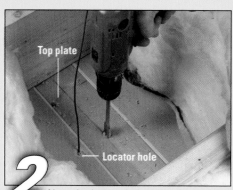

Top plate

Locator hole

2 Near the locator hole drill a ¾-inch hole through the center of the top plate. If your house has fire blocking, cut a hole into the wall and drill a hole through the blocking.

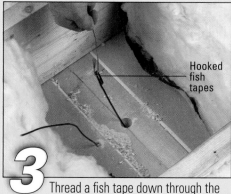

Hooked fish tapes

3 Thread a fish tape down through the attic hole while a helper threads a fish tape up through a box or hole in the wall. Once you snag the lower tape, pull up.

Code variations
Your building department may not allow running cable around a door frame or may require armored cable in finished walls and ceilings. Check local codes.

Through walls and ceilings

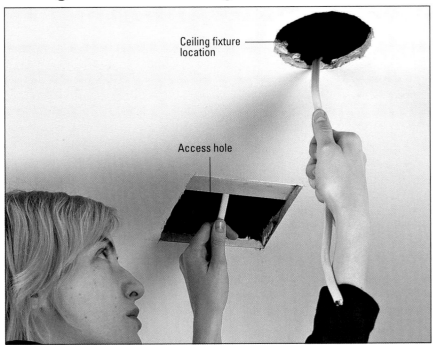

Ceiling fixture location

Access hole

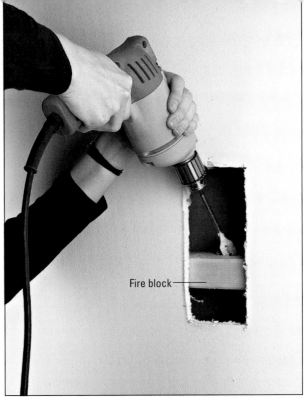

Fire block

Middle of ceiling: If you need to run cable across the middle of a ceiling or wall, find the joists or studs and cut holes that are large enough for your hand to fit into. (Save drywall pieces and use them to patch the holes later.) Drill holes and thread the cable through. Once the cable is run, install protective nailing plates.

Fire blocks: Some homes have fire blocks—horizontal 2×4s between the studs, usually 4 or 5 feet above the floor. Use a stud finder to locate one. Cut a hole into the wall and drill a hole through the fire block.

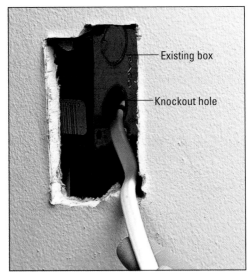

Existing box

Knockout hole

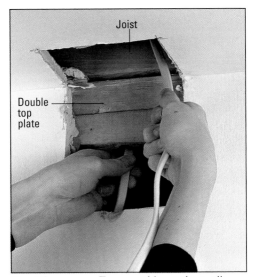

Joist

Double top plate

Behind a box: If the hole for a new box is behind an existing box on the other side of the wall, punch out a knockout slug in the existing box. Run fish tapes from both directions, hook them together, and pull through the box. Pull cable through the box to the hole.

No attic access: To run cable up the wall and across the ceiling, cut holes into the wall and the ceiling. Drill a hole up through the top plate. If a joist blocks the way, drill a hole through it as well. Bend the cable and thread it through the holes.

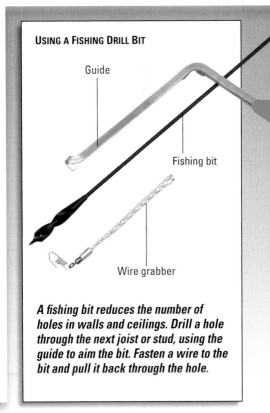

USING A FISHING DRILL BIT

Guide

Fishing bit

Wire grabber

A fishing bit reduces the number of holes in walls and ceilings. Drill a hole through the next joist or stud, using the guide to aim the bit. Fasten a wire to the bit and pull it back through the hole.

PATCHING WALLS

You probably will have to repair walls and ceilings after finishing your wiring. As you work cut holes into drywall as neatly as possible and save the cutouts to use as patches.

Allow plenty of time for patching. You may need to apply several coats of joint compound to achieve a smooth surface.

Dry-mix joint compound, which is strong but hard to sand, comes in bags labeled "90," "45," or "20." The numbers indicate roughly how many minutes it takes for the product to harden. Ready-mix joint compound, which comes in buckets, is easier to apply and sand but is not as strong. A good plan is to apply dry-mix compound for the first coat and use ready-mix for subsequent coats.

PRESTART CHECKLIST

☐ **TIME**
About 1 hour to install a patch and apply the first coat of compound; several 15-minute sessions on following days, to sand and apply additional coats

☐ **TOOLS**
Drywall saw, utility knife, hammer, putty knife, drill, taping blades, corner trowel, drywall-sanding block with 80- and 100-grit sandpapers or screens

☐ **SKILLS**
Cutting drywall, applying joint compound, painting

☐ **PREP**
Make sure the wiring is correct and have it inspected, if required, before you cover it up. Spread a drop cloth on the floor below.

☐ **MATERIALS**
Drywall screws, drywall for patching, 1×4 scraps, mesh tape, joint compound

1 Where there is no framing member to attach the drywall, slip a 1×4 or backer piece behind the hole so half its width is behind the wall surface and half is visible.

1×4 scrap

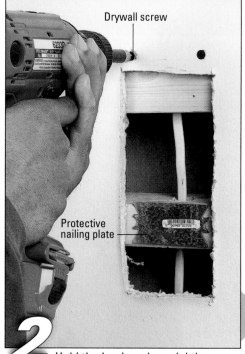

Drywall screw

Protective nailing plate

2 Hold the backer piece tightly against the back of the drywall and drive 1¼-inch drywall screws through the drywall and into the backer piece. Drive each screw until the backer piece is drawn tightly to the drywall.

Patching plaster walls

1 Pry or chip away loose plaster around the damaged area. If the whole wall has loose plaster, call in a professional plasterer.

2 Buy drywall that's no thicker than the plaster. Cut a piece to fit the hole and screw it to the lath.

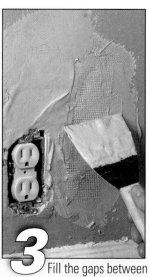

3 Fill the gaps between the patch and the wall with joint compound. Apply tape and joint compound as described above.

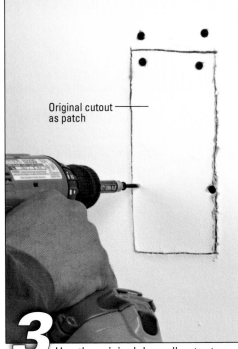

Original cutout as patch

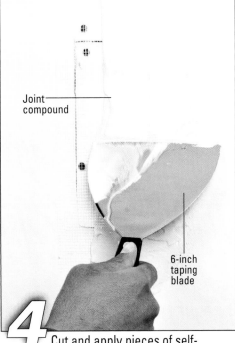

Joint compound

6-inch taping blade

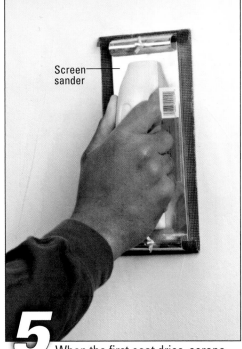

Screen sander

3 Use the original drywall cutout or cut a new piece to fit. Cut off any dangling scraps of paper. Attach the patch with drywall screws. Screw heads must sink below the surface of the drywall without tearing the paper.

4 Cut and apply pieces of self-sticking fiberglass mesh tape. With a taping blade apply enough joint compound to cover the tape. Smooth the compound.

5 When the first coat dries, scrape away high spots and apply a second coat, feathering out the edges a bit farther. When it dries, sand it. Apply and sand as many coats as needed to achieve a surface that looks and feels smooth. Prime and paint.

Patching at a corner

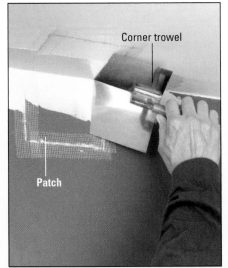

Corner trowel

Patch

A smooth corner is difficult to achieve. Use a corner trowel to form a perfect inside corner when applying the first coat. Use a straight trowel to smooth the wall and ceiling during subsequent coats.

Blending with textured surface

A textured wall surface may have been applied with a special tool. Patterns vary from one applicator to another. Try this trick: Make the cutout carefully, then replace it and caulk rather than tape the joints.
To mimic a texture practice on scraps of drywall, experimenting with various tools. (Sometimes it helps to add a handful of sand to a gallon of joint compound.) If a ceiling has a blown-on "popcorn" or "cottage cheese" surface, buy special patching compound, which can be sprayed on or applied with a trowel.

Need a small piece of drywall?
Most home centers sell broken pieces of drywall at a fraction of their original price.

COVER IT BEAUTIFULLY

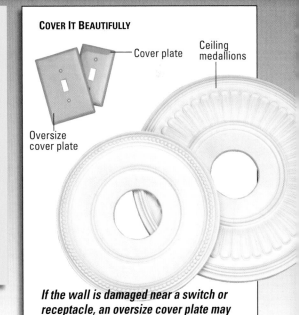

Cover plate

Ceiling medallions

Oversize cover plate

If the wall is damaged near a switch or receptacle, an oversize cover plate may hide the blemish and save patching work. To conceal a damaged ceiling near a light fixture, install a medallion, which you paint to match the ceiling.

INSTALLING NEW FIXTURES

Any wiring project should begin with a detailed plan. The chapter "Planning New Electrical Service" (pages 140–155) helps you prepare a thorough, easy-to-read description. Make sure existing or new circuits can handle the new installation (pages 148–149). Present your plans to the local building department and receive a permit before beginning work.

Getting ready

Your inspector may approve NM cable, or you might have to install conduit or armored cable. Metal boxes may be required; plastic may be allowed. Determine how ground wires should be connected (page 146) and how cable should be clamped to the boxes (page 22).

Most projects call for two-wire cable, but some require three-wire cable or even four wires running in conduit or Greenfield. Buy plenty of cable; it's easy to underestimate how much you need.

Unless you face special circumstances, use 12-gauge wire for 20-amp circuits and 14-gauge wire for 15-amp circuits. If your existing service uses armored cable or conduit, you can usually switch to NM cable if the cable runs into a box and the ground wire is connected according to code.

Test all new receptacles with a receptacle analyzer (page 32). It tells you instantly whether the receptacle is properly grounded and polarized.

Some building departments require that lights be on dedicated lighting circuits rather than share a circuit with receptacles. Other departments allow circuits to combine the two.

Planning a remodeling project

If a wiring project is part of a larger job, plan the work so different tasks and contractors do not collide. The first order of business is removing wall surfaces and any framing. Then comes rough plumbing, then rough electrical—installing boxes and running cable. If you install receptacles and switches at this point, protect them with tape. Better yet wait until after the walls and ceilings are drywalled (with openings cut) and painted before installing receptacles, switches, and fixtures.

Make your home more convenient and appealing by adding new receptacles and light fixtures.

CHAPTER PREVIEW

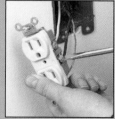

Adding a receptacle
page 182

Adding a 240-volt receptacle
page 184

Two-circuit receptacles
page 186

Split receptacles
page 187

Cable for wallmounted fixtures can run from below (through a basement or crawlspace) or from above (through an attic) to minimize damage to the ceiling and wall.

New light fixtures add style and illumination. Bathrooms are often prime candidates for new fixtures, especially when you can grab power from an overhead switched fixture.

Switched receptacles
page 188

Installing a new switched fixture
page 190

Installing three-way switches
page 194

Undercabinet fluorescents
page 198

Recessed cans
page 200

Wallmounted lighting
page 204

ADDING A RECEPTACLE

Tap power for a new receptacle from an existing receptacle. If doing this may cause the circuit to overload (pages 148–149) or if there is no conveniently located receptacle, tap power from a junction box in the basement or a nearby light fixture or switch (pages 166–167).

If one or more new receptacles supply heavy power users, run cable all the way to the service panel and install a new circuit (pages 278–279).

When connecting to a 15-amp circuit, install a standard receptacle and #14 wire. When connecting to a 20-amp circuit, use #12 wire and a special 20-amp receptacle.

PRESTART CHECKLIST

☐ **TIME**
About 2 hours to run cable and make connections (not including cutting a pathway for cable and patching walls)

☐ **TOOLS**
Voltage tester, drill, saw, hammer, fish tape, screwdriver, strippers, long-nose pliers, lineman's pliers, utility knife, stud finder, torpedo level, tape measure, pry bar, perhaps a drywall saw or jigsaw

☐ **SKILLS**
Stripping and connecting wires to terminals, installing boxes, running cable through walls and ceilings

☐ **PREP**
Lay a drop cloth on the floor below.

☐ **MATERIALS**
New receptacle, cable, remodel box and clamps, wire nuts, electrician's tape, protective nailing plates, cable staples

Existing receptacle · Voltage tester · Baseboard access for running cable

1 **Shut off power to the circuit.** Cut and drill a pathway for the cable. Pull out the receptacle you're grabbing power from and test to make sure power is not present (page 48). Move the receptacle to the side or disconnect and remove it.

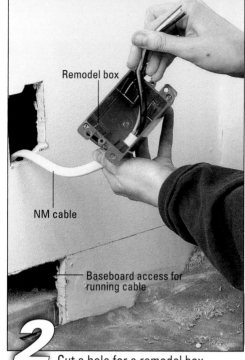

Remodel box · NM cable · Baseboard access for running cable

2 Cut a hole for a remodel box. Run cable from the area near the existing box to the hole, clamp the cable to the box, and install the new box.

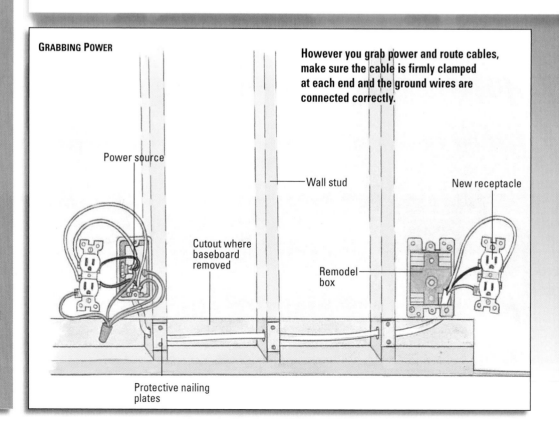

GRABBING POWER

However you grab power and route cables, make sure the cable is firmly clamped at each end and the ground wires are connected correctly.

Power source · Wall stud · New receptacle · Cutout where baseboard removed · Remodel box · Protective nailing plates

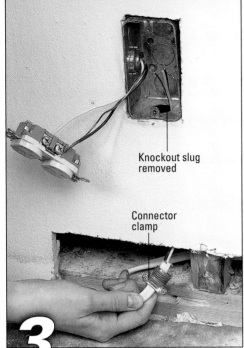

Knockout slug removed

Connector clamp

3 Pry up a knockout slug in the old box and twist it out with pliers. (If you can't do this, remove the box and replace it with a remodel box.) Remove the sheathing from the cable, strip the wires, and attach a connector clamp to the cable. Push the cable into the box and fasten the clamp.

Wrap tape around receptacle before pushing into box

Locknut tightened

4 Strip and run cable into the existing box and tighten the cable clamp. Connect the new wires to existing wiring. Attach the ground wires using a pigtail. Connect the white wire to the available silver terminal and the black wire to the brass one.

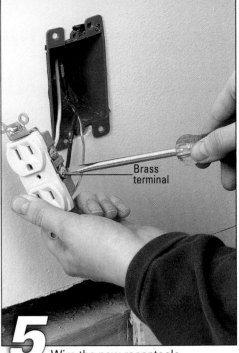

Brass terminal

5 Wire the new receptacle. Connect the ground wire to the ground screw, the white wire to the silver terminal, and the black wire to the brass terminal.

REFRESHER COURSE
Wiring a GFCI

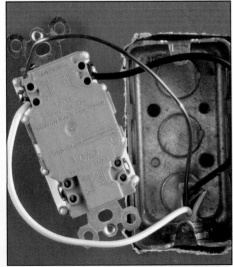

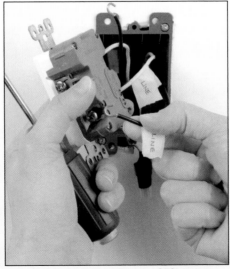

To wire a ground fault circuit interrupter (GFCI) at the end of a run, connect wires to the LINE terminals as marked on the back of the device.

To protect receptacles after the GFCI, connect wires supplying power to LINE terminals; connect wires leading to other receptacles to LOAD terminals.

EXISTING WIRING
Wiring a middle-of-run receptacle

If the existing receptacle box has two cables and there are no available terminals on the receptacle, disconnect all the wires. Hook up pigtails and connect the pigtails to the terminals.

ADDING A 240-VOLT RECEPTACLE

Electric water heaters, dryers, ranges, and other large appliances use 240 volts. Each appliance needs a separate double-pole breaker. (See pages 278–279 for how to install a new breaker.)

Various 240-volt receptacles are made for specific amperages and appliances. Buy the right one for your application. Some older receptacles use only three wires; codes now call for four wires—black and red hot wires, a white neutral wire, and a ground wire. Use 12-gauge wire for a 20-amp circuit, 10-gauge for 30 amps, 8-gauge for 40 amps, and 6-gauge for 50 amps. Check local codes for requirements.

Work with extreme caution: 240 volts can cause serious bodily harm.

PRESTART CHECKLIST

☐ **TIME**
About 3 hours to run cable (not including cutting and patching walls) and connect a breaker and receptacle

☐ **TOOLS**
Voltage tester, drill, saw, hammer, nonconductive ladder, flashlight, fish tape, groove-joint pliers, screwdriver, strippers, long-nose pliers, lineman's pliers

☐ **SKILLS**
Stripping and connecting wires, installing boxes, running cable

☐ **PREP**
Lay a towel or drop cloth where you cut into walls; cut a pathway for cable.

☐ **MATERIALS**
240-volt (or 120/240-volt) receptacle, wire of correct size, Greenfield, conduit or NM cable (if allowed), wire nuts, clamps, double-pole circuit breaker

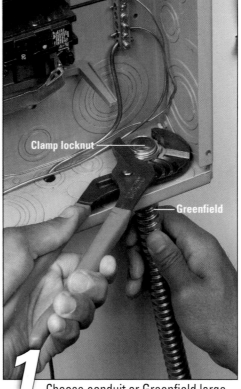

1 Choose conduit or Greenfield large enough so the wires can slide easily. Remove a knockout slug from the service panel (make sure it's the right size) and clamp the conduit or Greenfield to the panel.

2 Run the conduit or Greenfield from the service panel to the receptacle location (pages 158–163, 174–177) and attach a clamp. You may need to drill 1-inch holes. The receptacle may be mounted on the floor or in a wall box.

Air-conditioner receptacles

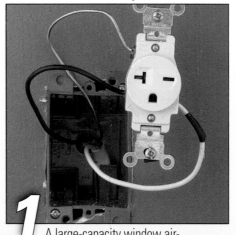

1 A large-capacity window air-conditioner calls for a 20-amp, 240-volt receptacle. Route 12/2 cable from the service panel to a receptacle box (pages 166–177). Mark the white wire black. Connect the white and black wires to the receptacle terminals. Connect the ground wire.

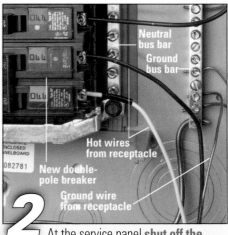

2 At the service panel **shut off the main breaker**. Make room for a double-pole breaker. Connect the ground wire to the ground bus bar and the black and the white-marked black wires to the breaker. Snap in the breaker.

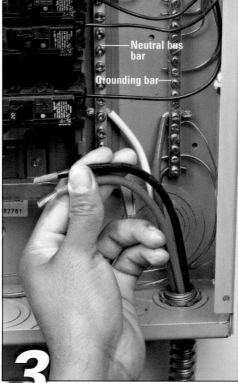

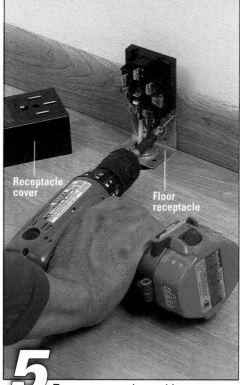

3 Shut off the main breaker. Fish wires (page 165) from the receptacle location to the panel. Attach the white wire to the neutral bus bar and the ground wire to the grounding bar.

4 Connect the red and black wires to the breaker terminals. Snap the breaker into the service panel. (See pages 278–279 for more detailed instructions.)

5 To connect a wire to this type of receptacle, strip the wire end, poke it into the terminal hole, and tighten the setscrew. Fasten the receptacle body to the floor or wall and install the cover.

Dryer receptacle

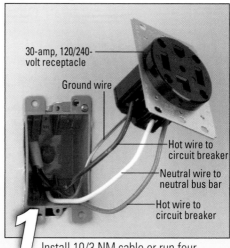

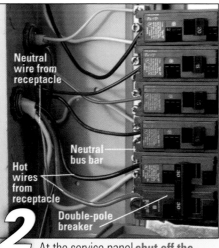

1 Install 10/3 NM cable or run four 10-gauge wires through conduit or Greenfield from the service panel to a receptacle box (pages 158–163). Connect the wires to the terminals of the receptacle.

2 At the service panel shut off the main breaker. Connect the ground wire to the ground bus bar and the neutral wire to the neutral bus bar. Connect the black and red wires to a double-pole breaker and snap in the breaker.

Use a whip

To connect to a cooktop or a wallmounted oven, run cable from the service panel to a junction box. Connect an appliance whip—a short length of armored cable—to the junction box and the appliance (page 277). Some new appliances come with a whip already attached.

Keep it neat—and safe

If wires enter the service panel far from the breaker, route them around the perimeter of the panel. This eases future work in the panel, clarifies the circuitry, and avoids strain on connections.

TWO-CIRCUIT RECEPTACLES

Code may require that adjacent receptacles be on different circuits. You can split receptacles (opposite) to achieve the same effect.

Run three-wire cable from the service panel to the boxes for the two circuits. Codes may call for connecting both circuits to a double-pole breaker. That way an overload on one circuit shuts off both, deadening all wires in each box.

PRESTART CHECKLIST

☐ **TIME**
About 3 hours to install several receptacles (not including cutting and patching walls)

☐ **TOOLS**
Voltage tester, drill, saw, hammer, fish tape, lineman's pliers, screwdriver, strippers, long-nose pliers

☐ **SKILLS**
Running cable; stripping, splicing, and connecting wire

☐ **PREP**
Run three-wire cable from service panel to boxes, two-wire between last two boxes.

☐ **MATERIALS**
Receptacles, three-wire cable, two-wire cable, boxes, double-pole breaker, wire nuts, tape

Reds spliced

Blacks to brass terminals

1 **Shut off power to the circuits.** At the first receptacle splice the red wires. Connect the grounds. Attach the white wires to the silver terminals. Connect the black wires to the brass terminals.

Blacks spliced

Reds to brass terminals

2 At the second receptacle splice the black wires. Connect the grounds. Attach the white wires to the silver terminals. Connect the red wires to the brass terminals.

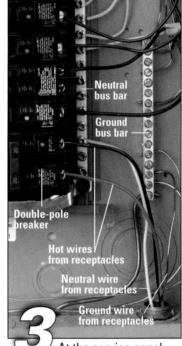

Neutral bus bar

Ground bus bar

Double-pole breaker

Hot wires from receptacles

Neutral wire from receptacles

Ground wire from receptacles

3 At the service panel **shut off the main breaker.** Attach the white wire to the neutral bus bar and the ground wire to the ground bus bar. Connect the red and black wires to a double-pole breaker, and Install it.

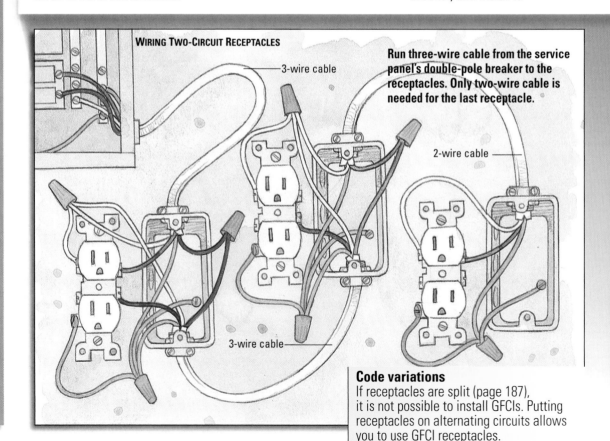

WIRING TWO-CIRCUIT RECEPTACLES

3-wire cable

2-wire cable

3-wire cable

Run three-wire cable from the service panel's double-pole breaker to the receptacles. Only two-wire cable is needed for the last receptacle.

Code variations
If receptacles are split (page 187), it is not possible to install GFCIs. Putting receptacles on alternating circuits allows you to use GFCI receptacles.

SPLIT RECEPTACLES

If a receptacle is split, its two plugs are on separate circuits. It's also possible to split a receptacle and have one outlet controlled by a switch (pages 188–189).

Run three-wire cable from the service panel to the receptacle boxes. Codes also may call for connecting both circuits to the same double-pole breaker. That way if one circuit overloads, both circuits shut off, ensuring that all hot wires in each box are dead.

PRESTART CHECKLIST

☐ **TIME**
About 3 hours to install several receptacles (not including cutting and patching walls)

☐ **TOOLS**
Voltage tester, drill, saw, hammer, fish tape, screwdriver, strippers, longnose pliers, lineman's pliers

☐ **SKILLS**
Running cable; stripping, splicing, and connecting wire

☐ **PREP**
Run three-wire cable from service panel to boxes.

☐ **MATERIALS**
Receptacles, three-wire cable, boxes, double-pole breaker, wire nuts, electrician's tape

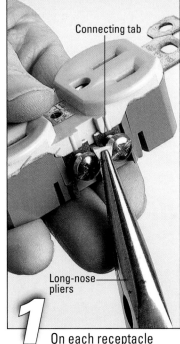

Connecting tab

Long-nose pliers

1 On each receptacle twist off the tab that connects the two brass terminals. Now the two outlets are disconnected from each other.

2 Make certain no power is present in the cable or boxes. At each receptacle pigtail the red, black, and white wires. Connect the red and black pigtails to separate brass terminals and connect the white pigtail to a silver terminal.

Double-pole breaker

3 At the service panel shut off the main breaker. Connect the white wire to the neutral bus bar and the ground wire to the ground bus bar. Connect the red and black wires to a double-pole breaker. Snap in the breaker.

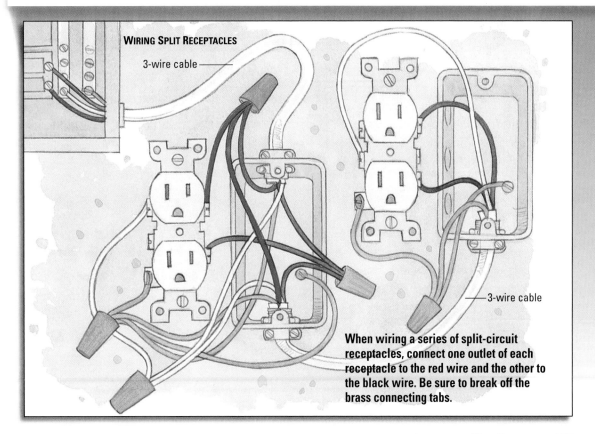

WIRING SPLIT RECEPTACLES

3-wire cable

3-wire cable

When wiring a series of split-circuit receptacles, connect one outlet of each receptacle to the red wire and the other to the black wire. Be sure to break off the brass connecting tabs.

SWITCHED RECEPTACLES

A receptacle can be split so a wall switch controls one of its outlets while the other is hot all the time. A lamp plugged into the switched outlet can be turned on as you enter a room. Many codes allow a bedroom without a ceiling light if it has a switched receptacle.

The steps on these pages show how to split and switch an existing receptacle that is wired normally. If you need to install a new receptacle and switch, see the illustration opposite.

If the wall is covered with drywall or plaster, most of the work consists of running cable and perhaps patching the wall afterwards (pages 172–179).

PRESTART CHECKLIST

☐ **TIME**
About 3 hours to run cable a short distance (not including cutting a pathway for the cable and patching walls), install a wall switch, and wire the receptacle

☐ **TOOLS**
Voltage tester, drill, saw, hammer, nonconductive ladder, fish tape, screwdriver, strippers, long-nose pliers, lineman's pliers

☐ **SKILLS**
Stripping, splicing, and connecting wires to terminals; installing boxes; running cable through walls

☐ **PREP**
Lay a drop cloth on the floor below.

☐ **MATERIALS**
Single-pole switch, receptacle (if you want to replace the old one), two-wire cable, wire nuts, remodel box, cable clamps, electrician's tape

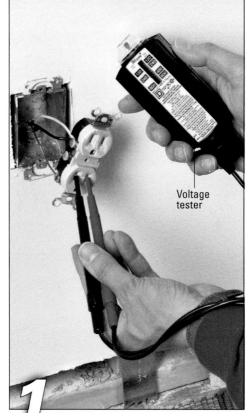

1 **Shut off power to the circuit.** Without touching the terminals carefully pull out the existing receptacle and test for power.

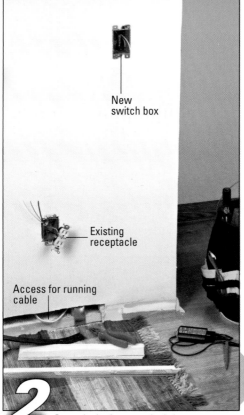

Voltage tester

New switch box

Existing receptacle

Access for running cable

2 Cut a hole for a switch box, run cable from the hole to the existing receptacle box, and clamp the cable to the box (pages 166–177).

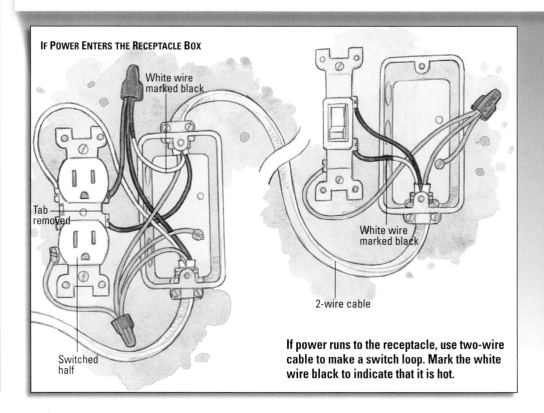

IF POWER ENTERS THE RECEPTACLE BOX

White wire marked black

Tab removed

Switched half

White wire marked black

2-wire cable

If power runs to the receptacle, use two-wire cable to make a switch loop. Mark the white wire black to indicate that it is hot.

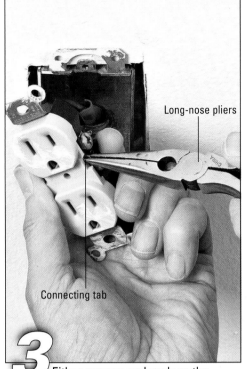

Long-nose pliers

Connecting tab

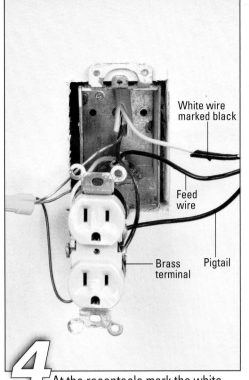

White wire marked black

Feed wire

Brass terminal

Pigtail

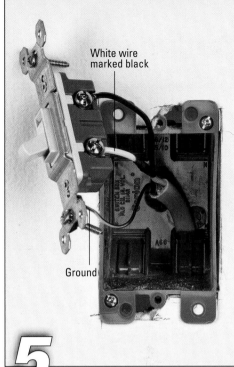

White wire marked black

Ground

3 Either remove and replace the receptacle or continue to use the existing one. Remove the tab that connects the two brass terminals; the two outlets are no longer connected to each other.

4 At the receptacle mark the white switch wire with black tape and connect the grounds. Splice the feed wire with the black-marked wire and add a pigtail. Connect the pigtail to a brass terminal, the remaining black wire to the other brass terminal, and the white wire to a silver terminal.

5 If only one cable originally entered the switch box, connect the ground and mark the white switch wire with black tape. Connect the wires to the appropriate switch terminals.

If power enters the switch box

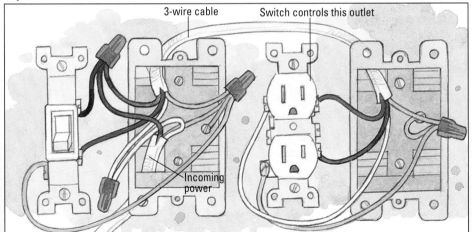

3-wire cable

Switch controls this outlet

Incoming power

If you install a new receptacle and switch, this is the most common configuration. Bring power to the switch box with two-wire cable and run three-wire cable between the boxes. Connect the grounds. At the switch box splice the white wires. Splice the black wires together with a pigtail and connect the pigtail to a terminal. Connect the red wire to a terminal. At the receptacle connect the red and black wires to brass terminals and the white wire to a silver terminal.

WHAT IF...
A receptacle is middle-of-run?

Tab removed

If two cables originally entered the receptacle box, connect the grounds and mark the white switch wire black. Attach the black switch wire to one brass terminal. Splice the remaining black wires and the white switch wire together with a pigtail. Connect the pigtail to the other brass terminal. Connect the remaining white wires to silver terminals.

INSTALLING A NEW SWITCHED FIXTURE

A switched fixture can be wired as a through-switch circuit (shown in the steps at right) or a switch-loop circuit (shown at the bottom of page 191). In a through-switch circuit power enters at the switch box. It comes into the fixture box in a switch-loop circuit.

Both methods work equally well. Unless your inspector has a preference, choose the wiring method that makes for the easiest cable runs. For various combinations see pages 192–193.

PRESTART CHECKLIST

☐ **TIME**
About 2 hours to run cable and install a switch and a receptacle (not including cutting a pathway for the cable and patching walls)

☐ **TOOLS**
Voltage tester, drill, saw, hammer, nonconductive ladder, fish tape, screwdriver, strippers, long-nose pliers, lineman's pliers

☐ **SKILLS**
Stripping, splicing, and connecting wires to terminals; installing boxes; running cable into boxes

☐ **PREP**
Lay a drop cloth on the floor

☐ **MATERIALS**
Single-pole switch, light fixture or ceiling fan, two- and three-wire cable, ceiling box, cable clamps, wall box, wire nuts, electrician's tape

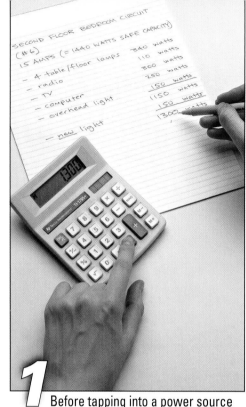

1 Before tapping into a power source (pages 166–167), list all the electrical users on the circuit and add up the wattages to see whether there is room on the circuit for a new light switch. See pages 148–149.

Hole for switch box

Power source

2 Cut a hole for the switch box and run two-wire cable from the hole to a power source. In this example a receptacle directly below the switch makes for an easy cable run. Pages 166–177 show how to install boxes and run cable.

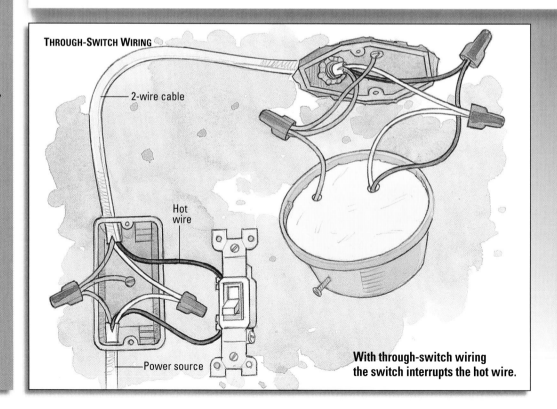

THROUGH-SWITCH WIRING

2-wire cable

Hot wire

Power source

With through-switch wiring the switch interrupts the hot wire.

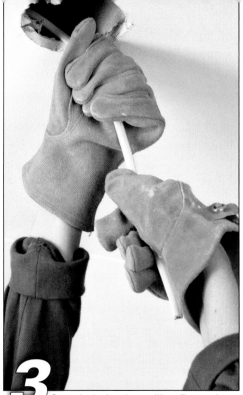

3 Cut a hole for the ceiling fixture box and run two-wire cable from that hole to the switch hole.

Blacks to terminals

4 At the switch hole feed the cables into a box, install the box, and clamp the cables. Strip the cables and wires. Splice the white wires and connect the black wires to the switch terminals. Splice the grounds with a pigtail to the ground on the switch or box.

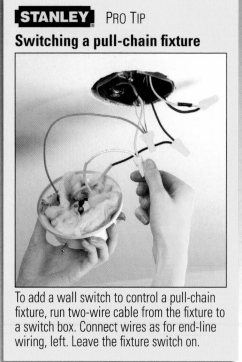

5 Feed the cable into the ceiling box and install the box. Clamp the cables and strip the cable and wires. Splice the white wire to the white fixture lead and the black wire to the black lead. Connect the grounds.

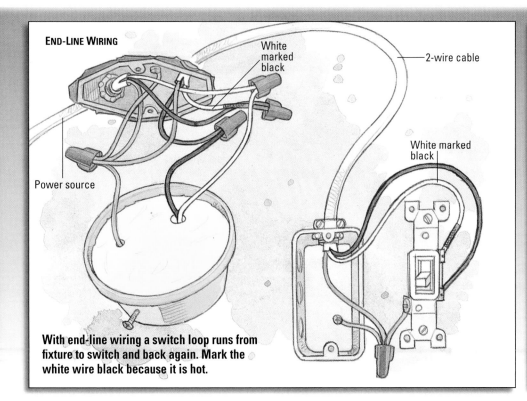

END-LINE WIRING

White marked black

2-wire cable

White marked black

Power source

With end-line wiring a switch loop runs from fixture to switch and back again. Mark the white wire black because it is hot.

STANLEY PRO TIP

Switching a pull-chain fixture

To add a wall switch to control a pull-chain fixture, run two-wire cable from the fixture to a switch box. Connect wires as for end-line wiring, left. Leave the fixture switch on.

Switch, light, and receptacle

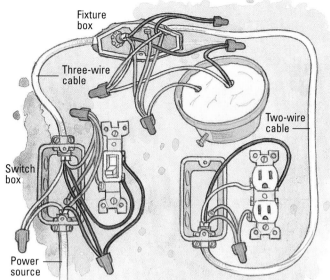

This circuit is a switched fixture and an unswitched receptacle. Bring power into the switch box with two-wire cable. Run three-wire cable to the fixture and run two-wire cable from the fixture to the receptacle. Connect all the grounds. At the switch box connect the black and red wires to the switch terminal and splice the white wires. At the fixture box splice the black wires, splice the white wires together with the white fixture lead, and splice the red wire to the black fixture lead. Wire the receptacle.

END-LINE OPTION

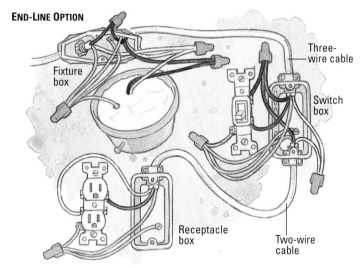

Bring power to the fixture with two-wire cable. Run three-wire cable to the switch and run two-wire cable from the switch to the receptacle. Connect all the grounds. At the fixture box splice the black wires, splice the white wires together with the white fixture lead, and splice the red wire to the black fixture lead. At the switch box splice the white wires, splice the black wires together and add a pigtail, and connect the black pigtail and the red wire to the switch terminals. Attach the black and white wires to the receptacle.

Two fixtures on two switches

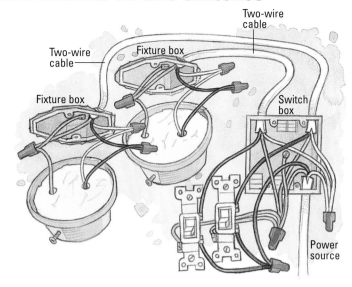

Two switches, each controlling a separate light, share a double-gang box. Bring power into the switch box with two-wire cable and run two-wire cable to each fixture. Connect all the grounds. At the switch box connect the black power wire to the switches using pigtails. Connect each black fixture wire to a switch and splice the white wires. Wire the fixtures.

END-LINE OPTION

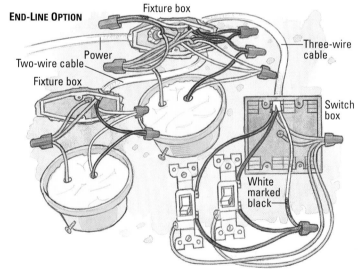

Bring power to the first fixture box with two-wire cable. Run two-wire cable between the fixtures; run three-wire cable from the first fixture box to the switch box. Connect the grounds. At the first fixture box mark the white switch wire black and splice it to the feed wire. Splice the other two black wires. Splice the remaining white wires with the white fixture lead. Splice the red wire with the black fixture lead. Wire the other fixture. At the switch box connect the red wire to one switch and the black wire to the other. Mark the white wire black and connect it to the switches with pigtails.

Switch and two or more fixtures

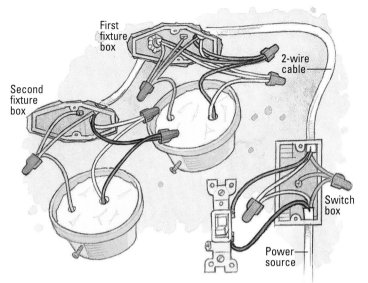

A single switch controls two fixtures. Run two-wire cable into all the boxes. Connect all the grounds. At the switch box splice the white wires and connect the black wires to the switch terminals. At the first fixture box, splice the two black wires with the fixture's black lead and splice the two white wires with the fixture's white lead. Wire the second fixture.

END-LINE OPTION

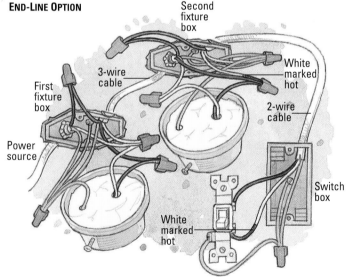

Bring power into the first fixture box with two-wire cable. Run three-wire cable between the fixture boxes and run two-wire cable from the second fixture box to the switch box. Connect all the grounds. At the first fixture box, splice the black wires, splice the white wires together with the white fixture lead, and splice the red wire with the black fixture lead. At the second fixture box, splice the black wires; mark the white wire from the switch black and splice it together with the red wire and the black fixture lead. Splice the white wire to the white fixture lead. Wire the switch, marking the white wire black.

Switch and receptacle

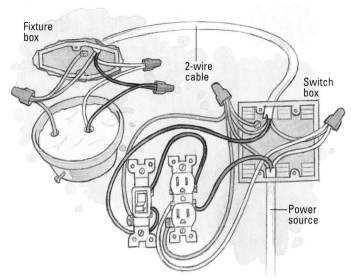

An always-hot receptacle and switch share a double-gang box. Run two-wire cable to both boxes. Connect all the grounds. At the switch box connect the black power wire to a brass receptacle terminal, run a short black wire from the other brass terminal to a switch terminal, splice the white wires together with a pigtail, connect the pigtail to a silver receptacle terminal, and connect the black fixture wire to the other switch terminal. Wire the fixture.

END-LINE OPTION

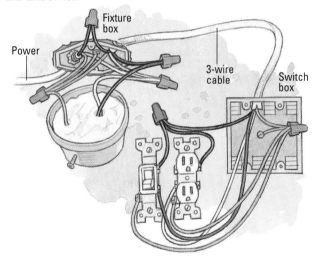

Bring power to the fixture box with two-wire cable. Run three-wire cable from the fixture box to the switch box. Connect all the grounds. At the fixture box splice the black wires, splice the white wires together with the white fixture lead, and splice the red wire with the black lead. At the switch box connect the black wire to a switch terminal and a brass receptacle terminal using pigtails. Connect the red wire to a switch terminal and connect the white wire to a silver receptacle terminal.

INSTALLING THREE-WAY SWITCHES

A pair of three-way switches control a fixture from two locations, such as the top and bottom of a stairway. A three-way switch has three terminals: two traveler terminals and one common terminal, which is darker in color. The toggle is not marked on and off.

These pages show how to wire a three-way switch with power entering a switch and traveling through the fixture to the other switch. Pages 196–197 show three more circuits and discuss four-way switches as well. Choose the setup that makes it easiest for you to run the cable.

PRESTART CHECKLIST

☐ **TIME**
About 4 hours to run cable and install a light and two switches (not including cutting a pathway and patching walls)

☐ **TOOLS**
Voltage tester, drill, saw, hammer, screwdriver, ladder, fish tape, strippers, long-nose pliers, lineman's pliers

☐ **SKILLS**
Stripping, splicing, and connecting wires to terminals; installing boxes; running cable through walls and ceilings

☐ **PREP**
Check that a new fixture doesn't overload the circuit and tap into a power source. Lay a drop cloth on the floor below.

☐ **MATERIALS**
Two-wire and three-wire cable, ceiling fixture, two three-way switches, switch and fixture boxes, cable clamps, wire nuts, electrician's tape

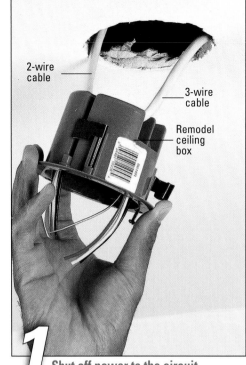

2-wire cable

3-wire cable

Remodel ceiling box

1 Shut off power to the circuit.
Cut holes for two wall boxes and a ceiling box. Run two-wire cable from the power source to the first switch box, three-wire cable to the ceiling box, and three-wire cable to the second switch box (pages 166–177.)

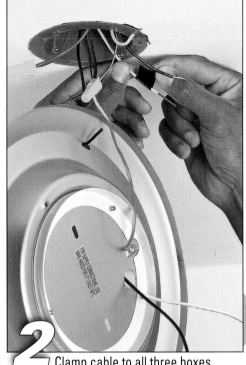

2 Clamp cable to all three boxes.
Install all the boxes and connect all the grounds. At the fixture box splice the red wires. Mark the white wire from the second switch with black tape.

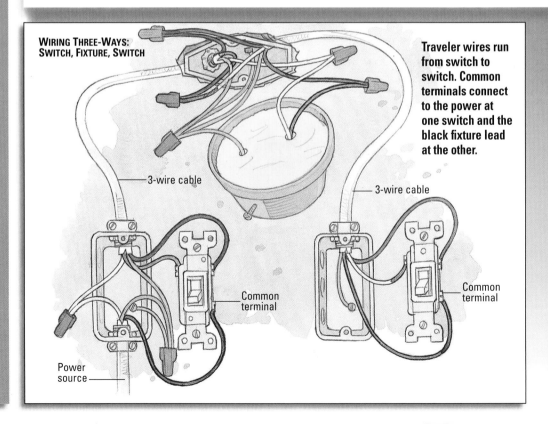

WIRING THREE-WAYS:
SWITCH, FIXTURE, SWITCH

Traveler wires run from switch to switch. Common terminals connect to the power at one switch and the black fixture lead at the other.

3-wire cable

3-wire cable

Common terminal

Common terminal

Power source

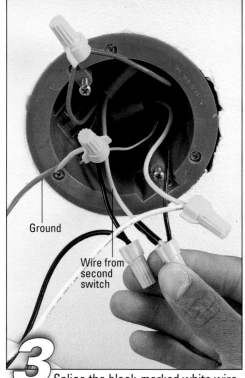

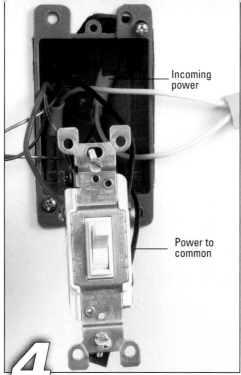

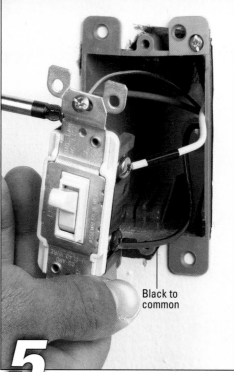

3 Splice the black-marked white wire with the black wire from the first switch. Connect the remaining black and white wires to the fixture's black and white leads.

4 At the first switch (where power enters), splice the white wires. Connect the black power wire to the common terminal and the red and black wires in the three-conductor cable to the traveler terminals.

5 At the second switch mark the white wire with black tape. Connect the black wire to the common terminal. Connect the red wire and the black-marked white wire to the traveler terminals.

How three-ways work

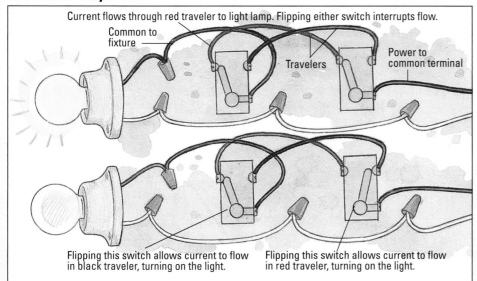

Current flows through red traveler to light lamp. Flipping either switch interrupts flow.

Common to fixture

Travelers

Power to common terminal

Flipping this switch allows current to flow in black traveler, turning on the light.

Flipping this switch allows current to flow in red traveler, turning on the light.

In a three-way circuit, the light is turned on when power can flow through both switches to the fixture. If the circuit is broken at either switch, the light is turned off. Traveler wires run from switch to switch and do not connect to the fixture. Common wires bring in power and carry it to the fixture.

STANLEY PRO TIP

Three rules for three-ways

If a wiring diagram gets confusing, pause minute and ponder these rules:
■ Route traveler wires so they run from traveler terminals to traveler terminals and never to the fixture or power source.
■ Attach the power feed wire to the common terminal of one switch.
■ Connect the black lead from the fixture to the common terminal of the other switch.

Where three-ways are required
Codes require three-way switches for lights in hallways and stairways.

Switch, switch, fixture

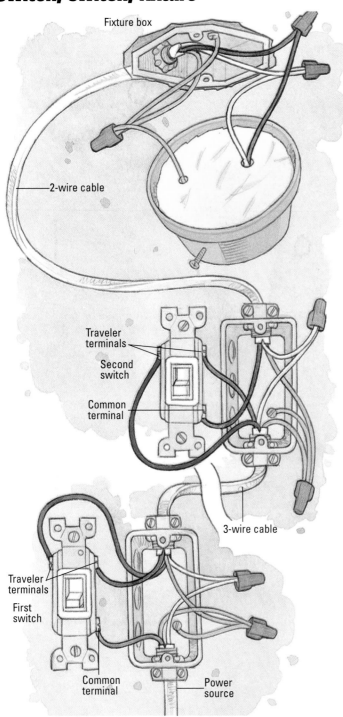

Fixture, radiating to switches

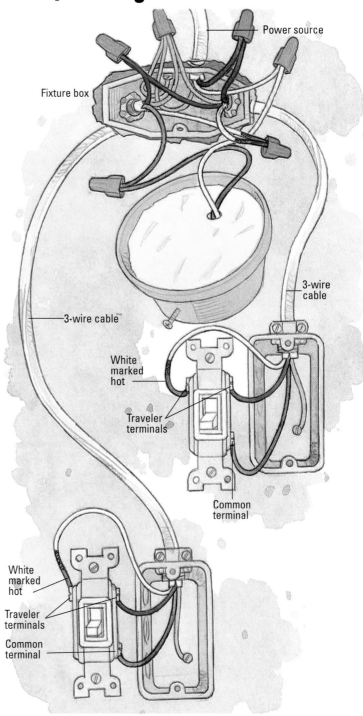

At the first switch connect the black power wire to the common terminal, splice the white wires, and connect red and black wires to traveler terminals. At the second switch connect the traveler wires to the traveler terminals and the black wire from the fixture box to the common terminal. At the fixture box splice the white fixture lead with the white wire and splice the black fixture lead with the black wire from the switch's common terminal.

At the fixture box splice the black power wire to the black wire that runs to one switch box and splice the white wire to the white fixture lead. Splice the black fixture lead to the black wire coming from the other switch box. In each switch box connect the black wire to the switch common terminal, connect the red wire to a traveler terminal, and mark the white wire as hot, then connect it to the other traveler terminal on the switch.

Fixture, switch, switch

Power source

White
marked hot

2-wire cable

White
marked hot

Traveler
terminals

Common
terminal

First switch

White
marked hot

Second
switch

Traveler
terminals

Common
terminal

3-wire
cable

Four-way wiring

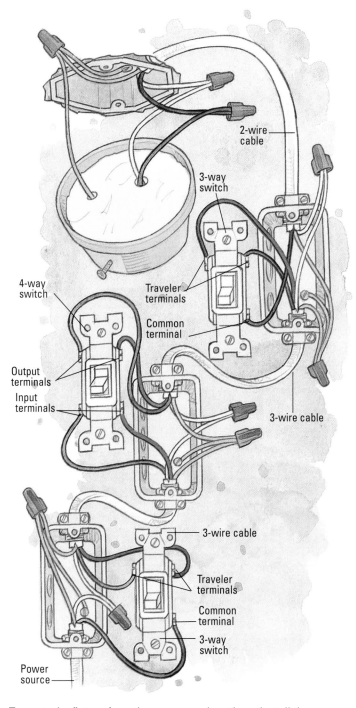

2-wire
cable

3-way
switch

4-way
switch

Traveler
terminals

Common
terminal

Output
terminals

Input
terminals

3-wire cable

3-wire cable

Traveler
terminals

Common
terminal

3-way
switch

Power
source

In the fixture box splice the black wires, splice the white power cable wire to the white fixture lead, and mark the other white lead as hot and splice it to the black fixture lead. At the first switch connect the black wire from the fixture to the common terminal, connect the red wire to a traveler terminal, and mark both white wires black and connect as shown. Wire the second switch as shown. Connect all grounds.

To control a fixture from three or more locations, install three-way switches at each end and one or more four-ways in between. A four-way switch has only traveler terminals and no common terminal. Connect wires from the first switch to the "input" terminals; wires connected to the "output" terminals lead to the third switch.

UNDERCABINET FLUORESCENTS

Undercabinet fluorescent lights are ideal for lighting countertop work areas in a kitchen. Home centers sell plug-in undercabinet lights that are easy to install (pages 133–136) but not as convenient as a string of fluorescent lights controlled by a single wall switch.

When remodeling a kitchen the wall cabinets are removed (shown). If wall cabinets are in place, see page 199 for tips on snaking cable to minimize wall damage.

Some undercabinet fluorescent lights have a single outlet. Thin fixtures (1-inch thick) are more difficult to wire than standard (1½-inch thick) fixtures.

(pages 133–136)

PRESTART CHECKLIST

☐ **TIME**
About 4 to 6 hours to cut holes and run cable and another half-day to install the lights after the cabinets are up

☐ **TOOLS**
Voltage tester, drill, hammer, drywall saw, level, stud finder, fish tape, screwdriver, strippers, long-nose pliers, lineman's pliers

☐ **SKILLS**
Stripping, splicing, and connecting wires to terminals; installing boxes; running cable through walls and ceilings

☐ **PREP**
Find power source and check that the new lights don't overload the circuit (pages 148–149). Clear the room of all debris and lay a drop cloth on the floor.

☐ **MATERIALS**
Fluorescent undercabinet fixtures, cable, remodel box with clamps, single-pole switch, wire nuts, tape

1 Draw the cabinet locations on the wall with a level. Determine how the lights will fit onto the cabinets; you may need to cut a lip at the bottom of the cabinets. Cut access holes into the walls. Make sure the cabinets cover all holes.

2 Shut off power to the circuit. Run cable from the switch hole to a power source (pages 166–167). Run cables from the switch box to the fixture holes (pages 172–177). Leave at least 16 inches of cable hanging out from each fixture hole.

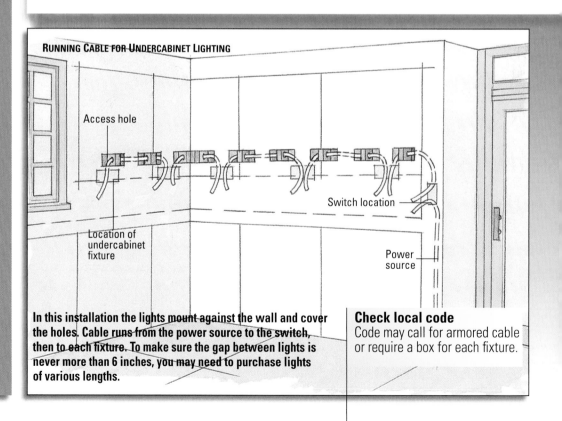

RUNNING CABLE FOR UNDERCABINET LIGHTING

In this installation the lights mount against the wall and cover the holes. Cable runs from the power source to the switch, then to each fixture. To make sure the gap between lights is never more than 6 inches, you may need to purchase lights of various lengths.

Check local code
Code may call for armored cable or require a box for each fixture.

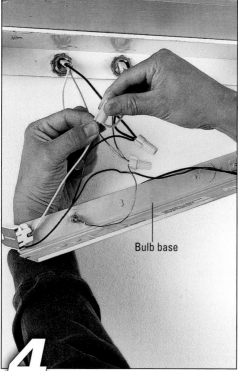

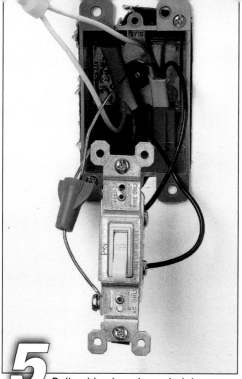

Fluorescent fixture body

Bulb base

3 If the cabinet has a lip at the bottom, cut or drill a hole in it for the cable to pass through. After the cabinets are installed, strip sheathing and clamp the cables to the fixture body.

4 At each fixture connect the grounds. Splice black wires with the black fixture lead and white wires with the white fixture lead. Once connected position and fold the wires carefully so they do not touch the ballast.

5 Pull cables into the switch box, install the box, and wire the switch. Connect the grounds and splice the white wires together. Connect the black wires to the switch terminals.

Two ways to run cable with cabinets in place

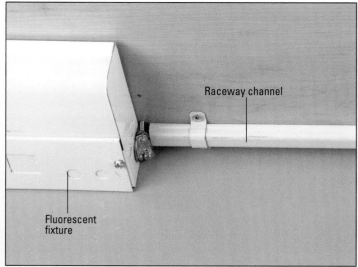

Raceway channel

Fluorescent fixture

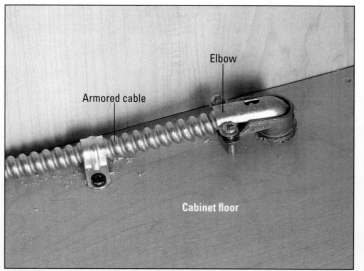

Elbow

Armored cable

Cabinet floor

If removing the cabinets is not practical, consult with your inspector for the best way to run wiring. One option is to run wires through metal or plastic raceway channels attached to the underside of the cabinets.

Running armored cable through the inside of the cabinet is another choice. Use elbows to bring the wiring into the light fixtures from the top rather than the side.

RECESSED CANS

The most inconspicuous lighting is recessed canister lights. Install a grid of lights spaced 6–8 feet apart, with eyeball lights for accent lighting. Install them as task lights over a countertop and position a watertight fixture above a tub or shower.

Recessed canister lights are easy to install in finished walls. Running cable is not too difficult because lights usually space only two or three joists apart. Using a fishing drill bit (page 177), you may need to cut only a few holes into the ceiling.

See page 202 for tips on buying recessed lights. Most inexpensive recessed cans are rated to use only 60-watt bulbs.

PRESTART CHECKLIST

☐ **TIME**
About a day to cut holes, run cable, and install six to eight lights with a switch

☐ **TOOLS**
Drill, spade bit or fishing drill bit, stud finder, ladder, drywall saw, level, hammer, fish tape, screwdriver, strippers, long-nose pliers, lineman's pliers

☐ **SKILLS**
Precision cutting of drywall or plaster; stripping, splicing, and connecting wires to terminals; installing boxes; running cable through walls and ceilings

☐ **PREP**
Find power source and make sure the new lights don't overload the circuit (pages 148–149). Clear the room of all obstructions and lay a drop cloth on the floor.

☐ **MATERIALS**
Recessed canister lights, cable, switch box and clamps, wire nuts, electrician's tape

A. Rough-in the wiring

Mark center of fixture.

1 Plan the locations for the lights and draw lines marking the center of each. Use a stud finder or a bent wire (opposite) to see whether a joist is in the way. You can move the light several inches to avoid a joist—the inconsistency isn't noticeable.

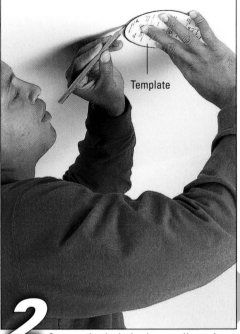

Template

2 Center the hole in the cardboard template over your location mark. Holding the template in place, mark your cutline.

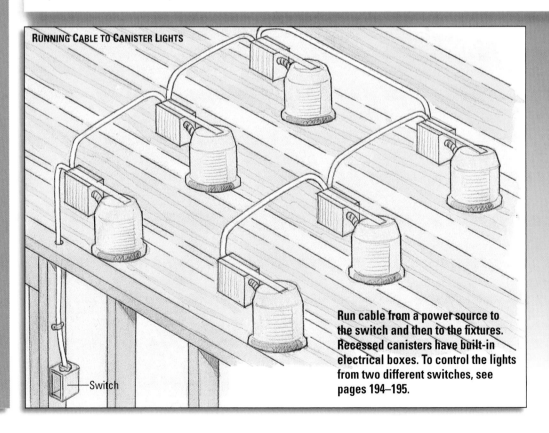

RUNNING CABLE TO CANISTER LIGHTS

Switch

Run cable from a power source to the switch and then to the fixtures. Recessed canisters have built-in electrical boxes. To control the lights from two different switches, see pages 194–195.

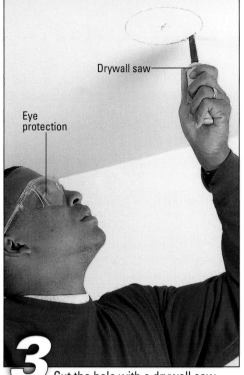

Eye protection

Drywall saw

¾-inch spade bit

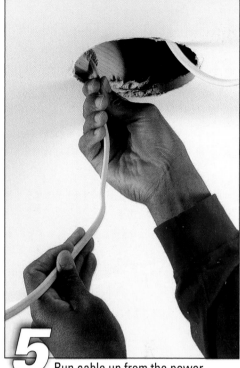

3 Cut the hole with a drywall saw. Wear safety glasses because drywall dust stings terribly if it gets in the eyes. If the ceiling is plaster, see page 172 for cutting tips. Cut precisely—the canister trim leaves little room for error.

4 Drill holes for the cable as far up the joist as possible so drywall nails cannot reach the cable. See pages 172–177 for tips on running cable through walls and ceilings.

5 Run cable up from the power source to the switch box, then run cable to each fixture hole (see the illustration, opposite). Allow at least 16 inches of cable to hang down from each hole.

STANLEY PRO TIP

Bent wire test

To make sure the fixture does not bump into a joist, use a stud finder. Or drill a ¼-inch hole, insert a bent wire, and spin it around to see whether you encounter an obstruction.

WHAT IF...
The ceiling framing is exposed?

If the ceiling joists are not covered with drywall or plaster, install a new-work can light. Adjust the light to accommodate the thickness of the drywall to be put up later. Slide the mounting bars out and hammer each tab into a joist. Slide the light on the bars to position it precisely.

Mapping can lights

With a standard flood bulb, a recessed light illuminates an area about as wide as the ceiling is high. Make a scale drawing of your room and map a grid of lights that are spaced fairly consistently.

If your ceiling is 8 feet high, a typical recessed light shines on a floor area with a diameter of 8 feet (a radius of 4 feet). To light the room install a grid of lights spaced no more than 8 feet apart. Perimeter lights should be no more than 4 feet from the walls. Lights placed closer together— perhaps 6 or 7 feet apart and only 2–3 feet from the walls—more fully light the room.

If you have a 10-foot ceiling, lights can be 7–10 feet apart and as much as 5 feet from the wall.

B. Install the lights

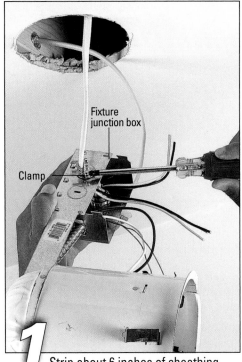

Fixture
junction box

Clamp

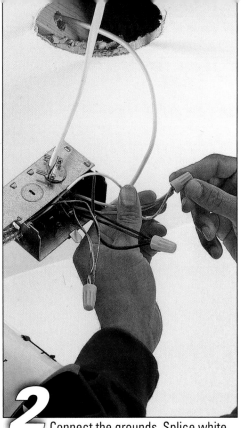

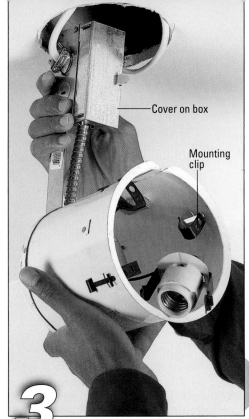

Cover on box

Mounting
clip

1 Strip about 6 inches of sheathing from the cable. Remove the cover from the fixture junction box and twist off a knockout for each cable. Slide the cable in and clamp the cable.

2 Connect the grounds. Splice white wires with white leads and black wires with black leads. Fold the wires into the junction box and replace the cover.

3 Pull the mounting clips inside the can so they aren't in the way when you push the canister into the hole. Without tangling the cables guide the junction box through the hole and push in the canister.

If insulation comes within 3 inches of a recessed light, be sure to install a fixture rated "IC" (insulation compatible). A non-IC light overheats dangerously.

WHAT IF...
The ceiling is sloped or space is tight?

If the ceiling slopes buy special canisters you can adjust so the light can point straight down.

If the vertical space above the ceiling is less than 8 inches, buy a low-clearance fixture. Some are small enough to fit into a space only 4 inches high.

Compact low-voltage halogen can lights are expensive, but they present new style options and produce an intense light.

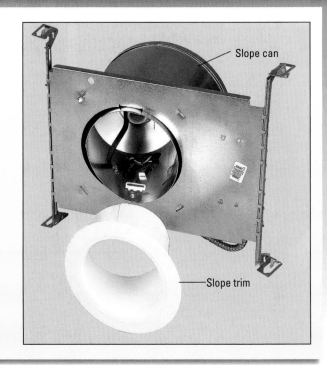

Slope can

Slope trim

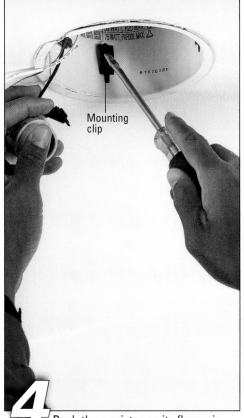

Mounting clip

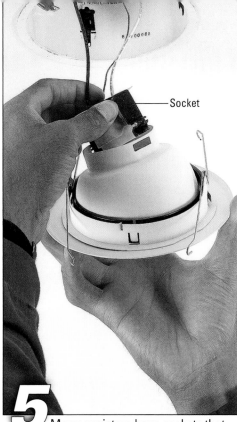

Socket

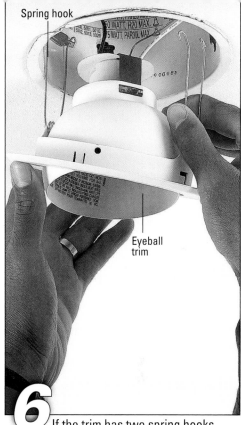

Spring hook

Eyeball trim

4 Push the canister so its flange is tight to the ceiling. With a slot screwdriver push up each mounting clip until it clicks into place, clamping the canister to the drywall or plaster.

5 Many canisters have sockets that attach to the trim with two spring clips. Slip one clip into the notch provided and rock the socket so the clip engages.

6 If the trim has two spring hooks, squeeze and guide their ends into the slots provided, then push up the trim until it snaps into place. Twist an eyeball trim to face in the desired direction.

WHAT IF…
The canister has a spring hook?

To mount trim that attaches with coil springs, hold the trim in place against the ceiling. Insert a pencil tip into the looped end of each spring and guide it up into the hole in the side of the canister.

Trim options

Baffle trim (white or black) diffuses the light, while reflector trim increases the brightness of a bulb. With open trim the flood bulb protrudes slightly downward. For above a tub or shower, choose a watertight lens.

An eyeball (or fish-eye) trim rotates to point where you want it; a wallwasher highlights the texture of a brick or stone wall.

Baffle trim

Reflector trim

Open trim

Flush watertight lens

Wallwasher trim

Eyeball trim

Extended watertight lens

WALLMOUNTED LIGHTING

Wall sconces provide indirect lighting for hallways or stairways or as wall accents. Place them just above eye level.

Use a ceiling box and wire, just as you would a ceiling light. Most sconces mount with a center stud so you can level the fixture even if the box is not level.

Install fixtures on both sides of a mirror. A strip of lights over a bathroom mirror or medicine chest calls for a similar method (see opposite). Such fixtures use low-wattage bulbs to reduce glare while providing plenty of light.

PRESTART CHECKLIST

☐ **TIME**
About 3 hours to run cable and install a switch and two sconces (not including cutting a pathway for the cable and patching walls)

☐ **TOOLS**
Voltage tester, drill, saw, fish tape, screwdriver, strippers, long-nose pliers, lineman's pliers

☐ **SKILLS**
Stripping, splicing, and connecting wires to terminals; installing boxes; running cable through walls and ceilings

☐ **PREP**
Find power source and make sure the new lights do not overload the circuit (pages 148–149). Spread a drop cloth on the floor below.

☐ **MATERIALS**
Sconce(s), ceiling boxes and a switch box with clamps, cable, switch, wire nuts, electrician's tape

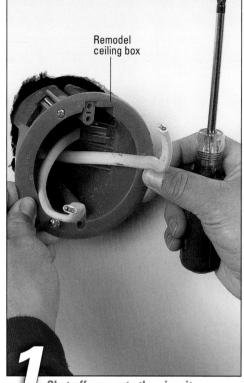

1 **Shut off power to the circuit.** Cut wall holes for the sconce boxes and the switch. Run cable from the power source to the switch, then to the sconces (pages 172–177).

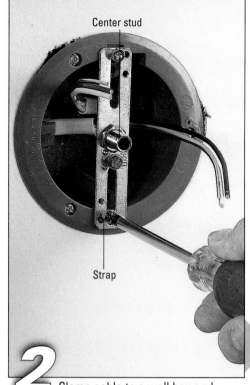

2 Clamp cable to a wall box and install the box. Most sconces come with all the necessary hardware—usually a strap with a center stud. The strap also helps carry heat away from the fixture.

SCONCE INSTALLATION

2-wire cable

2-wire cable

Remodel box

Switch

Sconce

Power source

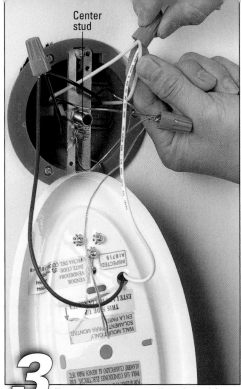

Center stud

3 To wire a sconce splice the white fixture lead to the white wire and the black lead to the black wire. Connect the grounds.

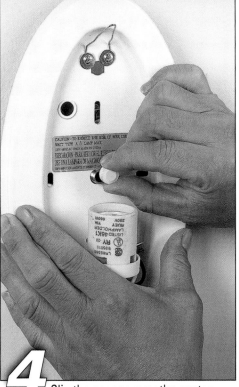

4 Slip the sconce over the center stud and start to tighten the nut. Stand back and check that the base is plumb and then tighten the base.

5 Install the lightbulb, making sure it does not exceed the manufacturer's recommended wattage. Clip the lens into place. Wire the switch (pages 190–197).

Lights mounted on a mirror

To install a bathroom strip light, center the box over the mirror or medicine chest. Attach the fixture over the box, wire the fixture, and attach the cover.

To install a light fixture directly onto a mirror, have a glass supplier cut three holes to match the fixture: a large hole for the electrical box and two smaller holes for mounting screws. Wire the fixture. Apply a thin bead of clear silicone caulk to its back to act as an adhesive. Attach with mounting screws but don't overtighten them—you might break the mirror.

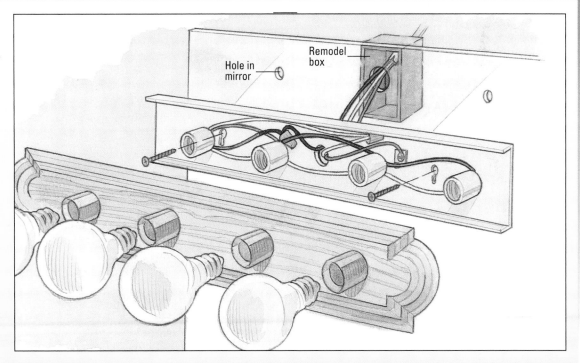

Hole in mirror

Remodel box

INSTALLING FANS & HEATERS

Fans that pull air through a room, an attic, or even the whole house contribute to making your home more comfortable, and they reduce energy costs. Small vent fans in the bathroom or kitchen expel unwanted fumes and moisture. Each requires relatively simple wiring; the fan and ducts or vents require the most time.

An attic must breathe

When the weather is hot and sunny, a stuffy attic can heat up to higher than 100°F, making it difficult to cool a house. In cold weather an attic that is too warm collects moisture that can damage insulation. It also can cause snow on the roof to melt, leading to ice dams at the eaves, which can damage roofing,

sheathing, and interior walls and ceilings. The solution to both problems is a well-ventilated attic.

Outside air must circulate freely through an attic. Modern building codes specify types and sizes of attic vents, but an older home may be inadequately vented. An attic should have vents below, at the eaves or the soffit, and above, on the roof, at the ridge, or in the gable. A gable fan or roof fan pulls hot air out of an attic but only if the eaves or soffit vents can sufficiently allow the air to easily escape.

Choosing the right fan

Ask local builders or home center employees to determine which fan or combination of fans works best in your house. If your attic

is not adequately vented, a gable fan (pages 212–213) usually is the easiest way to get the air moving. Install a roof fan (page 214) if a gable fan is not feasible. To keep a house cool without turning on the air-conditioning, a whole-house fan (pages 208–211) can work wonders. Consult with a dealer to find out which size fan or fans works most effectively.

If a bathroom stays steamy or a kitchen stays smoky even with a vent fan on, poorly designed or blocked ductwork may be the culprit (pages 215 and 218). Or you may need a more powerful fan. Add warmth to a bathroom or other areas with radiant floor heating or an electric heater (pages 224–229).

Built-in fans can reduce cooling costs, remove moisture, and vent unpleasant smoke and odors.

CHAPTER PREVIEW

Whole-house ventilating fan
page 208

Gable fan
page 212

Roof fan
page 214

Range hood
page 215

If your home does not have adequate eaves, roof, or gable venting, install vents before adding an attic fan. An eaves vent is the easiest to install. Cut a rectangular hole in the soffit, then fasten the vent screen in place with corrosion-resistant screws.

Eaves vent screen

In a well-ventilated attic, air moves up through eaves vents and out through vents on the roof, at the ridge, or in the gable. As an alternative two large gable vents may do the trick. Always clear vents of insulation and check that items stored in the attic do not block airflow.

Over-the-range microwave
page 218

Bath vent fan
page 220

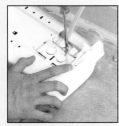

Installing electric heaters
page 224

Installing electric radiant heat
page 226

WHOLE-HOUSE VENTILATING FAN

A whole-house fan pulls fresh air through every room that has an open door or window and sends it out through the attic.

The attic must be vented and doors or windows must be open in the rooms below. Locate the fan in the ceiling of a top-floor hallway. The one shown rests on top of an exposed joist. Other models frame an opening.

In winter make sure the fan's shutters close tightly, and place insulation over the fan so the house won't lose heat.

PRESTART CHECKLIST

☐ **TIME**
About 8 hours to run cable and install a fan with a wall switch (not including preparing a path for the cable)

☐ **TOOLS**
Voltage tester, stud finder, tape measure, drywall saw, drill, circular saw, hammer, fish tape, nonconductive ladder, screwdriver, long-nose pliers, lineman's pliers, strippers

☐ **SKILLS**
Splicing and connecting wires to terminals, installing boxes, running cable through walls and ceilings, cutting and attaching boards

☐ **PREP**
Find a power source and make sure the fan does not overload the circuit (pages 148–149). Spread a drop cloth on the floor. Enlist a helper for lifting and placing the fan.

☐ **MATERIALS**
Whole-house fan, remodel box, switch, electrical boxes with clamps, three-wire cable, wire nuts, electrician's tape

A. Install the fan

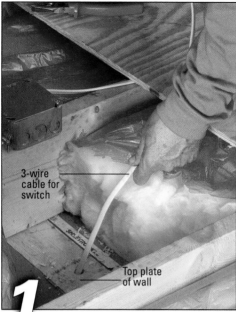

3-wire cable for switch

Top plate of wall

1 Cut a hole for the switch box into a wall below the fan. Run three-wire cable down through the ceiling plate to the hole.

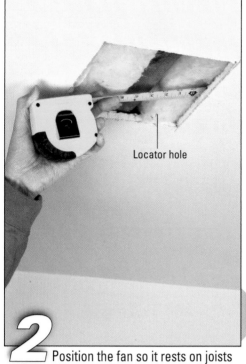

Locator hole

2 Position the fan so it rests on joists at either side; one joist runs through the middle. Use a stud finder to find the center joist, then cut a locator hole and measure to find the exact location of the joists.

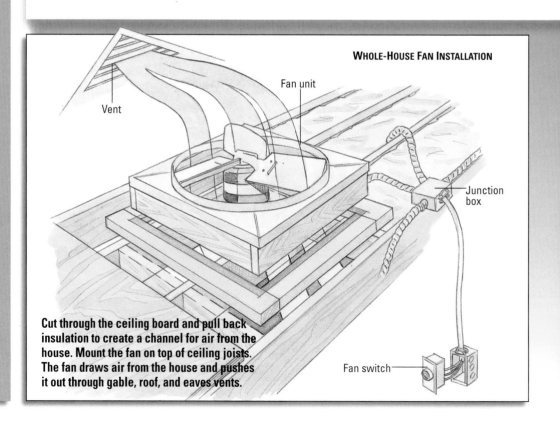

WHOLE-HOUSE FAN INSTALLATION

Fan unit

Vent

Junction box

Fan switch

Cut through the ceiling board and pull back insulation to create a channel for air from the house. Mount the fan on top of ceiling joists. The fan draws air from the house and pushes it out through gable, roof, and eaves vents.

3 Cut the hole according to manufacturer's directions. Lay pieces of plywood on the attic joists to provide a safe work surface. Work with a helper in the attic to lift the fan up into place.

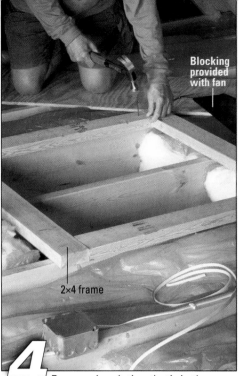

2×4 frame

4 Remove insulation that's in the way. If the fan does not come with blocking to fill gaps between the joists, cut blocking from lumber the same dimension as your joists. Build a frame of 2×4s, lay it flat and squarely on the joists, and fasten it firmly.

Blocking provided with fan

5 Center the fan over the frame. Attach it by driving wood screws (not drywall screws) through the brackets provided and into the frame.

STANLEY PRO TIP
Locating the fan

The best location for a whole-house fan usually is in a top-floor hallway. If the fan is in a room, that room's door must be kept open while the fan operates. To allow the fan to vent freely, provide at least 30 inches of vertical space between the joists the fan rests on and the roof rafters. If the attic contains loose insulation, cover it with plastic sheeting.

Open up
Open windows to promote airflow; otherwise the fan pulls air down through the fireplace, water heater, or furnace chimney, which could include carbon monoxide. The back pressure could even shut off a furnace.

Select size and capacity

To cool properly a whole-house fan should exchange the air in a house at least once every four minutes. The faster the air exchanges, the cooler the house.

Manufacturers offer several sizes of whole-house fans. Determine the total square footage of your home and consult with a salesperson or read the manufacturer's literature to choose the right size for your house. When in doubt buy the next size up; with a fan-rated multispeed switch, you can always adjust the power downward.

REFRESHER COURSE
Circuit analysis

Make sure your fan does not overload a circuit. Add up the wattages of all the electrical users on the circuit and then add in the fan's wattage. If the total exceeds 1,440 watts for a 15-amp circuit or 1,920 watts for a 20-amp circuit, the load outstrips safe capacity. If you cannot find a circuit with enough available wattage, you may need to run cable to the service panel and install a new circuit (pages 278–279).

B. Wire the fan

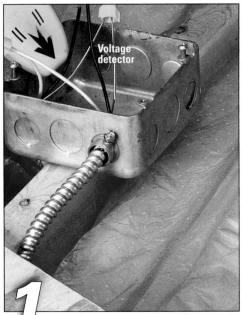

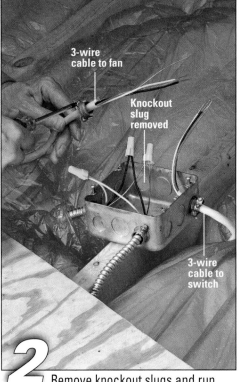

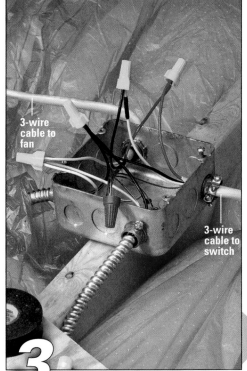

1 **Shut off power to the circuit** you use. If there is a junction box in the attic and its circuit can accommodate the fan, pull power from it. If several cables enter the box, **use a voltage detector to make sure all power is off.**

2 Remove knockout slugs and run two three-wire cables, one from the fan and one from the switch (shown below). If the fan has a cable whip that does not reach the junction box, run it to an intermediate box and run cable from there to the junction box.

3 In the junction box connect the grounds and splice all white wires in the box, except the one running to the switch. Mark it with black tape and splice it to the black wire running to the fan. Splice together the other black wires and splice the red wires.

SAFETY FIRST
Working safely in an attic

■ If an attic floor is unfinished with exposed insulation and joists, one misstep will put your foot through the ceiling below. Don't take chances; lay down sheets of plywood wherever you will be working.

■ Most insulation—whether fiberglass blankets or loose—causes eyes to smart and skin to itch. Wear protective goggles, a dust mask, and long sleeves when cutting or removing it.

Old attic wiring

If you find exposed wires running through porcelain knobs and tubes, the wiring is not necessarily unsafe. However do not try to take power from knob-and-tube wiring and take care not to disturb the wires.

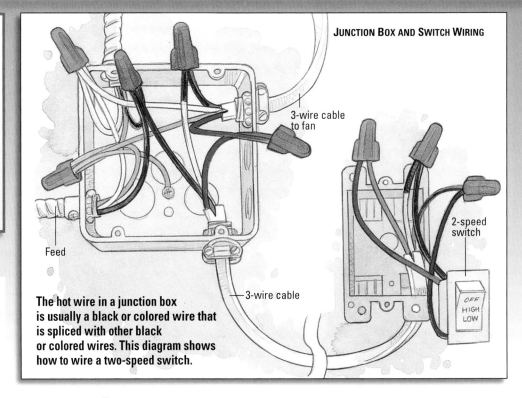

JUNCTION BOX AND SWITCH WIRING

The hot wire in a junction box is usually a black or colored wire that is spliced with other black or colored wires. This diagram shows how to wire a two-speed switch.

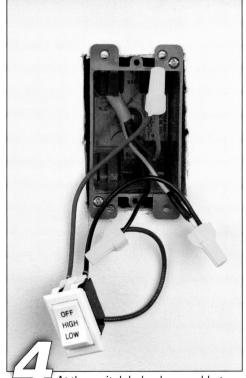

4 At the switch hole clamp cable to a remodel box and install the box. For the two-speed switch shown above (provided by the fan manufacturer), mark the white wire black with tape and connect it to the black switch lead. Splice the red wire to the red lead and the blue lead to the black wire.

5 Check the fan belt tension. When pressed it should deflect about ⅛ inch. If necessary follow the manufacturer's instructions for adjusting the tension. (Not all whole-house fans are belt-driven; some have blades powered directly by the motor.)

6 With a helper position the shutter so it covers the ceiling hole. Drive screws into joists to attach the shutter firmly to the ceiling. Restore power and test. Be sure the shutter freely opens and closes.

WHAT IF...
There is no power available in the attic?

If there is no usable power source in the attic, run power up through a wall switch and then on to the fan. Check that adding the fan to a nearby fixture or receptacle circuit does not create an overload (pages 148–149). **Shut off power to the circuit** and tap into the power source. Then run cable and install a switch box (pages 166–167). If using a fan-rated speed control, wire it as shown.

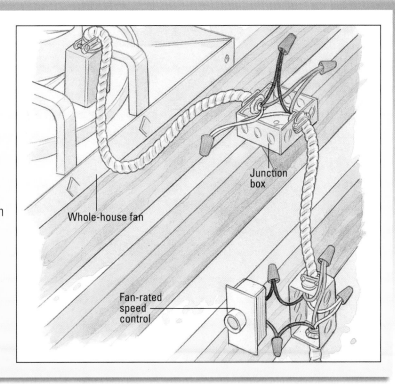

Whole-house fan

Junction box

Fan-rated speed control

Switch options

In addition to the two-speed switch shown in Step 4, switch options include a sliding control with a toggle (which returns to the power level when turned on and off), a three-level toggle switch, a three-level sliding switch, a timer, and a pilot light toggle. Make sure any switch is fan-rated.

GABLE FAN

If an attic has a gable (a vertical endwall often pointed at the top), it is usually easy to install a fan there. A gable fan is easier to install than roof-mounted fans or vents, which leak if not sealed correctly.

If your gable does not have a vent, install one. Plastic louvers are less attractive than fixed wooden units, but they seal out wind and rain more effectively.

Calculate the square footage of your attic and total the square footage of your eaves vents. These two figures help you buy a gable fan the correct size.

Gable fans have thermostats to turn on automatically when the attic gets too hot and turn off when it cools.

PRESTART CHECKLIST

☐ **TIME**
About 4 hours to run cable inside an attic and install a gable fan (not counting additional framing or cutting for gable vent)

☐ **TOOLS**
Voltage tester, drill, drywall saw, jigsaw or circular saw, hammer, screwdriver, strippers, long-nose pliers, lineman's pliers

☐ **SKILLS**
Stripping, splicing, connecting wires to terminals; installing rough wood framing

☐ **PREP**
Find power source and make sure the fan does not overload the circuit (pages 148–149). Lay sheets of plywood on the attic floor if the joists are exposed. Wear long clothes, protective goggles, and a dust mask.

☐ **MATERIALS**
Gable fan, cable, wood screws, wire nuts, cable clamps, electrician's tape

Junction box · Gable fan

1 If there is no gable vent, install one (opposite). If the studs are too far apart, add some framing. Cut 2×4s to fit between the studs and attach them with 3-inch screws.

Mounting flange · Thermostat

2 Mount the fan onto the framing by driving screws through the mounting flanges and into framing members.

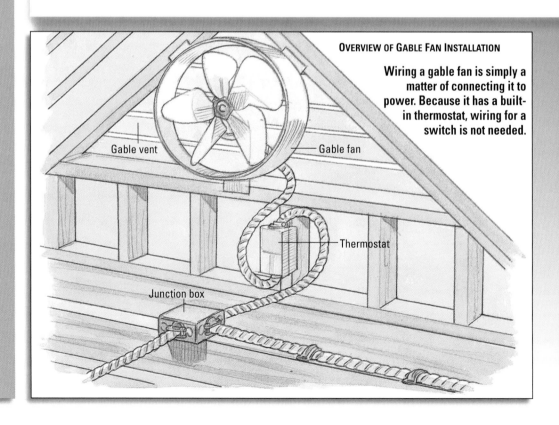

OVERVIEW OF GABLE FAN INSTALLATION

Wiring a gable fan is simply a matter of connecting it to power. Because it has a built-in thermostat, wiring for a switch is not needed.

Gable vent · Gable fan · Thermostat · Junction box

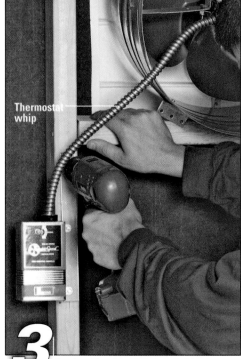

Thermostat whip

3 Fasten the fan thermostat to a framing member. The fan whip should be taut so it won't wobble and rattle against the framing when the fan runs.

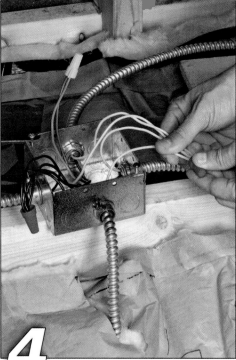

4 Shut off power to the circuit. Run cable from the thermostat into a power source. If no junction box is available in the attic, bring power up from a circuit in the floor below (page 176). Make sure the circuit can handle the additional load.

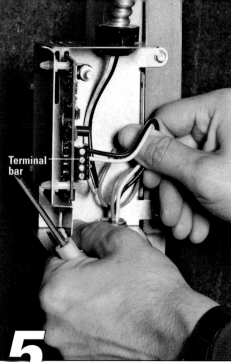

Terminal bar

5 Wire the thermostat following the manufacturer's directions. With the thermostat shown above, you insert stripped wire ends into a terminal bar and tighten the setscrews. Adjust the thermostat control and restore power.

WHAT IF...
No gable vent exists?

Jigsaw

To install a vent shutter, you need not cut or modify framing. Use a jigsaw or set a circular saw just deep enough to cut through the siding and sheathing.

Vent shutter

Cut a hole that the vent frame covers. Attach the louver by driving screws through its frame and into framing members.

Working with vinyl siding

Duct

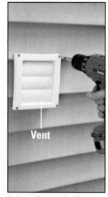

Vent

Cut vinyl with a fine-tooth handsaw, hole saw, or by repeated scoring with a utility knife. In some cases you may have to purchase a tool that unzips one course of siding from the next. For double protection install the duct and caulk around it. Then install the vent with galvanized screws and caulk around the vent housing.

Roof Fan

If it is not possible to install a gable fan (pages 212–213), a roof fan is the next best choice. Wiring is simple. Follow the manufacturer's instructions for cutting the hole and attaching the fan.

PRESTART CHECKLIST

☐ **TIME**
About 5 hours to cut a hole in the roof, install the fan, and run cable inside an attic

☐ **TOOLS**
Voltage tester, drill, bit, reciprocating saw or jigsaw, pry bar, utility and putty knives, screwdriver, strippers, long-nose pliers, lineman's pliers

☐ **SKILLS**
General carpentry, splicing wires and connecting wires to terminals, installing boxes, running cable in walls and ceilings

☐ **PREP**
Find power source and make sure the fan does not overload the circuit (pages 148–149).

☐ **MATERIALS**
Roof fan, cable, roofing nails, roofing cement, wire nuts, cable clamps, electrician's tape

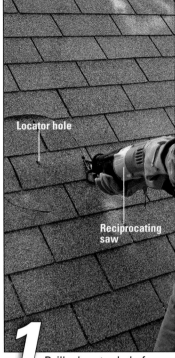

Locator hole
Reciprocating saw

1 Drill a locator hole from the inside of the attic to ensure that you do not cut through a joist. Mark the roof with the manufacturer's template and cut the hole with a jigsaw or reciprocating saw.

Flange

2 You may need to cut back some shingles. Slide the fan into place so that shingles cover the top half of its flange.

Roofing nail
Roofing cement

3 Drive roofing nails and cover them with roofing cement. Use roofing cement to seal down the roofing above and beside the vent. Wire the fan as you would a gable fan (pages 212–213).

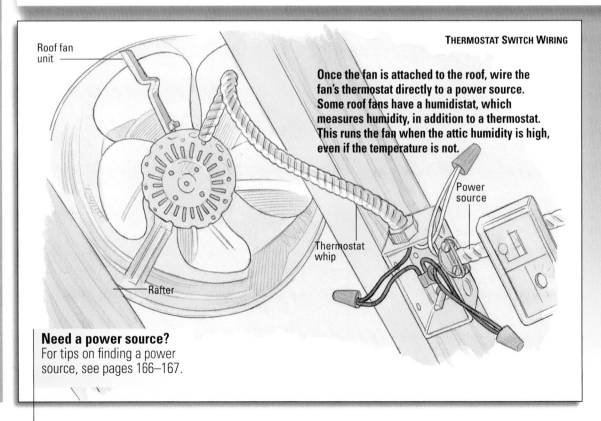

THERMOSTAT SWITCH WIRING

Roof fan unit

Once the fan is attached to the roof, wire the fan's thermostat directly to a power source. Some roof fans have a humidistat, which measures humidity, in addition to a thermostat. This runs the fan when the attic humidity is high, even if the temperature is not.

Power source

Thermostat whip

Rafter

Need a power source?
For tips on finding a power source, see pages 166–167.

RANGE HOOD

A range hood removes air over a cooking surface and may have lights too. Usually it attaches to the underside of a cabinet. The bottom of the hood should be about 24 inches above the cooktop.

Range hoods are rated for the amount of air they can move in CFM (cubic feet per minute). Ducts more than a few feet long or that make several turns to reach the outside reduce the flow. Consider purchasing a ductless unit, which filters the air and sends it back into the kitchen.

To replace a range hood, **shut off power** and remove the existing hood. Take the hood with you when you buy a new one to make sure the ductwork lines up.

PRESTART CHECKLIST

☐ **TIME**
About 6 hours to cut holes, run cable, and install ductwork and a range hood (not including cutting a pathway for the cable and patching walls)

☐ **TOOLS**
Voltage tester, drill, long bit, drywall saw, jigsaw, hammer, fish tape, long-nose pliers, screwdriver, strippers, tin snips, lineman's pliers

☐ **SKILLS**
Stripping, splicing, and connecting wires to terminals; running cable through walls; cutting holes into walls

☐ **PREP**
Find power source and make sure the range hood does not overload the circuit (pages 148–149). Spread a drop cloth on the floor below.

☐ **MATERIALS**
Range hood, cable and clamps, ducts, duct tape, sheet metal screws, wall cap, caulk, wire nuts, electrician's tape

Drywall saw

1 Remove the range hood electrical cover and punch out the knockouts for the duct and for the electrical connection. Hold the hood in position and mark the wall for two holes. Cut a hole in the wall for the duct.

Long bit for locator holes

2 If necessary drill a hole for the cable. With a long bit drill locator holes through to the outside of the house.

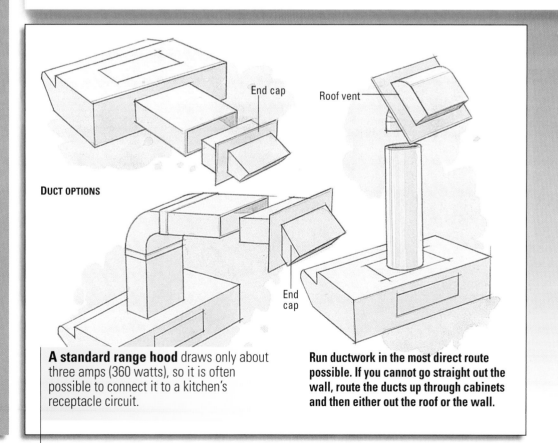

End cap

Roof vent

DUCT OPTIONS

End cap

A standard range hood draws only about three amps (360 watts), so it is often possible to connect it to a kitchen's receptacle circuit.

Run ductwork in the most direct route possible. If you cannot go straight out the wall, route the ducts up through cabinets and then either out the roof or the wall.

RANGE HOOD *continued*

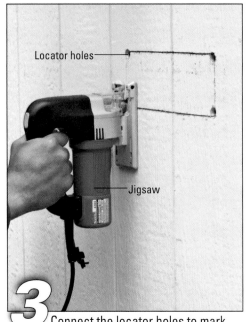

Locator holes

Jigsaw

3 Connect the locator holes to mark the cutout. Make sure the hole is the right size for your duct. Cut through siding using a jigsaw, reciprocating saw, or circular saw.

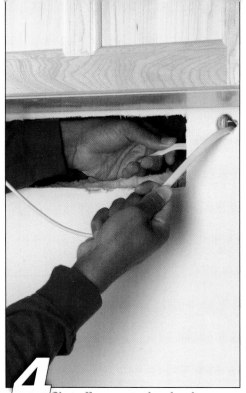

4 **Shut off power to the circuit.** Connect cable to a power source and run it up through the cable hole. You may use the cutout for the duct to help access and handle the cable, but make sure the cable is not in the way of the duct.

Caulk bead

End cap

5 Measure from the outside to the inside wall and cut a piece of duct to fit. Attach the duct to the end cap. Apply a bead of caulk around the hole on the outside and slide the duct and cap through the wall. Attach the cap with screws.

FOR VENT HOLE IN CABINET

Duct through cabinet

Knockout

If the duct runs upward, remove the knockout on top of the hood and install the damper unit. Cut cabinets carefully to make room for the duct.

STANLEY PRO TIP
Bending sheet metal

To join a duct to a range hood (left), you may have to cut the duct to size and bend your own flange. For a straight, neat angle, score the bend with the end of a screwdriver, clamp on two 1×2s as shown above, and bend the flange.

Cutting and attaching to a masonry wall

Use a masonry bit to drill the locator holes in Step 2. To cut through brick drill holes every inch or two, then chip away with a hammer and cold chisel. An older home may have two thicknesses of brick.

Caulk

Self-tapping masonry screw

Purchase masonry screws along with a masonry bit of the appropriate size for the screws. Drill a pilot hole and drive the masonry screw into the block.

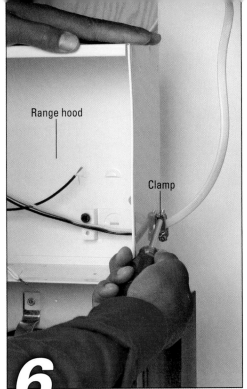

Range hood

Clamp

6 Stuff insulation into the cavity around the duct. Strip and clamp cable to the range hood.

7 Position the range hood so the duct fits snugly over the hood's damper unit. Attach the hood with screws driven up into the cabinet above and/or into the wall studs.

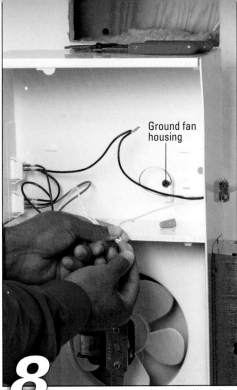

Ground fan housing

8 Connect the grounds, including the pigtail, to the hood housing. Splice the hood's lead wires to the house wires. Reattach the electrical cover.

WHAT IF...
A stud is in the way?

If a stud is in the way of the most direct route for the duct, try working around it with flexible ductwork. Another option is to cut a wall opening large enough to install a header but small enough that it is covered by the range hood and the cabinet above it. Cut the stud and install a header made of two 2×4s with ½-inch plywood between them.

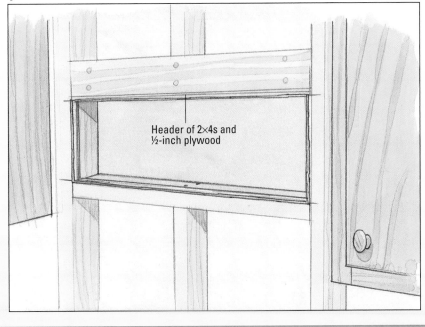

Header of 2×4s and ½-inch plywood

OVER-THE-RANGE MICROWAVE

Over-the-range microwaves are conveniently placed and do double duty as range vents. You need a microwave designed especially for the job, as well as a vent to carry away exhaust fumes from the stove. The vent is built into the wall and is easiest to install when you're building or remodeling the kitchen. But if you're good at drywall repair, you can install one in a finished kitchen. You also need a cabinet the microwave hangs from. The cabinet not only provides support but it also contains the wiring for the microwave and may contain part of the venting.

PRESTART CHECKLIST

☐ **TIME**
About 2 hours to hang the microwave from the wall and cabinet; longer if venting and wiring is required

☐ **TOOLS**
Screwdriver, tape measure, stud finder, drywall saw, wire cutters, needle-nose pliers, strippers

☐ **SKILLS**
Measuring and finding framing, wiring if outlet needed, ability to install vents, if required

☐ **PREP**
Move range, if it's in the way; install microwave cabinet.

☐ **MATERIALS**
Over-the-range microwave; cable; outlet boxes; receptacle; cover, if new outlet needed; vent, if needed

1 Install the vent and cover it with drywall. Cut through the drywall with a drywall saw to access the vent.

2 Over-the-range microwaves hang from a cabinet. Install an outlet for the microwave inside the cabinet.

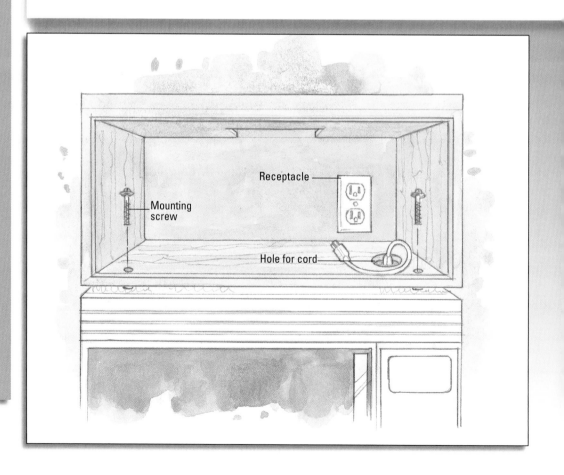

Mounting screw

Receptacle

Hole for cord

3 The microwave can vent through the wall or the roof. On some microwaves you'll adjust the vent to channel the air in the right direction. On others, including this one, you'll position the fan to channel the air.

4 A mounting plate attached to the wall and bolts through the bottom of the cabinet into the top of the microwave support the unit.

5 Many microwaves come with a template for mounting. Tape the template to the wall, drill where shown, then remove the template. If there is no template, follow the manufacturer's directions to lay out the mounting holes.

6 Attach the mounting plate to the wall. The exact method depends on where the studs fall and on the design of the plate. You need to attach to at least one stud but can probably use toggle bolts elsewhere. Follow the manufacturer's directions.

7 Make sure the door is latched and have someone help you hang the microwave on the mounting plate.

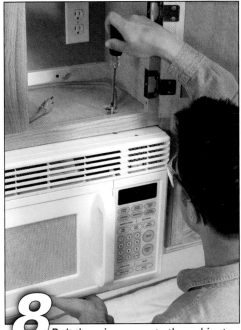

8 Bolt the microwave to the cabinet following the manufacturer's directions and plug it in.

BATH VENT FAN

Plan the installation so the vent duct is as short as possible and makes as few turns as possible (opposite).

In addition to a vent fan, a bathroom unit may have a light, nightlight, or heater. A heater uses more power than a light and fan, so it may need to be on its own circuit.

A fan or a unit with a light and fan that come on at the same time require only two-cable wiring. Wiring becomes more complex with separate function controls and additional functions. To replace an existing fan, check the wiring; you may need to replace two-wire cable with three-wire cable or even two cables.

PRESTART CHECKLIST

☐ **TIME**
About 7 hours to install ducting, a fan, and a switch (not including cutting a pathway for the cable and patching walls)

☐ **TOOLS**
Voltage tester, pry bar, drill, drywall saw, jigsaw, hammer, ladder, fish tape, screwdriver, strippers, long-nose pliers, lineman's pliers

☐ **SKILLS**
Cutting through siding or roofing; stripping, splicing, and connecting wires; installing boxes; running cable

☐ **PREP**
Find the shortest path for the ductwork. Find power source and make sure the new fan does not overload the circuit (pages 148–149). Spread a drop cloth on the floor below.

☐ **MATERIALS**
Vent fan, switch, ductwork, duct tape, sheet metal screws, cable, clamps, switch box, wire nuts, electrician's tape

A. Install the vent fan housing

Pry bar

Old ceiling box

1 To replace an existing ceiling light with a fan/light, **shut off power to the circuit.** Remove the light and pry out the ceiling box. If you cannot work from above, cut carefully around the box before prying. You may need to cut through mounting nails.

Fan housing

2 Disassemble the new fixture and use the housing as a template to mark for the opening. The fan must be securely mounted; if there is no joist to attach it to, install blocking nailed to nearby joists.

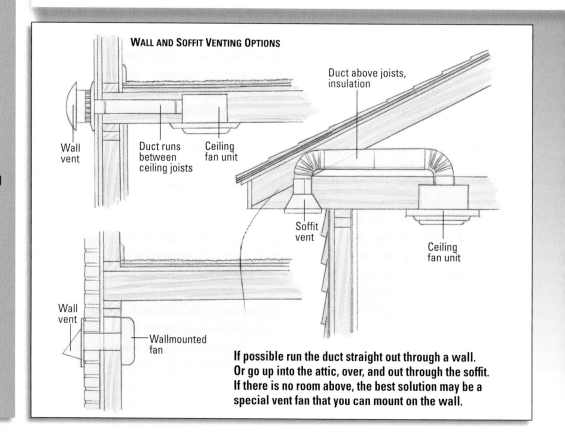

WALL AND SOFFIT VENTING OPTIONS

Wall vent

Duct runs between ceiling joists

Ceiling fan unit

Duct above joists, insulation

Soffit vent

Ceiling fan unit

Wall vent

Wall-mounted fan

If possible run the duct straight out through a wall. Or go up into the attic, over, and out through the soffit. If there is no room above, the best solution may be a special vent fan that you can mount on the wall.

Blocking

Drywall saw

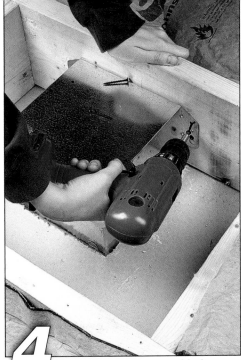

Locator hole

Jigsaw

3 If necessary install blocking to keep the insulation away from the fan. Cut a hole with a drywall saw or reciprocating saw. If the ceiling is plaster, drill locator holes at the four corners and cut the opening from below.

4 If necessary run new cable from the switch to the box (pages 174–177). (The fan shown has separate controls for fan and light and requires one three-wire cable.) Screw the fan to a framing member.

5 For the wall vent drill a locator hole from the inside through the outside wall. Outside cut a hole for the duct.

WHAT IF…
You must work from below?

If you cannot access an attic space above, cut the hole next to a joist. If the duct can run parallel to a joist and the outside wall is not too far away, use a long bit to drill the locator hole.

STANLEY PRO TIP

Ducts should be short, wide, and smooth

The shorter, smoother, and wider the ductwork, the more freely air can move through it. Most ductwork for bathroom fans is 4 inches in diameter; don't use anything narrower. Solid ducting is the smoothest and most efficient, but it may be difficult to install in tight places. All-metal flexible ducting is bendable and fairly smooth. Plastic-and-wire ducting is the easiest to install but is the least efficient.

At every joint use sheet metal screws or clamps to make tight connections, then cover the joint completely with professional-quality duct tape.

Venting through the roof

Roof jack

To install a roof jack (page 222), follow the manufacturer's instructions exactly to prevent leaks. First cut through the roof, then cut back shingles. Install the jack and cover its top half with shingles. Cover all nails with roofing cement (page 214).

A. Install the vent fan housing *continued*

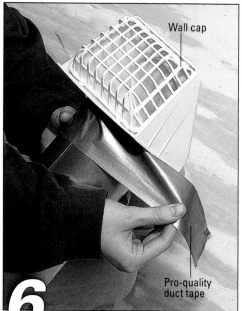

Wall cap

Pro-quality duct tape

6 Measure from the outside to the fan. Attach a piece of solid duct to the wall cap so it is long enough to reach the fan or as close as possible. Fit the duct to the cap, drill pilot holes, and drive sheet metal screws to hold it in place. Cover the joint with professional-quality duct tape.

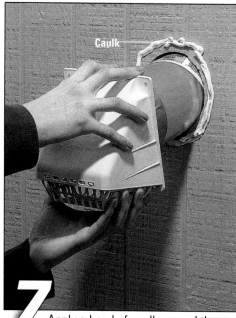

Caulk

7 Apply a bead of caulk around the exterior hole. Slide the duct through the hole and fasten the cap to the wall with screws.

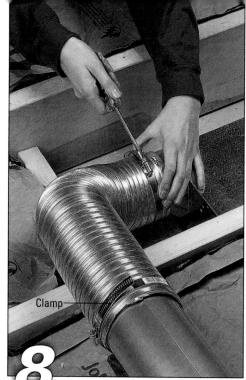

Clamp

8 Fill any gap between duct and fan with another piece of solid duct or with flexible metal ducting. Clamp each joint and wrap with duct tape.

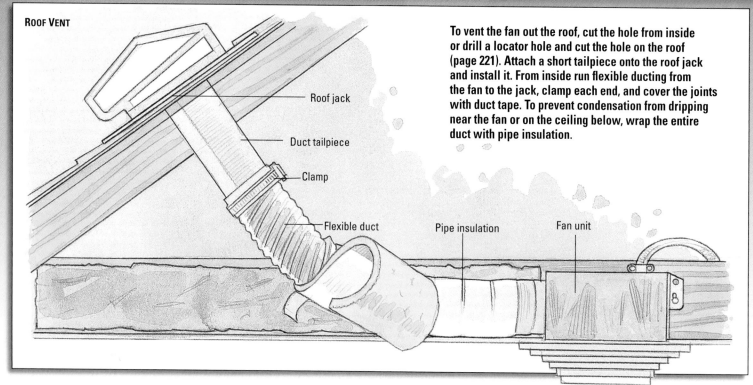

ROOF VENT

Roof jack

Duct tailpiece

Clamp

Flexible duct

Pipe insulation

Fan unit

To vent the fan out the roof, cut the hole from inside or drill a locator hole and cut the hole on the roof (page 221). Attach a short tailpiece onto the roof jack and install it. From inside run flexible ducting from the fan to the jack, clamp each end, and cover the joints with duct tape. To prevent condensation from dripping near the fan or on the ceiling below, wrap the entire duct with pipe insulation.

B. Wire the fan

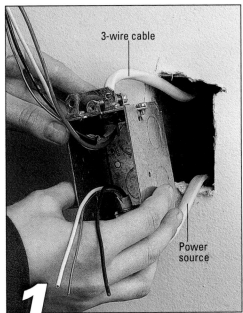

3-wire cable

Power source

1 If necessary run the correct cable or cables to the switch box. As shown above power enters the switch box. If power enters the fan, see the manufacturer's instructions.

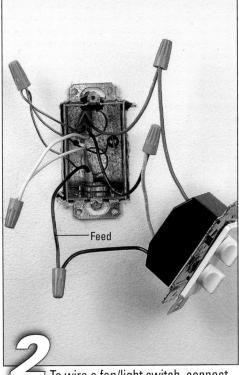

Feed

2 To wire a fan/light switch, connect the grounds and splice the white wires. Connect the red and black wires from the fan to the fan and light terminals. Connect the feed wire to the remaining terminal.

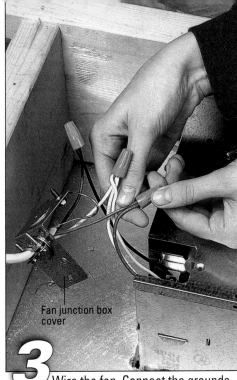

Fan junction box cover

3 Wire the fan. Connect the grounds and splice the white wires. Splice the black wire to the black fan lead and the red wire to the colored lead. Attach the junction box cover. In the bathroom install the light and the fixture canopy.

Timer switch for a fan with a heater

Leaving the fan heater on wastes energy and creates a hazardous situation. To avoid this install a timer switch (above) along with a two-function switch for the fan and light. To do so install a double-gang box.

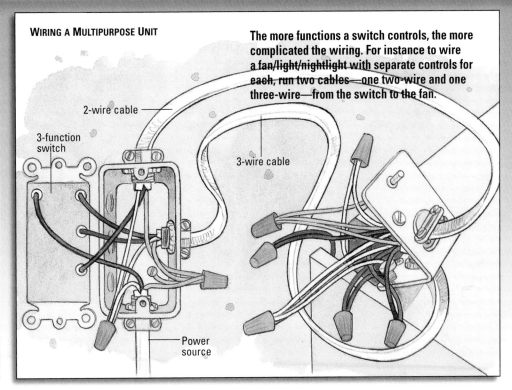

WIRING A MULTIPURPOSE UNIT

2-wire cable

3-function switch

3-wire cable

Power source

The more functions a switch controls, the more complicated the wiring. For instance to wire a fan/light/nightlight with separate controls for each, run two cables—one two-wire and one three-wire—from the switch to the fan.

INSTALLING ELECTRIC HEATERS

Adding an electric baseboard or wall heater can be a cost-effective way to bring heat to a cold spot or an area that gets only occasional use.

Plan 10 watts of heater capacity per square foot of room area. Check local codes for circuit requirements; some municipalities require a dedicated circuit protected by a 20-amp double breaker. In some cases you can add heaters to existing 120-volt circuits—see page 150. Confirm that the circuit voltage matches the heater voltage.

Place heaters on outside walls below windows. Never locate a heater beneath a receptacle. Follow the manufacturer's recommendations for placing furniture and drapes near the unit. In general baseboard units are best for supplemental heat; blower-heaters are best for intense heat of short duration.

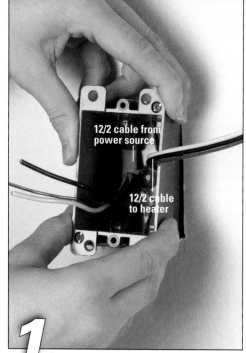

12/2 cable from power source

12/2 cable to heater

1 Cut an opening for a large-capacity remodel box. Run 12/2 cable to the location of the thermostat. **Do not connect the cable to its power source.** Run cable from the opening to the heater location. Strip cables and clamp them into the box. Install the box.

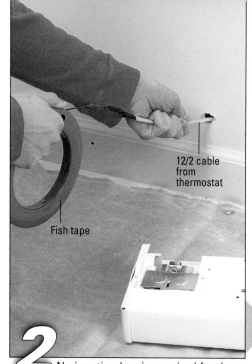

12/2 cable from thermostat

Fish tape

2 No junction box is required for the cable running to the heater—the box is built into the unit. Strip the incoming wires. (You also can run the feeder line directly to the heater and then to the thermostat. Check the manufacturer's instructions.)

PRESTART CHECKLIST

☐ **TIME**
About 3 hours to run cable and install a baseboard heater and thermostat; about 2½ hours to run cable and install a blower-heater

☐ **TOOLS**
Voltage tester, drill, ½-inch bit, drywall saw, fish tape, screwdriver, stripper, long-nose pliers, lineman's pliers

☐ **SKILLS**
Cutting into walls; stripping, splicing, and connecting wires to terminals; installing boxes; running cable into boxes

☐ **MATERIALS**
Heater, box for thermostat, 12/2 cable, electrician's tape, wire nuts

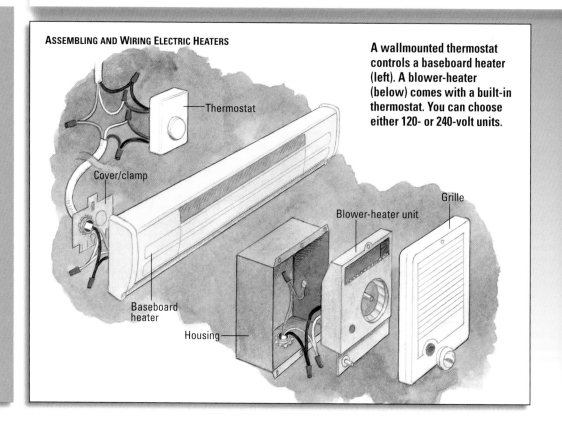

ASSEMBLING AND WIRING ELECTRIC HEATERS

A wallmounted thermostat controls a baseboard heater (left). A blower-heater (below) comes with a built-in thermostat. You can choose either 120- or 240-volt units.

Thermostat

Cover/clamp

Baseboard heater

Grille

Blower-heater unit

Housing

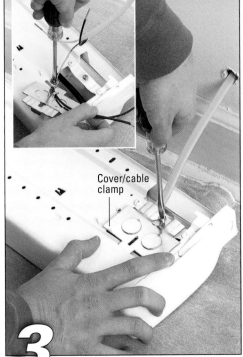

Cover/cable clamp

3 Place the heater face down on the floor and remove the cover/cable clamp. Attach the house ground line to the green screw on the heater (inset). Using wire nuts connect incoming lines to the heater leads. Close and fasten the cover/clamp.

4 Locate and mark wall studs. Push the cable into the wall. Attach the unit with at least two 1½-inch drywall screws. Tighten, then back off a half turn to allow for the expansion and contraction of the metal housing when the unit is turned on and off.

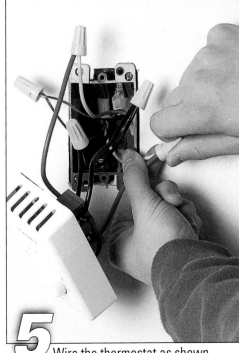

5 Wire the thermostat as shown (opposite), using wire nuts and electrician's tape. Install the thermostat and snap on its cover. Connect to the power source or new circuit (pages 278–279) and test the unit.

WHAT IF…
You're installing a blower-heater?

A blower-heater unit fits between wall studs and is somewhat simpler to wire because it has a self-contained thermostat. The unit shown runs on 240 volts. (To learn how to hook up a new 240-volt circuit, see pages 278–279. Check local codes for requirements.)

A blower-heater must be a safe distance from nearby walls and furnishings. When choosing a location for the heater, maintain 12 inches from any adjacent walls. For safe and effective operation, locate the box 12 inches above the floor and keep the area 3 feet in front of the box clear. Check the manufacturer's recommendations before locating the unit.

Before cutting an opening for the unit, drill a finder hole and use a wire to check that the wall cavity is clear of pipes and wires (page 201). Use a drywall saw to cut the opening. Run the recommended cable to the opening.

1 Remove one of the knockouts in the housing. Insert a clamp and pull 10 inches of cable into the box. Clamp the cable and fasten the housing in place with 1-inch (longer if needed) drywall screws. Strip incoming wires.

2 Attach the incoming wires to the heater leads (see opposite). Fasten the heater unit into the housing, being careful that the wires do not get caught between the motor and the housing. Attach the grille and thermostat knob. Connect to the power source.

INSTALLING ELECTRIC RADIANT HEAT

Electric radiant heat, installed directly over cement board, plywood, a mortar bed, or a concrete slab, is a plastic mat with interwoven heater cable. The mat is imbedded in thinset before the final flooring material is installed. A wallmounted thermostat or timer controls the heat.

The 120-volt circuit or power source for the radiant heat mats must be GFCI-protected. Mats are available in a variety of lengths. Check the manufacturer's specifications for the wattage your situation requires. See page 148 for determining whether a circuit can handle the demand.

PRESTART CHECKLIST

☐ **TIME**
About 8 hours to install mat, wire, and tile for an average bathroom

☐ **TOOLS**
Digital ohmmeter, drill, ½-inch bit, drywall saw, fish tape, chisel, hot-glue gun, ⅜-inch trowel, screwdriver, stripper, long-nose pliers, lineman's pliers, tools for laying the flooring, jeweler's screwdriver

☐ **SKILLS**
Stripping, splicing, and connecting wires to terminals; installing boxes; running cable into boxes; setting tile

☐ **PREP**
Rough-in the plumbing; install the subfloor.

☐ **MATERIALS**
12/2 cable, mat, box, armored power cable, thermostat and/or timer, thinset, flooring, mortar or grout

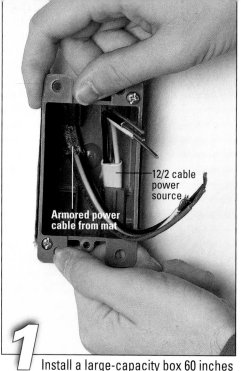

1 Install a large-capacity box 60 inches above the floor for the thermostat. Using 12/2 cable add a new circuit (pages 278-279) or extend an existing circuit (pages 166–167) but **do not connect the power source.** Pull cable provided with the mat to the box.

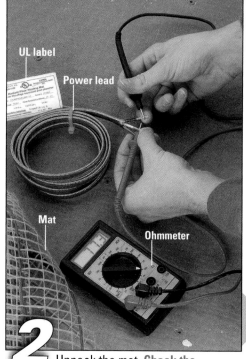

2 Unpack the mat. **Check the resistance using a digital ohmmeter.** The reading should be within 10 percent of the rating shown on the UL label. This is your benchmark for confirming that the heat cable is not nicked during installation. Write the reading down.

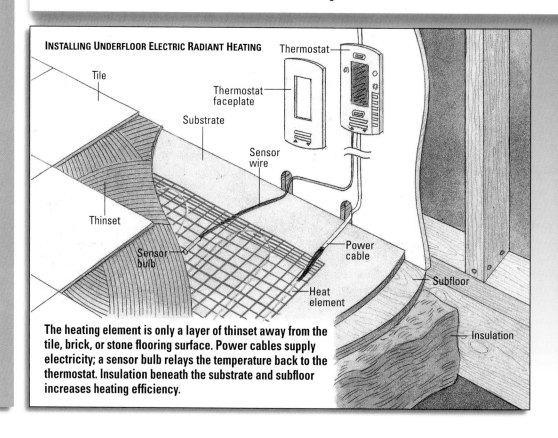

INSTALLING UNDERFLOOR ELECTRIC RADIANT HEATING

The heating element is only a layer of thinset away from the tile, brick, or stone flooring surface. Power cables supply electricity; a sensor bulb relays the temperature back to the thermostat. Insulation beneath the substrate and subfloor increases heating efficiency.

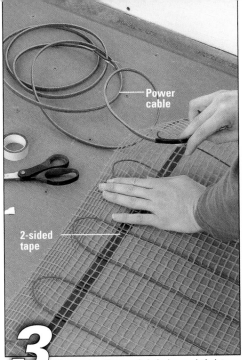

Power cable

2-sided tape

Channel for power cable connection

Cold chisel

Power cable

Hot-glue gun

3 Clean the floor of debris and tighten any protruding screw or nailheads. Roll out the mat and position it. Check that it is no closer than 3–6 inches to walls and fixtures. Attach double-sided tape to the floor, but do not attach the mat to the tape yet.

4 The armored power lead connection is thicker than the mat and must be sunk into the substrate. (Cement board is shown here.) Trace around the connection; use a cold chisel to cut a channel for it.

5 Glue the power cable connection into the channel with hot glue. Mark along the power cable and slide it to one side. Working a few feet at a time, run a continuous bead of hot glue. Press the lead into the hot glue.

REFRESHER COURSE
Strategies for running cable through walls

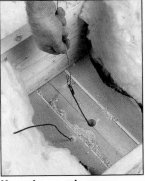

Go downstairs for power by drilling a finder hole directly in front of the wall through which you want to run the cable. Use a wire to mark the spot. Drill a ¾-inch hole and use a fish tape to pull the cable to where it is needed. (See page 176.)

Cut away drywall (save the piece for replacing and taping later) so you can run cable horizontally. This allows you to tap into a receptacle in the same room. (Check that the circuit can bear the additional load. See page 148.)

If you have attic space above, drop power down to the room where you need it. Drill a finder hole to locate the wall plate. Drill an access hole, run fish tape, then pull cable to extend a circuit or create a new circuit. (See page 176.)

WHAT IF...
You're working in tight quarters

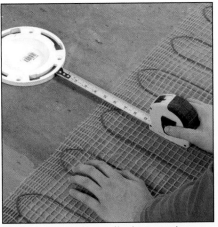

Mats can run under a toilet but must be 3 inches from the toilet ring. In addition a mat can run beneath the kick plate of a vanity. Never overlap mats, cut a mat to fit, nor attempt to repair a cut or nicked heating wire. If the wire is damaged you must replace the entire mat.

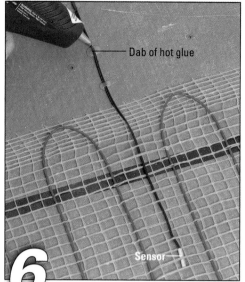

Dab of hot glue

Sensor

Thinset

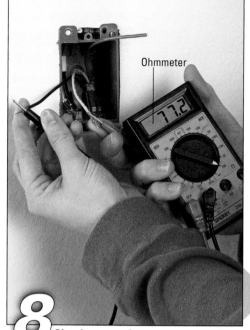

Ohmmeter

6 Press down on the tape to adhere it to the cement board, then pull off the backing and firmly press the mat onto the tape. Weave the sensor bulb between two heating elements. Adhere the sensor bulb wire with dots of hot glue. **Check resistance with an ohmmeter. Record the reading.**

7 With the flat side of a ⅜-inch notched trowel, apply thinset over an area of the mat. Then turn the trowel over and rake the thinset to ¼-inch uniform depth. Be careful not to snag the mat. Do not clean the trowel by banging it on the mat. Tile the area of the floor covered with thinset.

8 **Check mat resistance once again** using the ohmmeter. If the ohm reading is either 0 or infinity, the heating element has been damaged. The tile must be removed and the mat replaced.

LAYOUT ALTERNATIVES

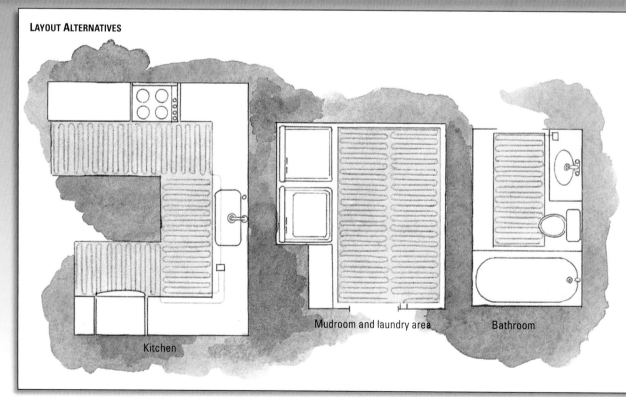

While this type of electric radiant heating can only be used indoors, it can be installed wherever a tile, brick, or stone surface makes sense: bathroom, mudroom, or kitchen.

Kitchen

Mudroom and laundry area

Bathroom

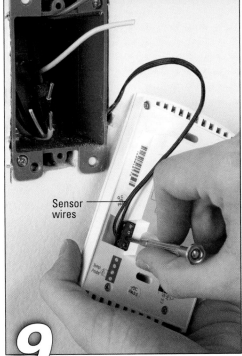

9 The control shown above has built-in GFCI protection. Using a jeweler's screwdriver attach the two sensor wires to the screw terminals on one side of the control. Connect the ground from the mat power lead directly to the house ground.

Sensor wires

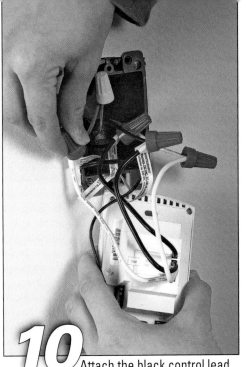

10 Attach the black control lead marked LINE to the incoming black wire. Connect the white control lead LINE to the incoming white wire. Attach the control leads marked LOAD to the wires connecting to the mat, black to black and white to white. Fold the wires into the box.

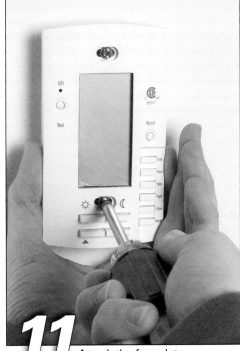

11 Attach the faceplate. Connect to the power source or connect the line to a new breaker (pages 278–279). Turn on the power and follow the manufacturer's instructions for setting the thermostat.

ADDING A TIMER

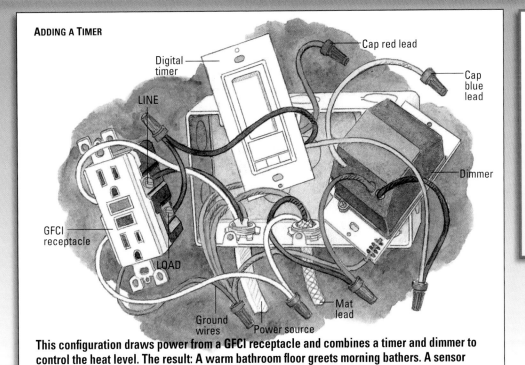

Cap red lead

Digital timer

Cap blue lead

LINE

Dimmer

GFCI receptacle

LOAD

Mat lead

Ground wires

Power source

This configuration draws power from a GFCI receptacle and combines a timer and dimmer to control the heat level. The result: A warm bathroom floor greets morning bathers. A sensor bulb and line are not needed with this approach.

SAFETY FIRST
Don't overload circuit or components

Checking the amperage a new installation demands tells you whether an existing circuit can carry the load or if you have to install a new circuit. Each square foot of electric radiant heating mat draws 0.1 amp. That means adding radiant heating mats to the work area of an average-size kitchen adds only five or six amps to the circuit (50–60 square feet of mat). Each component in the system, such as a dimmer or timer, must be rated to take the amperage.

HOUSEHOLD VOICE, DATA & SECURITY

Peek under any computer desk or behind the armoire that holds audio and video equipment, and you'll likely see a tangle of wires and cables. Stapled to the baseboard and popping out of holes drilled into the floor, such wires have been added over the years to meet the demands of new types of communication. These include speaker wire, phone lines, coaxial cable, and maybe the recent addition of high-speed, high-capacity Category 5 or 5e cable. These lines make up the other wiring found in your home—low-voltage communication lines.

Household networking

Taming the tangle is easier with newly available control panels and outlets designed specifically for household use. They help you wire your house for the present—and future—communication technology. They help ensure that bad runs or poor connections don't compromise the quality of signal. In addition they allow you to alter your communication network easily.

The heart of the system is a control panel installed in a central location. Incoming phone, cable, and satellite lines connect to it. Out of it run telephone, data, and video lines to various areas of the house. By using an attic, crawlspace, or basement, you can run Category 5 (and the higher-capacity Category 5e) and coaxial lines to outlets designed for phone, computer, fax, and video hookups.

This chapter shows you how to install just such a system. If your needs are more modest, it also shows how to extend a phone line, run coaxial cable, or install a wall speaker.

Fire and break-in protection

A growing number of municipalities require that smoke and carbon monoxide detectors be wired in a series so all units sound a warning. This chapter explains how to install such devices. In addition it explains how to plan and install a wide range of interior and exterior security fixtures and how to shop around for professionally installed and monitored security systems.

Low-voltage upgrades are safe to work with and can vastly improve household communication.

CHAPTER PREVIEW

Installing a media network
page 232

Installing a wireless network
page 236

Installing phone lines
page 238

Installing TV cable
page 241

Installing a home theater
page 243

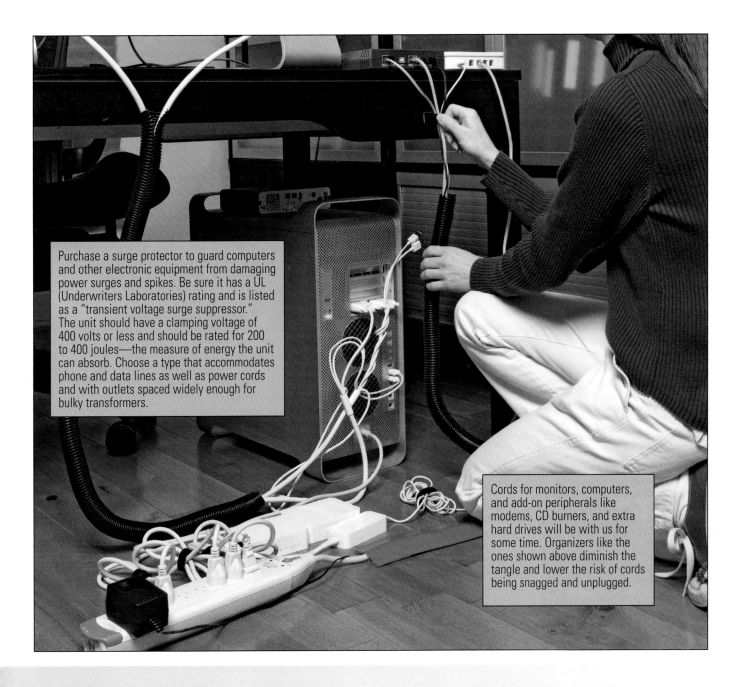

Purchase a surge protector to guard computers and other electronic equipment from damaging power surges and spikes. Be sure it has a UL (Underwriters Laboratories) rating and is listed as a "transient voltage surge suppressor." The unit should have a clamping voltage of 400 volts or less and should be rated for 200 to 400 joules—the measure of energy the unit can absorb. Choose a type that accommodates phone and data lines as well as power cords and with outlets spaced widely enough for bulky transformers.

Cords for monitors, computers, and add-on peripherals like modems, CD burners, and extra hard drives will be with us for some time. Organizers like the ones shown above diminish the tangle and lower the risk of cords being snagged and unplugged.

Planning security
page 248

Installing hardwired smoke detectors
page 250

Installing a garage door opener
page 251

Home automation
page 254

Installing a surge protector
page 256

Emergency generators
page 257

INSTALLING A MEDIA NETWORK

Installing a media network panel with modules for phone, data, and video lines provides flexibility and the assurance that you have reliable connections.

Planning the network

Choose a central location for your network panel, away from any electrical breaker panel or subpanel. Avoid attics or garages, where temperatures and humidity vary widely. Make sure no lines have to reach more than 300 feet from the panel. Check with service providers for special requirements. Place several outlets in each room, no more than 12 feet from each other. Each should have at least a telephone and cable outlet. Draw a plan, noting the length of cable run and parts needed.

PRESTART CHECKLIST

☐ **TIME**
About 1 hour to run each cable, about 4 to 6 hours to install the panel

☐ **TOOLS**
Drywall saw or reciprocating saw, cable connector crimpers, type-F connector crimpers, stripping tool, drill, fish tape, longnose pliers, diagonal cutter

☐ **SKILLS**
Planning, making electrical connections, running cable

☐ **PREP**
Plan the installation; clear space for installing the panel and outlets.

☐ **MATERIALS**
Panel; cable and telephone distribution modules; power module, Cat. 5e and coaxial cable with connectors; outlets

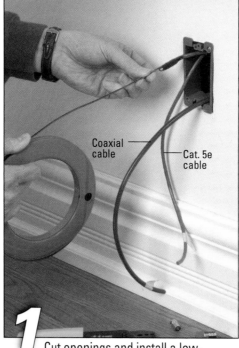

1 Cut openings and install a low-voltage box at each outlet location. Between two studs cut an opening for the network panel. Run Category 5e cable for phone and data lines and coaxial cable for broadband or satellite lines. (See how to run cable on page 169.) This is the hardest and most time-consuming part of the job.

Labels: Coaxial cable, Cat. 5e cable

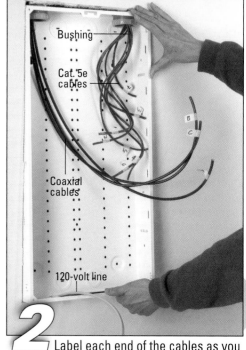

2 Label each end of the cables as you pull them. Leave 12–18 inches of excess cable at each opening. Run a 14/2 electrical cable from the breaker panel to the network box opening. Remove knockouts and fit the box with bushings to protect the cables. Feed the cables into the box and fasten them to the studs.

Labels: Bushing, Cat. 5e cables, Coaxial cables, 120-volt line

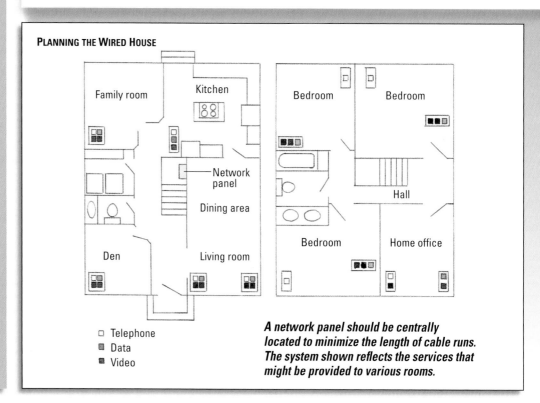

PLANNING THE WIRED HOUSE

Rooms: Family room, Kitchen, Bedroom, Bedroom, Network panel, Hall, Dining area, Den, Living room, Bedroom, Home office

☐ Telephone
☐ Data
☐ Video

A network panel should be centrally located to minimize the length of cable runs. The system shown reflects the services that might be provided to various rooms.

Punch tool provided with connector

3 Purchase Cat. 5e connectors, selecting colors to indicate use (blue for data lines and white for phone lines for example). Strip about 2½ inches of cable jacket and straighten the wires. Using the A color key on the eight-conductor connector, push the wires into their color-coded slots. Press them into place using the punch tool provided.

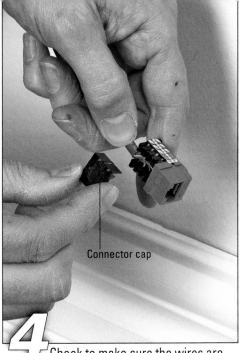

Connector cap

4 Check to make sure the wires are positioned correctly and then trim any excess wire with a diagonal cutter. Push the connector cap into place. Fit the coaxial cable with type-F connectors, following the steps shown on page 241.

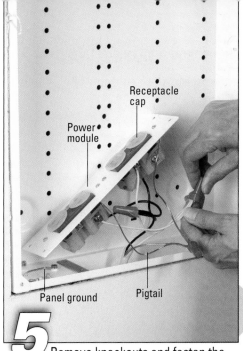

Receptacle cap

Power module

Panel ground   Pigtail

5 Remove knockouts and fasten the surge protector and GFCI power module into the network box. Strip the 14/2 cable and connect the module following the manufacturer's instructions. Fasten the module into place using screws provided. Leave caps in place to guard against debris falling into the receptacles.

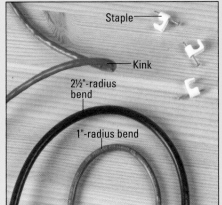

STANLEY PRO TIP

Avoid kinks and bends

Staple

Kink

2½"-radius bend

1"-radius bend

You can safely bend Category 5 and 5e cable to a 1-inch radius. Avoid kinks or strains— Cat. 5 and 5e cable cannot be spliced if damaged. Bend coaxial cable to no less than a 2½-inch radius. Secure wires with single-wire staples where accessible.

Attaching modular plugs on Cat. 5 and Cat. 5e cable

Modular plug

1 Use stripping pliers to strip about 2 inches of jacket. Straighten each wire. Check packaging for recommended wire order.

2 Trim wires to ½ inch. Fan them in the order they go into the modular plug. Push the wires into the plug.

Crimping tool

3 Use a crimping tool to fasten the wires into the plug. Give the plug a firm tug to make sure it is tight.

INSTALLING A MEDIA NETWORK continued

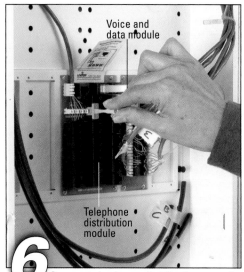

Voice and data module

Telephone distribution module

6 Snap a telephone distribution panel into place. It routes incoming telephone lines. Attach a voice and data module (or more if you need them—each module serves six wall outlets). Wire each household extension line to this module. Connect patch cords between these modules and the appropriate plug-in.

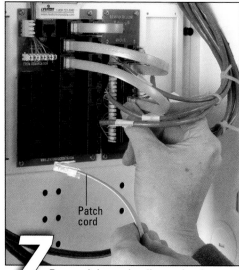

Patch cord

7 For each incoming line strip about 2½ inches of cable jacket from the Cat. 5e cable. Following the manufacturer's instructions straighten and fan the wires and place them into the color-coded brackets adjacent to the appropriate module. Press them into the brackets with a punch tool and snip off the excess.

Internet gateway

8 Snap the Internet gateway into place. Connect the incoming modem line to the WAN (wide-area network) port with Category 5e-rated patch cords. Connect computer lines to the gateway. Configure the gateway using the software provided on a CD packaged with the Internet gateway.

MAKING THE CONNECTIONS

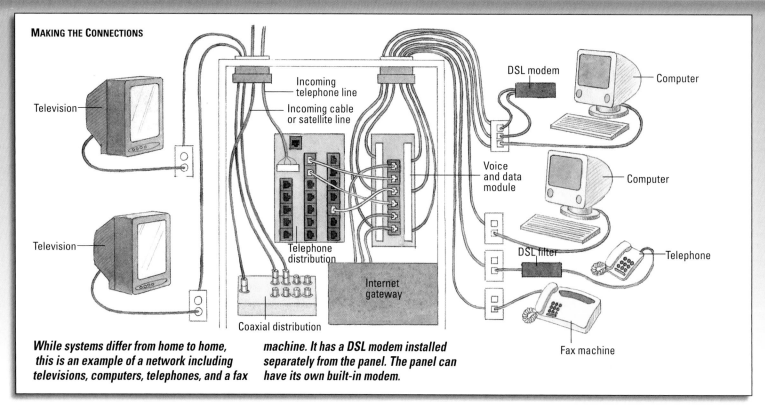

Incoming telephone line

Incoming cable or satellite line

Television

Television

Telephone distribution

Coaxial distribution

Internet gateway

Voice and data module

DSL modem

Computer

Computer

DSL filter

Telephone

Fax machine

While systems differ from home to home, this is an example of a network including televisions, computers, telephones, and a fax machine. It has a DSL modem installed separately from the panel. The panel can have its own built-in modem.

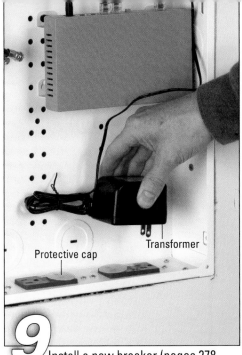

9 Install a new breaker (pages 278–279) to power the dedicated 15-amp lines. Test for power (see page 48). Remove a protective cap from one of the GFCI receptacles and plug in the Internet gateway transformer.

Protective cap

Transformer

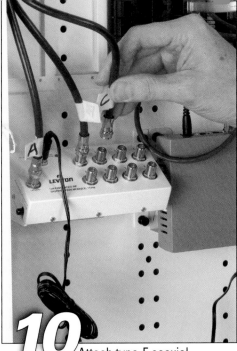

10 Attach type-F coaxial connectors to each incoming coaxial line, using coaxial stripping and crimping tools (page 241). Attach the incoming service cable to the CATV/ANT connection. Attach the other lines according to their labels. Plug the module transformer into the power module.

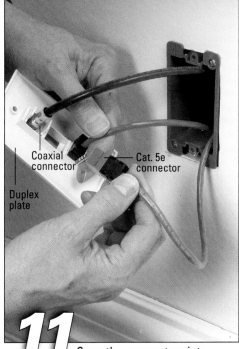

11 Snap the connectors into the duplex plate. (You can choose from plates that have from two to six openings.) Test each line (see box below). Gently feed the cables into the wall and attach the plate to the outlet box.

Coaxial connector

Cat. 5e connector

Duplex plate

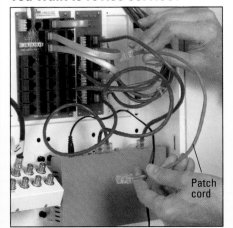

WHAT IF...
You want to revise service?

Patch cord

If a bedroom with only phone and video service is to become a home office requiring a fax/modem line or a network connection, changing is easy. As long as you've already pulled an extra Category 5 or 5e cable into the room, you can simply add a patch cord to add the service.

Testing the system

1 With an inexpensive walkie-talkie, an assistant, and the testing device shown, you can quickly test each new line. This tester has plugs for coaxial, four-pair phone lines, and Cat. 5 and 5e lines. Have your helper check the plan to identify the line being tested and then announce the line number to you.

2 At the network panel find the cable being tested and touch the tester to it. If the line is correct, the tester emits a high-pitched sound. If there is no sound, check other lines until you find the connected line. Adjust the connection at the panel to correct any mistakes.

INSTALLING A WIRELESS NETWORK

network usually consists of at least two computers. To be wireless the computers should exchange information and connect to the Internet without any extra wires coming out of the computer. But even if your network consists of a single computer, being wireless has its advantages. If you're working on a desktop computer, you cut down on the clutter of wires coming and going out of your computer. If you have a laptop, you can work away from your desk and still send email, connect with the Internet, and listen to music over the Web.

You won't need much to do it. You need a wireless router, and each computer needs a wireless card so it can communicate with the router. Most new computers come with wireless cards installed, and adding one into an older computer isn't complicated. The router itself is available online, at computer stores, and in some cases from your Internet service provider.

PRESTART CHECKLIST

☐ **TIME**
About 30 to 45 minutes to install and set up a system

☐ **TOOLS**
Screwdriver if installing card

☐ **SKILLS**
Plugging and unplugging USB cables

☐ **PREP**
Clear your desk.

☐ **MATERIALS**
Router, wireless card for each computer that doesn't already have one

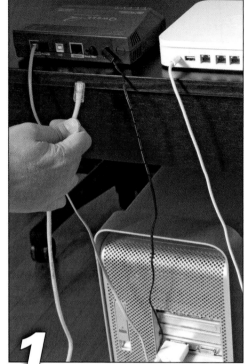

1 Turn off your computer and disconnect all cables running into and out of the computer and modem. Although you only have to make minor wiring changes, it's best to start from scratch so you can keep track of how things stand.

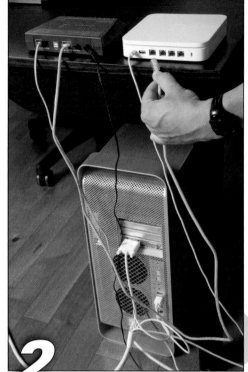

2 Run a cable from the modem to the router. The router enables devices on the network to "talk" with each other and to go online, so the router is the modem cable's first and only stop.

Wireless cards

New computers usually are set up for wireless service. If you have an older desk computer, you may need to install a PCI wireless card.

An older laptop may require a PCMCI wireless network card, which slips into a slot in the side of the computer.

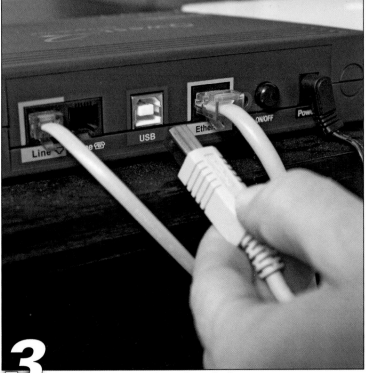

3 Plug in the router and turn it on. It diagnoses your system and sets itself up largely without requiring added information. Follow the on-screen "wizard" to set up security, choose a password, and name the system. Unless your printer has wireless capability, plug the printer cable into the router.

4 Touch the chassis to discharge static electricity that could ruin the card. Remove the screw that holds the cover over one of the empty PCI slots.

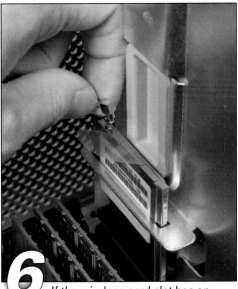

5 If your computer doesn't have wireless capability, install a wireless PCI card. On a notebook the card fits into a slot on the side. On a desktop unplug the computer and remove the cover by loosening the screws that hold it on. Push the card into the slot and screw it in place.

6 If the wireless card slot has an antenna, attach it to the card. Replace the computer cover.

INSTALLING PHONE LINES

Delivering telephone service to the house is the telephone company's business. For a fee the telephone company also runs lines and adds jacks inside, but you'll save money—and get exactly what you want—doing it yourself.

Telephone wiring is straightforward, but running cable so it is hidden takes time and effort. Before running and stapling cable, plan the entire run. Extra effort may save trouble and eliminate an eyesore. For instance running cable through a wall may mean you do not have to run it around a door.

For easy and secure connections, buy telephone cable that has solid-core 24-gauge wire. Cheaper cables have stranded wires that are difficult to handle.

PRESTART CHECKLIST

☐ **TIME**
   About 3 hours to tap into a junction box, run cable, and install a jack

☐ **TOOLS**
   Screwdriver, drill, strippers, lineman's pliers, round-topped stapler, flat pry bar, stud finder, voltage detector, drywall saw

☐ **SKILLS**
   Stripping and connecting telephone cable, running cable

☐ **PREP**
   Find the best route for the phone wires; if possible avoid having to go around a doorway.

☐ **MATERIALS**
   Telephone cable or Cat. 5 cable, phone jacks, round-topped staples or plastic-coated staples

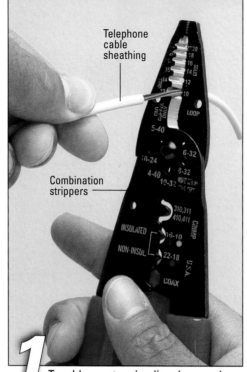

Telephone cable sheathing

Combination strippers

1 To add an extension line, loosen the screw and remove the cover from an existing phone jack. Using strippers remove about 2 inches of sheathing from the new cable using the tool's "10" slot.

2 Strip about ½ inch from each wire using the 22/20 slot on the strippers. Loosen each terminal screw, remove the wire attached to it, and twist it together with the new wire of the same color.

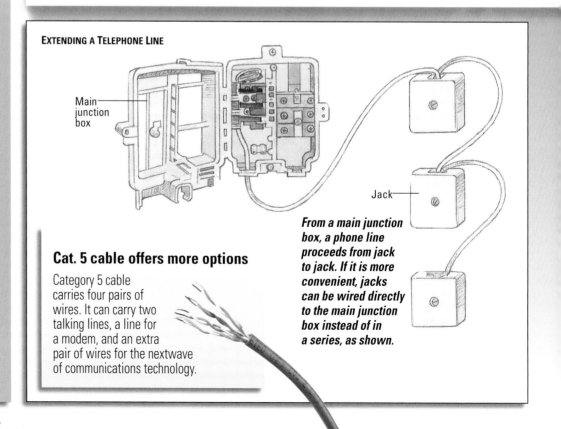

EXTENDING A TELEPHONE LINE

Main junction box

Jack

Cat. 5 cable offers more options

Category 5 cable carries four pairs of wires. It can carry two talking lines, a line for a modem, and an extra pair of wires for the nextwave of communications technology.

From a main junction box, a phone line proceeds from jack to jack. If it is more convenient, jacks can be wired directly to the main junction box instead of in a series, as shown.

3 Loop each pair of wires clockwise around the terminal of the corresponding color. Tighten the screws and push the cable into the hole provided. You may have to snap out a breakout tab.

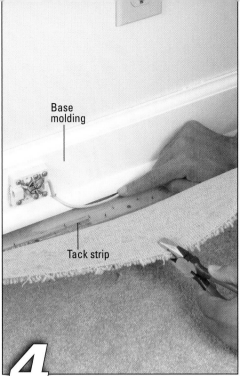

Base molding

Tack strip

4 Cable can run under wall-to-wall carpeting. Use lineman's pliers to pull back a short section at a time and run the cable between the tack strip and the molding.

¼" bit

5 To run cable through a wall, drill a hole through both sides of the wall using an extended ¼-inch drill bit. Use a stud finder to avoid running into a framing member. Before drilling use a voltage detector to check walls for electrical cable.

Tapping into a junction box

It may be easier to run cable discretely by starting at a junction box rather than a phone jack. Many houses have a junction box, like the one above, attached to the exterior. One section of the box is accessible to the homeowner; attach wires as you would in a phone jack (Step 3).

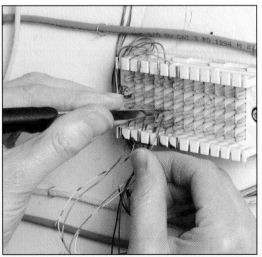

An indoor junction box or phone jack may have slide-on connectors. Do not strip the wires. Slide the wires end down onto the metal slit, using a thin slot screwdriver or a dull knife.

STANLEY PRO TIP

Running two or more lines using one cable

When installing a new line, it may be possible to piggyback on existing cable rather than running new cable. A phone line uses one pair of wires. With two-pair cable the red and the green wires are used for the first line, and the yellow and black wires for the second. Three-pair cable, as well as four-pair Category 5 cable, is also available.

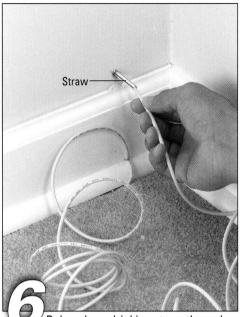

6 Poke a long drinking straw through the hole and fish it around until it pushes through the hole in the wall on the other side. Feed the cable through the straw. Remove the straw from the other side of the wall.

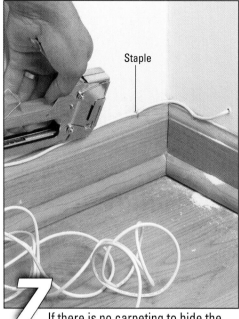

7 If there is no carpeting to hide the line, staple it to the top of the base molding. Use round-topped staples or staples made specially for phone line.

8 Attach a new jack to the base molding by drilling pilot holes and driving screws. To attach to a drywall or plaster wall, drill holes, insert plastic anchors, and drive screws into the anchors. Connect wires and attach the cover.

WHAT IF...
You want a jack for a wallmounted phone?

1 Use a stud finder to make sure the opening doesn't overlap a stud. Cut a hole into the drywall with a drywall saw. With plaster walls cut with a utility knife first, then use a jigsaw. Slip a low-voltage (LV) ring into the hole and tighten the screws to secure the ring to the drywall or plaster.

2 Attach a weight, such as a nut, to a string and guide it down the hole until it hits bottom. Leave plenty of extra string at the top.

3 Drill a ½-inch hole into the wall near the floor directly below the opening you cut for the wall jack. Insert a bent piece of wire, snag the string (jiggle the string to help snag it), and pull a loop through the hole. Attach the phone cable to the string with tape and pull it up through the hole.

4 Strip and connect wires to the terminals of a wall jack. Mount the jack to the LV ring and install the cover plate.

INSTALLING TV CABLE

Coaxial cable used for cable and satellite TV installations uses special male/female connectors and splitters. Twist-on connectors are available but do not provide as solid a connection as a crimp-on connector. You need a special crimping tool to work with those connectors (see below). For outdoor locations use watertight connections. All are available at electronics or hardware stores.

Run cable into a low-voltage (LV) ring, which is like an electrical box without a back (page 242).

Have the service provider do as much of the work of running the cable as possible. If service technicians run the cable into your house, provide specific instructions to route the cable, requesting that they adequately hide it. Or ask them to leave a coil of cable that you can install yourself.

PRESTART CHECKLIST

☐ **TIME**
About 3 hours to install a splitter or two, run about 40 feet of cable, and install a jack

☐ **TOOLS**
Drill, long ½-inch bit, screwdriver, strippers, utility knife, crimping tool, drywall saw

☐ **SKILLS**
Stripping cable, crimping cable, running cable through walls or behind moldings

☐ **PREP**
Spread a towel or drop cloth below where you cut the wall.

☐ **MATERIALS**
RG6 coaxial cable, cable staples, male connectors, splitters, LV ring, wall jack

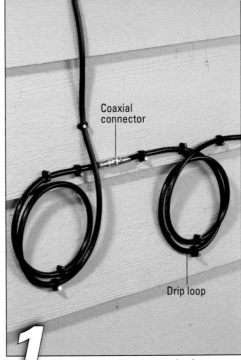

1 Where the cable enters the house, there are a watertight metal connector or possibly a splitter and a drip loop that carries water away from the connector. To split the line outside rather than inside, ask the cable company to provide the fitting and the cable.

Coaxial connector

Drip loop

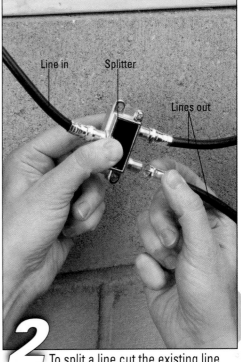

Line in   Splitter   Lines out

2 To split a line cut the existing line at a convenient location. Make male ends on both cuts and on the new line (below). Screw the three male ends into a splitter and attach it to a wall or joist with screws. If you're attaching to masonry, drill holes and use plastic anchors with screws.

STANLEY PRO TIP: **Making the male end**

1 Strip ½ inch of outer sheathing. With strippers or a knife, barely cut through the sheathing—don't cut through the wire mesh that lies inside. Pull the outer sheathing off with your fingers.

2 Push back the wire mesh. Strip ⅜ inch of plastic insulation from the center wire end. Slip a crimp-on connector onto the cable end. Push until the wire protrudes beyond the front of the connector by about 1/16 inch.

3 With a special coaxial crimping tool (don't try to use pliers), squeeze the connector sleeve tightly onto the cable.

INSTALLING TV CABLE continued

3 To run cable up from a basement or crawlspace, cut a hole into the wall for a low-voltage (LV) ring (Step 4). With an extended ½-inch bit, drill a hole down through the floor inside the wall.

Extended ½" bit

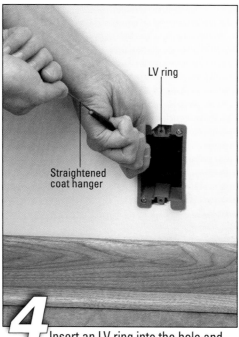

4 Insert an LV ring into the hole and tighten the mounting screws. Poke a wire hanger down through the hole in the floor. From below attach the end of the cable to the hanger with tape. Pull the cable up through the holes.

LV ring

Straightened coat hanger

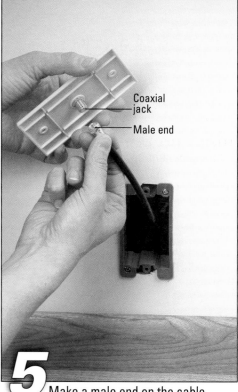

5 Make a male end on the cable (page 241) and screw it tightly to the back of a coaxial wall jack. Screw the jack into the LV ring.

Coaxial jack

Male end

Antenna alternatives

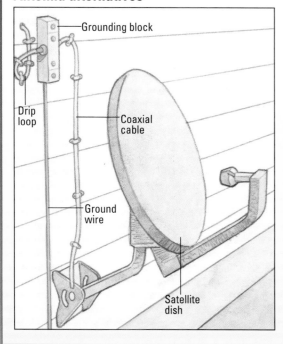

Grounding block

Drip loop

Coaxial cable

Ground wire

Satellite dish

Some satellite dishes are suitable for do-it-yourself installation. From a grounding block run RG6 cable down an exterior wall, staple it in place with plastic staples, and connect it to the dish. Attach a grounded copper wire to the grounding block. Run the ground wire to a grounding rod (page 29). Make a drip loop where the cable enters the house. Inside run the cable to a wall jack and plug the dish receiver into the jack. Follow manufacturer's instructions for pointing the dish.

Even with a satellite dish, an outdoor TV antenna may be needed to receive local channels. Some antennas have a coaxial connection. Others have a twin-wire lead. Use an adapter, available from an electronics store or home center, to connect a twin-wire antenna lead to coaxial cable.

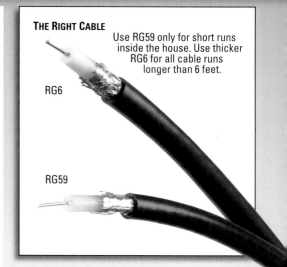

THE RIGHT CABLE

Use RG59 only for short runs inside the house. Use thicker RG6 for all cable runs longer than 6 feet.

RG6

RG59

Fuzzy reception?
If reception is fuzzy on one or more TVs, inspect all the splices and tighten if needed. If the problem continues ask the cable company about having a signal amplifier installed.

INSTALLING A HOME THEATER

A home theater combines the latest technology to change television into an experience that rivals the movie theater. A large-screen, high-definition television delivers a large, crystal-clear picture. A sophisticated audio system divvies up the sound and delivers it to a series of speakers that surround and seemingly place you in the middle of the action.

While the TV screen is clearly the heart of the experience, the true theater feeling comes from "surround sound," created by an audio system that takes stereo to the extreme. A typical system has a receiver/amplifier capable of parceling the audio from DVDs and HDTV among several speakers or "channels." A typical system might have six speakers, each delivering sound from a particular part of the audio landscape. Speakers to the left and right of the screen deliver sounds that would occur to the left and right of the action. A center speaker delivers sounds from action in the center of the screen. Left and right speakers behind the viewing area deliver sounds that would occur behind a viewer sitting in the middle of the action.

The sound of *Star Wars* X-wing fighters flying toward the screen would zoom from the rear speakers toward the front speakers for example. A sixth speaker, called a subwoofer and placed anywhere in the room, would deliver the bass rumble of the engines. A setup like this, with five speakers and a subwoofer, is called a 5.1 system. There are also 6.1 and 7.1 systems, which have six or seven speakers and a subwoofer.

There's plenty of flexibility in even the most basic system—the television can be plasma, projection, or flat screen. The video can come from either a DVD player, cable, or satellite TV connection. The quality and number of speakers can vary. The system can come prepackaged in a box, or you can pick and choose from stand-alone video and audio systems to get something that matches both your needs and budget. The challenges you face installing any system, however, are basically the same—running and hiding wire to at least six speakers, connecting the components with each other, and making sure the power source is adequate and free of interference. See the following pages for more details.

PRESTART CHECKLIST

☐ **TIME**
Installation time depends on the complexity of the system. A simple system with wireless speakers can be installed in about 2 hours. Running wire for a more complex system can take a day or longer.

☐ **TOOLS**
Screwdriver, drill, stud finder, torpedo level, utility knife, hammer, drywall saw, rotary cutter, or jigsaw.)

☐ **SKILLS**
Measuring and cutting drywall, connecting wires

☐ **PREP**
Plan speaker location, carefully plan the routes for the speaker wires, make sure power supply is adequate.

☐ **MATERIALS**
Television, receiver, DVD player, speakers, speaker wire

Home theater systems recreate the big-screen experience on a slightly smaller scale with a top-notch screen and a surround-sound system similar to those used in movie theaters.

Wiring a home theater

Wiring a home theater revolves around two things: a power source and speaker wires. By and large the power system is simplest. The components of your home theater will plug into a multiple-outlet power supply that plugs into a standard wall outlet. With anywhere from 6 to 8 speakers, however, the speaker cable will be your biggest challenge. You'll need to know where each speaker goes and then figure out the best way to get wire to it.

The power source
A sudden spike in power can burn out audio and video equipment as quickly as it can burn out a computer. At the very least you need a high-quality power strip that provides surge protection for the outlets and for the cable/satellite hookup. If you have a digital video recorder such as TiVo you'll also need to protect the phone line it uses.

Beyond surge protection you may also want filters that remove magnetic and radio interference from the line. These filters, sometimes called power or line conditioners, remove snow and other interference from the screen as well as background noise from the speakers. Filters can be built into a surge protector, into special outlets, or they can be installed separately. The ultimate (and most expensive) in-line cleaning is a power regenerator, which converts the AC current into DC and then back into AC under tightly controlled conditions, stripping it of its noise in the process.

As a system gets more extensive, consider adding a battery backup, usually referred to as an uninterruptible power supply (UPS). Not only will it keep the system operating (and save your settings) during a power outage, it will protect sophisticated gear from stress that may be caused by improper shutdown. UPS systems provide backup for anywhere between 40 minutes and 8 hours, depending on the unit.

Choose your power supply once you've chosen the other components so you know your power system is large enough, provides adequate protection, and has enough outlets.

Positioning speakers
Before you lay out your speakers, choose a television and designate a listening area based on the size of the screen—the distance from the seating area to screen should be at least twice the screen width.

Start with the center speaker, centering it above or below the TV screen and putting the tweeters as close to ear level as possible. If above the TV align the front edge of the speaker with the front of the TV to minimize distortion.

When you position the left and right speakers, a line drawn from one speaker to the primary listening area and back to the other speaker should form a 45-degree angle. (If you'll be using the speakers primarily for music, rather than theater, go with a wider, 60-degree angle.) If only a few people will use the theater, place the left, right, and center speakers in an arc, equidistant from the primary listening area. For larger groups line up the speakers across the front of the room.

In a 5.1 channel system, position the rear speakers directly to the side or slightly behind the listening area. Hang them at ear level when you're standing, so that they don't overpower the other speakers in the system. A 6.1 system is set up like a 5.1 system, with the additional speaker behind the seating and in line with the front center speaker. A 7.1 channel system is also arranged like a 5.1 channel system, with the additional speakers equidistant behind the seating and half as far apart as the front speakers.

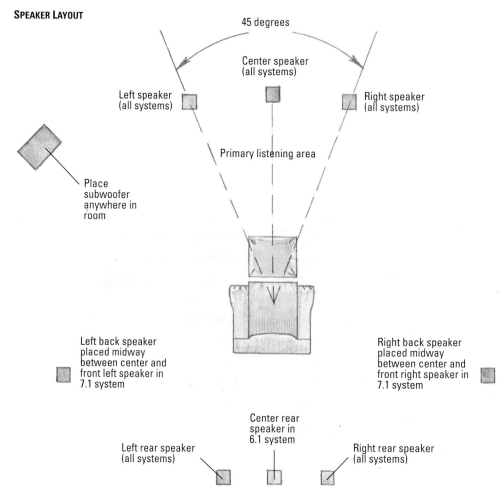

SPEAKER LAYOUT

45 degrees

Center speaker
(all systems)

Left speaker
(all systems)

Right speaker
(all systems)

Primary listening area

Place subwoofer anywhere in room

Left back speaker placed midway between center and front left speaker in 7.1 system

Right back speaker placed midway between center and front right speaker in 7.1 system

Center rear speaker in 6.1 system

Left rear speaker
(all systems)

Right rear speaker
(all systems)

Connecting your system

A home theater system requires an incredible amount and variety of wiring between the individual components, as well as between the system and the speakers. The wires you use largely will be determined by the components—an optical cable requires a system that produces an optical signal for it to carry. Likewise high-definition multimedia interface cables, which carry digital audio and video simultaneously, can only be used on a system that has the proper jacks. Nonetheless you should familiarize yourself with the various cables and their jacks so that you'll recognize them when you come across them.

Video cables

Composite video cables carry video signal once the television, DVD, or receiver has processed it. It carries the entire video signal in a single wire.

S-video cable carries the video signal in two streams—color and brightness—so that they can be processed separately.

Component video cable carries the video signal in three cables—one for brightness and two for color.

DVI cables

Digital Video Interface (DVI) cables use a pure copper cable to send a high-definition signal from your HD tuner to your screen.

HDMI

High-Definition Multimedia Interface cables (HDMI) carry both pure digital video and pure digital audio in the same cable. They can deliver up to 5 gigabytes per second—enough to handle both the video and audio in 7.1 channel systems. They're used to deliver a pure signal and minimize wiring between HDTVs, HD tuners, and high-definition disc players.

Audio cables

RCA patch cords have RCA plugs or jacks on the ends and are used to carry analog audio signals between components.

Digital coax cables have an RCA jack on one end, but the cable is designed to carry a wider bandwidth than non-digital cable. Digital coax is used in audio inputs or outputs on high-end equipment.

Speaker cable conducts the audio signal between the receiver and the speakers. If used inside a wall, it must be rated CL-2 or CL-3. Speaker wire is sold without connecters. Add connectors to match those on your receiver and speakers.

Optical cables transmit sound as light for a pure signal. You'll find optical cables on DVD players, CD players, and mini-disc recorders.

Radio frequency cable is 75-ohm coax cable that carries radio and television signals. It's used as an antenna wire and for connecting VCRs, cable, and satellite boxes. The inner core carries the signal; a layer of mesh underneath the jacket shields the cable from interference. RG-59 is the standard cable; RG-6 provides slightly better shielding.

Running speaker cable through the wall

A home theater system is much more enjoyable if it doesn't involve a maze of wires draped around the room. The best way to hide speaker cable is to run it through the walls—an easy enough job if you're doing it before the drywall is installed. Once the drywall is in place, however, you must follow the procedures for running electrical cable through a finished wall: cut into the wall selectively, drill holes through the studs, string the cable, and then repair the sections you cut away (pages 174–179). You can also hide wires effectively with some simpler techniques described on this page and the opposite page. Keep the following in mind:

■ Speaker wire must be approved for in-wall use. Local codes vary, but most call for a Class 2 or Class 3 wire, also known as CL-2 or CL-3.
■ The longer the speaker wire, the larger the wire you'll need. Generally speaking you will need 16-gauge wire for wire runs of less than 80 feet, 14-gauge wire for runs between 80 and 200 feet, and 12-gauge wire for anything more than 200 feet.
■ Run a continuous length of cable between the speaker and receiver. Once the wires are covered with drywall, splices that come loose are impossible to find.
■ Unless supported by studs cable must be supported every 4½ feet and within 1 foot of any junction box it enters. Use wire ties and tie plates to support the wires. Staples can damage the cable.

■ Don't drill holes within 2 inches of the top or bottom of a stud or within the middle third of the stud. Do not drill through glu-lams—structural beams made by gluing layers of wood together.
■ Cable pulls best through holes at least twice the diameter of the cable (or bundle of cables if you're running more than one cable through the hole.) Codes limit the size of the hole to one-third the thickness of the stud—½ inch is allowable for a 2×4, which is 1½ inches thick in actual dimension.
■ Do not run speaker or RF wires through holes that also contain electrical wires. The electrical wire will generate interference. Keep the electrical and speaker wires at least 2 feet apart if they run parallel for more than 5 feet. If wires must cross minimize interference by crossing them at right angles.

Wire ties and plates

Support speaker cable every 4½ feet with cable ties and tie plates. They offer a better solution than staples for supporting cable in walls.

Ties and plates are available at most home improvement centers.

Keep electrical and speaker wires at least 2 feet apart. Minimize interference by having wires cross at right angles.

Hiding cable in plain sight

Most home theaters are installed in finished rooms, where running speaker cable through the walls is a major job. Special materials and a couple of tricks make the job easier.

First you can always run cable along the wall, instead of through it. **Ultrathin cable,** a wide, flat cable only .006 inch thick, is made for the job. Stick the cable on the wall with the appropriate spray adhesive. When you're done paint or wallpaper over it to make it virtually invisible.

Wire mold is another way to run cable along the surface of the wall. The best way to hide it is to make it look like a part of the trimwork. Run along or just above the baseboard and painted to match, it is an unobtrusive way to hide the maze of wires created by a home theater system. It's available in vinyl, which paints well and is easy to trim, and comes with an adhesive backing that sticks to the wall.

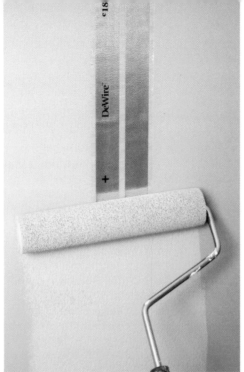

Ultrathin cable is so thin that you can make it disappear by painting or papering over it.

When you use wire mold to hide cable, make it look like part of the woodwork.

Running wire under carpet

While it's against code to run electrical cable under the carpet, running low-voltage speaker wire under the carpet is acceptable. Carpet that is glued down won't work, of course, but carpet held down by tack strips allows several possibilities.

Tack strips are the thin strips of wood that run around the edge of the room under the carpet; the points of the tacks point up to grab the carpet and hold it in place. The space between the wall and the strips creates a space perfect for housing a cable.

Instead of pulling up the carpet, fish the cable through the space with a **Fishtix YFT fish tape.** Be sure to get the thin one— it's only .11 (11/100) inch wide. Pull up neighboring corners of the carpet and feed the tape between them in the space between wall and the tack strip. Strip an end of the speaker wire, tape it to the end of the fish tape, and pull it back underneath the carpet.

If you'd rather you can fish tape under the body of the carpet with the help of another special fish tape, called an **undercarpet fish tape.** Pull up an inch or two or carpet anywhere along the wall and slide the tape between the carpet and pad.

Feed the tape across the room to the wire's ultimate destination. Pull up a couple inches of carpet where the tape reaches the other wall and fish the cable under the carpet. Use a flat cable to keep from creating a ridge in the carpet.

You can hide speaker cable along the edge of the room with the help of a narrow Fishtix YFT fish tape.

A flat fish tape lets you pull flat cable between the carpet and its padding.

PLANNING SECURITY

Before you decide on electrical and electronic features for home security, make sure you've covered the purely physical aspects. Install solid-wood or metal-clad exterior doors equipped with dead-bolt locks—not just the key-in-the-handle type of lock. Equip exterior doors with a peephole. (Don't bother with a door chain—the door can easily be forced open.) If you have recently moved into your home, have the locks changed. Secure sliding doors with locks or a thick dowel set into the track to prevent opening. Install key locks or slip-in pins on double-hung windows. Cover basement windows with grilles.

Secure the perimeter
Illuminate the outside of your house and any areas near the house where intruders could hide. A combination of switched lights, lights on timers, and lights triggered by photocells or motion sensors can create a protective buffer of illumination. A motion-sensor floodlight fixture can be installed as a complete unit, or you can retrofit a standard floodlight fixture with a motion sensor or a screw-in motion sensor. Existing exterior lights can be retrofitted with photocell controls. (Be a good neighbor by checking that such lights don't shine into nearby homes and aren't triggered by dog walkers going past on the sidewalk.)

Uplight trees with low-voltage floodlights to eliminate hiding places while providing an attractive landscape accent. Trim bushes and small trees to eliminate remaining hiding places. Trim tree limbs that might help someone climb into an upper-story window and lock in place any ladders stored outdoors. A wireless motion sensor placed outdoors can detect an intruder. A receiver, placed up to 400 feet from the sensor, chimes when it detects motion.

Illuminate each door so your path is visible while walking in and, more important, so you can see visitors before you open the door. Install two single-bulb fixtures or one dual-bulb fixture in case a bulb burns out. Add mushroom downlight fixtures or grazing lights along long or curving paths to eliminate tripping hazards. Light steps or stairways for safety too.

Make sure your house numbers are visible at night and readable from the street to speed the arrival of emergency personnel.

While you're away
In addition to covering the essentials—stop your newspapers and mail or make sure a neighbor gathers them for you—do what you can to create a credible illusion that you are still home. Plug in photocell light controls so lights switch on at dusk and off at dawn. (Such units must be exposed to natural light.) You can plug lamps into clock timers so they switch off and on in different areas of the house at different times. Lights left on through the night are better than leaving the house dark but still are a signal that the house might not be occupied.

Don't lower all the blinds and close all the curtains; make everything look occupied and as normal as possible.

Interior precautions
Window alarms can alert you to a break-in through a window. In the event of a power loss, battery-powered emergency backup lights in stairwells make an exit path less hazardous. Equip your home with adequate smoke and carbon monoxide alarms. Or consider getting a professionally installed and maintained security system (see opposite page).

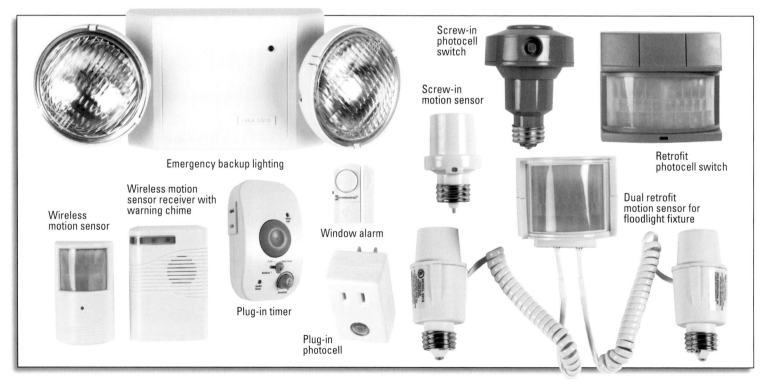

Emergency backup lighting

Screw-in photocell switch

Screw-in motion sensor

Retrofit photocell switch

Dual retrofit motion sensor for floodlight fixture

Wireless motion sensor receiver with warning chime

Wireless motion sensor

Window alarm

Plug-in timer

Plug-in photocell

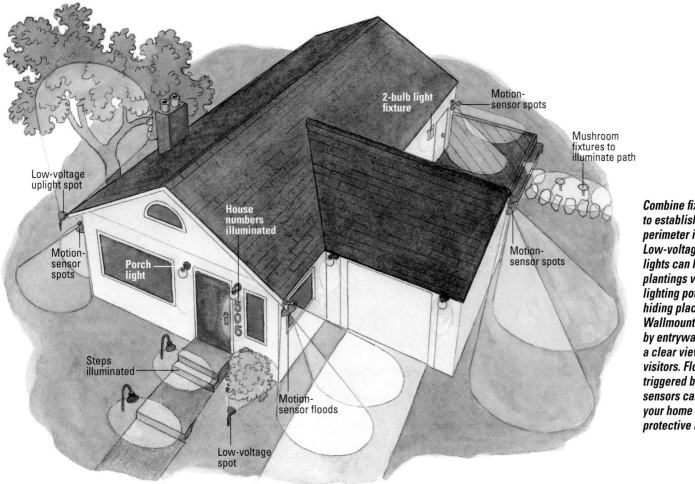

2-bulb light fixture

Motion-sensor spots

Mushroom fixtures to illuminate path

Low-voltage uplight spot

House numbers illuminated

Motion-sensor spots

Porch light

Motion-sensor spots

Steps illuminated

Motion-sensor floods

Low-voltage spot

Combine fixtures to establish protective perimeter illumination. Low-voltage accent lights can highlight plantings while lighting potential hiding places. Wallmounted fixtures by entryways give you a clear view of visitors. Floodlights triggered by motion sensors can surround your home with protective light.

Shopping for professional security

A professionally installed and monitored security system typically includes door and window contacts, motion detectors, and smoke detectors. If you are considering such a system, here are questions to ask and features to look for:

■ Be sure that the company is licensed, but be aware that licensing requirements in some states may be lax. Find out how long the firm has been in business—look for 10 years or more. Police or sheriff's departments don't officially recommend firms, but they can indicate whether your candidates are sound. Contact two or three firms.

■ Is your alarm system to be connected to police and fire dispatchers or to the company's monitoring center? If the former you need dedicated phone lines to police and fire departments. If the latter ask about staffing and response time—30 to 60 seconds is acceptable. And ask who does the monitoring—smaller firms contract it out.

■ Does the company offer a range of services, such as break-in, fire, carbon monoxide, low temperature warning, and sump pump high-water alarms? (You may not want all these features, but their availability indicates that a company can tailor a system to your needs.)

■ Can the company install alternate paths of communication (such as cellular or long-range radio) in case the primary line is interrupted? Consider this if you live in a remote area.

■ Be wary of anyone willing to provide a quote without seeing your home. Ask for a detailed, written description of the services. Avoid leasing the installation—that takes away your option of transferring to another monitoring service or changing equipment readily if your requirements change.

■ Beware of an overelaborate plan prone to false alarms. Most municipalities charge for false alarms beyond a maximum limit.

■ Check with your insurance agent to make sure the proposed system qualifies for a lower homeowner's insurance premium. Expect a 10–20 percent reduction.

■ Glass-break detectors should be secondary, not primary, defense. They shouldn't be placed in kitchens or baths and shouldn't be activated during waking hours. Dropped objects—even a yipping dog—can set them off.

INSTALLING HARDWIRED SMOKE DETECTORS

Hardwired smoke detectors with battery backup are required in some places. They are wired in a series so when one alarm sounds, all sound.

Running the cable is the hardest part of the job—the time required depends on the layout of your home. See pages 174–179 for instructions. In addition you'll need to tie in to a single source of power (pages 166–167).

PRESTART CHECKLIST

☐ **TIME**
About 5 hours to run cable and install three detectors

☐ **TOOLS**
Voltage tester, drill, ½-inch bit, drywall saw, fish tape, screwdriver, strippers, long-nose pliers, lineman's pliers

☐ **SKILLS**
Installing boxes; running cable into boxes; stripping, splicing, and connecting wires to terminals

☐ **MATERIALS**
Smoke detectors, boxes, 14/2 and 14/3 cable, electrician's tape, wire nuts

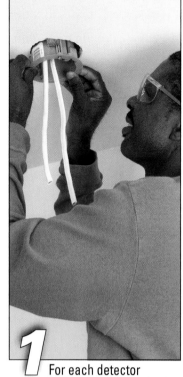

1 For each detector cut a hole for a standard 4-inch octagon or single-gang box. Run 14/2 cable to the first detector in the series, 14/3 cable thereafter. Install the boxes (pages 172–173).

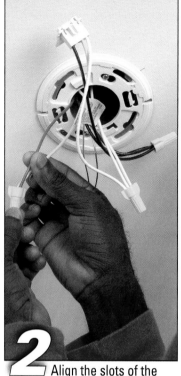

2 Align the slots of the mounting plate and attach the plate to the box. Gently pull the wires through the plate. After connecting the first box in the series (see below), connect wires as shown.

3 After securing the wire nuts with electrician's tape, gently push the wires into each box. Install the detectors, activate the backup batteries, and connect to the power source (pages 166–167).

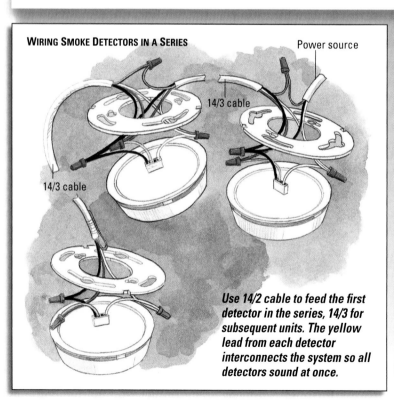

WIRING SMOKE DETECTORS IN A SERIES

Power source

14/3 cable

14/3 cable

Use 14/2 cable to feed the first detector in the series, 14/3 for subsequent units. The yellow lead from each detector interconnects the system so all detectors sound at once.

FOR EXTRA PROTECTION
Install a plug-in carbon monoxide alarm

Carbon monoxide, an odorless, colorless, poisonous gas, results from combustion. Faulty venting for appliances, wood or charcoal burners, or the incursion of auto exhaust can put your household at risk. Plug-in units like this have battery backup.

INSTALLING A GARAGE DOOR OPENER

Installing a garage door opener involves carpentry and mechanics as much as wiring. The wiring is about as simple as hooking up a doorbell. The power head usually plugs into an outlet, but check with your local building inspector to see whether it needs to be hardwired.

The carpentry and mechanics involve assembling a large piece of equipment and hanging it from the ceiling joists. It is a good idea to have a helper.

Garage door openers are available with screw-drive or chain-drive. A knowledgeable salesperson can help you choose the right opener. It helps to know what your door weighs, but you probably don't unless the door is brand new and you still have the packaging. Instead know the size of the door, what it's made of, and whether it's sectional or one-piece. You can take along a picture of it when you go shopping.

1 The opener's rail, which runs between the power head and the door, is shipped in pieces. Assemble as directed by the manufacturer.

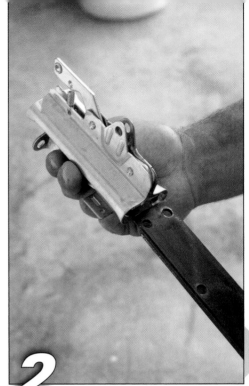

2 The carriage travels back and forth in the rail and connects to an arm that raises and lowers the door. Slip the carriage into its slot and attach the emergency cord.

PRESTART CHECKLIST

☐ **TIME**
  About 8 hours

☐ **TOOLS**
  Drill and bits, hammer, phillips head and slotted screwdrivers, tape measure, adjustable wrench, socket wrench, pliers, wire stripper, 6- or 7- foot stepladder

☐ **SKILLS**
  Wiring, basic assembly, minimal carpentry

☐ **PREP**
  The opener needs a nearby 120-volt outlet. The garage door should already be installed.

☐ **MATERIALS**
  Garage door opener

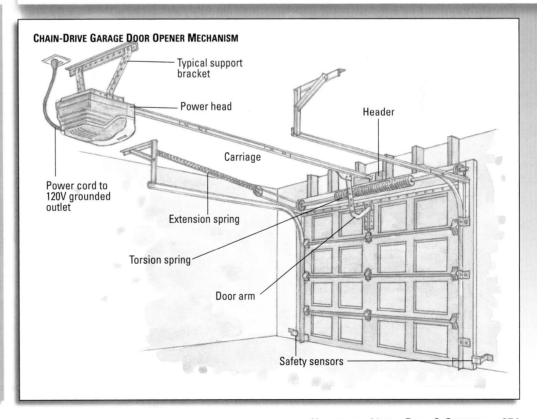

CHAIN-DRIVE GARAGE DOOR OPENER MECHANISM

- Typical support bracket
- Power head
- Header
- Power cord to 120V grounded outlet
- Carriage
- Extension spring
- Torsion spring
- Door arm
- Safety sensors

3 Bolt the rail to the power head following the manufacturer's instructions. Tighten all fasteners securely.

4 The limit switches attach to the rail. One of them is adjusted later so it cuts off the motor when the door has closed. The other is adjusted to cut off the motor when the door is completely open. For now attach but don't adjust them. Run the limit switch wires to the power head and connect them.

5 The bracket that holds the rail needs to attach to the framing. If necessary, nail in a new piece of framing to support the bracket. The framing can be either a vertical piece, as shown here, or a horizontal piece nailed to neighboring studs.

8 Attach the door arm to the door, then slide the carriage back and forth until it aligns with the upper end of the arm. Connect the arm to the carriage.

9 Power door openers have safety sensors that stop the door from closing if someone or something is in the way. Attach the sensors—a light and a photocell—to the garage door tracks as directed.

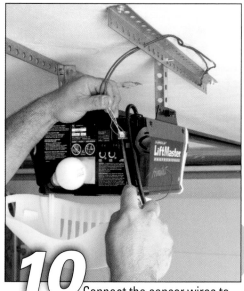

10 Connect the sensor wires to the power head. Route the wires so they will not interfere with the door or carriage.

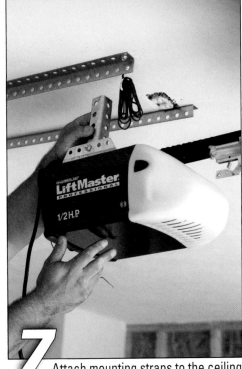

6 Attach the bracket that supports the rail following the manufacturer's directions. Then support the power head on a ladder, box or small table so that you can lean the rail assembly against its mounting bracket.

Attach the rail to the bracket, tightening the screws or bolts finger tight. Tighten them firmly once the power head is in place, or as directed by the manufacturer.

7 Attach mounting straps to the ceiling joists to hold the power head. The rail needs to be at a 90-degree angle to the door—if necessary add framing so the straps are properly positioned. Hang the power head from the straps. For more on squaring up the rail, see "The 3-4-5 Method."

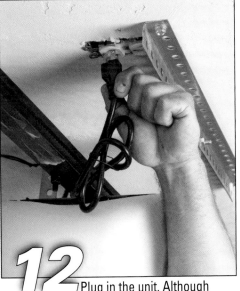

THE 3-4-5 METHOD

Use the 3-4-5 method to make sure that the rail is square to the garage door. The method is based on geometry: If the sides of a triangle measure 3, 4, and 5 feet, the angle opposite the 5-foot side is 90 degrees. Make a mark 3 feet along the door and 4 feet along the rail. The rail is at 90 degrees when the distance between the marks is 5 feet. This method works no matter the units—feet, yards, miles, inches, meters, or anything else—and with multiples, such as 6-8-10 or 12-16-20.

11 Garage door openers have switches mounted on the wall so you can open and close the doors from inside the garage. Attach the wall switches, run wires for them, and connect to the power head.

12 Plug in the unit. Although garage door openers can be hardwired into a junction box, most codes allow you to plug one into a dedicated outlet. Adjust the limit switches and safety sensors.

HOME AUTOMATION

*T*he smart house. You come home and the air-conditioner has been on just long enough to cool the house. The lamp is on by your favorite chair. If there had been an emergency, you would have been called and the plumbing or wiring would have been cut off as needed. When you go on vacation, the lights turn on in random order, fooling the curious criminal.

Smart-house technology has existed for years. Now hardware that can bring that technology into any home is becoming more readily available.

The system shown is Z-Wave, a radio-controlled platform used by a group of smart-house product manufacturers. Radio signals from a handheld transmitter control outlets plugged into your receptacles. A push of a button turns on a light at the far end of the house, activates a lighting scheme for the whole house, chooses a different scheme, or has your home theater up and running.

PRESTART CHECKLIST

☐ **TIME**
About 10 minutes to install a system of Z-Wave outlet adapters, and about 20 minutes for each Z-Wave switch you install

☐ **TOOLS**
To install a switch you need a screwdriver, current detector, wire cutters, wire strippers, and needle-nose pliers

☐ **SKILLS**
Wiring a switch

☐ **PREP**
Choose lights, appliances, and switches you want to control.

☐ **MATERIALS**
Remote control, outlet adapters, Z-Wave switches

1 Install outlet adapter dimmers for the lamps you want to control. The dimmer simply plugs into the outlet and controls up to 300 watts of lighting. Install high-power outlet non-dimming adapters for appliances of up to 1,800 watts. The button at the bottom of each adapter is for direct control—push for on and off. If it's a dimmer adapter, hold the button to dim. The adapter receives and acts on signals from the remote and forwards signals to other adapters.

2 Install dimmer switches for overhead lights you want to control. Remove the old switch and install the Z-Wave unit.

How it works

Everything you need to control a Z-Wave system is in a handheld remote control. The remote control sends radio signals to outlets, telling them what do: Turn on, turn off, dim this, or dim that. The remote can control as many as 64 outlet adapters, which can be set to provide 34 different lighting scenes—one for small dinner parties, say, and another for Monday night football. Any of eight built-in timers can be used in any scene, allowing you to make changes without touching the remote.

A system like this needs a reliable way of communicating and, as a result, not only can the remote talk to the outlet adapters but the adapters all talk with each other. If you're turning on the electric blanket from your basement workshop, the nearest adapter picks up the signal and relays it up the stairs. If there's an obstacle that interferes with the radio signal, like a brick wall or large refrigerator, the outlets figure out a route around it. Because each outlet acts as a repeater, the range of the remote is limitless.

3 Once you've installed an adapter, point the remote at it and push the button designated in the manufacturer's directions. The remote registers the adapter's presence. Plug in an appliance and you can turn it off or on with the remote. On dimmer adapters you can dim the light plugged into it.

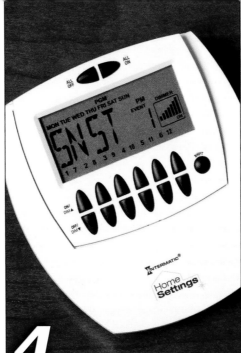

4 To control more than one unit at a time, you can create groups. Set the remote in group mode. Give the group a name and push buttons until the remote reads "add unit." Go to an adapter you want to add to the group and push the button on it. Repeat with other adapters you want to add. You now can turn the group on and off or dim it.

5 Scroll to the scenes menu and select the group you want to create a scene for. Press and release the button on the adapter you want to include and wait for the message on the remote telling you to set the level. Dim the light to the desired level, press OK on the remote, and set the next member of the group the same way.

The original home automation system

Z-Wave is only one of several automation systems. The first system was X10, which sent signals through the house wiring. Developed in 1975 it used one of the world's first integrated circuits. It's still in use today: The units it controls can plug into an outlet or replace the outlet. Operating through the house lines avoids having to run wires to control the system but has its drawbacks. Electrical distortion in the power lines can interfere with an X10 signal the way static interferes with your radio, and a command from the remote gets drowned out. Conversely an X10 receiver might interpret a bit of noise as a command. As the oldest system however, X10 now has a wide variety of accessories, from lawn sprinklers to leak detectors that shut off the water and call you in an emergency.

Outdoor lighting controls

Home automation isn't restricted to indoor lights and appliances. Two different devices let you control outdoor lights without ever leaving the house. The first is a simple screw-in device. It fits in outdoor light fixtures, is approved for use in dry, damp, or wet locations, and can handle up to 300 watt-bulbs in an open-air installation. (If the bulb is fully enclosed in a light fixture, the heat generated limits bulb size to 60 watts.) Operation with the base above the bulb is not recommended. Some lights, such as rope lights, Christmas lights, and temporary spotlights, plug in rather than screw in. For lights like these, you can use a weather-resistant outdoor appliance module. Plug the module's cord into an outdoor outlet and plug the lights into the module. Either the screw-in socket or the appliance module can be operated by a standard Z-Wave remote.

INSTALLING A SURGE PROTECTOR

Surge protectors protect electronic equipment—computers, DVD players, televisions—from the damaging electrical surges that occur when lightning strikes a power line. They are heavy-duty versions of plug-in protectors that protect your computer. When a surge travels through the line to your house, the surge protector directs it away from your wiring and into the ground—a single protector protects every circuit the box controls. There are three types of protector. One attaches to the meter and needs to be professionally installed. A second type mounts outside the breaker box. The third type resembles a double breaker and replaces two of the breakers in the breaker box.

PRESTART CHECKLIST

☐ **TIME**
About 40 minutes

☐ **TOOLS**
Voltmeter, slot-head screwdriver

☐ **SKILLS**
Adding and removing breakers, taking meter readings, removing knockouts, attaching external box to breaker box

☐ **PREP**
Obtain a powerful battery-operated light to help you see what you're doing when the power is off

☐ **MATERIALS**
Surge arrester, two 20-amp breakers

1 Remove the cover and look for two slots that are on opposite bus bars. Test by taking a meter reading with the power on. If you don't get a reading in the neighborhood of 240 volts, test other combinations of empty slots until you find two that give you the 240-volt reading.

2 **Turn off the power at the main breaker** and test to make sure it is off. Remove the knockout on the breaker box that gives you the shortest route to the open slots on the bus bar and attach the surge arrester to the box as directed by the manufacturer. Connect the ground wire to the ground bus and the white wire to the neutral bus. Make sweeping wire curves instead of sharp turns for best performance.

3 Connect the black wires to 20-amp breakers. Snap the breakers into place; remove knockouts for them in the panel cover and replace the cover.

Surge-protector breakers

Several companies make surge-protector breakers, which mount inside the box instead of outside. Unlike external surge protectors and the breakers they use, snap-in surge protectors do double duty— they protect your circuits and you can use them as regular breakers. This makes them perfect in a breaker box without empty slots. The downside—snap-in breakers don't protect you against as large a surge as external protectors. To install **turn off the power at the main breaker** and remove two breakers. Connect the wires to the surge protector breakers and snap into place. Most breakers are specific to the type and manufacture of the box you have—ask before you buy one.

EMERGENCY GENERATORS

Backup generators can be lifesavers in an emergency. A generator can keep the freezer going and the lights on when a storm interrupts power. And you can run a microwave or hot plate should the outage turn from hours to days. In rural areas an emergency generator provides power to well pumps and farm equipment.

The simplest arrangement, and the only do-it-yourself solution to emergency power, is an independent portable generator that delivers power to lamps or appliances through extension cords.

A more powerful integrated generator, on the other hand, connects directly to the home wiring system. An integrated generator may be powered by gasoline, diesel fuel, or natural gas. It is usually professionally installed.

Integrated units can be either portable or permanently mounted. A permanent unit should be mounted off the ground away from areas prone to flooding. A portable integrated generator connects to a special outdoor receptacle, which provides power to selected outlets inside the house.

Whether portable or permanent, an integrated generator must connect to the house wiring through a transfer switch that isolates the generator from the power grid. The code-required switch ensures power from your generator won't enter the utility lines and harm power company employees who are working on the wires. It also protects your generator, which could burn itself out trying to serve the load on the entire power network. It also is easy to reconnect to the utility system when the power comes back on.

In addition to taking your house off the power grid, the switch directs power from the generator to a subpanel that is connected to outlets and appliances that you've designated for emergency use. It's unlikely you would have a generator large enough to power all the outlets in the house. Plan ahead and decide where you want power. Work with an electrician to make sure your generator can handle the load and let the pros do all the wiring.

An integrated generator, which can be either a portable or a permanent unit, has the advantage of sending power directly to the home's electrical system.

A transfer switch removes an integrated generator from the power grid to protect both the generator and utility crews who may be working on downed power lines.

Portable dos and don'ts

An independent portable generator with a gasoline engine is the basic emergency power source. You set it up when needed to power a few appliances or lamps. While it's simple there are some rules that will ensure safe use:

A portable generator can safely provide emergency power if you pay attention to a few rules.

- Store the generator in a clean, dry place that's easily accessible when the lights are out. Set it up outside the house and away from open windows when running to prevent carbon monoxide from entering the house.
- Do not operate the generator when it is raining or snowing. Wet conditions are likely to result in shocks.
- Do not plug the generator directly into the house wiring. Use as few extension cords as possible.
- Attach a ground wire to the generator and ground the system properly. An ungrounded system is dangerous.
- Use fresh gasoline or add a stabilizer to the gas in the tank to make sure the engine will start. Start the generator once a month to keep it in running order. Do not add gasoline while the engine is running or hot.

Make sure your generator can handle the load

Before you buy a generator, make a list of what you want it to power. In the simplest case for example, you might want to power a couple of lights, the refrigerator, a portable heater, a radio, and a hot plate. Add up the wattage drawn by all things that don't have a motor in them—in this case everything but the refrigerator. For motorized items triple the wattage listed on the appliance. Starting a motor takes more power than running it. If you don't allow for it in your calculations, expect to trip a breaker on the generator. Don't plan on running sensitive electronic equipment, like computers or televisions, unless the generator has adequate surge protection.

OUTDOOR WIRING

L ow-voltage outdoor lights are inexpensive and easy to install. Kits typically include five or more lights, cable, and a transformer/timer. Some lights are mounted on stakes poked into the ground; others can attach to posts. The cable runs in a shallow trench or sits on top of the ground, covered with mulch; the transformer/timer simply plugs into a standard receptacle.

Low-voltage lights are bright enough to light a path, accent foliage, or provide lighting for an outdoor dining area. More extensive illumination or installing an outdoor receptacle requires extending household 120-volt wiring outside.

Choosing lights and switches

The first step in an outdoor wiring project is to decide where to place lights and receptacles. Pages 260–261 give some ideas. Gather more tips by consulting with neighbors and salespeople.

For switches there are four basic options: standard, timers, motion sensors, and photocells, which turn lights on at dusk and off at dawn. Motion sensors and photocells often are built into outdoor light fixtures such as floodlights, but you can also install them as separate devices that control several lights.

If you already have an outdoor receptacle and if its circuit isn't overloaded when you add new service (pages 148–149), tap power from it. If this is not possible, see pages 262–263 for moving power outdoors. Pages 264–267 show how to run lines and install fixtures.

Meeting code

A building permit is required for running line-voltage cable outside. Local codes vary considerably, so have your building department approve your plans before you start work. Be clear on what sort of cable and/or conduit is required, how deeply underground it must be buried, and what type of weathertight connections and fixtures are required. Contact utilities to locate underground cables and pipes before you start digging.

Exterior lights and outlets add safety and enhance a home's appearance.

CHAPTER PREVIEW

Planning outdoor lighting
page 260

Extending power outdoors
page 262

Running outdoor cable
page 264

Installing outdoor fixtures
page 266

Installing streetlight-style lamps
page 268

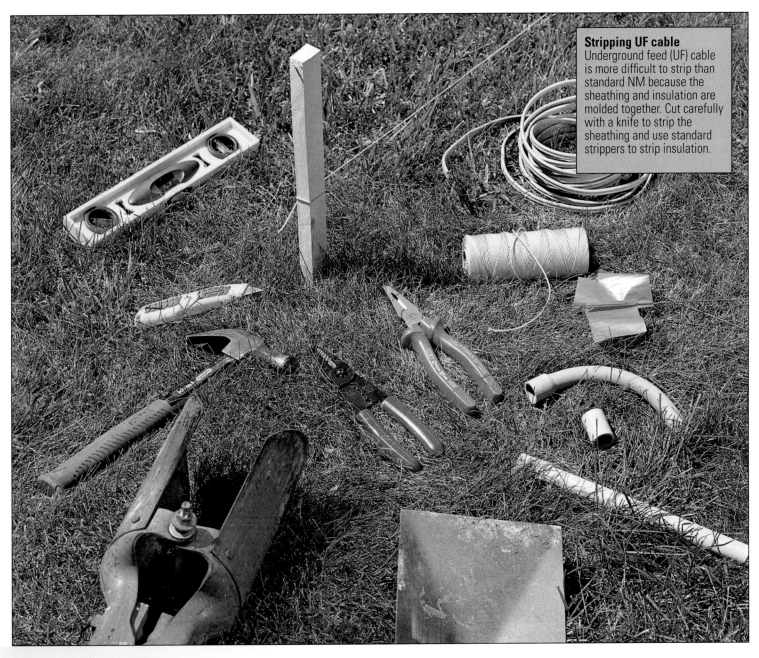

Stripping UF cable
Underground feed (UF) cable is more difficult to strip than standard NM because the sheathing and insulation are molded together. Cut carefully with a knife to strip the sheathing and use standard strippers to strip insulation.

The wiring for typical outdoor installations is simple. Burying cable and protecting fixtures from damage is difficult. You need not only standard wiring tools but also layout materials, a shovel for trenching, and possibly a clamshell digger for postholes.

Installing low-voltage outdoor lights
page 270

Installing stair riser lights
page 272

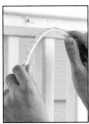

Installing rope lights
page 273

PLANNING OUTDOOR LIGHTING

Outdoor lights provide a pleasant setting for outdoor activities and also highlight interesting features of a yard or patio. They can light a pathway and make your home safer by deterring criminals. The most challenging stage of an outdoor lighting project is running cable from a power source inside your home and making sure the outdoor cable is protected. Otherwise the wiring is straightforward.

A system for all purposes

Aim for flexibility when choosing the type and number of outdoor lights and switches. For instance use low-voltage lights controlled by a timer or photocell to provide inexpensive lighting all night long.

For security and to light pathways when you come home at night, add bright line-voltage lights controlled by motion sensors.

For a dramatic effect aim accent lights at trees or foliage and control them with a standard switch or a timer. To provide lighting for outdoor dining or parties, hang decorative standard-voltage lights overhead and control them with a dimmer switch.

Choosing lights

Make scale drawings of your property, including foliage, sidewalks, and paths. Pencil in the type of lighting you want in various areas.

Take the drawing to a home center or lighting store and think through the possibilities. A wide selection of lights poke into the ground, mount on posts, attach to siding, or hang overhead. Mix and match fixtures.

Floodlights provide plenty of illumination for a small cost, so you may be tempted to light up your entire yard with them. However while floods are excellent for security purposes, most people find them too glaring for dining and entertaining.

Cable and conduit

Outdoor rooms are casual, so exposed conduit may not be considered unsightly. Plastic (PVC) conduit is pretty rugged, but metal conduit better resists hard knocks. Consider installing metal wherever it might get bumped—for example by a lawn mower. See pages 162–164 for instructions on running plastic and metal conduit. Codes prohibit exposed cable outdoors because it can be easily damaged.

Always use approved UF cable for outside wiring. Pages 264–265 show how to hide it underground. Though resistant to moisture UF cable is vulnerable to damage from a shovel or hammer, so protect it well. When installing an eaves or porch light, run standard cable through the attic or through a wall (pages 174–177). When installing a post light on top of a 4×4, run the cable through a groove in the post, then cover the groove with a 1×2.

Easy lights

In addition to permanent lights, you also can put up decorative lanterns or even a string of holiday lights, which can easily be moved. Miniature lights strung from trees render a magical feeling all year long. Exterior-rated rope lights can hang under railings or stair treads or over doorways. If stretched taut they have a high-tech look; draped in casual loops they make for a party atmosphere.

Holiday lighting

If you love outdoor holiday decorations, don't assume you can just plug all those colored lights and illuminated reindeer into any old receptacle. Typically these setups use lots of low-wattage bulbs. They quickly can add up to a circuit overload, especially if the circuit runs to a living room or family room where a home entertainment system is plugged in.

Plan for holiday lights as you would any electrical installation. Add up the wattages of all the bulbs and check to see that you don't overload a circuit. You may need to plug half the lights into a receptacle on one circuit and the other half into a receptacle on another circuit. Elaborate displays may call for a new circuit.

Shedding light on home security

Even the most brazen thief prefers the cover of darkness. By adding a combination of these security features, you can add an inexpensive layer of defense against home invasion:
- The brighter the light, the greater the deterrent. Replace dim bulbs with brighter ones, especially near doors.
- Surprise potential intruders with motion-sensor lights that turn on when they approach. However set your detector so it is not tripped by innocent dog walkers.
- Make sure all pathways—front and back—are illuminated.
- Have at least two lights pointed at each area of your lot, in case a bulb burns out.
- Place some lights out of easy reach; some thieves like to unscrew or break bulbs. High-placed porch lights or eaves lights fit the bill.
- An indoor light controlled by a motion sensor provides the greatest surprise, making it appear as if someone were home.

SAFETY FIRST
Check before you dig

Utility lines may be hidden under your lawn—the main water supply, the gas or propane line, or even an underground electrical line. Determine where all utility lines—water, gas, electricity, and telephone—run, as well as how deep they are buried, before you start digging trenches or postholes in the yard. Utility companies often provide one number to call for locating all lines.

Pole lamp

Floodlight with photocell

Bulkhead lamp

GFCI receptacle

Riser light

Low-voltage uplights

Low-voltage pathway lighting

When lighting a yard first make sure all pathways are lit and take care of security concerns (page 248). Then turn your attention to lights that enhance your yard's appearance at night. Upward-shining lights dramatically highlight bushes and trees. Smaller lights can spotlight lower plantings or shine from inside a hedge or flowerbed. Lights that swivel can be adjusted as foliage grows and seasons change. With its mixture of low-voltage and standard-voltage lights, this outdoor space can brighten an evening get-together and provide enough light for safety.

EXTENDING POWER OUTDOORS

Position an outdoor receptacle at least 16 inches above the ground. An in-use cover (Step 5) increases protection from the weather. A simple wooden box built around it shields it from bumps by the lawn mower or kids at play. Outdoor receptacles must be GFCI-protected. Check local codes for approved cable, conduit, and boxes.

The quickest way to extend power outdoors is to install a receptacle back-to-back with one inside the house (page 263). You also can drill through the wall from a basement or crawlspace and attach a receptacle on the side of a house using an extension ring (Steps 1 and 2).

PRESTART CHECKLIST

☐ **TIME**
About 2 hours to install a new outdoor receptacle with extension ring and in-use cover (not including cutting a pathway for the cable, and patching walls)

☐ **TOOLS**
Voltage tester, screwdriver, shovel, hammer, drill, long drill bit, saw, lineman's pliers, long-nose pliers, strippers

☐ **SKILLS**
Stripping, splicing, and connecting wires to terminals; installing boxes; running cable through walls and ceilings

☐ **PREP**
Make sure the new service does not overload the circuit (pages 148–149)

☐ **MATERIALS**
GFCI receptacle, outdoor box with extension ring and in-use cover, cable, conduit, fittings, wire nuts, electrician's tape

1 Find the easiest path for cable to reach an outside wall, perhaps through a basement or crawlspace. Use a long drill bit to drill a locator hole. If the location is inconvenient or does not satisfy code, install an LB fitting (opposite) rather than a receptacle to run power elsewhere.

Rim joist

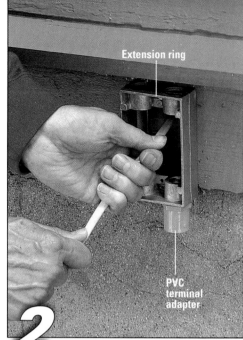

2 Using a reciprocating saw or keyhole saw, cut a hole for a remodel box. If the exterior is masonry, see page 216. Run cable through the hole and into a remodel box. Install the box and add an extension ring and a terminal adapter if using PVC, shown.

Extension ring

PVC terminal adapter

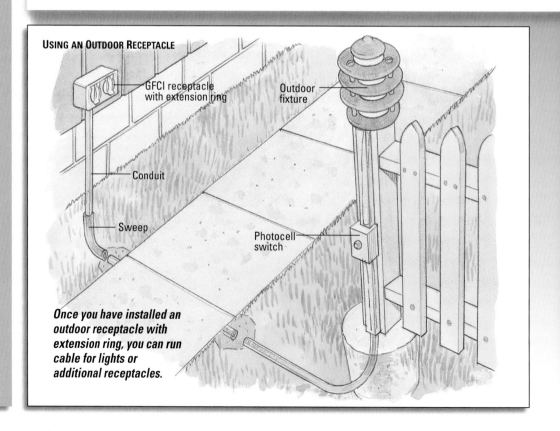

USING AN OUTDOOR RECEPTACLE

GFCI receptacle with extension ring

Outdoor fixture

Conduit

Sweep

Photocell switch

Once you have installed an outdoor receptacle with extension ring, you can run cable for lights or additional receptacles.

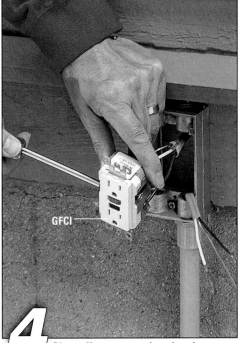

3 Beneath the box dig a trench deep enough to satisfy local codes. **Call before you dig.** Using PVC or rigid metal conduit, attach a length of pipe to a sweep. Cut the pipe to fit, attach it, and anchor the conduit with straps.

4 **Shut off power to the circuit.** Connect the black and white wires from the power source to the LINE terminals of a GFCI receptacle. After you run cable for the new service (pages 264–265), connect those wires to the LOAD terminals so the new service is GFCI-protected. Connect the power source.

5 Install an in-use cover, which protects the receptacle from moisture even when a cord is plugged in.

METAL CONDUIT

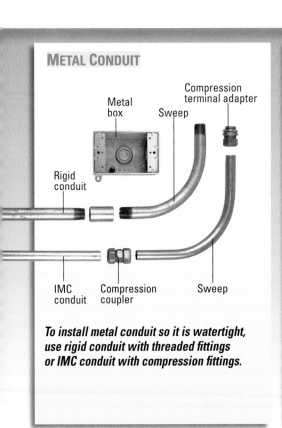

To install metal conduit so it is watertight, use rigid conduit with threaded fittings or IMC conduit with compression fittings.

Back-to-back wiring

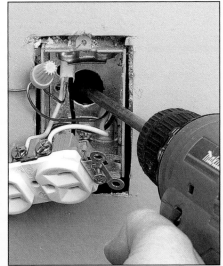

One way to bring power outdoors is with back-to-back receptacles. **Shut off power,** pull out an indoor receptacle, and drill a locator hole through the wall to the outside.

WHAT IF...
You don't need a receptacle?

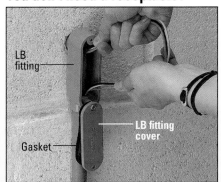

To make the transition from indoor to outdoor wiring, use an LB fitting. Essentially a watertight pulling elbow, it is ideal for connecting to conduit.

Ground fault circuit interrupter (GFCI)
A GFCI receptacle isn't necessary if the circuit is protected with a GFCI breaker or if the new line taps into a GFCI receptacle.

RUNNING OUTDOOR CABLE

Some building departments require metal or plastic conduit for all underground wiring, but most codes call for conduit only where the wiring is exposed or in a shallow trench. (Condensation can moisten wiring in watertight conduit. UF cable offers the only protection against water damage.)

Before you dig have utilities mark the location's underground lines. Most have a toll-free number available.

A square-bladed spade handles short runs. If you need to dig more than 50 feet of trench, rent a powered trench digger.

Check local building codes. Some allow a shallower trench if the cable or conduit is covered with a 2×6 pressure-treated plank.

PRESTART CHECKLIST

☐ **TIME**
Once power is brought outside (pages 262–263), about 8 to 12 hours to dig trenches, run 60 feet of cable, and install several lights (pages 266–267)

☐ **TOOLS**
Shovel, posthole digger, hammer, drill, fish tape, pliers, garden hose or sledgehammer

☐ **SKILLS**
Laying out and digging trenches, fishing cable through conduit

☐ **PREP**
Install a receptacle or LB fitting, bringing power to the outside, and check that the new service does not overload the circuit (pages 148–149). Call the utility company to mark lines.

☐ **MATERIALS**
Conduit and fittings, conduit clamps, stakes, string line

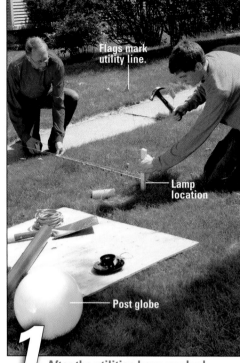

1 After the utilities have marked the location of any underground lines, plan a route that stays several feet away from them. Use string lines and stakes to indicate the path for the underground cable.

2 Cut the sod carefully with a square-bladed shovel so you can replace it later. Dig a trench deep enough to satisfy local codes. If you encounter a large root or rock, consider running the cable under it.

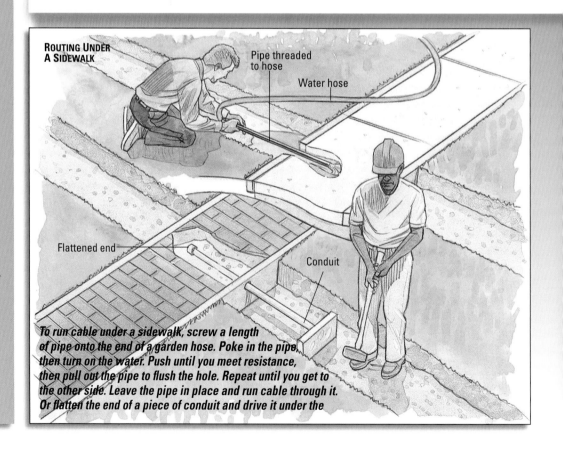

ROUTING UNDER A SIDEWALK

Pipe threaded to hose

Water hose

Flattened end

Conduit

To run cable under a sidewalk, screw a length of pipe onto the end of a garden hose. Poke in the pipe, then turn on the water. Push until you meet resistance, then pull out the pipe to flush the hole. Repeat until you get to the other side. Leave the pipe in place and run cable through it. Or flatten the end of a piece of conduit and drive it under the

3 Run metal conduit under the sidewalk (use the method shown on page 264) and attach a protective bushing to each end. Push the UF cable through the conduit.

Protective bushing

UF cable

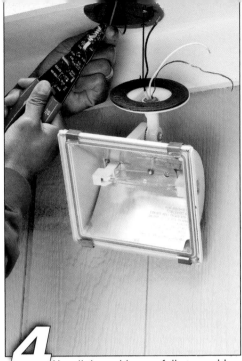

4 Unroll the cable carefully to avoid kinks. Have a helper feed it through the conduit as you thread it through the trenches all the way to the power source.

5 When running cable to a lamp post, be sure to set the post so its access hole faces the trench (see pages 266–267 for more on setting fixtures). Carefully push the cable into the access hole and up the body of the post.

Light post set in concrete

Access hole

Bushing at end of conduit

Bushing

Codes typically require a bushing at the end of the conduit to protect the cable sheathing. This is especially important when using metal conduit, which can easily slice through plastic sheathing.

Sink that cable

Local codes specify how deep cable or conduit must be buried. Some codes require conduit for underground cables.

Running wires through metal conduit

Outdoor box

If codes call for a continuous run of metal conduit, purchase watertight boxes and fittings. Take care to tighten each fitting; one bad connection can result in water leakage.

Tape wire to hook.

Fish tape

Run wire through the conduit using a fish tape, as shown on page 165.

INSTALLING OUTDOOR FIXTURES

Home centers stock a variety of outdoor light fixtures. Those that use standard incandescent bulbs provide plenty of light for most residential purposes. Outdoor fluorescent fixtures may save energy costs but are usually more effective in an enclosed space like a garage. (Some may not function in cold weather.) For the brightest illumination install mercury vapor or halide fixtures.

Whatever fixture you install pay attention to its gasket. When you attach the cover, sandwich the gasket tightly to seal out all moisture.

These two pages show how to set posts into concrete. In many areas filling the hole around the post with well-tamped soil is considered just as strong.

Some lights come with cylindrical metal posts. Install these in much the same way as the post light shown here.

PRESTART CHECKLIST

☐ **TIME**
Once cable is run about 4 hours to install a post and light; less time for other types of lights

☐ **TOOLS**
A posthole digger, post level, screwdriver, hammer, drill, chisel, strippers, long-nose pliers, lineman's pliers

☐ **SKILLS**
Running cable outdoors; stripping, splicing, connecting wires to terminals

☐ **PREP**
Run cable and connect it to a circuit that is not overloaded by the new service.

☐ **MATERIALS**
An outdoor fixture, conduit, post, wire nuts, electrician's tape, concrete mix

GFCI receptacle

1 Don't start digging until the utility company has marked lines. Plan locations of fixtures and trenches to avoid utility lines. Dig a trench to the fixture location (pages 264–265). Use a clamshell digger to bore a hole at least 36 inches deep, including the depth of the trench.

2 Set the post into the hole. Plumb it with a level and brace it firmly with 1×4s. Fill the hole with concrete, leave the braces in place, and allow a day or so for the concrete to cure.

Gentle lighting options

Outdoor lights range from familiar low-voltage tier lights and undereaves floodlights to light-equipped, outdoor-rated ceiling fans. For a subtle effect consider the following options:

Low-voltage **post lights** mount to the top of a 4×4 post, linking into a low-voltage run for their power.

Some **rope lights** are designed for outdoor use. Staple them to the underside of railings or decking overhangs or drape them from above.

For deck lighting without glare, use low-profile **edge lights** or **surface lights** to illuminate traffic areas and stairways or simply to add an accent.

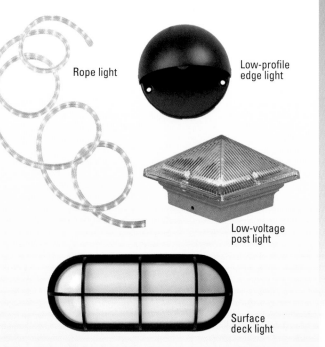

Rope light

Low-profile edge light

Low-voltage post light

Surface deck light

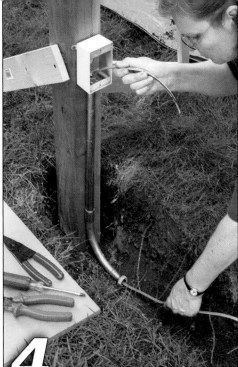

3 After the concrete has cured, attach the conduit and sweep to the box and fasten the box to the post. Attach a bushing to the sweep (page 265).

4 Strip about 8 inches of sheathing from the UF cable and push the wires up through the conduit into the box. Run the cable to the power source, removing any kinks and laying the cable flat in the trench. Connect a GFCI receptacle (page 183) to the wires.

5 Fold in the wires and fasten the receptacle to the box. Place the gasket around the receptacle and fasten the outdoor receptacle cover.

Receptacle and post light

Using a ¾-inch bit, bore a channel down from the top of the post to the level of the box. Drill from the side to connect the hole. Run cable through the channel and through a punch-out hole in the back of the box.

Undereaves light

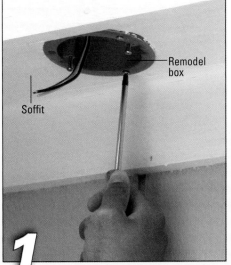

1 To install a light that hangs under the eaves, cut a hole into the soffit for a round remodel box. Run cable to the hole and clamp it to the box. Install the box.

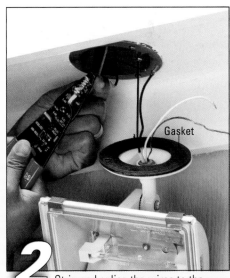

2 Strip and splice the wires to the fixture's leads and attach the fixture. Check the gasket to make sure it is seated evenly and securely around the box to seal out water.

INSTALLING STREETLIGHT-STYLE LAMPS

Streetlight-style security lamps cast light over a broad area, turn on automatically at dusk, and turn off at dawn. Mounting a light on a utility pole is more work than a home electrician can undertake, unless you're willing to install a pole and able to run overhead wiring. Mounting the light on the side of a building is simple, however. Code does require two things: First the light must be 10 feet above finished grade or 15 feet above a driveway or parking area. Secondly the wires running to the light must be housed in conduit.

Install the conduit completely before you fish the wires. While it might be tempting to piece the conduit together at the same time you run wires, it's against code because you might pinch one of the wires while fastening conduit. Besides it's no harder and perhaps even a little bit easier to do it the right way.

PRESTART CHECKLIST

☐ **TIME**
About 6 hours to hang and wire the light

☐ **TOOLS**
Screwdriver, drill and bit, pliers, wrench, wire strippers, wire cutters, fish tape, voltage tester

☐ **SKILLS**
Basic wiring and agility on a ladder

☐ **PREP**
Tap power from an exterior box or run a circuit from inside the house to a weatherproof box where you can connect wires from the light

☐ **MATERIALS**
Streetlight; conduit; white, black and green conduit wire; pulling lubricant; electrician's tape; wire nuts

1 Drive at least one mounting bolt into the building's framing. You may have to locate the studs from inside the building and measure to mark them on the outside. Lay out holes for the mounting screws using the template that comes with the light. Drill holes to match the mounting bolts as specified in the manufacturer's directions.

2 Install the two bottom mounting screws but don't drive them all the way in. Leave enough room to slip the fixture over them. At this point you also may want to drive in the top screw and then back it out. This makes it easier to install later.

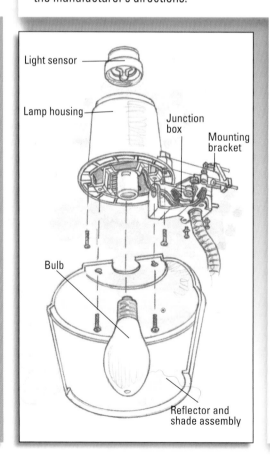

Light sensor

Lamp housing

Junction box

Mounting bracket

Bulb

Reflector and shade assembly

6 Feed a fish tape from the light back to the junction box. Attach the wires to the fish tape, apply pulling lubricant, and pull the wires up through the conduit.

3 The light sensor usually is a separate assembly that plugs into the top of the light. Align the plug in the base of the sensor with the slots in the stop of the light, making sure the largest prong is over the largest slot. Push down to plug it in and turn the sensor clockwise to attach it.

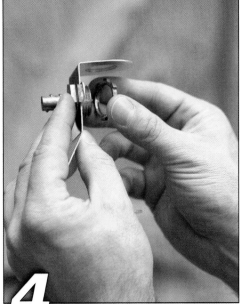

4 The connection between the light and the incoming wiring takes place in a built-in junction box between the light and mounting bracket. Remove the cover to the box and install a conduit connector on the back. Hang the light.

5 Run conduit between the conduit connector on the lamp and the junction box that provides power to the light.

7 Attach the conduit's ground wire to the light's green ground screw. Pull the wires from the light into the built-in junction box. Strip the white wires as needed, twist them together, and cover with a wire nut. Wrap electrician's tape around the wire nut and a short section of wire. Repeat with the black wires.

8 Replace the junction box cover and attach the reflector to the light. Install the bulb and attach the globe to the reflector.

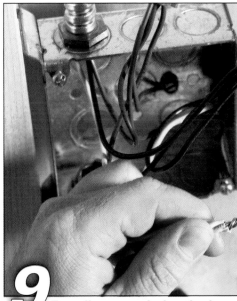

9 Turn off power to the junction box that powers the light. Connect the light ground wire to the cable ground wire and run a pigtail to the grounding screw on the box. Connect the white to the white and the black to the black. Put caps on all three and cover each cap and a bit of the wire with electrician's tape.

INSTALLING LOW-VOLTAGE LIGHTS

Low-voltage outdoor lights are on stakes that stab into the ground. The cable can be hidden under groundcover or covered with soil or mulch. Place the transformer nearby and plug it into an outdoor outlet. To connect cable to a light, snap together components.

Choose from a variety of light fixtures: tiered or flower-shaped lights to mark a pathway, floodlights to accent foliage or provide security, and deck lights for vertical surfaces such as step risers.

Add up the wattage of the lights you want to use and choose a transformer/timer that supplies enough power. For instance eight 18-watt lights and five 20-watt lights add up to 244 watts. A 250-watt transformer can handle the load, but you lose the option of adding lights—so you may want to buy a larger transformer.

1 Insert the tip of each lamp stake into the ground and push it in. If the soil is hard, cut a slit with a gardening trowel, then push in the stake.

2 Run the cord from the house receptacle to each lamp. Hide the cord under groundcover, dig a shallow trench for the cord, or cover it with mulch. On a deck or porch, staple the cord where it is out of sight.

PRESTART CHECKLIST

☐ **TIME**
About 4 hours to install 10 to 15 lights and cover the cable

☐ **TOOLS**
Screwdriver, lineman's pliers, hammer, gardening trowel, perhaps a drill

☐ **SKILLS**
Stripping and splicing wires

☐ **PREP**
If there is no outdoor receptacle, have one installed. Or plug the transformer into an indoor receptacle and drill a small hole for the cable to run through to the outside.

☐ **MATERIALS**
Low-voltage outdoor light kit, including lights, transformer/timer, and cable (you may buy additional lights and cable)

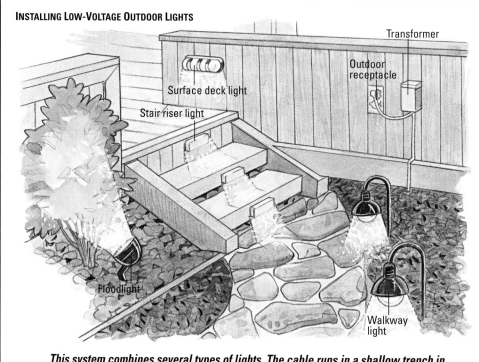

INSTALLING LOW-VOLTAGE OUTDOOR LIGHTS

Transformer

Outdoor receptacle

Surface deck light

Stair riser light

Floodlight

Walkway light

This system combines several types of lights. The cable runs in a shallow trench in the ground or stapled to the house or deck.

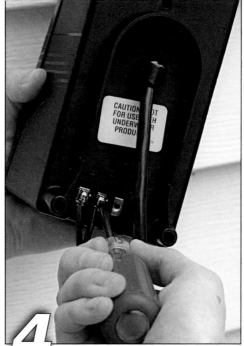

3 To connect a light to power, slip the two parts of the light's connector around the cord and snap them together. They pierce and pinch the cord to make the connection.

Snap-on connector

4 Mount the transformer near a receptacle where it can stay dry and undamaged. Strip the cord's wire ends and connect them to the transformer terminals, following the manufacturer's instructions.

5 Plug in the transformer. Most models turn lights on automatically when it gets dark and allow you to set the lights on a timer. Follow the manufacturer's instructions for programming.

WHAT IF...
There is a HI/LO switch?

A HI/LO switch allows you to change the power to the lights. Turn on the lights with the switch set to LO. If some lights do not come on or if they are too dim, flip the switch to HI.

REFRESHER COURSE
Use a GFCI outdoors

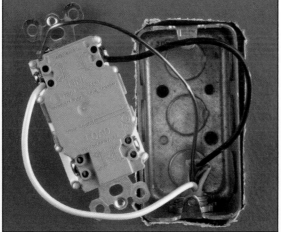

Any receptacle that is exposed to moisture should be a GFCI. To replace a standard receptacle with a GFCI, **shut off power** to the circuit, remove the old receptacle, and restrip the wire ends. If only one cable enters the box, connect the wires to the LINE terminals. If two cables enter the box, connect the wires that bring power into the box to the LINE terminals and connect the other wires to the LOAD terminals. See page 108 for more instructions.

SOLAR LIGHTS

Solar-powered lights are easy to install. Just push them into the ground; no wiring is required. Solar lights are handy for spots far away from a power source. The light must receive at least three or four hours of sunlight a day to provide light at night. It generally takes a few days for the battery to charge. A solar light may not work well during prolonged periods of cloudy weather and gives little light anytime.

INSTALLING STAIR RISER LIGHTS

Outdoor stairways can be dangerous at night. Mounting a light in the riser makes steps safer and provides accent lighting too. A low-voltage light is the easiest type to install. It operates off the same kind of transformer that landscape lights use.

If you have a landscape lighting system, it may power riser lights. Add up the wattage of the lights and compare it with the transformer wattage to see whether there is enough capacity. If so you can splice onto the light cable with a silicone-filled cap, sometimes called a grease cap. Strip the wires, twist the connector over them, and fold the wires and connector inside the silicone cap. If your transformer is at or near capacity, buy a new one for the riser lights. You can add more landscape lights with the additional capacity.

PRESTART CHECKLIST

☐ **TIME**
About 30 minutes per step

☐ **TOOLS**
Screwdriver, tape measure, drill and bit, saber saw

☐ **SKILLS**
Basic woodworking, elementary wiring

☐ **MATERIALS**
Low-voltage riser lights, transformer, connecting wiring

1 Remove the faceplate from the light and insert the bulb, which is usually packed separately.

2 Lay out the cutout for the light, using the dimensions in the manufacturer's directions. The light usually is centered in the riser.

3 Drill a hole slightly larger in diameter than the width of a saber saw blade in each inside corner of the hole you laid out. Start the cut in one of the holes and cut along the line from hole to hole until you've made a cutout for the light.

4 Attach the feed wire to the transformer and run it to the steps you're lighting. If you plan to add additional lights, continue running the line to where they will be.

5 Reach through the opening and temporarily pull the feed wire through. Attach the clip at the end of the light's wires to the feed wire. Run the line to the next riser and repeat until you've installed all the lights.

6 Screw the box into place and replace the cover.

INSTALLING ROPE LIGHTS

Rope lights are a series of small lights encased in a flexible PVC tube. The tube is waterproof so you can use the lights outdoors as well as indoors. They're popular outdoors to outline a deck or gazebo, adding safety without ruining the mood. The lights operate at line voltage—110–120 volts— so there's no transformer. The lights plug in to the nearest outlet, which should be GFCI-protected.

Install the lights with the clips that are provided. Avoid using nails and staples, which can puncture the PVC tubing and expose the lights and wiring to the weather.

1 The light rope is held in place by clips. Predrill holes for the screws that hold the clips. Screw the clips into place roughly every 2½ to 3 feet or as directed by the manufacturer.

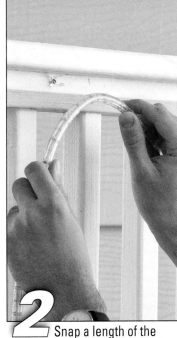

2 Snap a length of the rope into the clips starting at the end near the outlet or extension cord that powers it.

3 If installing outdoors plug the rope into a GFCI outlet. You can plug it into a regular outlet for indoor use.

Extending the length of rope lights

1 You can connect several lengths of rope lights together to receive more light or cover a greater distance. Maximum length varies from rope to rope, so read the directions and don't link too many ropes into a strand. To connect one rope to another, unscrew the cap at the end of one rope. At the beginning of the other rope, the plug splices onto the first rope. Unscrew the nut that holds the splice together.

2 Plug the uncapped beginning of one rope into the uncapped end of the other. Slide the nut from one rope over the threads on the other rope and tighten.

APPLIANCES & NEW CIRCUITS

Wiring an electrical appliance such as a dishwasher, disposer, or electric water heater often is the easiest part of a job—moving the unit in and connecting the plumbing takes most of your time. This chapter shows how to install many of the most common types of major household appliances. It also walks you through how to run a new circuit if the appliance requires it.

Whenever you add a new appliance or upgrade an old one, check the wattage ratings to make sure you don't overload a circuit (pages 148–149). With an upgrade you may be surprised to find that your new appliance actually reduces the load. The reason is that many new appliances— refrigerators, toasters, microwaves, dishwashers, and water heaters, for instance—use less power than the older models they replace.

Installing a new circuit

Some new appliances—spas, baseboard heaters, or window air-conditioners—may need a new circuit. As long as your service panel has room for a new circuit, the wiring is not difficult. Running the cable consumes most of your time. Pages 278–279 show how.

Before adding a new circuit, consult page 148 to make sure your basic electrical service can handle the extra load. If not have an electrician upgrade your service.

Adding a subpanel

If the service panel does not have enough room for a new circuit but your basic service can handle the added load, install a subpanel with room for a number of new circuits (pages 280–281).

Some of these projects involve 240-volt circuits. The wiring is no more complicated than wiring a 120-volt circuit, but the danger is much greater. A 240-volt shock can be very serious, even fatal. Check your plans with a building inspector. **Double-check to see that power is shut off** before beginning any work. Call in a professional electrician to advise you or have a pro do the work if you are at all unsure.

Here's how to add new circuits to a panel and connect permanently installed appliances.

CHAPTER PREVIEW

Hardwiring appliances
page 276

Hooking up a new circuit
page 278

Installing a subpanel
page 280

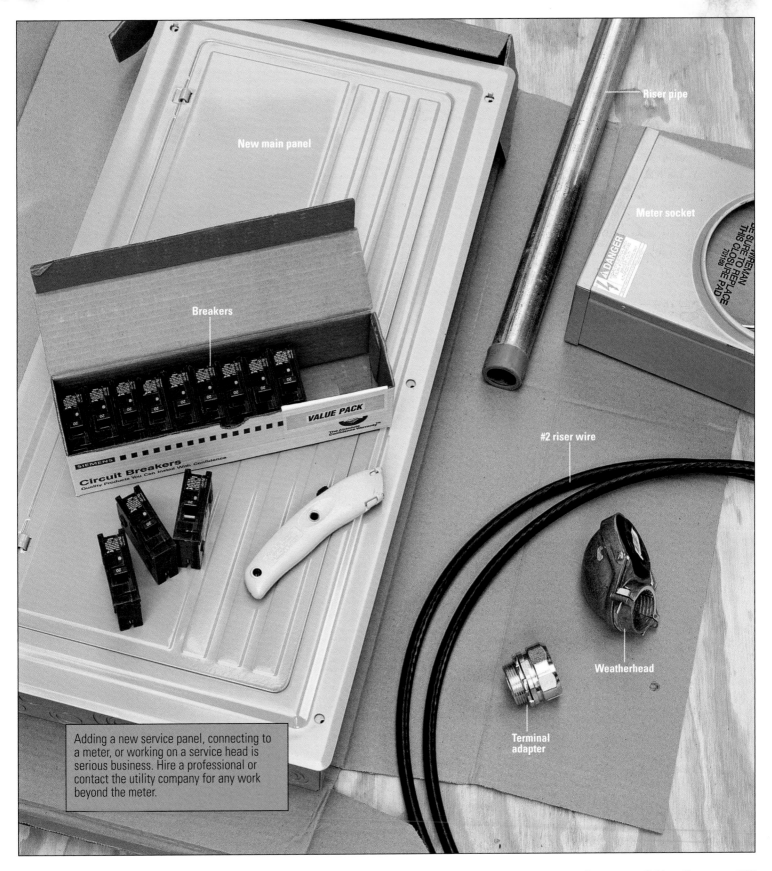

New main panel

Breakers

VALUE PACK
The Attached
Confidence Warranty™

SIEMENS
Circuit Breakers
Quality Products You Can Install With Confidence

Riser pipe

Meter socket

⚠ DANGER

BE SURE TO REMAIN
THIS CLOSURE TO REPLACE
CLOSURE PAD

#2 riser wire

Weatherhead

Terminal
adapter

Adding a new service panel, connecting to
a meter, or working on a service head is
serious business. Hire a professional or
contact the utility company for any work
beyond the meter.

HARDWIRING APPLIANCES

Most 120-volt appliances simply plug into standard receptacles. Some 240-volt appliances plug into special 240-volt receptacles (pages 184–185). Other appliances—those that use 240 volts and are stationary—are hardwired, meaning that cable attaches directly to the circuit. Garbage disposers and dishwashers may be either plugged in or hardwired.

Shut off power to the circuit before installing any appliance. These pages give general directions for some typical installations. Consult the manufacturer's instructions before wiring—wire colors and cable connections may vary.

Appliance disconnects
If you shut off a circuit breaker to work on a 240-volt appliance, another person may mistakenly flip the breaker on while you are doing the wiring, creating a very dangerous situation. That is why building codes may require a hardwired appliance to have a disconnect—basically an on/off switch. The disconnect must be positioned within sight of the appliance. An alternative is to install a circuit breaker with a lockout feature, which allows you to lock the breaker shut to prevent an accident.

PRESTART CHECKLIST

☐ **TIME**
About 1 hour to make most connections once cable has been run

☐ **TOOLS**
Screwdriver, flashlight, strippers, lineman's pliers, long-nose pliers

☐ **SKILLS**
Stripping, splicing, and connecting wires to terminals

☐ **PREP**
See that the new appliance does not overload the circuit (pages 148–149). Remove the old appliance or run cable for a new appliance.

☐ **MATERIALS**
Appliance, wire nuts, electrician's tape

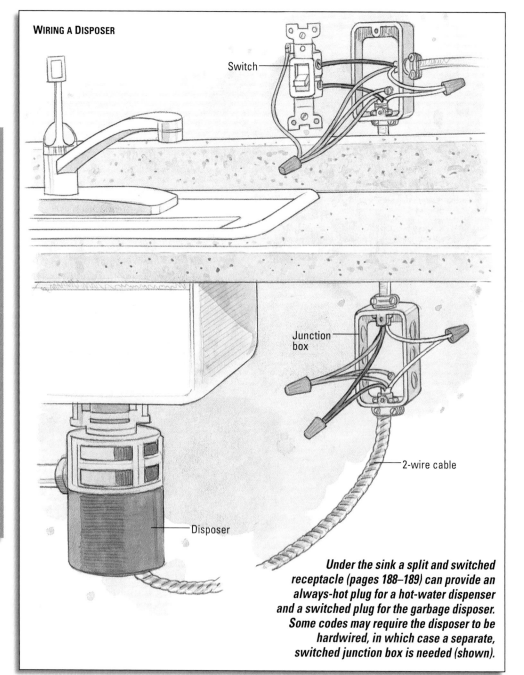

WIRING A DISPOSER

Switch

Junction box

2-wire cable

Disposer

Under the sink a split and switched receptacle (pages 188–189) can provide an always-hot plug for a hot-water dispenser and a switched plug for the garbage disposer. Some codes may require the disposer to be hardwired, in which case a separate, switched junction box is needed (shown).

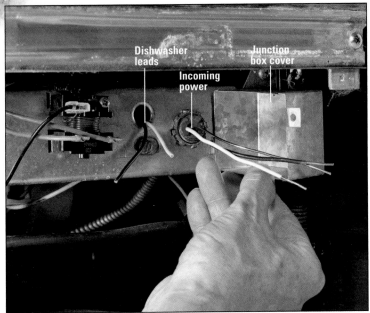

Dishwasher: Codes may require a dishwasher to be on a dedicated circuit. Some models plug into receptacles, but most are hardwired. Provide a cable that can reach to the front of the dishwasher. Slide the dishwasher into the space and make the plumbing connections. Open the dishwasher's junction box and splice wires to the dishwasher's leads. Replace the junction box cover.

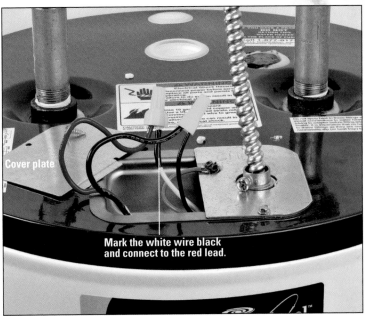

Electric water heater: A water heater requires a dedicated 240-volt circuit. Check the unit's amperage rating and make sure the circuit can handle at least 120 percent of the rating. For most homes a 30-amp circuit with 10/2 cable is sufficient. Because of the heat the unit generates, use Greenfield or armored cable rather than NM cable. Remove the cover plate, splice the wires (note that a neutral is not required), and replace the cover plate.

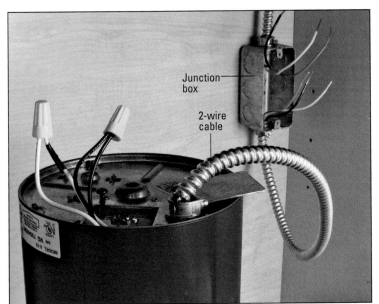

Garbage disposer: Garbage disposers are sold without cords so they can be wired directly to a junction box (hardwiring) or to an appliance cord with a plug. Install armored cable (shown above) or buy a cord that can handle the disposer's amperage rating. Splice the wires to the disposer first. Install it under the sink. Then hardwire or plug the disposer into a switched receptacle. A disposer should not be on a light circuit, or lights dim when it starts.

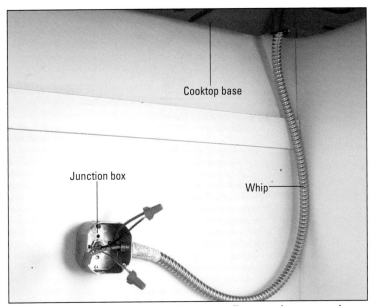

Electric cooktop: An electric cooktop or wallmounted oven requires a 120/240-volt circuit—120 volts to power lights and timer, 240 volts for the heating elements. A cooktop and an oven can be wired to the same circuit. Run cable to a nearby junction box. An electric oven or cooktop usually has a short length of armored cable, called a whip. Clamp the whip to the junction box; make the splices. Make sure the wire and breaker are big enough for both.

HOOKING UP A NEW CIRCUIT

Connecting a new circuit is no more difficult than the other projects in this book. You'll spend most of your time running cable from the new service to the service panel (pages 168–177).

Make sure that adding a new circuit does not overload your electrical system. Review pages 150–151 and talk with an inspector or an electrician about your plans. If the service panel cannot accept another circuit, install a subpanel (pages 280–281). If your system cannot accommodate a new circuit, have an electrician install a new service panel.

If there is an available slot for a new circuit breaker in your service panel, you can add a breaker there. If not you may be able to replace a regular circuit breaker with a tandem breaker (below right).

PRESTART CHECKLIST

☐ **TIME**
About 2 hours to make connections for a new circuit once cable has been run

☐ **TOOLS**
Flashlight, hammer, screwdriver, strippers, lineman's pliers, long-nose pliers, voltage tester

☐ **SKILLS**
Figuring loads on circuits, stripping sheathing and wire insulation, connecting wires to terminals

☐ **PREP**
Install boxes for the new service and run cable from the boxes to the service panel.

☐ **MATERIALS**
New circuit breaker and cable

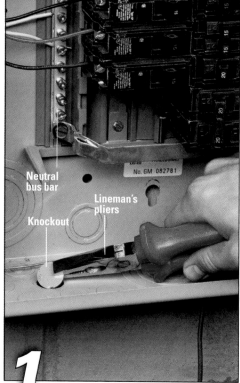

1 **Shut off the main breaker** and remove the panel's cover. Remove a knockout slug from the side of the cover.

2 Run cable to the box, adding at least 2 feet extra for wiring work within the service panel. Strip enough sheathing from the cable to allow wires to travel most of the way around the panel. Slide the wires through the knockout hole and clamp the cable in place.

TWO FOR ONE WITH A TANDEM BREAKER

A tandem circuit breaker makes it possible to install two circuits into the space of one. Unlike double-pole breakers (page 279), tandem breakers can be switched off and on individually. Some panels do not allow for tandem breakers. Others allow only a certain number of tandems. Get an inspector's OK before you install a tandem.

REFRESHER COURSE
When do you need a new circuit?

If new electrical service—lights, receptacles, or appliances—uses so much wattage that it cannot be added to an existing circuit, a new circuit is called for. See pages 148–149 for the calculations.

Extra protection
An arc fault circuit interrupter (AFCI) protects against fire caused by frayed or overheated cords. It is installed in place of a standard circuit breaker and is required for bedroom wiring.

Breaker

No. GM 082781

3 Route the wires so they skirt the perimeter of the panel and stay far away from hot bus bars. Strip ½ inch of insulation from the neutral wire and connect it to the neutral bus bar (shown in photo 1). Connect the ground wire to the ground bus bar.

4 Bend the hot wire into position along the side of the panel, cut it to length, and strip ½ inch of insulation. Poke it into the breaker and tighten the setscrew.

5 Slide one end of the breaker under the hot bus bar and push the breaker until it snaps into place and aligns with the surrounding breakers. Twist out a knockout slot in the service panel's cover and replace the cover.

WHAT IF...
There is only one neutral/ground bar?

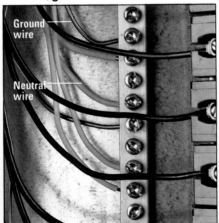

Ground wire

Neutral wire

Some service panels have separate bus bars for neutral and ground wires. Others have only one bar that serves both. Connect neutral and ground wires in any order.

STANLEY PRO TIP
Double-pole breakers

A double-pole breaker takes up twice the space of a single-pole breaker. You need it for 240-volt circuits and with two-circuit and split receptacles (page 187). Connect the ground and neutral wires to bus bars and connect the hot wires to the breaker.

GFCI breaker

A GFCI circuit breaker protects all the receptacles, lights, and appliances on its circuit. Connect the hot and neutral wires from the circuit to the breaker. Connect the breaker's white lead to the neutral bus bar.

INSTALLING A SUBPANEL

If the service panel does not have room for new circuit breakers and you cannot use tandem breakers (page 278), a subpanel may be the answer. Before installing one consult with an inspector to make sure you do not overload your overall system.

A subpanel has separate bus bars for neutral and ground wires and typically has no main breaker. It may not be labeled "subpanel" but instead be labeled "lugs only." It may be a different brand than the main panel.

Have the inspector approve the subpanel, the feeder cable, and the feeder breaker (page 281).

Shut off the main breaker in the service panel before you begin.

PRESTART CHECKLIST

☐ **TIME**
About 4 hours to install a subpanel with several new circuits, not including running cable for the new circuits

☐ **TOOLS**
Screwdriver, hammer, voltage tester, flashlight, strippers, lineman's pliers, long-nose pliers

☐ **SKILLS**
Stripping sheathing and wires, connecting wires to terminals

☐ **PREP**
Run cables for the new circuits to the subpanel location. In the main service panel, make room for the double-pole feeder breaker.

☐ **MATERIALS**
Subpanel, mounting screws, approved feeder cable, staples or cable clamps, approved feeder breaker, breakers for the new circuits

1 Mount the subpanel about a foot away from the main service panel. Determine how far the wires will have to travel in the subpanel and pull wires (shown above) or add cable and strip sheathing accordingly. Remove a knockout slug, slide the wires through, and clamp the cable.

2 At the main service panel, plan the routes for the four wires: ground, neutral, and two hot wires (black and red). Strip the sheathing, remove a knockout slug, and clamp the cable. Route the neutral and ground wires carefully and connect them to their bus bar(s).

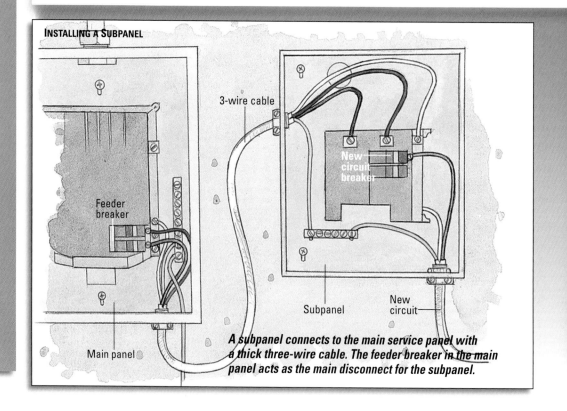

INSTALLING A SUBPANEL

A subpanel connects to the main service panel with a thick three-wire cable. The feeder breaker in the main panel acts as the main disconnect for the subpanel.

3 Route, cut, and strip the red and black wires. Connect them to the feeder breaker. Snap the breaker into place.

MAIN PANEL

Feeder breaker

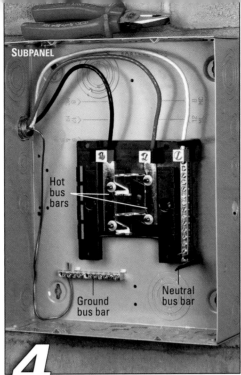

4 In the subpanel route the feeder wires, cut and strip them, and connect to terminals. Connect the black and red wires to the hot bus bars, the neutral wire to the main neutral terminal, and the ground wire to the ground bus bar.

SUBPANEL

Hot bus bars

Ground bus bar

Neutral bus bar

5 Run cable for new circuits into the subpanel and clamp the cable. For each circuit route wires around the perimeter, connect the ground wire to the ground bus bar, the white wire to the neutral bus bar, and the hot wire to a circuit breaker.

SUBPANEL

New circuit cable

New circuit cable

Choosing a feeder breaker and cable

Buy a subpanel larger than you need so you're ready for future electrical improvements. The three parts—subpanel, feeder breaker, and cable—should be compatible in capacity.

To figure sizes add up the wattages of all the new electrical loads (pages 148–149) and add 20 percent to allow a safety margin. Then divide by 230 to find the amperage you need.

If the new service totals 4,000 watts, for example, add 20 percent (multiply by 1.2) to get 4,800; then divide 4,800 by 230 to get 20.9 amps. A subpanel supplying 30 amps of service will work.

To supply up to 5,700 watts of new power, install a 30-amp subpanel, a 30-amp feeder breaker, and a 10/3 feeder cable. To supply up to 7,500 watts, install a 40-amp subpanel, a 40-amp feeder breaker, and 8/3 cable.

Cable with 8-gauge wires may be difficult to find. If a home center does not carry it, call an electrical supply dealer.

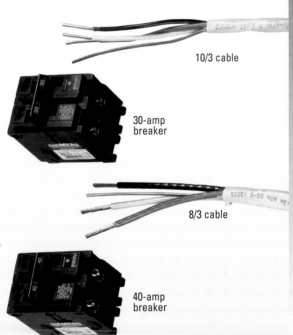

10/3 cable

30-amp breaker

8/3 cable

40-amp breaker

GLOSSARY

For terms not included here, or for more about those that are, refer to the index on pages 284–287.

Amp: Short for ampere. A measurement of the amount of electrical current flowing through a wire or appliance. An amperage rating tells the greatest amount of current a wire, device, or appliance can carry.

Antioxidant: A paste applied to aluminum wires to inhibit corrosion and maintain safe electrical connections.

Armored cable: Flexible cable, containing two or more wires, with a protective metal sheathing. See *BX cable* and *MC cable*.

Box: A metal or plastic container with openings for cable. All electrical connections must be made inside a code-approved electrical box.

Bus bar: A set of terminals inside a service panel. Circuit breakers or fuses connect to hot bus bars, neutral wires connect to neutral bus bars, and ground wires connect to ground bus bars. Some service panels have separate bus bars for neutral and ground wires (required in Canada), while others have only one neutral/ground bus bar.

BX cable: Armored cable containing insulated wires and no ground wire; the sheathing acts as the grounding path.

Cable: Two or more insulated wires wrapped in metal or plastic sheathing.

Circuit: Two or more wires carrying power from the service panel to devices, fixtures, and appliances and then back to the panel. A circuit breaker or fuse in the service panel protects each circuit from overloading. Also called a branch circuit.

Circuit breaker: A protective device in a service panel that shuts off power to its circuit when it senses a short circuit or overload. See *Overload* and *Short circuit*.

Codes: Local regulations governing safe wiring practices. See *National Electrical Code (NEC)*.

Common terminal: On a three-way switch, the darker-colored terminal (often marked COM) to which the wire supplying power or leading to a fixture is connected.

Common wire: In a three-way switch setup, the wire that carries power to the switch or to the fixture.

Conductor: A carrier of electricity, usually a wire, or a material that carries electricity.

Conduit: Plastic or metal pipe through which wires run.

Continuity tester: A device that tells whether a circuit is complete and capable of carrying electricity.

Cord: Two or more insulated stranded wires encased in a flexible sheathing.

Current: The flow of electrons through a conductor.

Device: An electrical receptacle or switch.

Duplex receptacle: The most common type of receptacle; has two outlets.

Electrical Metallic Tubing (EMT): Thin rigid metal conduit suitable for residential use. Also called Thinwall.

End-line wiring: A method of wiring a switch in which power runs to the fixture box. Also called switch-loop wiring.

End-of-run: A receptacle at the end of a circuit.

Feed wire: The hot wire that brings power into a box.

Fixture: A permanently attached light or fan rather than plugged into a receptacle.

Four-way switch: A switch with four terminals, used when three or more switches control a fixture.

Fuse: A safety device located in a fuse box that shuts off an overloaded circuit.

Greenfield: Flexible metal conduit.

Ground: Wire or metal sheathing that provides an alternate path for current back to the service panel (and from there to a grounding rod sunk into the earth or to a cold-water pipe). Grounding protects against shock in case of an electrical malfunction.

Ground fault circuit interrupter (GFCI): A receptacle that shuts off to reduce the chance of electrical shock.

Hardwired: An appliance wired via cable directly into a box rather than having a cord that plugs into a receptacle.

Hot wire: The wire that carries power; it is either black or a color other than white.

Junction box: An electrical box with no fixture or device attached; used to split a circuit into different branches.

Kilowatt (kW): 1,000 watts.

Knockout: A round slug or a tab that is punched out to allow room for a cable or circuit breaker.

LB fitting: A pulling elbow for outdoor use.

Lead: A wire (usually stranded) connected to a fixture.

MC cable: Armored cable that has a ground wire and at least two insulated wires.

Middle-of-run: A receptacle located between the service panel and another receptacle. Wires continue from its box to one or more other receptacle boxes.

Multitester: A tool that measures voltage of various levels, tests for continuity, and performs other tests.

National Electrical Code (NEC): The standard set of electrical codes for the United States, updated every few years. Local codes sometimes vary from the NEC.

Neon tester: See *Voltage tester*.

Neutral wire: A wire, usually covered with white insulation, that carries power in the circuit back to the service panel. See also *Hot wire* and *Ground*.

Nonmetallic (NM) cable: Usually two or more insulated wires, plus a bare ground wire, enclosed in plastic sheathing. Older NM cable may have cloth sheathing and no ground wire. See also *Romex*.

Old-work box: See *Remodel box*.

Ohmmeter: A device that measures electrical resistance in ohms, the unit of resistance.

Outlet: Any point in an electrical system where electricity may be used. Receptacles, fixtures, switches, and hardwired appliances are outlets.

Overload: A dangerous condition caused when a circuit carries more amperage than it is designed to handle. Overloaded wires overheat. A circuit breaker or fuse protects wires from overheating.

Pigtail: A short length of wire spliced with two or more wires in a box so multiple wires can attach to a single terminal.

Plug: A male connection at the end of a cord designed to be inserted into a receptacle outlet.

Polarized plug: A plug with its neutral prong wider than the hot prong. It can be inserted into a receptacle outlet in only one way, thereby ensuring against reversing the hot and neutral sides of a circuit.

Raceway: Surface-mounted channels made of plastic or metal through which wires can be run to extend a circuit.

Receptacle: An electrical outlet into which a plug can be inserted.

Recessed can light: A light fixture that contains its own electrical box designed to be installed in a ceiling so it is flush with the ceiling surface.

Remodel box: A metal or plastic electrical box that clamps to a wall surface (plaster or drywall) rather than being fastened to framing. A remodel box must have an internal clamp to hold the cable.

Rigid conduit: Metal conduit that can be bent only with a special tool.

Romex: A common name for nonmetallic cable, from a trade name.

Service entrance: The point where power enters the house. A service entrance may be underground or at or near the roof.

Service panel: A large box containing fuses or circuit breakers. Power enters the service panel, where it divides into branch circuits. Also called a panel box or main panel.

Short circuit: A dangerous condition that occurs when a hot wire touches a neutral wire, a ground wire, a metal box that is part of the ground system, or another hot wire.

Splice: To connect the stripped ends of two or more wires, usually by twisting them together and adding a wire nut.

Stripping: Removing insulation from wire or sheathing from cable.

Subpanel: A subsidiary service panel, containing circuit breakers or fuses and supplying a number of branch circuits. A subpanel is connected to the main service panel.

System ground: The method by which an entire electrical system is grounded. Usually a thick wire leading to one or more rods sunk deep into the earth or to a cold-water pipe.

Three-way switch: A switch with three terminals, used when a fixture is controlled by two switches.

Through-switch wiring: A method of wiring a switch in which power runs to the switch box. Also called in-line wiring.

Transformer: A device that reduces voltage, usually from 120 volts to between 4 and 24 volts. Doorbells, thermostats, and low-voltage lights use transformers.

Traveler wires: In a three-way switch circuit, the two wires that connect the two switches. See *Common wire*.

Underwriters knot: A special knot used to tie the wires in a lamp socket.

Volt (V): A measure of electrical pressure.

Voltage detector: A tool that senses electrical current even through insulation and sheathing.

Voltage tester: A tool that senses electrical current when its probes touch bare wire ends. Some voltage testers (often called voltmeters) also tell how many volts are present.

Watt (W): A measure of how much power an electrical device, fixture, or appliance uses. Watts = volts × amps.

Wire nut: A plastic cap that screws onto twisted-together wires to secure and insulate a splice.

INDEX

METRIC CONVERSIONS

U.S. UNITS TO METRIC EQUIVALENTS			METRIC EQUIVALENTS TO U.S. UNITS		
To convert from	Multiply by	To get	To convert from	Multiply by	To get
Inches	25.4	Millimeters	Millimeters	0.0394	Inches
Inches	2.54	Centimeters	Centimeters	0.3937	Inches
Feet	30.48	Centimeters	Centimeters	0.0328	Feet
Feet	0.3048	Meters	Meters	3.2808	Feet
Square inches	6.4516	Square centimeters	Square centimeters	0.1550	Square inches
Cubic inches	16.387	Cubic centimeters	Cubic centimeters	0.0610	Cubic inches

To convert from degrees Fahrenheit (F) to degrees Celsius (C), first subtract 32, then multiply by $5/9$.

To convert from degrees Celsius to degrees Fahrenheit, multiply by $9/5$, then add 32.

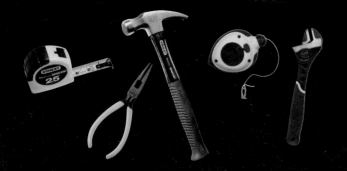